Praise for

FROM PLAIN TO PLANE

"This candid memoir set in a Mennonite childhood concerns the lasting damage of early traumas, but also recovery from them . . . an inspirational account of transcending limitations and succeeding despite the odds."

—*CLARION REVIEWS*

"The author tells her story in fluid, open prose that captures both the naïve worldview of her younger self and the observant eye of the woman she became . . . the tale of a girl raised under incredibly odd circumstances that ultimately feels quite universal, touching on the weight of community, the flaws of parenting, the messiness of family, and the drive to achieve more than what is expected."

—*KIRKUS REVIEWS*

"Patty Bear's captivating memoir, *From Plain to Plane*, recounts her tumultuous childhood as a member of the Reformed Mennonite Church and her remarkable triumph over troubled circumstances . . . a gripping story—one sure to resonate with anyone who believes in the power of the underdog."

—*BLUEINK REVIEW*

from PLAIN
to PLANE

ALSO BY PATTY BEAR

House of the Sun:
A Visionary Guide for Parenting in a Complex World
with Pat Shannon

from plain *to* plane

My Mennonite Childhood,
a National Scandal,
and an Unconventional
Soar to Freedom

by
PATTY BEAR

BARNSTORMERS PRESS

Published 2021

ISBN: 978-0-9975735-0-3 (paperback)
ISBN: 978-0-9975735-4-1 (hardcover)
ISBN: 978-0-9975735-5-8 (ebook)

Library of Congress Control Number: 2020914747

Published by
Barnstormers Press

For inquiries, please address:
barnstormerspress@gmail.com

Editing and book design by Stacey Aaronson
Cover photo of bonnet by Jonah Brandt

In order to maintain privacy, some names have been changed,
including when mentioned in newspaper articles.

Printed in the United States of America

For my guides on this journey

David, *who championed principles that would startle and awaken me, and who talked me into flying and mentored me in the practical expectations of the outside world.*

Mr. Phil T. Matthews *(deceased), because you saw with the eyes of your heart and did something about it.*

Col. William Etchberger *(deceased), because you acted scrupulously fair and unbiased toward a girl in an arena and a time when that was uncommon.*

The Ancestors

I am, and always will be, a hopeless admirer of badass souls. When I was a child, a library card was my ticket to sit at the feet of these colorful, formidable, inspiring Elders. Among them:

Harriet Tubman, Sojourner Truth, Annie Sullivan, Helen Keller, Annie Oakley, Lucretia Mott, Abraham Lincoln, Abigail Adams, George Washington Carver, Frederick Douglass, Elizabeth Cady Stanton, Geronimo, Pocahontas, Alexander Graham Bell, Lewis and Clark, Tecumseh, Florence Nightingale, Susan B. Anthony, Sitting Bull, William Penn, Clara Barton, Dolley Madison, Lotta Crabtree, Daniel Boone, Stephen Decatur, Louisa May Alcott, George Washington, Thomas Edison, Paul Revere, Amelia Earhart, Betsy Coleman, The Wright Brothers, Sacagawea, Davy Crockett, Albert Einstein, Benjamin Franklin, Booker T. Washington, Teddy Roosevelt, Eleanor Roosevelt, Crazy Horse, Mark Twain, Molly Pitcher, Babe Didrikson Zaharias,

And finally . . .

My beloved spirit Guides *who whispered and warned, who closed some doors and opened others, who nudged me to do the work that was needed . . . and who conducted show and tell, instructed me in the themes of this drama, and tutored me in the magic of dreams and of universal law.*
Without you, what would I have become?

PREFACE

*Lies can only persist by violence. The bolder and falser the lie, the more
insistent the calls to conformity and the elimination of dissent . . .*
—ALEKSANDR SOLZHENITSYN

OUTSIDE THE WINDOW LIES A FROZEN AND FORBIDDING LANDSCAPE.
Stretching to the horizon and disappearing beyond is an infinite sea of hard-
edged snow waves. No tree or home dares to interrupt the march of the wind
as it blows the tips of the snow into a white veil across the land. So little sep-
arates me from this harsh and deadly terrain that an involuntary shiver
sweeps through my shoulders and neck at the thought. And yet I am intensely
curious about this landscape. I lean my forehead against the heated window
to gaze at the vast Siberian wilderness thirty-five thousand feet below. We
are passing over the land of the gulags, I muse, where dissident exiles were
sent to brutal forced-labor camps.

The summer between my junior and senior year of high school, I had
been assigned to read twelve books for my fall AP English class, including
The Gulag Archipelago by the Soviet dissident Aleksandr Solzhenitsyn. All
twelve books were important, but somehow, I would only remember this
one. Smuggled out in bits and pieces from the Soviet Union and published in
1973, the author's description of the violent inhumanity of the gulags and
his commentary on a culture were as revealing as an x-ray.

Perhaps, too, at some deep unconscious level, his features—with the
long face and full scraggly beard and hair—connected me to one tributary of
my Anabaptist ancestors who were also dissidents. Fleeing religious persecution in Europe, they became the diaspora of Amish and Mennonites seeking
religious freedom in other lands. Invited by Catherine the Great in 1763,

some would find shelter in Russia. Their descendants, however, would not escape the violence of the gulags established after the 1917 revolution. Their coded letters that somehow found their way out to the US and Canada would be described by a British newspaper as Postcards from Hell.

A year after that senior class assignment, Korean Air 007, with 269 souls on board, would be shot out of the sky without warning by fighter jets when it inadvertently wandered into Soviet airspace. Thirty-seven years prior, the land passing below had been called the USSR, our arch enemy and fearsome Cold War rival.

Marveling at what the passage of time has brought, I look at the instruments of the Boeing 777 cockpit and strain to understand the Russian air traffic controllers. The radio is scratchy and their accent so thick it sounds like they have golf balls in their mouths. But today—and every day—American commercial carriers crisscross this territory, passing behind what once was called the "Iron Curtain."

Four decades of flying have taken me to places big and small: Beijing, Kuwait, Dubai, Rome, Tokyo, Frankfurt, Sao Paulo, London, Paris; Cedar Rapids, Boise, and Presque Isle—all so far from where I began and so profoundly at odds with my upbringing.

I was raised to be a wife and a mother. Raised to be silent, submissive, obedient. To know a woman's place in a man's world. And yet, here I sit, part of the five percent of airline pilots who are women, and an even smaller number who are captains. Though I *will* become a wife and mother, and they will define me to an extent, I won't be defined *only* by my relationship to others as my female ancestors were. Yes, I am a woman in a man's world, but the lies that once bound me no longer rule my life.

From a high altitude the landscape stretches before me to the horizon, and it is obvious how distant locales, histories, and characters are related, all interwoven like some grand, colorful, ongoing tapestry in the larger story of life. As a child, walking a country lane or a farm field, I was able to witness up close the patches of the quilt and the small stitches that held it all together, the tree-lined dirt roads, the gentle mound of a hill that blocked the horizon, all forcing me to see the details by the side of the road. I was constantly drawn to the magic underfoot, to the flowers I knew by name that became cherished friends, to the pebbles that seemed to look like all the others but were unique and beautiful, to the cool feel of newly plowed earth squeezing deliciously through my toes, to the astringent smell of walnuts that had fallen from a tree and beckoned me to crack open their bright green outer shell, then urged me to go beyond the sticky black interior that stained my fingers for days to find its treasure. I can still smell the steaming cow patties in a nearby pasture, see playful tadpoles skittering beneath the water's surface, inches away and yet somehow a world away. There, in the closeness of nature, I felt the emotions of each season: the giddy joy of spring as the grass became an exuberant green and the teacher taped cheerful cutouts of Peter Cottontail and yellow chicks to the windows; the intoxication of summer with its bouquet of fragrances, vivid colors, and soulful breezes; the subtle sadness of fall as the colors intensified and then dropped to the ground in sodden masses, surrendering to rain and relentless gray skies; the bleakness of winter, its beauty revealed in the stark bones of shrubs and dry-stone walls. And because I noticed these details, because I felt them, each one became a part of who I was.

I'd never *wanted* to leave that bucolic life of bare feet on a country dirt road, the chorus of birds in the meadow, or swinging on a rope above the creek and jumping off at the highest moment in exultation. I'd never dreamed of being anywhere but there. I certainly never imagined being here in this place or this job. And yet sometimes I still shudder thinking how narrowly I escaped that life. What might have been if it hadn't been for my father? For there is no logical route from that time and place to this moment and this place.

Sometimes, though, like now, I wonder if I'm delusional. Did I merely imagine the events that catapulted me out of one world and into another? Self-doubt, my one constant, had migrated with me between those two worlds. Just because I had attained this lofty position didn't mean the ghosts of the past had gone away.

I look once again at the instrument panel and then back to the whiteness passing far below at a barely discernible six hundred miles an hour.

Inside.

Outside.

What is the truth?

Did I imagine all those long-ago events?

I shake my head to clear the fog. *No, you're not crazy*, I reassure myself as I think of the stack of newspaper articles, court cases, and media I've unearthed.

People magazine featured my father twice, and national newspapers wrote about his cause for over ten years. Our local newspapers and radio shows featured him. He graced the front page of the *New York Times*, and was featured several times in the *Washington Post*. He was written up in the *Boston Globe*, the *San Francisco Examiner*, and the *Philadelphia Inquirer*, among others. His story even found its way to the *World News* in Bangkok, Thailand. We had heard he was interviewed on *Good Morning, America*, though we had no television to watch it. People would write letters to us or approach us and ask, "Are you any relation to *the* Robert Bear?" I'd stammer as my cheeks flushed red. The pervasiveness of the publicity had been devastating as a child. There is a sense of feeling crazy, of questioning one's own reality, when a public branding is so different from the private reality.

Despite the fifty intervening years, that paralyzing self-doubt can still appear out of nowhere, overwhelming my knowing. Ironically, today those public records serve a healing purpose. They help to organize the parts of my memory that became fragmented and to validate a chaotic reality that has been denied, rationalized, minimized, and whitewashed for a long time—even by me.

I will tell you about the public record and our family's private reality, but deeper than that was another story. My most cherished one. A narrative about fate and destiny quietly recorded by the turning points of life. That story is about the path toward liberation. Accompanying me on some of the darkest passages and most triumphant moments were my faithful companions and divine Guides.

When I was doing research for *House of the Sun*, the book I wrote with Pat Shannon, I came across James Hillman's book *The Soul's Code*. In it he talks about the "acorn theory"—how beneath the acorn's cap lie all the instructions to become a mighty oak tree, that *every* seed comes coded with instructions for the flowering of its destiny, and that this is true of each human being. Within every one of us is the seed of something unique that asks for expression; we are born with a destiny that seeks to bloom, and we each have an inner tutor, something the ancient Greeks called a daemon, Christians call a guardian angel, and others call a spirit guide.

This daemon urges us and guides us on our life path, helping us to circumnavigate obstacles, accompanying us through the darkest passages of life to our unique destination. This destiny leads not only to *our* happiness, but to the treasure of gifts we bring to offer the world. Just as the oak tree provides shade, lumber, paper, and a home for many animals, the rose provides beauty and fragrance, and the potato feeds the body. So, too, does the flowering of our destiny offer something for the world. Each one of us is a channel for something. Each has a purpose and carries a Gift. The oak tree is never told it should try to be more like a pansy. A petunia is never told it has no worth in the world because it's not useful like the cotton plant. Both follow their inner instructions. They don't have to contend with confusion around those instructions or be shamed out of the intrinsic worth of their purpose in the world—they simply *are*. But humans almost always do. We get conditioned. We ingest distorted opinions about what has value and what, and who, are worthless. We may grow in fields that are not fertile for our gifts, that do not nurture and support. We may become twisted and confused by the opinions of others, and in the process, lose touch with those precious inner instructions we carry. Through both good and self-serving intentions, those who surround us may try to control our minds and our lives, take possession of our destinies. Sadly, the voices of our Guides are often drowned out by the noise of the world.

Memory is a strange thing. It is sometimes haunting and unrelentingly brutal, sometimes elusive and mysterious. In a family of six children, you learn about the relationship between memory and reality. Most of the skeletal facts in this book were either recorded in court or featured in newspapers, or their outlines were generally agreed upon among my siblings. But what one remembers, and how it is remembered, can sometimes vary. I've been stunned to discover major elements I've forgotten, and found it interesting that what was catastrophic for one sibling sometimes never registered as a blip on another sibling's Richter scale—or that they remembered the tone and intentions differently. I've wondered about events that take place with multiple witnesses and questioned how there could be so many disparities. Is someone right and the other wrong? Are one person's senses or memories faulty? Is the memory influenced by how much a person was bothered—or thrilled—by it?

In trying to accurately record the past, I have run into these conundrums. What's true? Who's right? And *why* do we remember what we do?

Specific past events and how I remembered them created a framework for my life—the memories became a container that raised questions about and agitated the truth hidden beneath them. Some questions stood out clearly, demanding a decision; in those cases, a choice was made, a path chosen, and life was forever altered. Those crossroads I remember vividly. Other memories laid down markers for the future, as if an agitation that would one day ask to be resolved, healed, or relinquished.

I see the soul itself as a dissident. It's always pressing for the truth and questing for a greater understanding of oneself and the larger world around us. The events of life and the memories that stand out in neon lights beckon for some distortion to be confronted, some illusion to be pierced, some truth to be embraced.

For me, it was a quest to gather up those memories like a thousand shards and glue them back together to reveal what the original container looked like. Once reassembled, the vessel—being me—carried the scars of that shattering. It is difficult to predict whether a shattered vessel will be left weaker, or if, like broken bones knitted together, it will become stronger.

I believe one's memories and the triggering events of life that differ so greatly among individuals vary precisely because behind those events are where *your* truths are hidden, where *your* path lies. Even painful truths, if they are genuine, lead to healing, freedom, and power. It is in this noble struggle that the pilgrimage to one's destiny is walked. The agitation is the compass. True north lies in one's inner mysteries and reveals one's spiritual DNA. It unfolds and catalyzes the blooming of your Gift.

All suffering is bearable if it is seen as part of a story.
—ISAK DINESEN

My father told his story extensively for nearly five decades without interruption. Each of my brothers and sisters and my mother have their own untold stories of the tumultuous time that this book illustrates, of the narrative that shaped *their* lives. I have tried to balance speaking about what I witnessed without telling their stories, as they are not mine to tell.

Instead, I am telling *my* story, the one that has arisen from what I witnessed and how that drove my choices. This is the narrative that shaped my life, made it bearable, and radically transformed my trajectory.

I spent countless hours researching newspaper articles and court cases to fact-check my memories. Having access to this documentation was fortunate, as I was able to cross-check to locate when something happened and how it happened. The stories that never showed up in the newspapers or court cases, and that my siblings were fuzzy on timing and I could not independently verify with a date, I have placed where logic dictated they must have occurred.

They say you should focus on one thing at a time. I've never had the attention span for that. I've always been a multitasker and this book is no different. It is part memoir, part prosecution of a cold case, and part window into the nature of divine guidance. Toward those ends, I write this for three audiences and three reasons dear to my heart.

First, it is for each of my two children and for my nieces and nephews, so they might have a coherent history, a narrative to understand the confusing labyrinth of stories and ghosts of trauma that haunted their parents and extended family. It is also to make sense of what they witnessed, to exhume the truth buried alive that cries out from beyond the grave, to organize the chaos with a timeline and thus understand the crimes that were committed, to give it proper acknowledgment so it might finally be put to rest.

Second, I write for seekers on the Path. This is the diary of a little girl's pilgrimage, of her education in the collaboration of the practical and the mystical. I had been aware of the presence of my own inner tutors, my spirit Guides, since early childhood, but until Hillman I'd never heard anyone talk about this path the way *I* had experienced it. In their telling, when God spoke, it seemed he always validated what they already believed. Yet, that was not my experience at all. The guidance I received led me over hill and dale, turned me upside down and inside out. Plus, my Guides were not an authoritarian presence, commanding me what to do and demanding unquestioning obedience; I somehow always understood I was responsible for what I did with the guidance I received. But although this guidance carried a distinct vibration of integrity, there were many times when it made no sense to me at the time. Only later would I understand its meaning.

Last, I write to offer justice for the little girl who so often longed for this —for the child who was offended by the lies and silently outraged by unaccounted-for crimes, the child who hoped someone, *anyone*, would speak up, would call down the waters of righteousness and justice.

> *To everything there is a season,*
> *and a time to every purpose under the heaven:*
> *A time to keep silence, and a time to speak.*
>
> —ECCLESIASTES 3:1–8

It is time to speak.

CHAPTER ONE

A Child's Picture of Paradise

There is a voice that doesn't use words: listen.
—RUMI

NINETEEN SEVENTY-TWO WAS THE BEGINNING OF TIME FOR ME.
That year bolts into my consciousness with the force of a natural disaster.
Prior to that spring of second grade, my life was comprised of a collection of
memories, rarely anchored in specific years. Months and dates meant birthdays and holidays, but the years themselves were invisible. It was during this
hazy swirl of childhood days that blended one into the next that the world
we lived in was laid out before me—its dynamic, its conditioning, its paradise. These are the memories that shaped me until I was eight, the ones
that would precede my lifelong journey toward individuation. Of course, I
didn't know what individuation was as a child, and for that matter neither
did any of the adults I knew. To the extent that they might have known, they
would have highly discouraged it.

Conforming was what we did better than virtually anyone around us
except the Amish, but we were right up there with them. The Amish and
Mennonites, we are kind of like cousins because we come from the same
religious root. There are many kinds of Mennonites now: liberal Mennonites
who look like ordinary people, and others who wear regular clothes except
that the women wear a small white lace piece for a head covering. But my
mother wore the same attire as all the women in our Church: ankle-length
dresses in severe shades of blue or gray with black shoes. Every woman also

wore her hair exactly the same: parted in the middle and pulled up into a bun tucked beneath a prim, white cap custom made to embrace the bun. Over the cap, they wore a black bonnet, tied primly beneath the chin. For Sunday meeting, all the men dressed in identical black suits and wore a hat —straw with a black grosgrain ribbon in the summer, and black-on-black felt in the winter. This is why we're known as members of the Plain People of Pennsylvania: because of how we dress and live. Simply, humbly, separate.

This uniform meant that when we went to town—or even as far away as Lancaster where there were more Plain people like us—we could immediately spot who we belonged to and who we didn't, which was important because our members were considered "the one true Church." Even the other kinds of Mennonites and the Amish weren't going to heaven because they didn't believe what we did.

Unlike the Amish, we had electricity and cars, but we had some strict rules: we could use electricity, but we were forbidden from having a television or going to the movies. Everybody's car had to be black too. Nothing flashy or fancy was allowed. Being worldly was a grave sin.

But that's the world I knew. And despite the severity of all the rules, that's the world I loved.

Little Fan

Mother would read to us amidst the loads of work she had to do on one condition: if we agreed to rub her legs. It was a fair bargain because she liked to read, and she'd read for a good long time. So, we would take turns rubbing her ankles, calves, and feet through her black stockings. Sometimes we massaged her aching back too. Looking back, I think it must have felt good because it was probably the only affection she ever got. Daddy was never the romantic type, even without the biblical reinforcement that women were there to serve men's needs. So, we willingly granted her wish while she read.

Often, she'd read the Children's Bible. I hated those horrifying stories. I imagined Daniel surrounded by ferocious lions, waiting to tear him to pieces and no way to escape. Then there were Shadrach, Meshach, and Abednego, three youths thrown into the fiery furnace. That they survived didn't matter.

They were burned alive. And Abraham and Isaac, Abraham raising a knife to murder his own son at the bidding of God. Only at the very last second was Isaac granted a stay of execution. *What kind of God would even ask such a thing?* I wondered. My mother said that parents owed their first allegiance to God, even if it meant sacrificing your children or family.

Somewhere (I'm pretty sure it wasn't in the Children's Bible), I saw an illustration of a magnificent, luminous, marble staircase that spiraled right into the wispy clouds of heaven. I liked that image better. I would remember it forever.

We also subscribed to several magazines, which sometimes Mother read to us and other times we just looked through until we learned to read. My favorite was *Ranger Rick*. It was in those pages that I fell in love with impossibly exotic and colorful puffins, and where I reacted with shock and wonder—and a curious feeling of familiarity—to pictures of two-story-high carved totem poles from Alaska. Volumes of the distinctive orange-yellow *National Geographic* came to our home too. Here, we frequently traveled through the pages to countries around the world like Africa, where our eyes bugged out seeing women with eight or ten rings elongating their necks so high and thin that they couldn't hold their head up anymore without them, or where they scandalously wore no shirt and walked around bare-breasted. We'd crack the pages open just a hint so our parents wouldn't see us sneaking a look. Scantily clad men, wearing nothing but a flimsy cloth like underwear, were shown too, with ominous red, white, and black paint on their bodies. Sometimes huge buttons swallowed up their earlobes until it seemed they would be forever stretched out of shape. None of it looked very comfortable, but it was an exciting peek into the world beyond our farm.

Perhaps my favorite, though, was when Mother would read from the twelve volumes of My Book House series, which were, to my mind, a door into pure magic. Each of the twelve volumes was covered in a hardened stem-green linen-like fabric, with a different picture on the front distinguishing each one. Even after I was old enough for the later volumes, one of my favorites was *In the Nursery*. It had rhymes from all around the world: Ireland, South America, Estonia, Finland, Czechoslovakia, Switzerland, Spain, Norway, Russia, Germany, and France. The pictures were gloriously colorful, like a Crayola box brought to life. The children's clothes from myriad countries were so different from each other and from mine. Some rhymes we memorized, like "Mary, Mary, Quite Contrary," depicting a character who secretly reminded me of one of my sisters. Another favorite was, "To market, to market, to buy a fat pig, home again, home again, dancing a jig." Old Mother Hubbard and Old Dan Tucker populated story time with people Mother might describe as "quite a character." But everyone's most cherished was a rhyme we begged to hear over and over. It went like this: "Teddy Bear, Teddy Bear, turn around. Teddy Bear, Teddy Bear touch the ground. . . ." On it went until Teddy Bear went up the stairs to say his prayers, turn out the light, and say good night. Partly we liked it because Teddy Bear was so adorable, and partly because we were Bears too.

As we grew older, My Book House stories became longer and more advanced, with the pictures just as detailed and the experience no less magical. Now, they featured knights, kings and queens, dragons, trolls, evil people, and castles whose flag-bedecked turrets disappeared into the clouds. Paul Bunyan, Snow White, Hiawatha, Don Quixote, Robin Hood, Johnny Appleseed, Joan of Arc, and William Tell all enchanted me, as well as the story "The Twelve Dancing Princesses," featuring a youth with an invisibility cloak. My imagination was treated to a royal feast and still I hungered for more.

But Mother wasn't reading any of these on the day I chose a lifetime role by accident.

McGuffey's Reader was a series of compact books with maroon spines and saddle-brown covers inlaid with intricate blue and white swirls. They looked like elegant but overgrown vines crawling up the cover, with a sailing ship enclosed in a small circle at the center. McGuffey's Readers had been textbooks used in one-room schoolhouses. Delightful in a different way from My Book House stories, each one contained tales that taught about life, each one with a moral that I eagerly digested. But it was *Which Loved Best* that would define my new role for the next four decades.

"I love you, Mother," said little John;
Then forgetting work his cap went on,
And he was off to the garden swing,
Leaving his mother the wood to bring.

"I love you, Mother," said rosy Nell;
"I love you better than tongue can tell";
Then she teased and pouted full half the day,
till her mother rejoiced when she went to play.

"I love you, Mother," said little Fan;
"To-day I'll help you all I can;
How glad I am that school doesn't keep!"
So, she rocked the baby till it fell asleep.

Then stepping softly, she took the broom,
and swept the floor, and dusted the room;
Busy and happy all day was she,
helpful and cheerful as a child could be.

"I love you, Mother," again they said—
Three little children going to bed;
How do you think that mother guessed
Which of them really loved her best?

–JOY ALLISON

Almost before Mother finished the story, I got it. I knew what the moral of the story was—and what to do. I would be little Fan! The one who loved Mother best. The one who would "help all I can."

The truth was, our parents always said they loved us all equally, but I don't think any of us believed that. We knew who the favorites were, for both parents shared the same opinion on this. One boy and one girl, both of whom were handsome and beautiful, smart as well as clever, athletic, and agile. It seemed right that they would be favored, so I didn't mind. After all, they were indisputably the ideal boy and ideal girl.

The day prior to reading this story, my two younger sisters (the youngest had not yet been born) and I had been playing on the porch. Mother waxed poetic about her ideal girl with a routine that I could recite from memory: "Oh, your curly dark hair, your rosy red cheeks, your pearly white teeth," she exclaimed in rapture. It made me think, *What about my hair, Mommy? Is it pretty too?* I wanted to know. Her answer came so quickly it surprised me. "No," she said definitively, "your hair is reddish and it's straight and coarse like a horse's hair." She loved horses, so I wanted to believe that this was a good thing, but from her tone it didn't sound so.

For years I would tell myself that my hair was titian. Though I wasn't sure exactly what color that was, it sounded exotic. Mother would say the red tints in my hair reflected my Irish temper and tell about how when I was very small, my brothers would pick on me. And then she laughed and said I wasn't afraid—I chased after them with a tea towel, shrieking at them as they dashed away from me. As she told that story, I detected a touch of admiration in her voice, and I secretly found this fiery little girl charming too, like a character in one of our stories. But by then I didn't recognize her, for I had already determined I would be a very good girl and had long forgotten her existence.

Though we all had chores and Mother endeavored to keep us continually busy with work, I noticed how much she had to do and was determined to make a difference. For one thing among many, Mother was responsible for rototilling the acre of garden in the field behind our house. We children helped, of course, but she sowed all the seeds, weeded, fertilized, tended, and harvested all the crops. And then she would can or freeze everything we ate at home. In the summer, we picked cherries, blueberries, and strawberries, and Mother froze them or made them into jam. She also boiled apples and turned them into applesauce, and she preserved peaches, pears, and apricots in thick syrup and sealed them in glass jars. In addition, she sewed most of our clothes and cooked three meals a day. Spring-cleaning, fall-cleaning, and everyday cleaning consumed large amounts of time. Laundry for a farm family of eight was an all-day affair with heaps of dirty clothing that covered the entire floor. Add to that darning socks, sewing buttons, and repairing seams . . . the amount of work was overwhelming, and Mother's work was never done. It was amazing she had time to read to us. The only day she might have some adult company was on Sunday, albeit while she cooked and cleaned the mass of dishes after a company dinner.

Once I'd made the vow to become like little Fan, I became indignant that the other children didn't seem to notice how overworked Mother was. When we worked at home, we would ask what she wanted us to do next, and she'd often say with exasperation, "Look around and see what needs to be done," as if it was obvious.

I quickly began doing just that and acquired the skill of seeing what she needed. In time, I became so good at it that I huffed and fumed and herded my siblings with guilt, not that they were impressed with my exhortations. In short order, I settled solidly, reliably, and more quietly into the role of Mother's helper, which seemed to perfectly reflect the meaning of my name, Patricia, a moniker Mother said was derived from "patrician" and meant nobility. I liked this description and took pride in helping Mother shoulder her burdens with a quiet sense of nobility.

To this day I remember sitting by her knee as she read the story about little Fan for the first time, and how exciting it was when the lightbulb in my head lit up, how spontaneous it was. In the beginning, I'd been drawn to the moral of the story because I wanted to do what was good and be helpful. I didn't know it then, but my choice that day, watered over the years by my mother's genuine appreciation, would gradually become a defining role.

I was a quick study for the role of Good Girl. It meant, above all else, having no expectations, no personal needs. These things distracted one from being attentive to the needs of others. A Good Girl never said no, never showed anger, never complained. She was always cheerful, always helpful, always sweet. She was the angel in the house.

The Good Girl's reward, I came to understand, was the freedom from disappointment. Divorced from one's own needs meant not expecting anything from others and thus liberated one from unrealistic hopes. As such, I relished the grateful approbation of those I served, or at the very least, reveled in the fact that my service made me indispensable, which offered me a sense of worth. I made this serviceable bargain cheerfully, with little contemplation. And it was not a particularly unique or clever strategy—millions of women had chosen it before me, and millions more would choose it after me. In my case, the role was a perfect fit for my nature—plus, I had chosen it so young that I was scarcely aware of having made a choice at all. I would practice it so long that it grafted onto my being and I forgot that it was something I had adopted.

After I became indispensable to my mother, I wasn't "Patty" as often. Now I was "sweet Tricia," the one who saw my mother's plight and lightened her load. The one who loved Mother best, her Good Girl, and I liked that. Now she talked about *me* with pride.

As time wore on, Mother occasionally shared that when her mother would see her growing belly bump, she'd exclaim, "Oh, Gale, you're not pregnant *again*?" She even shared how, with three children under the age of three, a home to clean, freezing, canning, baking, sewing, and always having meals on the table on time for my father, she had been so exhausted that one time she lay down in the grass in our backyard and just sobbed and sobbed.

When I heard that, I knew I could help so that never had to happen again.

And it wasn't just for my mother that I did these things. My yearning to be good was fed by something else too, something bigger that I couldn't place in a single event or story. Something in the air.

Goodness in the Air

"Stop climbing on the gravestones, it's disrespectful to the dead," Mother scolds as we play tag in the graveyard after Sunday meeting and clamber up the big gravestone that dominates all the other markers. I picture the dead people lying stiffly below in the silent darkness for all eternity while the cold and rain seep down like a tenacious detective, finding the way to their brittle bones. I feel sad that no warm sunshine or loving touch will sneak down there to chase away the gloom and boredom.

If I were dead, I would love the sound of happy children playing on my grave.

But I don't say that out loud. I know better than to talk back.

This one gravestone—wider, taller, and fancier than the rest—sits in the middle of an old, well-kept stone-walled cemetery next to our meeting-house. It's surrounded by a field of compact, plain white tablets jutting up from the grass, making it the perfect place to climb. A lower granite ledge acts like a stool, letting me step up so I can boost myself to the top where a rounded dome like a horse's back holds several children riding at once. What sets it apart, other than its size, is the name on it: HERSHEY.

Our primary meetinghouse is in Middlesex, Pennsylvania, but sometimes we drive to other meetinghouses in our area when we get invited to dinner by another member. Today we are attending the Hershey meetinghouse. Most people would call this building a church, but we don't. The *building* is the meetinghouse. The *religion* is The Church. And because it's only open occasionally in the summer, it always feels like a treat to come here. Its rich dark brown and tan stone with immaculate mortar joints and a slate shingle roof give it a soft, timeless dignity. Massive sycamore trees stretch their canopies over the grass and dirt parking lot to protect the collection of black cars gathered from the burning sun. Path stones placed in the grass lead from the road beside the parking lot to a sizable granite stoop that leads into a long wooden-floored anteroom. On one side of the anteroom are benches with pegs mounted above in an obedient row, holding a long line of black bonnets on one side and an equally long row of hats on the other. Opposite the hats and bonnets on the outside wall of the anteroom is a row of wooden outhouse doors. Most of our other meetinghouses have an outhouse too, but Hershey is unusual. It has several, and they are all inside, beneath the main roof.

Daring to open one of the wooden outhouse doors, I'm met with an overpowering stew of heat and odors that curl my lips and nose and water my eyes. A flat wooden board with a hole carved in the middle, the edges softened—and splintered—by many years of use, reveal the graphic details of the person who has just visited. I try not to dry heave at the smell and sights. Plus, I worry I'll fall through that adult-sized hole and drown in that horrible muck, so I "hold my water" (as my father says) for as long as I can.

Turning right past the anteroom and through the middle door is the main section where Sunday worship is held. Long wooden pews with a timeless shade of brown line the room. My two older brothers, David and Benny, usually sit on the men's side of the church, and my two younger sisters, Leah and Susie, sit with Mother and me on the women's side. A wood stove is parked against the left wall that once provided heat in the winter when the congregation was large enough to be open year round.

Overall, the room has the peaceful feel and smell of a bygone era, as if we're on a field trip visiting a historical site. The walls are clean, soft, white plaster, unadorned except for a couple of round tin plates near the ceiling, maybe covering holes from where the wood stove used to exhaust. A low, simple dais at the front is where the ministers sit solemnly while they wait to preach.

Many of the ministers and bishops are rather unimaginative speakers. They repeat the same canned phrases in their sermons year after year, so I end up silently finishing their sentences before they do. The thing they say the most is that "we are the one true Church" and impress upon us the importance of unity. Also, that we are born sinners, that God loves us as he loved his only begotten son, and that any who do not believe in him will be sent to hell to burn in the hottest fires for all eternity. They describe eternal damnation, the torture of the fire, and the worms that eat you in such awful detail that I sometimes want to put my fingers in my ears and go "la, la, la, la, la, la" loudly and methodically like I do when my brother calls me names. I also think about the people on some remote island in the ocean who haven't had the opportunity to hear about our religion and wonder if God would really send them to hell. It doesn't seem very fair.

Some adults fall asleep in meeting, especially when it's warm. When it gets too boring or frightening, I daydream. But Uncle Glenn is one of the best speakers, and I'm not just saying that because I'm related to him. I know he works hard on his sermons because I've seen his notes. Plus, he's smoother than the rest, which is a relief. I figure it must be because he went to college, which is kind of unusual. Higher education is discouraged because you might get educated away from the Truth and then you would go to hell. Daddy has told us many times he doesn't want any of us going to college. He says eighth grade was good enough for him and it's good enough for us too.

Sitting in the pew beside Mother, I spend many Sundays squinting hard at the space just above Uncle Glenn's head while he's preaching. The ministers are supposed to be the inspired mouthpiece carrying the word of God directly to the congregation and therefore infallible. I've seen pictures of Jesus and the halo over his head. I reason since Uncle Glenn is God's representative here on earth, he must have a halo over his head too. But just when I think I'm getting close to capturing his ring of light, my eye muscles get tired and let go. I never seem to be able to see it. It must be there, though, and I am determined to try harder next Sunday.

On this particular day, the shutters and side doors are all flung open to let in the light breeze and keep the meetinghouse cool. Summer's creatures—birds and crickets, grasshoppers, and cicadas—along with the sound of the wind, provide a cheerful and soothing background hum that melds into the sound of hymns being sung until I feel intoxicated.

Singing a cappella hymns and playing afterward are my favorite part of church. When the meeting is over, we find our cousins and the other children and go outside to play while our parents visit with the other members. Today, I bolt out the open side door to the walled graveyard, where the big, fancy tombstone my mother doesn't like us to climb on looms in the middle.

I look up at the massive grave marker and read HERSHEY chiseled in large letters. Milton Hershey's father was buried here at our church before his son moved his body to the Hershey cemetery. Though Milton Hershey never joined our Church, he grew up in it, and his parents were members. My father remembers the stories he was told that occasionally, Milton Hershey would pull up to the church in his black chauffeured limousine to attend the service with his mother. We were supposed to be humble, I knew, and not to think too highly of ourselves or be prideful about anything. But secretly, I was *very* proud that our people were connected to someone so famous and good.

Milton Hershey left a legacy that I notice every time we pass through this town. For one thing, the streetlights in town are enchanting. Lining the main street are silver poles holding metal Hershey's Kisses that cap each light, and the silver Hershey wrapper peeks from the top like a flag. We always roll down the windows as we pass through town, even in the winter. It's like inhaling a cup of creamy cocoa through the nose.

But perhaps what gives me the best feeling about this association is the story Mother told us about the almost identical oversized farmhouses that dot the countryside around Hershey. Mr. Hershey and his wife could not have children, so instead, he transferred most of his wealth and control of his company to a trust that would provide a boarding school for orphaned boys. In these distinctive farmhouses, they found a stable home, performed chores, learned responsibility, and were taught vocations. He also endowed a nursing home for the elderly members of our church in Lancaster. I love how, perched on a high ridge beside what is now the Hershey Hotel and above the Hershey amusement park, the school he built for these children has its name spelled out in hedges on the hill. Whenever we drive to and from meeting here, we are surrounded by the prosperity generated by a man who put quality first—and who believed that better living conditions nurtured better workers.

I guess chocolate is what that kind of goodness smells and tastes like.

And I guess goodness has a shape too. At least that's how I always saw Lancaster County.

The Shape of Goodness

If goodness had a body, I think it would look like Lancaster County. The undulating curves of its country roads wind through fertile farmland, bursting with life and exuberant colors. I always looked forward to attending the away meetinghouse called Longenecker's because of that magical drive.

Gazing out the car window, I would search for the colorful folk art known as hex signs that hung like jewelry on certain barns we passed. Bold geometric designs in bright oranges, reds, blues, greens, and a touch of black —all contained within a circle—stood out against the meticulously maintained white sheds and barn walls. Incorporated in the designs were tulips, birds, lovers, and a variety of other symbols meant to bring prosperity, good luck, protection, and happiness, as well as to ward off evil. Of course, the Amish and Mennonite farmers didn't have hex signs on their barns. We were forbidden from wearing jewelry or makeup. And we didn't believe in magic.

Their brand of magic must have worked, though, because this wholesome, prosperous land produced a breathtaking range of abundance on display in the farmers markets and roadside stands. I saw an array of delights on those trips: produce plucked fresh from the bright green fields; simple mouthwatering baked goods like shoofly pie, sticky buns, whoopie pies, funnel cakes, homemade cookies, and fudge; a smorgasbord of fresh meats alongside potato and macaroni salads, cabbage slaw, and sauerkraut; and colorful quilts, with designs featuring tumbling blocks, interlocking wedding rings, broken stars, and pinwheels, all in the same bold colors as the hex signs, flapping on clotheslines with for-sale signs. They also had loads of solidly crafted cupolas, birdhouses, small sheds, and furniture for tourists and locals alike who flocked here for what had become increasingly scarce: homemade, handmade, well-made items.

The landscape vista in every direction looked like the cover of a coffee-table book. In the fields, vibrant green crops were tended with tractors and horse-drawn plows. Bold yellow straw, gathered in large bales and waiting to be collected, dotted the lively hills. Small ribbons of country roads divided acres of farmland that clambered over gentle hills, and horses pulling black buggies clip-clopped peacefully along the shoulder of the road toward their Sunday services.

Sometimes on the drive, Mother played "I Spy with My Little Eye" with us. Other times she told us how to spot which were Amish farms—no electricity lines plus a windmill, and they were not allowed to have landscaping. (I figured landscaping must have been like jewelry for the house.) And she instructed that married men had beards, while unmarried men were clean shaven. I also knew that clotheslines filled with black pants and aprons, interspersed with deep purple and royal blue dresses, were a dead giveaway for an Amish farm.

This part of the land was called Pennsylvania Dutch country because the people who settled here came from Holland, Switzerland, and Germany (Deutschland). They were (and still are) regarded by outsiders as peaceful, gentle people who lead quiet, slow, even idyllic lives removed from the hustle and bustle of a noisy, complex world. But the *city* of Lancaster was mostly comprised of non-Plain people, or "worldly" people as we called them.

Grandma Gross, Mother's mother, was from Lancaster. Her father started Cope's Corn, a landmark business in Lancaster. Daddy sold a little corn to Cope's—and we bought some of their famous dried corn to make a yummy baked corn casserole every Thanksgiving.

Yes, Lancaster, the county and the city, had the shape of goodness to me. Something about the timeless architecture of the graceful stone homes on tree-lined streets gave it the feeling that one could count on it to always be there. With my nose pressed against the car window, I would marvel at the perfectly proportioned lines, the careful workmanship, the broad, generous porches with white swings, the quietly elegant molding, the gracefully trimmed hedges, and the dignified ivy that casually climbed the stone corners. Mother called these "quality homes," meticulously maintained houses that carried an unpretentious grandeur. I didn't have words for what I felt when I looked at this architecture, but later I would understand it as a kind of integrity.

Food, Glorious Food

We lived on a four-hundred-acre farm beside the Conodoguinet Creek. (Daddy said the creek got its name because the Indians asked the white men, "Can a dog go in it?" It actually means "a long way with many bends," but that was a good way to remember the name and, later, how to spell it.) We grew corn, cantaloupe, watermelon, pumpkins, and cabbage on our land—but our biggest crop was potatoes. The one hundred acres that lay on one side of the creek was what we called the "Home Farm," and the three hundred acres on the opposite side of the creek we called the "Other Farm." The Home Farm looked out on the meadow by the creek and toward the lane leading up to the house. Nestled behind a small hill and winding a long stretch from the main road, it was completely hidden from view from both the neighbors and the cars on the road. The privacy was one reason we loved it so much.

Our family always got invited to dinner when we went to an away meeting. Lancaster was the farthest, aside from Illinois and Canada where we had relatives. Other families were usually invited as well, so these dinners were large affairs. Tables, as well as guests, were donned in their Sunday best: white tablecloths, the good china and silverware, and plenty of good food. Maybe because we were forbidden a lot of worldly things, the quality and quantity of food was important, if not an obsession. But then again, maybe it was because farm work made us so hungry.

The extended table would groan beneath a platter of roast beef, which was placed before the head of the household to await his expert slicing. Mounds of creamy mashed potatoes erupted from bowls that graced either end of the table, and a lipped bowl of beef gravy waited patiently to deposit its riches in the little volcano hole we carefully carved when the potatoes were finally passed to us. In between these delicacies lay an assortment of vegetables: green beans, Harvard beets, and creamed corn. There was always a large plate featuring a Jell-O salad too, which had been carefully extricated from an intricate mold. Our favorite was Reception Salad, which was made with cream cheese, chopped walnuts, and a layer of orange Jell-O. Though it was a salad it actually tasted like dessert. Baskets of homemade Parker rolls swaddled in embossed white linen would make the rounds, followed by a procession that included a butter plate with its own special knife, then a small crystal bowl and tiny spoon with either black raspberry, strawberry, apricot, or peach jam—or sometimes two varieties. On Sundays, there was always dessert, and since most all the women were good cooks, and everything was made from scratch, the desserts were worth waiting for.

On the Sundays when members came from the large congregations in Lancaster, Chambersburg, or Waynesboro—or even from Illinois or Canada—to attend services at our local church in Middlesex, they were invited to Sunday dinner either at our home or one of a local member. (Our favorite visitor for Sunday dinners was "the donut lady." As good manners dictated that everyone who came to dinner brought a gift for the hostess, the donut lady—who worked at Dunkin Donuts—always brought a dozen in the trademark pink-and-white cardboard box.)

We'd spend days preparing for these company dinners. First, we'd add the extensions to the rectangular table in the dining room, which we only used for company. (It was a Pennsylvania House solid cherry table, which my mother reminded us when we dusted it every Saturday. She didn't think much of other types of wood, except perhaps walnut, and oak was considered so unrefined that we had none of it in the house.) I'd help iron the long linen tablecloth, and we'd lay a thick, clear plastic over it to protect it and the table from spills. Then, we'd lay out the bone china with its dainty blue flowers that looked like forget-me-nots at each place setting, along with ironed and folded linen napkins. Last, we'd open the wooden box that held a set of silver-plated cutlery and place the fork on the napkin to the left of the plate and the knife and spoon on the other. We had service for twelve, but if we invited more members, we'd add white plates and extra chairs. Adults sat in the living room while the children ate in the kitchen at the children's table— which was fine with us because adults asked us too many questions and we would have to stop eating to answer.

We all knew how to set the table and who to offer the dish to first. My father always got served first at home, but for some reason when we had company, the oldest woman was served first. We couldn't always tell who that was, so we'd move toward our best guess and look at Mother until she nodded silently.

In preparing for these feasts, Mother would make the desserts in advance. We rarely had dessert during our family meals, so we looked forward to company meals. Mother made dinner rolls from scratch a day prior, and then on Sunday, she would place a roast in the oven to cook while we went to church. On the occasions we were having company for dinner, we'd leave church early and rush home to make the mashed potatoes and vegetables before our company arrived. During the week, we made mashed potatoes with their skins on, but for company we always peeled them. After dinner the men would retire to the living room, the boys would run outside to play, and the women and girls would wash, dry, and put away all the plates and cutlery. Then everyone would go to the living room to visit and sing hymns.

One Sunday, my sister and I rode to church with Uncle Glenn and Aunt Mary Ellen—who didn't have any children—and afterward they took us to Howard Johnson's for dinner. I ordered the mashed potatoes, but as soon as I put a spoonful into my mouth, I spit them out into my napkin. "Ugh! What's wrong with these?" I asked. Aunt Mary Ellen gave me a curt smile as she reminded me of my manners and explained they came from a box.

All I could think was, *Whoever heard of such an awful thing?*

You couldn't expect to get something like boxed potatoes past us Bear kids. Living on a potato farm, we ate potatoes at least twice a day. Aside from dessert, potatoes were probably my favorite food: it didn't matter if they were scalloped, fried, mashed, or baked. I loved them every which way. "If nobody wants their potato skin," I'd announce, "I'll take it." But potato skins were prized, and no one ever gave them up. We even had a ritual for the baked potatoes: first scoop out the white flesh, then plunk a big hunk of butter into the hollow of the crisp skin, sprinkle salt on it, and plop it into your mouth. Only then would we flatten the rest of the potato and slather butter over it.

Yes, potatoes were the heart of most meals, but there were other foods we all agreed on too. One of them was watermelon. Since Daddy grew them, we could eat as much as we wanted. Sometimes in the summer, we would each get a quarter of a large watermelon and have that for lunch with peanut butter on top. That meal we'd have to eat outside on the picnic table because it was so messy.

Peanut butter and raisin sandwiches were a favorite too. I once stayed overnight at Grandma and Papap Bear's house, probably while Mother was having another baby, and Grandma asked me what I wanted for breakfast. I told her I wanted a peanut butter and raisin sandwich—which I didn't think she would agree to at that time of day, but she did!

Other favorites were fresh green beans cooked just till they made your teeth squeak; peanuts in the shell; wild black raspberries straight off the prickly stems that stained our fingers and lips; and of course, strawberry shortcake and fresh coconut cake.

I guess now you know why I said food was an obsession.

A Robbery

Lancaster county, with all its warm and wonderful memories, also held another, less savory one.

On this particular Sunday, we had attended church in Lancaster and were the guests of members there. Following the big meal, the post-meal visit, and the playing, we children arranged ourselves in a sleepy backseat tangle for the long drive home.

Awakened by the crunch of gravel as we turned into our lane, Daddy announced, in his typical jaunty manner, "Home sweet home." I popped up and was greeted by the big bushes that hid our secret play places at the entrance to the lane, where we had carved imaginary houses and paths, and where we would invite each other over for mud pies or imaginary tea or be ambushed by cowboys and Indians carrying rubber-band guns.

As we drove up the lane, I searched for my green tricycle where I left it on the grassy hill. On my third birthday, I'd come down from my nap and opened the door at the bottom of the stairs to see Mother smiling beside that shiny little trike. "Happy Birthday!" she said. But I could tell immediately from the way it was painted that it wasn't new. My disappointment must have shown because Mother said sternly, "You should be ashamed of yourself. Be grateful for what you get. It's a nice tricycle." In the time since, I did become very grateful, and I loved riding that tricycle on the driveway and down the lane, turning this way and that, with the feel of the wind in my hair and the freedom to drive anywhere I wanted. We had to share most of our toys among the five—and eventually six—of us, but this was mine alone. My prized possession.

The day before, just prior to dusk, my eldest brother David had yelled up to me while I was happily pedaling my tricycle in circles on the driveway. "I need help carrying something back to the house," he insisted. I protested that I didn't want to but conceded anyway. "Don't worry," he said, "I'll help you carry your tricycle back to the house when we're done." But it got dark, and so it was still sitting there atop the hill beside the lane when we drove to meeting on Sunday.

But as Daddy steered the car up the lane, the tricycle wasn't there, and I couldn't imagine where it might have gone.

As soon as we walked into the house, Mother and Daddy sensed something was wrong. They went from room to room until they came to the small office where our toy chest sat on one wall and the desk where my parents did the books for the business and paid the bills sat on the other. On the middle wall was a filing cabinet, whose top drawer was partially—and suspiciously—open.

The next morning, Daddy was climbing onto the tractor to go to the Other Farm when I appealed to him for help.

"Daddy, I can't find my tricycle. I left it right there. I know I did." I pointed anxiously toward the hill along the lane as the blackbirds with their insistent "caw, caw" and the sound of the tractor competed with my pleading voice.

"I don't have time for this, Patricia," Daddy said irritably. "I have work to do."

As he rumbled off, David appeared and took me aside. "Daddy's angry because someone who works for us on the farm stole all the money in the filing cabinet." My eyes grew wide. "They knew we were going to an out-of-town church and that we'd be gone all day. They also knew Mother and Daddy wouldn't call the police."

My heart dropped. I didn't know how much money was in that filing cabinet, but I imagined it was a lot. It wasn't long before each of us kids discovered that our piggy banks had been emptied too.

I knew our faith insisted that we "turn the other cheek" and be nonviolent. Men don't even serve in the military because we believe in nonresistance. (When they're drafted, they declare themselves "conscientious objectors.") David said Daddy would fire the man who stole from us, but he wouldn't call the police because pressing charges was forbidden, as was suing anyone.

Alarmed, I ran into the house and right up to Mother. "If someone killed us, would they get away with it?"

She laughed slightly. "No. The state would press charges, but under no circumstances are we allowed to. We are to be *in* the world but not *of* the world."

As I dejectedly walked away, it occurred to me that the robbers didn't only steal money. They stole my tricycle too. And I was never going to see it again.

Root, Little Pig, or Die

"Rise and shine," Mother announced cheerfully as she yanked the covers off David. He hunched into a fetal position and shivered, but still he slept. After a couple more shakes, I knew the cold water poured over his feet would come. I hoped he'd get up before that happened to him.

Six o'clock was breakfast, after which we'd head to work in the field, usually up at the Other Farm where most of the potatoes were grown.

According to Daddy, nothing was more important than learning to work. Daddy often quoted his father: "It was 'root little pig, or die.'" It meant something like "pull yourself up by your own bootstraps." In any case, you were on your own; that much was clear. Daddy tweaked his father's version for us, saying: "You don't work, you don't eat," and we knew he meant it literally. If we didn't perform satisfactorily, he would see to it that we didn't get food—or get less of it—according to how we worked.

Training Daddy's future farm crew began early in life. Around age three or four, we'd started working in the fields, picking up potatoes that had been plowed to the surface. We'd put them in half-bushel baskets placed along the rows, and my father would come pick them up. We earned a nickel a bushel, which we were required to save. "A penny saved is a penny earned," Daddy would quote Ben Franklin. He'd also quote, "Early to bed, early to rise, makes a man healthy, wealthy, and wise."

As the business grew, Daddy bought a potato harvester that was much quicker than manual labor. He drove the big John Deere 4020 linked to the potato harvester, where three or four workers would stand before a conveyor belt that brought a continual procession of potatoes. Their job was to cull rocks and clods of solid dirt from whatever was too big to fall through the holes in the metal-link transport. (This was how David found a large Indian tomahawk roughly five inches long and an inch thick. We marveled at this treasure unearthed from the ground. Since David found it, it was his to keep, and though we'd unearth plenty of smaller flint-stone arrows, we'd never find another like that tomahawk.)

Beside the potato harvester, one of Daddy's hired men drove another tractor pulling a large wagon. The potatoes exited the side of the potato harvester onto a conveyer that deposited them in the wagon. Before we got big enough to stand on the potato harvester, our job was to ride in the wagon and throw out the rocks and hard clods of dirt that the main workers had missed. As the pile of potatoes in the wagon climbed, we did too to avoid being buried. It was mostly boring, but at the same time, it was kind of fun to keep climbing that potato mountain. Once the wagon was full, it would be driven to the large barn located on the Other Farm. As we sat atop our big pile on our way to the potato barn, we'd try to hit the telephone poles with a well-aimed clod as we passed, careful that Daddy didn't look back and notice.

At the farm the load would be dumped into a square pool used to wash the dirt off the potatoes before they were sorted and packed in bags. Large conveyor belts would rise out of the muddy water, carrying potatoes into a dryer, then dumping them onto another conveyor belt inside the barn where workers in assembly-line fashion would quickly grade the potatoes as they passed by. The potatoes called "seconds"—those that were too small, had a gash, or were defective in some way—would be culled from the group and set aside to be sold at a lesser price. The remaining potatoes were transported to piles three stories high for storage through the winter. As orders came in, they would be filled from these piles and packed into ten-, twenty-, or fifty-pound bags. Each bag had a little mesh section to allow air to reach the potatoes and prevent rotting, and the front of the bags carried our logo: a cute little bear cub smiling and resting his paws on the circle that held him, with the name BEAR in big letters.

My father's reputation as a boss was legendary, at least according to the stories he told us, and I never heard anyone contradict him. He treated people fairly and demanded hard work, and because of that, employment with my father conferred instant credibility. When someone who'd worked for my father applied elsewhere, they were told, "Well, if you can work for Bobby Bear, I know you can work. You're hired."

Daddy's command of work-related sayings was unique and legendary too. For example, he would quiz a new hire—whether an adult or teenager—by asking, "How do you spell work?" The older hands who knew the answer would try to stifle their smiles as the green hand would answer a perplexed "w.o.r.k."

"No," my father would boom with a big smile. "It's spelled capital W, capital O, capital R, capital K."

He always laughed with delight when he told that story.

He'd also ask, "How can you tell who's the manager in a group of workers? He's the one standing around not working and telling everyone else what to do."

Daddy didn't think much of managers who ran their businesses like that. He believed bosses should work just as hard as those they were supervising—and that's exactly what he did. He had the hands to prove it too; years of work since he was a child had left him with permanent calluses and fingers an inch thick. I would stare at them aghast, wondering if a person could build muscles in their fingers alone. I never did have the nerve to ask.

What I did know, however, was this: Daddy taught all of his children to be obedient little ones who knew how to root . . . or perish.

Fundamental Flaws

Although Daddy demanded prompt and absolute obedience from his workers, he told us children emphatically and repeatedly that we needed to think for ourselves. When it came to David, however, it was clear that Daddy went against his own maxim.

David was the firstborn, and for whatever reason, he seemed to be a lightning rod for Daddy's aggravation. Maybe because he was so bright, David noticed everything about twenty years before the rest of us: contradictions, hypocrisy, annoying patterns, unfairness. He definitely thought for himself—but it was nonstop and he almost always verbalized it, which got on our father's last nerve. You could say that what most parents would deem a point of pride in a child was, for my father, more of a fundamental flaw.

Throughout most of our childhood, I maneuvered my way to the back of the pack of kids, where I could remain safely out of reach of my father. "Please shut up, David," I would silently breathe. But he rarely did. Instead, he became quite adept at spotting my father's meaty hand arcing toward his cheek and ducking just in time.

My father's management style, while demanding, could be measured and jaunty with the adult hired help. With David, though, it ranged from physical brutality to pervasive and penetrating contempt. Poor David never did anything worthy of praise in my father's estimation. He didn't even walk fast enough to please our father. "What's the matter with you?" he'd bark. "Pick up the pace." Then he'd lunge threateningly and mock, "Always walking with your Big Spring stroll." Big Spring was the local high school, so Daddy's taunt was both a personal condemnation of my brother's work ethic and a dig at higher education. He made it clear that intellectual abilities were worthless on a farm. While Daddy was a smart person, he frequently lashed out in the direction of the educated.

What I observed, even at a young age, was that David was far more brilliant than Daddy—than any of us for that matter. Mother would say he was too smart for his own good, and from the way Daddy treated him, that certainly seemed to be true. David probably knew he was smarter than most, and he wasn't going to let our father keep his mouth shut.

Daddy had attended a rough-and-tumble one-room schoolhouse until eighth grade, where he had done well in his studies, as well as with his fists in the schoolyard. As I mentioned before, Daddy often reminded us that eighth grade was good enough for him, and it was good enough for us too. He was convinced that education made people soft and saddled them with too many ideas. This, he believed, was what led to working for someone else, the idea of which he disdained. "You should always work for yourself," he insisted.

Daddy would also sometimes say things without any clear reference to whom or what he was referring, as if they'd just popped into his head for some reason. One rather ominous story he frequently repeated was how the Romans would throw babies with birth defects over a cliff. He said it so matter of factly that it came across as a practical and ideal solution to an inconvenient problem.

Was he thinking of David? I wondered.

David couldn't walk until he was two. Thinking he might be mentally retarded, Mother and Daddy took him to several doctors. It turned out he had such a big head that it threw off his balance when he was a baby. His head was so big, in fact, that by the time he was ten, he'd outgrown Daddy's church hat. It's a horrible notion to entertain, but perhaps Daddy was so humiliated by the possibility of having a defective child that he frequently contemplated how other cultures solved this problem, and sometimes his ideas escaped his head in words.

And that wasn't the only fundamental flaw Daddy had ideas about; he felt that way about sickness too. He saw being sick as a sign of weakness and having a poor constitution. Oddly, he attributed most illness to overeating, so when we got sick, "the doctor" prescribed no food. Sometimes Mother went along with it, but when Daddy wasn't around, she'd fix us poached eggs on shredded wheat with peas.

I couldn't help but wonder if it wasn't only David whom Daddy thought the Romans would have thrown over a cliff; I wondered if he'd thought the same about me. I had such a constant rotation of ailments as a child that one of the nicknames my siblings gave me was Sicky. Constant sore throats, scarlet fever, earaches, strep throat, anemia, allergies—it seemed I always had something. "Cherry or Grape?" was the morning question for most of my early childhood, which meant, what flavor medicine did I want? My tonsils were so large that I couldn't speak properly; I had to have a speech therapist in second grade because the teacher couldn't understand me. This was not common then, and I was profoundly embarrassed to need this help, especially because Daddy had made it clear that to be sick meant there was something wrong with you, some weakness of character that everybody saw.

Between David's irreverent verbal observations and my propensity for illness, I imagine my father had seemingly no end to his risk of shame by association with his family and what he considered our fundamental flaws.

I never realized until later that Daddy's true frustration probably had nothing to do with us, but rather with something deep inside himself that fed a feeling of inferiority.

Foreshadowing

One day, Daddy was showing David and Benny how to shoot the .22. I thought I might get a chance after they were done, so I tagged along. Benny was steadying the rifle on the fence post, pointing at a tin can placed in the meadow, when David wondered aloud why Daddy did something a particular way in farming. I didn't hear the whole question; I only saw Daddy's hand snake toward David's face. "You think you know better than me?" he sneered. "Show a little respect." David's chin retracted into his neck as he slid out of reach. Daddy must not have been too upset this time because he didn't pursue it further.

As an observer, I was intensely disturbed by the way Daddy treated David. I couldn't help but notice how David always wore the same face in the aftermath of these incidents—a slightly amused smirk with red tinted cheeks, hollow eyes, and a studious attempt to appear uncaring. I also couldn't help but notice the way David ravenously attacked his fingernails afterward. I didn't know how he could even reach them with his teeth anymore; they'd become so tiny that the flesh of his fingers clambered over top of the nail bed as if to protect it from any more raiding. Even if the nails wanted to grow back, I didn't see how they could with the wall of flesh that had grown on the tips of his fingers.

I wished I was big enough and brave enough to protect my eldest brother from Daddy.

Instead, I could only plead repeatedly inside myself, *Please shut up, David. Please.*

Little Dummy

Anytime we weren't in school—which included before school, after school, and during the summer—we worked on the farm.

"Pleeeaaase let me go to kindergarten," I'd begged Mother when I was five, nearly six. It sounded wonderful, and I'd have been the first in my family to attend.

"No," she said, "I need you at home."

So, I waited another year and started school in the first grade.

On one non-school day, I was out in the field and feeling hungry. I could never eat much at one time, and because of that, I felt hungry most of the time. We weren't allowed to spoil our appetites by eating between meals, but because it seemed like it should almost be dinnertime, I asked Daddy what time his watch said.

"Why, Paaaatricia," he said, with the "a" in my name as one long windup that ended with an emphatic crack of disgust. "Whatever's the *matter* with you?" The pronunciation signaled I'd done something terribly wrong. And though that tone was familiar, it still paralyzed my chest and yanked my breath to a halt. Like a cornered animal I froze, hoping the stillness would forestall annihilation. *At least he got my name right*, I thought. Most days when he wanted to talk to us, it was as if he couldn't quite settle on any one name. He'd run through the list of children's names aloud before at last returning to settle on the one he wanted to address.

Finally, he said, "Why, both your brothers could tell time by the first grade. What's the *matter* with you?"

I stared at him wordlessly, my trapped mind racing frantically to make sense of his response.

I just started first grade. I reasoned. *Was I supposed to know how to tell time? Nobody taught me. Everybody else knows something I don't. I should know this. Did someone tell me, and I missed it? I don't even have a watch.*

My chaotic thoughts were interrupted when a wide smile spread across Daddy's face, as if a brilliant observation had just become delightfully obvious to him. "You're the dummy of the family," he declared.

I am? I wondered. *I didn't know that. Am I dumber than all my brothers and sisters? Even the younger ones? Are they all smarter than me? Can this be true? I never knew I was dumb. It is horrifying to think how dumb I must be.*

It was then that I decided this must be the solution to the puzzle my mind had been trying to solve: I can't tell time yet because I'm dumb.

My father's explanation seemed to resolve his tension, and I watched his face get lighter. "You're my little dummy," he said to me, softer, kinder.

Despite the sentiment he attached to the statement, my heart dropped.

My father never liked to be called Bobby. He always preferred Robert, and he never called us by anything except our full names either: David, Benjamin, Patricia, Leah, Susan, and Sharon. But for me, he made an exception and thereafter took to affectionately calling me "My little dummy."

All I could think was that my father must have known what he was talking about, so I tentatively accepted his judgment. Inside, though, I felt hollowed out, as if a bomb decimated everything but my outside shell.

And the shock and numbness didn't entirely subside in the days that followed.

For forty years, I would remain convinced that I must be dumb.

Loafing

One of the most consistent themes of my childhood was the huge emphasis placed on work ethic. In fact, it was so strong in our house that loafing when we were supposed to be productive was considered a mortal sin.

All of us kids were expected to work in the fields, as well as perform chores around the house. The chores included washing and drying dishes, setting the table, everyday house-cleaning, spring and fall cleaning, mowing the lawn, tending the large garden, weeding, cooking, and mending clothes. But just *who* should do *which* chores was a heated disagreement I remember Mother and Daddy getting into.

"The boys shouldn't have to do housework," Daddy asserted. "That's women's work."

"No," Mother countered, "the boys have to learn how to cook and clean too."

Daddy grumbled about it, but Mother won the argument. Mostly.

The boys had to clean their room, and they had to wash and dry dishes on the weekdays, but on Sundays when company came, they took their cues from the men. The women and girls always cooked the large meal; afterward, they cleared and washed the dishes while the men retired to another room and the boys were allowed to run and play.

My brothers did take stabs at cooking, though. The clear winner in that category was Benny. After learning how to make excellent chile con carne, he'd take a pan down into the meadow where David and Benny had built a fort, and they'd camp out while Benny made his signature meal over a fire.

But I digress . . .

Born in 1929, my father had grown up during the Depression and the Second World War. He spent his entire childhood working hard, providing vital food supplies for the war effort. But I suspect that war or no war, he'd have toiled just as diligently.

Working hard defined my father, and he wanted it to define us. Even the breaks he took were short. Daddy always came home for lunch, and afterward he'd lie down on the floor, place his red bandana over his eyes, and take a nap—usually for thirty minutes. Hoping he'd sleep longer so we wouldn't have to rejoin him in the fields so soon on the days we weren't in school, we'd go outside and play quietly to make sure the house was as serene as possible. He rarely overslept by more than ten minutes, but we always held out hope.

Finding opportunities to loaf, without getting caught and paddled for it, became a game for us siblings. For example, after Daddy would show the four eldest kids—David, Benny, Leah, and me—what to do on the backside of the big potato hill, such as moving irrigation pipe or hoeing weeds, he'd walk off to supervise another part of the farm. We often worked long, hard days in the fields, but we always looked for opportunities to give ourselves a break.

After working for a while, one of us would act as a scout to see where Daddy was. That person would creep up to the top of the hill and poke a head over the ridge, where we had a sweeping view of the Other Farm in all directions. If the coast was clear, we'd drop our tools and lie on the ground, one ankle casually resting on the opposite knee, and nonchalantly "smoke" the sweet stem of a foxtail plume. We'd seen the grown men who worked for my father chewing these weeds as they walked, and "smoking" them made us feel like we were grownups too. Sometimes we'd take the foxtail leaf, turn it sideways, and use the thin edge to make a sharp whistle. I was never very good at that, but Benny was an expert. He could also whistle with two fingers in his mouth, which I could never do either.

Although we had to be ready to jump at a moment's notice and get back to work if Daddy was spotted, loafing was delicious. Looking up at the sky, we could see the orchestrations of another world as airplanes painted lazy white paths, appearing on the horizon and then disappearing again, going who knows where. I loved the hypnotic drone of the engines as they grew louder and then faded away. If I'd been able to, I would have drifted off to that soothing sound with the warm sun and light breeze on my face.

One day, during one of our loafing sessions, I remember staring into the clouds, thinking of the story Mother had read from the My Book House series about a child who dug and dug with his spade and pail until he reached China on the other side of the world.

If I dug a hole all the way through the earth, I wondered, *would I come out the other side?*

It seemed to make sense to me, but I never had enough loafing time to test it out.

Ice Cream

On certain occasions, after we'd worked for hours late into the evening, Daddy would surprise us by quitting just before the little gas station and convenience store in Bloserville closed. We'd rush the few miles there in the pickup truck, and Daddy would buy each of us a popsicle of our choice. It was always nice for him to treat us, but I'm not sure who loved ice cream more—us kids, or him.

Throughout the summer, ice cream was a staple in our house. Each fruit crop—strawberries, raspberries, peaches—was another reason to pull out the hand-cranked ice cream maker. Mother would mix up the ingredients and pour them into the long, round metal container, affix the crank, and pour in rock salt and ice. One child would sit on a towel on top of the barrel to hold it steady while another would crank until his or her arm got too tired. Then we'd switch places, each of us clamoring for who got the treat of licking the beaters when the ice cream was finished.

When Daddy was experimenting with a new health idea —which he did often—he'd restrict his eating to as little as possible and would refuse to be tempted even by his favorites, which included his beloved ice cream. Even as a teenager, Daddy had been very health conscious. (He once told us he was abstaining from food when his mother made his usual birthday dinner and cake, and he had refused to eat it.) As a boy, he had to work so hard and so long that the lack of eating left him weak, so when he couldn't take it any longer, he'd "break down and enjoy some food" as he described. Those "gorges" became how he would mark the end of his health campaigns, after which his brothers teased him about going overboard.

As an adult, his ritual had not changed. Only now, his abstinence was usually broken by a half gallon of butter pecan ice cream. He would pull the tab that released the top of the carton, then carefully separate the sides from the top and lay them flat so that the frozen rectangle sat fully exposed on all sides. Crowded around him like hungry hyenas, we'd watch as he meticulously scraped a spoon along the top in rows, then down each side before turning it over so that the melting bottom was also exposed. When we would ask if we could have some, he would irritably say, "No, this is mine." So we would be left to begrudgingly hope he'd change his mind as we watched the rectangle get smaller and smaller.

As if reproaching the disappointment on our faces, he would quote his dead brother: "George always used to say, 'You can't please everybody, so you've got to please yourself.'"

As a quintessential "good girl," hearing this phrase shocked me. It had never occurred to me that pleasing myself was an option.

To Market to Market

Even though my father sold everything on our farm wholesale, going to market was a longstanding tradition in our family. Daddy grew up taking produce to market; his mother was a popular vendor due to her personable and kind ways; and Grandma Gross had a deli stand at the Lemoyne Farmers Market, where she sold the prepared foods she made in her basement, like potato salad, coleslaw, and tapioca pudding, plus fresh breaded haddock for the Catholics who couldn't eat meat on Friday. Papap Bear even had a farm market in the carport of his house, where he sold tomatoes and radishes, and sometimes lettuce and celery, along with whatever was not needed from the garden for freezing or canning.

One spring, Daddy decided it was time for us to learn how to grow our own little commodities. "You should never work for someone else," he repeatedly asserted. So we children were given garden space, a plan for what to grow, and seeds. The boys were to grow vegetables and the girls were to grow flowers. All summer we tended our crops, watering, hoeing, and weeding, and Mother sewed four identical blue-and-white short-sleeved checked dresses with white aprons to slip over top for us girls to wear to market. Leah, Susie, and I were excited about our matching dresses, and Leah and I were proud that we were old enough to embroider our initials on the pockets of our aprons.

While our crops were still growing, Benny took Daddy's words to heart and asked to start his first business, a small roadside market that would also be good practice for all of us for the big day when we would go to market. Daddy helped Benny set up a series of crates facing the road behind the big potato shed at the Other Farm. This was so he could create an outdoor market that shaded us from the sun and where we could practice selling the watermelon, cantaloupe, and sweet corn we grew to any cars that passed by (which was almost none).

What I remember most about that practice day was that the heat was wilting, despite the shade of the crates, and that we sold very little. But it was practice for manning a stall at the Carlisle Farmers Market, and that was the important thing.

When the day came to officially peddle our wares, we girls donned our new dresses, and the boys wore their cleanest work clothes and combed their hair neatly. Daddy showed us how to set up our cashbox and to make change, and Mother showed us how to arrange our offerings.

"David's in charge," we were reminded. That was no surprise. The hierarchy was that when Daddy was there, he was in charge because he was the head of the household; if he wasn't present, Mother was in charge; and if neither of them was around, the order of authority was David, Benny, me, Leah, and finally Susie. (Susie couldn't oversee anyone that day because the only person below her was Sharon, and even though Sharon had a blue checked dress too, she was only a year old, so our parents took her with them.)

After Mother and Daddy left, we eagerly awaited our customers. Vegetables sold much better than flowers, and the boys made a good dent in their inventory. We girls, however, still had lots left over as the busy time of market faded. The hottest item with the longest line seemed to be the big cookies from the stand in the middle of the market, and we all looked at each other with the same thought. Our cashbox had money in it, and being away for a few minutes probably wouldn't hurt anything. So we headed over to the cookie stand to see what our money would buy. Only our secret plan was foiled. Just as we were making our way back to our stand, Mother and Daddy arrived.

"You left your cashbox unattended," Daddy said furiously, as if he couldn't fathom such a thing. "Anybody could take your money."

Luckily, nobody did.

Middlesex Makes Me Swoon

While I liked the meetinghouse at Hershey, and Lancaster was fine too, it was Middlesex that made me swoon. Not because it was a newer brick building. Not because it was the only meetinghouse without an outhouse (although I did heartily approve of the clean, modern, indoor bathrooms). And not even because I liked the newer oak pews and the smell of the reed fans advertising the local funeral home as we waved them on a warm summer day. No, this meetinghouse made me swoon because of what was outside: the breeze that blew softly through the open windows and the view of a particularly special tree.

One particular day, the jumble of Bible quotes was all about Adam and Eve—how Eve tempted Adam and caused the fall of all mankind . . . how Eve was responsible for all the evil in the world . . . how women are supposed to be silent, submissive, and selfless . . . how men are supposed to rule over them . . . how women are supposed to be obedient to their husbands . . . how women are never supposed to lead, only follow meekly. I guess this was all to justify why women didn't have any roles in our Church and only men could be ministers, and why women's opinions didn't matter. I had heard the minister's phrases so many times that I tuned him out until it was time to start singing the hymns.

I turned my attention to the chorus of nature singing joyfully beyond the windows. Savoring the soft, fragrant whisper of the breeze as it graced the congregation, I was lost in ecstasy. Then, turning toward the window across the aisle beyond the men's side, I found myself filled up so full I never wanted to come back. There, a willow tree swayed gently. Though I could only see the top of it, I knew it was blissfully, lazily, dangling its pale green fingers in the cool creek passing by its feet, drinking in the radiance of that day just like me.

Storytellers and Story-Makers

Though Daddy worked harder than anyone I knew (besides Mother), and he could be tough on us, he also had the heart of a little boy. In the spring-time, he expressed this by buying us kites—traditional kites, box kites, flying dragons—allowing us to choose whichever style and design we wanted. One by one, as each spring followed another and we children grew up, he would show the youngest how to get a running start and let out the string gradually so the kite would take flight.

But perhaps Daddy's childlike heart shone through most when he would occasionally tell us stories in the evenings before bedtime, keeping us spell-bound with adventures he made up as he went along. We'd gather in my brothers' room and crowd around as Daddy spun heroic tales of two boys named Harry and Larry—characters who resembled David and Benny.

"One more story," we'd plead, "one more," and he would usually oblige.

But as we got older, Leah and I noticed the stories were always about boys, and we wanted our own stories.

"Make up one about us too, Daddy, please?" we begged.

"Oh, all right," he said good-naturedly.

And so the adventures of Ann and Irene were born.

They, too, were bold and adventurous, getting into and out of scrapes. And we were happy to be part of the story.

The world of heroes and adventurers broadened when Mother took us to obtain our prized library cards from the Bosler Free Library in Carlisle. Within those doors awaited a whole cast of colorful, bold American men and women who would come to life through the Childhood of Famous Americans series. "Think for yourself," my father always insisted. Now, here amongst these pages, were all kinds of people who thought for themselves: inventors, explorers, writers, artists, abolitionists, suffragettes, healers, leaders, reformers, liberators, pioneers. Stories of patriots of all kinds filled the shelves, one favorite of which was Molly Pitcher, a fearless hometown hero who took over her husband's cannon during the Revolutionary War as he lay dying, and whose statue of undaunted resolve in combat stood in the Carlisle graveyard.

I learned about more heroic people than I ever imagined possible. George Washington Carver, born into slavery, who would develop hundreds of products using peanuts and the practice of crop rotation (which was unknown at the time and which my father used on the farm). Clara Barton, who founded the Red Cross. Abraham Lincoln, whose harsh early life in the backwoods gave way to a man of patience and wisdom when his country needed those virtues the most (not to mention he was the author of the famous Gettysburg address, which I would memorize by heart). Sitting Bull. Daniel Boone. Jim Thorpe. Davy Crockett. Kit Carson. Meriwether Lewis. The wit and plain-spoken wisdom of Benjamin Franklin (which I was already familiar with through the many quotations by Daddy). The irrepressible Dolley Madison. Flag maker Betsy Ross. Aviators Charles Lindbergh and Amelia Earhart. Women's rights activists Susan B. Anthony, Elizabeth Cady Stanton, and Lucretia Mott. Sharpshooter Annie Oakley. Military leaders Ethan Allen and the Green Mountain boys, Stephen Decatur, and Frances Marion, the "Swamp Fox." Louisa May Alcott. Robert Byrd. Helen Keller and Annie Sullivan. Eleanor Roosevelt. Frederick Douglass. Pocahontas. Dorothea Dix. The audacious bravery of liberator Harriet Tubman. The breathtaking confidence and spiritual mission of Sojourner Truth and her "Ain't I a Woman?" speech. The list seemed to go on forever of men and women of character and initiative, of resolve, ingenuity, and spirit. I wanted to meet them all, but we were only allowed to take out seven books at a time.

Later, when we studied history in school, I already knew who these people were, why they mattered, and what period of history they belonged to because they'd come so vividly to life for me. Even more important, the qualities of these men and women inspired me. Though I had been taught from the day I was born that the place of women was to be subservient to men, and that to step into my predestined role was what my future held—

and even what I believed I wanted—I was profoundly drawn to these people who had forged their hardy characters through difficulty, who had made bold choices and taken daring initiative, who possessed steely resolve, who had irrepressible spirits and colorful lives.

Each one of them lived inside me like a cadre of mentors for the person I had no idea I would grow up to be.

Heaven on Earth

I've given glimpses of the expansiveness of our farm, and a few of the details of it, but the panoramic landscape of it for me really was heaven on earth.

From my bed, I could look out the window and see beyond the millrace bridge to the meadow where the sycamore trees—whose trunks were so thick two grown men couldn't touch their fingertips if they stood opposite each other—guarded the creek edge. At night it was so black down there it terrified me, as if that fog of darkness might creep up toward the house and get me. But in the daytime, it was peaceful and beckoning.

In the spring, I kept watch for weeks by this window for the bluebells. They rose on masses of green stalks that flooded the entire meadow, then sprouted tops that became a sea of blooms. You couldn't see the first blossoms from my window, though. For that you had to visit the meadow every day and watch the tight pink buds unfurl into delicate blue bonnets that drooped from fragile stems. Even then, you could hardly smell the faint fragrance of the masses of flowers unless you dropped to your knees and buried your face in them. That's how the meadow was. You had to get close to fully experience its wonders.

At the feet of the sycamores nestled scores of violets, along with pale pink, almost transparent, flowers with delicate purple veining. The millrace bridge that connected our lane to the meadow was as utilitarian as they came, but it was softened by trailing succulents that clambered over the concrete walls and embankment. I would sit beneath the metal guardrails and dangle my bare feet over the edge while watching the millrace community: frogs on lily pads, and tadpoles skittering just beneath the surface (with the hope I didn't see a green snake slithering upward). Besides the flowers, my favorite sight was the daring aerial display the iridescent dragonflies put on as they chased each other over the water.

Perched on the edge of the bridge, looking farther up the bank where it got steeper, I could sometimes spot an isolated patch of surviving Sweet William. This was the spot where we threw our kitchen scraps over the wire fence and where Mother discarded the spent annuals and biennials from her garden. I would stare at them, amazed that the bright pink and darker maroon petals amidst the garbage looked happy, even though they were supposed to be dead. Because the fence stood between us, though, I could only long to get closer to their scent that I cherished.

In our front yard a long, deep flower garden lined the sidewalk, filled with perennials of every sort. I delighted in the tart-smelling mustard-yellow yarrow paired with airy baby's breath; the pink and white peonies interspersed like exotic luxuries; the small persimmon tree that punctuated where the sidewalk met the driveway; the mysteriously named bleeding heart growing in the shade beneath it—and marigolds and petunias bordering every walkway.

In the back garden, Mother's prized rose named "Sutter's Gold" reigned over the marigolds at its feet and was guarded by the cedar tree with its tiny, fragrant pinecones. Morning glories climbed the posts toward the second-story porch off the girls' bedroom, and at the juncture where the back sidewalk descended below the horizon stood a lone wisteria bowing beneath a wealth of fragrant purple racemes. At the boundary between the backyard and the field where the greenhouse sat was an enormous lilac tree—one that partially concealed the thick irrigation pipe that leaked cool water in the summer. And on the other side of the house was a series of shabby white barns decorated with hollyhocks, giving them an old-fashioned charm.

Beyond these well-tended gardens lay more of nature's wealth and endless bouquets: Queen Anne's lace, purple aster, yellow buttercups, honeysuckle, the blue daisy-like petals of chicory, and puffy yellow wildflowers looking exactly like a fairy's pocketbook. I couldn't decide which I loved best: wildflowers or those that grew in the garden.

Both my grandmas loved flowers too. Whenever anyone came to our house to visit, the person brought some kind of gift, and we did the same. Grandma Bear's gift was always flowers from her garden, usually snapdragons or dahlias. Most of her garden was a utilitarian patch of vegetables that stretched from the front of her house to the lane, but she reserved one long, straight row of flowers at the road's edge to welcome visitors. She would cut dozens of stems, lay them diagonally on dampened newspaper, then roll it up to swaddle the blooms for presentation. Whenever she would show up on our porch with her offering, I would open my arms to receive it and promptly sink my face into those glorious blooms as if to inhale their very essence into mine. Though Grandma would hand them to me so I could find a vase, and I *knew* they were for everyone, I didn't think it would hurt to pretend for just a little bit that they were all mine.

The back of Grandma and Papap Gross's house had no vegetables. It was just one giant, colorful flower garden with a massive sycamore tree guarding it. It was one of my favorite playgrounds. In the fall, seeds from the tree descended like toy helicopters, and winding flagstone paths edged in boxwood transported me through the various garden rooms and out to the alleyway behind the house. The garden was populated with bird feeders, and with statues of a gnome and of a little man fishing in the pond beneath a waterfall. (Grandma was actually admonished once because one of the ministers thought her garden was verging on too worldly.)

Maybe my love of flowers comes from my grandmothers because I can't think of anything I love more. But Mother was an inspiring influence too— she loved pretty much everything in nature. On Sunday afternoons, she would sometimes take her binoculars and bird book and tromp through the brambles and brush, with us following behind like little ducks. She taught us how to recognize the sound of a yellow warbler, and she took us on walks in the country where we learned the names of trees, roadside plants, and flowers. "Look," she might exclaim excitedly, "there's a pileated woodpecker." We also learned how to spot the riches of wild black raspberries hiding in plain sight, and the patches of apple mint by the side of the road that we used to make minted lemonade, an old family recipe. In the fall, we gathered pinecones and bought colored pipe cleaners to make Thanksgiving turkeys, and Mother would get permission from a neighboring farmer to climb over their pasture fence to harvest nuts from their shellbark trees. As winter settled in, we would spend those long, chilly nights cracking shellbarks and walnuts to our hearts' content.

Clearly, nature played a pivotal role in my childhood, and while flowers were my favorite components, the vegetable gardens made our farm seem like we had the best of two worlds.

Behind the back lawn was a huge vegetable patch where we grew regular and cherry tomatoes, and where zucchini and acorn squash sprawled out in all directions. (Daddy grew the watermelon and cantaloupe on the farm, so we didn't have to tend to that in this garden.) Sweet corn that we would eat by the cob or spend a whole day cutting off to make creamed corn to freeze loomed on its stalks, and peas we would harvest in wash pans and shell sitting on the back porch grew snugly in pods. Pole beans of every kind proliferated this garden too, including lima beans, which we would cook with a little milk and butter, or let dry to make baked beans like Grandma Bear did.

Tending to this garden year round was part of Mother's job, and all of us helped her with it. One day, I recall weeding lima beans when it was so hot I felt like I would melt into the ground. It was on that day that heaven and earth first merged into one.

Looking up at the expansive blue sky, I thought, *This must be where God and the angels live. It looks so lovely . . . I wish I could live up there too.* The clouds looked firm enough to skip across, and I imagined the angels walking in hidden hallways formed by the intersections of giant clouds. Enraptured, I stopped weeding and mentally traveled there to live with them.

First, I placed God off to the left by himself. I felt a little guilty about this, but from the description in church, he seemed like such a scary, mean old man. They were always talking about how he was jealous and possessive and vengeful, and how he needed to be worshipped all the time or else, and how he punished those who disobeyed, and how we were always supposed to fear him. They also said in church that he loved us, but I was not so sure about that part. Plus, the ministers were always saying that God knows everything we do—that he could see everywhere, and that he even knows everything we think. I felt terrible thinking these bad things about God; I didn't want him to feel bad and thought maybe I was wrong. Still, it seemed safer if he was a little distance away. Plus, I imagined God probably had lots of work to do so he maybe wouldn't notice me.

And so, ensconced in paradisiacal luxury well above the ordinary plane, I forgot about my siblings still weeding under the scorching sun and skipped off happily to the right with the angels to explore among the clouds. It wasn't until Mother noticed my daydreaming and ordered me back to my task at hand that I was shaken from my nirvana in the sky to return to the sweet pea blossoms that awaited me on the ground.

Both worlds suited me beautifully, but the elevated one was sure nice to escape to during those hot summer days.

To Everything There Was a Season

Farm life was largely governed by seasons, which gave it a comforting rhythm, and spring was the busiest of all.

It would begin with spring cleaning, which meant scrubbing the whole house thoroughly until it smelled new. We moved every piece of furniture and cleaned behind and beneath; we removed the screens from the windows and made sure the glass was cleaned to a sparkle inside and out; we laundered the curtains, emptied the cupboards, and reorganized the shelves; and we donated any clothes no longer in use to Goodwill. In late spring, we began planting both in the fields and in the large vegetable garden. We would butcher and freeze chickens too. They'd arrive alive in crates and be unpacked behind the barn by our home. My father would bring out a hatchet and set to work, with a tree stump that stood on end serving as the final resting place for the chicken's neck. My sister Leah liked to wield the hatchet too, but I couldn't bear to watch the beheading, or the way the poor birds sometimes ran around headless and spurting blood. Because I was squeamish, Daddy, with a look of disgust, would send me into the house to pluck chickens and help the women in the kitchen.

Making chicken corn soup was an all-day affair. We would make it in bulk and add it to the growing wealth in the freezer, which included a steer we would share with my uncle's family. (We once went to a neighboring farm to select our steer, and when I saw the bloody carcasses hanging on steel meat hooks, I started dry heaving at the sight and would only peck at red meat for decades.) Since we couldn't fit all of the meat in the freezers along with everything else, we rented freezer space in Carlisle.

When summer arrived, it brought bounty from the brambles on the farm and the sides of the road. We picked wild black raspberries that stained our hands purple. Those raspberries were my first source of independent income—twelve dollars of harvested berries bought my first bicycle, a used green Schwinn from the bike store in Carlisle. We also picked loads of strawberries, peaches, plums, and apricots that we made into jam, froze, or canned. Mother would take us to local orchards to pick cherries too. We enjoyed climbing the trees and filling our buckets. We froze the cherries whole and packed them in school lunches.

Fall brought more to our overflowing freezers. Shellbark nuts, which look like a small pecan but with sharper flavor, were used in the reception salad we made for company and for birthday cakes. Each birthday we got to request a favorite meal and a favorite cake. Coconut cake was a strong contender, but shellbark cake with cream cheese icing was a favorite too.

In winter we rested somewhat. My father repaired machinery and delivered potatoes from the storage shed. Mother mended clothes, gathered seed catalogues to plan the gardens, and sewed new clothes. And we children read by the fireplace or worked on indoor projects and hobbies: David might make candle tapers from the antique mold he acquired; Benny might carve rubber-band guns; and we girls busied ourselves with embroidery projects or reading. But on certain days, when the weather permitted, we would build opposing snow forts outside and have a huge "battle." As much as we each delighted in our individual projects, those snowball-hurling days of all of us playing together and then warming up by the fire with hot cocoa became some of our fondest collective memories of winter.

A Treasure Chest of Skills

Mother began preparing us girls early for her life—which would be our life too. Beginning with sewing buttons that had fallen off and darning socks that acquired holes, we learned basic sewing. As our fingers became more capable of fine stitches, we graduated to embroidery with simple cross-stitch patterns, decorating the wide hem of pillowcases. Once we'd learned all the different embroidery stitches, we practiced them on increasingly complex projects: long bureau scarves that adorned and protected the top of our dressers, round ones that graced side tables in the living room, and embellishments on clothing. Once we became proficient in that, we would move on to crewel projects, like the hanging calendar I got for a birthday present that used metallic gold accent threads. Eventually, we would be allowed to take on the final exam of embroidery: a sampler.

Samplers were a demonstration of the mastery of this particular skill, as it displayed an encyclopedia of stitches. (Tiny stitches and consistency of length were an indication of skill level and character.) The composition and artistry of the entire piece reflected another aspect of the future wife—her dedication to the art of housekeeping. Samplers were often the size of a poster, with a wide embroidered band framing a display of each letter of the alphabet and each number. Often a Bible verse or rhyming verse was placed at the top or bottom, while in the middle a Pennsylvania Dutch folk art–style home might be surrounded by birds, animals, and flowers with a tree of paradise. Once completed, the girl's name and date of completion were embroidered at the bottom and the sampler was framed and hung.

The sampler would go with a young woman to her new home as a wife, and the pillowcases, bureau scarves, quilts, and other useful home items she'd made would be stored in a hope chest to provide a foundation of the essentials when she began housekeeping. Mother had a Lane cedar hope chest filled to the brim with items from her life, along with stories that went with them.

I was eager to make a sampler and start my own hope chest, but once we got a new sewing machine, I was enraptured. I watched Mother's fingers expertly guide the fabric past the needle, furiously flying over some new outfit. I wanted to join her in pinning the Butterick and McCall's patterns to fabric, cutting them out, and producing dresses.

"How about starting with a pair of pull-on shorts?" she suggested.

The straight lines, and the absence of pockets and a zipper, were a simple first project that I loved. Pretty soon I would be making simple shirts, then graduating to more complicated projects.

By the time I entered my teen years, I would be well on my way to possessing the skills of a productive wife and mother.

Saturday's Child

Not only were our seasons markers of time, but our weeks were divided into neat categories of tasks assigned to specific days.

Monday was wash day, when we brought all the clothes down to the utility room and sorted them into piles by color. By this time we had an automatic washing machine, but I could still remember the wringer washing machine Mother had set up in the garage before we got an automatic. My job had been to hand items of clothing to her so she could drown the clothes in the large metal bucket and then feed them through rollers to dry. We were both relieved when that automatic washer arrived. Doing laundry for our entire family was still a lot of work, but it certainly made things easier. (We got an automatic dryer too, but Mother said it used too much electricity.) Once the clothes were washed, we hung them outside—no matter the season—on four long washing lines strung between sturdy metal poles.

Wednesday was bread day. Mother would gather five pounds of white flour, five pounds of whole wheat flour, and a few other ingredients. (One day she showed me how to test the temperature of the water on my wrist to make sure it was warm enough to get the yeast to rise, but not so hot that it killed it.) Then, Mother would knead the mixture to mash it all together, let it rise, punch it down, knead it more, then let it rise again. This seemed to go on for quite some time. After she was finished kneading, she would form the dough into ten smooth loaves, cover them, and let them rise. Once that phase was over, they would be baked. When the loaves came out warm and steaming, we would butter a piece and add black raspberry jam or honey. There was nothing like freshly baked bread from our oven.

Friday was shopping day. (More on that to come.)

Sunday was always a day of rest; nobody was permitted to work except for cooking and cleaning up the dishes. The only time I remember us working on a Sunday was when the weather turned cold much earlier than expected, and our crops would have been ruined by frost if we didn't bring them in. Because it was a dire circumstance, we got special dispensation from the bishops to work all day Sunday and into the night.

Saturday, though, was cleaning day, particularly if we were inviting company for Sunday dinner. One Saturday I was on my hands and knees scrubbing the kitchen floor. (We didn't use mops because scrubbing was the only proper way to wash a floor.) I remember thinking how I couldn't understand why our chores were never-ending, and my wondering drifted out of my mouth.

"Why do we have to work so hard all the time?" I asked Mother, who was supervising my scrubbing.

But before she could reply, I spotted the cloth calendar beyond her shoulder, hanging over the basement door on its wooden dowel. Every year we got a new calendar with a colorful design and the old one became a dish-drying towel. One year, the calendar told the fate associated with one's day of birth, and I had memorized it.

> *Monday's child is fair of face*
> *Tuesday's child is full of grace*
> *Wednesday's child is full of woe*
> *Thursday's child has far to go,*
> *Friday's child is loving and giving,*
> *Saturday's child has to work for a living,*
> *But the child that's born on the Sabbath is fair and wise and good and gay.*

We had each wanted to know the day of our birth, and as I recalled mine in that moment, I had the answer to my question.

"Oh," I exclaimed with delight as the awareness struck, "I'm a Saturday's child. *That's* why I have to work so hard."

Mother chuckled, and I happily went back to my scrubbing.

If there was a good reason—some meaning I could latch on to—I found myself accepting my circumstances and, despite the hard work, even enjoying them.

Shopping Day

Fridays were days of both adventure and observation. Mother would take us into town in the car, with the radio tuned to the same channel: one that featured a smooth, deep, confident voice delivering the news. I enjoyed these trips—except for the drive there. The back roads had undulations that must have been made for a slower speed because when we went over them, my stomach would go flying and I'd feel sick by the time we got to the grocery store.

We always went to the A&P on shopping day. While we roamed the aisles and Mother checked off her grocery list, we kids were careful to be good. Mother always said she received lots of compliments on our behavior, that people said we were just like little adults. That pleased her. People often stared at her like she was weird because of her clothes and bonnet, though, which seemed very rude to me. When that happened, I would want to stick my tongue out at them from behind my mother's skirts, but I had to be satisfied with merely giving them the squinty-eye look; if I got caught with my tongue out, I would be in big trouble. Mother would warn, "If you make me hit you in the store, you'll really get a paddling when we get home."

Shopping days were usually just for buying groceries, but occasionally Mother needed some things at Montgomery Ward. She would allow us to plop down on the floor in front of the rows of televisions for sale while she shopped, and because television was forbidden to us at home, we didn't much care what was playing so long as we could watch.

The main doors to Montgomery Ward spilled out into the MJ mall. Sometimes, if the show wasn't that interesting, my mind would wander toward three curiosities that often fascinated me just beyond those doors. One was the large, shallow water fountain in the center of the main walkway that was covered in pennies at the bottom from people investing in their wishes. *What do people wish for when they throw in their penny?* I pondered. Another was the food stand that sold soft pretzels. I could never figure out what possessed the customers who kept buying those mediocre imposters of the real pretzels you could get in Lancaster. They didn't even smell good. *Why don't the customers wise up?* I wondered. And right beside the pretzel stand was the Army recruiter who was always trying to rope people into signing their life away. When young men would walk up, some stayed only briefly and asked a couple of questions. I figured those were the ones who got away, and that the ones who stuck around got captured for life by the recruiter. *What would happen to them?* I contemplated with a mixture of worry and sadness. *Would they become prisoners of war, like the soldiers talked about in such somber tones on Mother's news station in the car?*

And then Mother would appear with her bags in hand, and I'd have to wait until she needed more things from Ward's to engage in the curiosities of the outside world that comprised my ongoing saga.

Learning the Hard Way

Both Mother and Daddy believed it was necessary to paddle us children as a disciplinary measure, but they each had different reasons for doing it.

With Daddy, it would happen mainly for disobedience to him, or for dishonesty. He always said that honesty was a hugely important virtue and to remember that it takes twenty lies to cover up one lie. (Mother added that actions spoke louder than words.)

"Your word should be your bond," Daddy would say. "Your reputation is all you really have." He also said, "Two wrongs don't make a right." That one always made sense to me.

Daddy used a belt or a paddle—and for the paddle we had to pick out the piece of wood and carve it ourselves. I thought it horribly unjust to have to select our own paddle, and I guess my brothers did too because we chose a piece of balsa from my brother's model airplane kits. That did not go over so well.

Daddy had such strong ideas about disciplining children that even when I was a baby, he thought corporal punishment for crying was justified. Mother wrote in her diary that when they brought me home from the hospital, I had colic and would not stop crying. Daddy didn't like this because he had to get up and go to work. He said he'd paddle me and that would take care of that. Mother reported that it worked. I can't imagine an infant being hit and that that would stop her crying. I would have thought the opposite would happen. Oddly enough, I've never been much of a crier.

Mother's biggest reason for paddling was for talking back to her, or if we made her look bad in public. Once, while she was paying the cashier, I reached out and put a pack of Fruit Stripe gum in my pocket. All the candy had just been sitting there in front of me, so I didn't know I had stolen something until we got home. When I pulled the pack out and began to unwrap a stick, Mother suddenly looked up. "Where did you get that gum?"

"At the . . . store," I said hesitantly.

"Hand it over," she ordered. She then doled out a piece to each of my siblings. Instead of a piece for me, I got a paddling. Then she sent me to my piggy bank to retrieve the cost of the gum. Back we went to the store, where she marched me in to apologize to the clerk.

That's how I learned what stealing was.

There were times that both our parents would be too busy to stop and paddle, so we would get it later. On those occasions, we'd don ten pairs of underwear to pad the blows, hoping it wouldn't be a bare-bottom paddling.

Both Mother and Daddy were determined that we learn lessons for everything, even if we had to do it the hard way.

Daddy's Opinion List

At the A&P, there was a red coffee grinder at the end of the checkout lane that smelled heavenly. Mother must have thought so too because she occasionally purchased instant coffee, even though she wasn't supposed to.

Daddy forbade Mother to drink coffee. He didn't think it was healthy. But sometimes, when he was working at the Other Farm, she would make a cup. We children wanted to know how this forbidden drink tasted, so we would clandestinely take green plastic dinner glasses, add hot water to some granules, then add milk and lots of brown sugar till it tasted good. Then we'd sneak outside and sit out of sight on the bank behind the pine tree in the front yard until the evidence of our misdeed was consumed.

Daddy had other opinions about Mother too. Even though she was 5'7" and weighed only 125 lbs., he said she was fat. To try to slim down even further, she would run a couple of miles down along the creek and then back up the lane every day she was able. Her gray skirts would swish back and forth against her ankles while her black shoes rhythmically pounded the macadam. When we weren't in school, we would follow along, trying to keep up.

Daddy also didn't like her talking on the phone to her mother, Grandma Gross. He not only complained about the cost of the long-distance calls, he was always finding fault with her family, as if his was the ideal. He scorned her on more than one occasion, saying, "You've never grown up. You're still tied to your mother's apron strings." I didn't know what that meant but it didn't sound good. He also said she was the runt of her family, like he had gotten a defective product at the store.

Papap Gross had been admitted to the State Mental Hospital for a spell after having a nervous breakdown, which gave Daddy more ammunition to criticize Mother's family. I never understood why Daddy was the one who took us to visit him or why Mother never came along. I did enjoy the visits, though. The property had a broad grass lawn dotted with peaceful sycamores, and we would bring a brown paper bag full of peanuts to feed the squirrels. Papap Gross would sit on the lawn with a blanket over his legs.

It seemed like almost everybody in our family had a nervous breakdown at some time or another. Grandma Gross had one too, when she and Papap almost went bankrupt when Mother was little. Papap was a poor businessman and too stubborn to admit it. That's when Grandma Gross got permission from the Church to start her business at the Lemoyne Farmers Market so the family would have some income. Turns out that Grandma was as good at business as Papap was poor at it.

Daddy continually berated Mother's family for being weak. But he was also irked to no end that Grandma was a strong woman and Papap wasn't more forceful and dominating. It wasn't supposed to be this way, he insisted. He told me that when my brothers were born, having all boys suited him pretty well. He wanted a large farm crew and boys were ideal for that. But then he added with a jolly smile, "When you came along, though, I decided little girls were all right too." I wanted to believe him, but Daddy didn't have much good to say about females, so I wasn't sure which story was true.

Daddy's father had had a nervous breakdown too, right after Daddy was born. Why that wasn't a show of weakness in Daddy's eyes, I never understood. Daddy merely claimed it was because of the strain of supporting his family and his parents, and that his father was never the same after that— not as strong or able to do as much work. (That never made sense to me, though, since Papap Bear did acquire four farms during the Depression years, so it seemed to me he must have done pretty well.) When Papap went to the sanatorium, Grandma Bear was left with the care of the farm and three little boys for several months.

Having a nervous breakdown must be normal, I figured. You go away to rest for six months, and then you come back. Grandma Bear appeared be the only one who hadn't collapsed under the stress of life by having a breakdown.

Looking back, I believe most of Daddy's opinions revolved around his need to win and feel superior; he viewed everything as inferior to his family (the Bears), his ways, and his values, not to mention to men in general. Later, the indoctrinated notion that we were superior in some way would sustain us. Though it wasn't true, it did urge us to hold our heads up in the darkest of times, and it set a standard that we all aimed for.

The Voice

Although we didn't know it at the time, we later learned that Mother tried to keep us constantly busy because she was afraid of losing control of six spirited kids. So, as soon as we walked up the lane from the school bus, we were immediately ushered to the back porch where a pan of lima beans, waiting to be shelled, was plopped onto our laps, or some other pressing task was waiting.

Mother sometimes had a list of things we were supposed to do for the day, but we also knew that it was often a kind of line-of-sight scheduling—meaning if you weren't seen, it was harder to be assigned something to do. (The truth was, with all the work she was constantly doing, trying to supervise a half dozen children was challenging. I imagine it was like herding cats; she simply couldn't always keep an eye on us.) So, if you were lucky *and* sneaky, you could avoid her spotting you and assigning a task, especially if you could navigate the open area between the house and the woods and end up safely out of sight. Even better, if you walked far enough down the meadow so that you couldn't hear her calling, you could honestly say that you never heard her and therefore be free for several hours.

Once we reached the woods and the meadows, we kids had access to a vast playground. Within the woods lay endless possibilities, one of which was created by the creek. A portion of the creek had departed the main part of the stream and wrapped an arm around a circle of land to the side. We called this our "island," and it was surrounded by a two-foot-wide moat. We made it accessible by placing a recovered plank of wood across the moat and became "pioneers" discovering untouched territory. Only children were allowed on secret expeditions to this island, and we often built small fires and had picnics there on Sundays.

Farther down the meadow and lane near the mailbox was a thicket of bushes that provided another place to construct our fantasy world. Dense branches obscured the interior from view from the outside, but once "inside," thinner branches allowed for the creation of an entire make-believe community of homes, stores, friends, and relatives.

Between our chosen hiding spots were winding roads that made for adventurous passages to and from the resting places we carved out of the magical place that was the Home Farm.

One gorgeous summer day, when I was around the age of six, I escaped Mother's eagle eye. Packing a brown bag lunch, I set out on the path that wound along the small ridge above the millrace.

The millrace had once diverted water from the creek to service a mill, but now it was so lazy and slow that bright green algae grew in thick, fascinating blankets on its surface. Snakes meandered by the concrete wall of the bridge my father constructed to carry his tractors from the home driveway to the meadow and passage to the Other Farm. Like a tiny canal, the millrace had a small bank on each side. On the ridge of one bank was a narrow path that wound through small saplings and along the tangle of bushes and brambles, worn to bare earth by traversing animals. This path was mostly hidden from view of the lane until it opened into a small clearing where the bank was free from branches and briars.

When I reached my destination, I sat on my haunches and placed my brown bag by my side. Wrapping my arms around my knees, I took in the scene before me. Enormous lily pads in bloom stretched from bank to bank, holding the algae at bay. Frogs gathered atop these flat thrones and croaked out their songs as the crickets and birds chimed in. On my left, bright yellow buttercups danced whimsically up the bank. As I surveyed the scene, intoxicated with the exuberant sounds and colors of summer, my eyes were drawn across the millrace tableau over the fence that bordered the lane, then up higher to a sky of mesmerizing blue. Perched there in the expanse was a series of billowy white clouds climbing on each other. They were crisp enough to support a person, I thought, but not so dense that dark shadows of a storm would appear anytime soon. So, I went up there to visit again, turning immediately to the right where the angels bustled in their daily activities. I imagined brushing up against the angels' robes and them smiling affectionately, after which I skipped from cloud to cloud and roamed all the secret hiding places there.

And then, abruptly and unceremoniously, I was jerked out of my trance by a firm, no-nonsense voice.

"You will have a bigger life."

I swiveled toward the shadows of the woods behind me.

Who had spoken? Where was this man?

I realized with growing alarm how isolated I was and became a little frightened. No one would hear me if I yelled; I was too far away from the house. My eyes darted left then right and behind me, tentatively searching amongst the saplings. But no one was there.

What did that mean? What was a bigger life?

"I don't want a different life," I thought indignantly.

The meadows and streams and fields of this farm were my favorite place. I couldn't imagine being anywhere else. My sister Leah and I had already decided we loved this farm and weren't going anywhere—*ever*. In fact, we vowed to plop a trailer down in Mother and Daddy's backyard and live right there on our farm forever.

"Oh, well," I shrugged. "Mother always did say I was a dreamer."

Though I wrote this incident off to my imagination at the time, it would for the rest of my life serve as an anchor to remind me that there had always been a plan—and that it was a sign to keep the faith, no matter what.

CHAPTER TWO

1972

Not all storms come to disrupt your life.
Some come to clear your path.
—UNKNOWN

A Big Christmas

My baby sister Sharon's second birthday rang in 1972. But before the New Year arrived, that Christmas of 1971 was the last one we would share before everything fell apart. The sounds of discord must have been in the air, but I don't remember them anymore. What I *do* remember is a highly unusual Christmas.

My father's business, with the help of expert advice from the Penn State extension service, had steadily increased and thrived far more than anyone had predicted possible. When other farmers suffered through the uncertainty of dry summers, the ample irrigation we enjoyed from the creek was evident in our lush green fields and bumper crops. With that came new tractors and increasingly specialized farm machinery, such as the large potato harvester that had taken the place of harvesting potatoes by hand. Daddy had also taken a trip to Ohio to haul back a large trailer stacked high with added irrigation pipe, along with acquiring a three-person cabbage planter where workers could sit while they fed small plants into pincers that inserted them into the ground, then gently tamp the surrounding soil.

My father also brought home a brand-new Ford Galaxie 500. It sat in the driveway all shiny and black. I wondered, after climbing inside and inhaling the unfamiliar but delicious smell of a new car, if it might be considered too fancy by the Church. I loved this car, so I hoped it was all right. Plus, Uncle Glenn and Aunt Mary Ellen had a slightly fancier car, so I figured we would be allowed to keep it.

These signs of abundance had been growing for years, but not until this Christmas had they reached us children. Usually, we received one present each, but this year there were more than six total, a pile we discovered hidden behind a large chair in the living room, all wrapped in bright colors. We were astonished to see so many, and curious too—so curious that while Mother and Daddy were out shopping, Benny and I carefully lifted the tape on the ends of the gifts and peeked inside. Apparently, we were not as careful as we thought, for our parents noticed as soon as they came home and threatened to take back everything if we did it again.

Though it was not new, we also felt abundant having a ventilator in our living room that poured out soothing, warm air from the wood fire to all corners of the room. A Christmas tree stood in one of them. (Looking back at the pictures, I realize it was a tall, skinny, scraggly cedar cut down from the woods and resting in a bucket of sand, but it didn't seem shabby at the time.) We knew to be grateful to have a tree, no matter its size or type. Christmas was supposed to be about the birth of Jesus, and there was some question whether a Christmas tree distracted from this message.

Mother said Grandma Gross justified her tree by saying it was for the children. It was no great secret, though, that Grandma loved Christmas and all the trappings that went with it. She would decorate for the holidays with prolific pots of poinsettias and put up a Christmas tree with all the trimmings. She even had an antique electric train that chugged around her tree, running along metal tracks over bridges and through tunnels. We were thrilled when she decided to gift that train to us. We would step carefully around it as we decorated our tree with the red and green construction paper garlands we made, and with the popcorn and cranberry garlands we had threaded sitting by the fire.

I always loved to see the Christmas decorations going up in town too. Green garlands would be strung across the Carlisle main streets, and large red candle-shaped lights adorned each lamppost. In the town square across from the new courthouse, Santa's house, intricately decorated with a warm yellow light glowing through a small window facing the street, welcomed the line of children waiting to enter and hand Santa their Christmas lists. The kids on the school bus talked about Santa and what he would bring them, but *I* knew something they did not: Santa wasn't real because Christmas isn't *supposed* to be about Santa. Still, I looked longingly at his little house on the square and wished I could visit and sit on his lap too.

All in all, we enjoyed an abundant holiday. Because both Susie's and Sharon's birthdays were so close to Christmas, they often got one present that was expected to do dual duty for both holidays. But this year, they got grander presents than normal. I specifically remember Sharon receiving a red and blue stuffed teddy bear almost as big as she was, as well as a red wagon with slatted sides big enough to haul our German Shepherd, Duke. The boys got lots of power tools, and I got a jumping jimmy that made me think of a witch jumping up to reach me on the top floor of my Rapunzel-like castle. Even Grandma and Papap Bear gave us large presents, which was out of the norm for them.

As an adult now looking back, I wonder about that Christmas and question, *What did the adults know that we kids didn't?*

A Surprising Trip

Another outcome of our growing abundance is that we took our first real vacation. We usually went to Ontario, Canada, where the other half of our church membership and cousins lived. (Daddy's brother's widow had moved back to Canada and remarried, and his only sister had married a Canadian man too, so we always had lots of catching up to do with our Canadian cousins.) Or we drove in the opposite direction to Illinois to visit our other relatives. But this time we drove down to Williamsburg, Virginia. We saw the wild horses at Chincoteague, marveled at the bridge and bay tunnel, saw the ships at Jamestown, and watched in fascination as artisans in period costume blew glass into beautiful shapes. We spent the day putting our heads in the public stocks, visiting the governor's palace, and seeing the armory and all the tradespeople plying their crafts. Tired and hungry, we begged for food, but my father said that restaurants inside Williamsburg were "too salty" (his term when he thought something was overpriced); plus, if we left, we would have to pay to re-enter. So, my parents bought a large gingerbread man at the period bakery and we shared it among the eight of us. I tried to quell the panic that arose, wondering how long it would be before we would get our next real meal. But even the memory of that hunger could not dampen the thrill of adventure I felt at discovering a wider world beyond the walls of our culture.

Two Sides of Spiritual Education

Second grade is one of several years of schooling where my memory was spotty. Of course I remember the humiliation of being singled out for speech therapy (which seemed one more piece of evidence that there was something profoundly wrong with me), and it being the year I got scarlet fever and Mother being worried I might die. I also clearly recall it was the year I hated anyone who beat me in tetherball, the year I wanted a maxi dress like the other girls more than anything (but knew it would probably never happen), and the year my siblings and I were called the Hare Bear Bunch at school after the television show. I wasn't sure if that was a good thing or a bad thing because I'd never seen it. So when talk of the show came up at recess, I would laugh and say, "Oh yeah, wasn't that so funny what happened on last night's show!" I reasoned that pretending I had seen it the night before would make the other children think we had something in common with them, and that they wouldn't consider us weird.

There was one area, though, where I did not mind standing out. One time, I overheard some kids talking about their parents on the school bus. One boy was upset because he said his parents lied to him, and another kid chimed in that this had happened to him as well. When I heard this, I was instantly relieved and grateful that my parents were Mennonites. They *couldn't* lie to us, I knew. They weren't allowed to lie to anybody because of our faith.

In the larger world, however, we did stand out; lots of things were considered too worldly for us, like jewelry and makeup and anything that looked fancy. My parents didn't even wear wedding rings, which made me worry that people at school might think my parents weren't married. We even kept a polite distance from people outside our Church because they might corrupt us with their worldly ways. I played with my brothers, sisters, and cousins, for instance, but I didn't have friends at school or go to their houses to play. The one time I was invited to a classmate's birthday party, I begged my mother to let me go. When she gave me permission, I became the first of my siblings to attend a birthday party.

My parents and virtually all our relatives on both sides of the family only congregated with members of our Church. The men who didn't have farms or small businesses often worked for other Church members, or in jobs that wouldn't be considered "too worldly" and might lead to their being corrupted and steered away from "the faith." The women, as I've already described, were all housewives who raised large families, cooked, sewed, cleaned, entertained visitors, and worked on the family farms.

Because we were so sheltered, besides those wonderful days of being plopped in front of the televisions at Montgomery Ward while Mother shopped and seeing snippets of whatever was playing, I had never seen an actual movie. But that changed in second grade.

Gathered with my classmates in the auditorium that doubled as a cafeteria, I was captivated when the lights went down and a bright, title image illuminated the portable screen. The movie was called *Paddle to the Sea*. I loved everything about it and would have happily watched it every single day if I could—even as an adult, I never forgot this sweet little film. It was about a young First Nation boy in the wilderness of Canada. One winter he sits, every night, by the crackling light of the fireplace, carving a canoe from a block of wood. All winter long he shapes and hones it until a man with long hair, sitting ramrod straight, begins to emerge from the canoe. When every detail has been whittled to perfection, the boy carefully paints the figure in bright colors. Then, he pours a molten bead of lead in a groove on the bottom of the canoe so that it will stay upright. Finally, he carves an inscription on the bottom with the name of the canoe, Paddle to the Sea, and instructions for whomever finds it: "Please put me back in the water." After that, he releases it on a snow-covered hill, and the spring thaw carries it to a stream downhill. Though the little boy will never leave the wilderness, he hopes his creation will find its way downstream and eventually to the sea.

Right away, Paddle to the Sea encounters obstacles. Raging rapids up-end him but he rights himself; a fire rages on either side of the creek as he floats through the inferno but he emerges unscathed; animals think he is food to eat but he escapes. Just when you think he's been through enough, he takes a stomach-churning ride over Niagara Falls and gets frozen amidst crushing blocks of ice. Luckily the springtime thaw frees him, and he moves on his way once again. The times he washes up on shore, the lapping waves either pull him back into the gently moving stream, or children want to keep him as a toy but obey the carved commandment on the bottom: "Put me back in the water." Somehow, against all odds, he *does* make it, journeying downstream until he reaches the great, wide ocean.

I loved this story and the way it unfolded, but truth be told, I would have watched *any* movie or television show and been happy. I loved the luxury of not having class, the treat of sitting in the dark and hearing the clacking reel on the back wall where the movie projector sat, and the magic of watching a story unfold. I even imagined the reel was playing tag with the teacher, trying to avoid capture and being forced into the projector. I hoped the teacher would win.

After that first introduction to cinema, school became the place my brothers and sisters and I sometimes got to watch full-length movies or television shows. I didn't care if some of them were strictly educational. I always looked forward to the times when the lights were dimmed and the television was rolled to the front of the class, or when the teacher said we were going to the auditorium to watch a movie.

But I would never forget how enchanted I was with that very first one, and how later I understood how that little canoe's path to the sea was a spiritual education of its own.

Journey Toward Individuation

I didn't set out to be an individual in 1972; in fact, I intended the exact opposite. I wanted more than anything to join the Church my ancestors and virtually all my living relatives belonged to. My father's genealogy book records his first ancestor (a persecuted Mennonite minister) coming here from the area near the Swiss-German border around 1720. William Penn would extend an invitation for our people to escape persecution and settle in Penn's woods—or Pennsylvania as it became known. On Mother's side I have no specific date, but it probably goes back a ways too.

I knew I would become a member eventually, but patience has never been one of my virtues. And unlike the Catholics who baptize children as infants, our people, as my mother often reminded me, refuse to do this. We let children choose whether they want to join. When she would read from *Martyr's Mirror*—a well-worn book at least six inches thick with pages as thin as onion skin—she'd remind us that our refusal to perform infant baptism was why the Catholics had persecuted us. The book catalogued stories of the gruesome deaths of those who died for their faith. They were hunted like animals by the authorities of their day, and when found they were burned alive, beheaded, drowned, or hung if they refused to renounce their faith. This detailed record of the convicted grace and courage of our most revered ancestors, the martyrs who were tortured and perished because of their loyalty to the Church, became part of the fabric of our being.

In the spring of my second-grade year, I asked Mother to please ask her brother, who was a bishop, if I could become a convert. Typically, someone becomes a convert in their late teens to early twenties, and then they get baptized as a member after a year or so. Once you join, though, you can never leave, or you will get excommunicated and shunned. I'd never seen an eight-year-old convert, but like I said, I tend to get ahead of myself. Plus, I usually knew what I wanted. And while I was at it, I told Mother what my wish was for my ninth birthday in November so that was not left up to chance: a real Bible. Not the Children's Bible she was always reading to us. I made that clear. I wanted a grownup Bible. My very own.

Mother promised she'd speak to Uncle Glenn about my becoming a convert but was noncommittal about the Bible. I was not exactly sure if she'd heard what I wanted, so I made sure to reinforce it from time to time over the weeks and through the summer to make sure it didn't slip through the cracks. She was also a bit distracted during that time for reasons we were soon to find out.

The W Word

That spring was when we children became aware of a series of meetings taking place at our house. Mother and Daddy refused to answer when we asked what they were for, but they were different from most of our gatherings. Normally we only had company on Sundays, but these meetings were on weekdays and no meals were served. Bishops and ministers came from Lancaster, Chambersburg, Middlesex, and Waynesboro, and even as far away as Canada. The meetings were conducted in our living room, and we kids were not allowed downstairs while they took place. We figured they must be having some kind of church service, so we set up a pile of books and placed a short oak lectern we found in the attic on top of them so that they could speak from an official pulpit. Strangely, my father insisted that some of these meetings include our neighbors and certain relatives from my father's family whom we had never met.

Before everyone arrived, we were sent upstairs where we promptly pressed our ears to the wooden floorboards. We all took turns, but none of us could make out nor understand what the adults were discussing.

Sandwiched between these secret meetings was a frightening argument that occurred between my parents that all of us kids were witness to.

"The ministry is a bunch of hypocrites!" Daddy spouted, which he had begun to say often. "*Hypocrites*! They say one thing and they do another. They constantly preach unity but they aren't even in unity with each other. It's so hypocritical!" He spat out the words "hypocrite" and "hypocritical" like bullets firing from the .22 he kept. Daddy continued talking loudly and jabbing his finger into his palm while making insistent arguments to Mother, and then he said a foreign word that caught our ears.

"Oh, Robert," Mother said with disgust. "Don't be so vulgar."

In our house any kind of bad word was punished severely. (Once, when I was five or six, I'd remarked, "Mommy, you know our neighbors the Hechendorns? Their name sounds like heck and darn." She said those words sounded too much like hell and damn and promptly washed my mouth out with soap and water.) The word Daddy spit out definitely sounded like a bad word, and Benny and I glanced at each other wide-eyed, wondering what it meant. Side by side, we headed straight for the dictionary on the shelf in the living room, flipped to W, and skimmed till we found it.

Whore.

We looked at each other in shock. Was he saying Mother was selling her body? He had also said something vulgar and graphic about her sleeping with the main bishop in our area. But that was Uncle Glenn, her own brother. That would be incest, we knew, so that couldn't be right. *What was he talking about?*

By June, the mysterious meetings ended.

Looking back, I wonder if Mother sensed things were about to change forever.

One day in late spring, she dressed us in our Sunday clothes, combed our hair carefully, and drove us to town. It was not a Friday, so we weren't going to the A&P. I thought maybe we were going to the library or to the bank to deposit some money in our savings accounts, but we went to neither of those places. Mother parked the car and we got out silently. Sidewalk sales offered racks of dresses and clothing hanging in the sunshine, as if the town was having a party. But Mother passed them by without even looking. Instead, she marched toward Dutrys, where we got our feet measured with the big metal sliding tool and bought all our shoes. *Maybe we were going there.* But we turned just prior to it and walked up a set of stairs to a second-story photographer's studio.

After Mother paid him, the photographer assembled the six of us kids—ranging from ages two to eleven—for our first official family photograph.

I didn't know it then, but I suspect my mother wanted to freeze time and record the image of goodness and family that she feared was slipping away from her.

Winning

I always looked forward to the last day of school for two reasons: one was the bus ride home, and the other was what was called "field day."

The bus ride home was special on this particular day because the driver would stop at a soft-serve ice cream store on our route and let anyone who had money get off and order a cone. I loved this ritual and always brought money from my piggy bank. But the even bigger treat on the last day of school was being outside the whole day and having the chance to win ribbons in the field day competitions.

For my final day of second grade, Mother made me a yellow dress, which was astonishing because our dresses were mainly navy blue, Kelly green, or brown, and more old-fashioned than what the other girls wore. This dress, however, with its delicate flowers sprinkled all over it was a purely happy dress. (Mother and Daddy made us girls wear dresses to school even though some other girls wore pants. We could wear shorts under our dresses on gym day and for field day, though.)

Because I loved winning ribbons so much, I signed up for every field day event that I could: the sack race, dashes of any length, the standing broad jump, the softball throw. Winning blue ribbons was my favorite, of course, but red ribbons were okay too. I kept my collection in a special box Grandma Gross once saw me admiring and said I could have—it was a large metal box stamped in a gold tone with German coats of arms on it and a picture of a model ship on the front. I think it was a cigar box. Anyway, I put all my treasures and keepsakes in it: cards from my third birthday (that one stood out as a particularly happy one for some reason), all the handkerchiefs I'd collected from Grandma Bear (she always, with her quiet smile, offered us colorful little handkerchiefs she kept hidden away in a drawer each time we visited her and Papap's house), some small embroidery or crewel projects I'd done, and of course, all my ribbons on top (well, the blue and red ones anyway . . . I filed the yellow ones on the bottom out of sight). I knew I would someday get a hope chest just like Mother had, but for the time being, that old cigar box suited me just fine. I loved placing special things in it, but I especially loved imagining it filled with first- and second-place ribbons from each field day until I had amassed a huge collection.

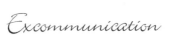

Excommunication

We went to church every single Sunday from as far back as I could remember—but that changed on June 11, 1972.

Out of the blue, Daddy forbade us to go with Mother, saying he did not want his children hearing the sermon where he got "excommunicated." We didn't know exactly what excommunication was or understand why we weren't going to church, but my father was adamant. He did not want his children witnessing his humiliation. And so, Mother went to church alone and Daddy took all us kids to Gettysburg battlefield, the high-water mark of the Confederacy. My father loved battlefields; we had been to Gettysburg many times before, and we often visited battlefields on our way home from trips. (Daddy grew up boxing with his brother and relished a good fight. I could not understand the appeal.)

Ten days later Hurricane Agnes rolled through Pennsylvania. It was the costliest hurricane in US history at the time. Almost seventy thousand homes and three thousand businesses were ruined. The governor's mansion on the banks of the Susquehanna was flooded, and 122 people perished. It was so destructive that the name was retired.

On the Home Farm we were flooded in, and the house, which had always seemed ample, now felt oppressive and threatening. The Condoguinet creek alongside our home was a swollen, raging, churning brown, carrying a parade of items once upstream from us, including cars, washing machines, and picnic tables. The deluge disdained all boundaries, swallowing up the meadow and the fort my brothers had built, and overflowing the millrace as if it were a thimble. These destructive rains didn't usually stop Daddy, though. He liked to go out in the canoe and ride the currents when it flooded because he found the challenge "exhilarating." In prior floods, my mother had put her foot down when he intended to take us children with him. It was too reckless, she insisted. And this time, even he must have agreed because the canoe remained tucked away in the barn.

After the waters receded, a neighboring farmer painted a three-foot line on his barn by the road, marking the high-water mark of Hurricane Agnes. (It would still be there years later when I drove by as an adult.) We children did not understand it yet, but we had just passed the high-water mark for our family too. After June 1972, my father would refer to events in one of two ways: "before the Trouble began" or "after the Trouble."

Scriptural Warfare

In July, barely a month after he had been "excommunicated," a term my siblings and I still didn't fully understand, Daddy shocked us with the purchase of a brand-new trailer that he placed on the opposite side of the creek on the Other Farm. On the day we visited and inspected it, I noted that even though it was new, it didn't seem very solid to me. The compact kitchen, two bedrooms, and flimsy doors and windows weren't particularly impressive, and I didn't understand why Daddy would purchase such a thing. But quickly enough, we discovered that Daddy intended to live in that trailer—to a point. He ate meals with us but often slept in the trailer, until he developed a pattern of unexpectedly announcing that he was coming back home to live for good. These homecoming pronouncements always foreshadowed trouble: they signaled that he was ready to blow his top and assert his rightful place as the head of the household, after which a terrible scene always followed.

"You're too hardheaded, Gale," he would say to Mother. "You need to be put in your place."

He would go on to complain that she listened to the bigwig bishops—including her brother, Uncle Glenn—her mother, and everybody else except him. He said that she should be obeying *him*, that she needed to learn who her rightful leader was. Daddy would then chase Mother round and round the kitchen table or the car in the garage, after which the scriptural pummeling would begin.

On this particular day, with the Bible resting on the splayed palm of Daddy's enormous hand, he thumbed quickly to one of his references and looked at Mother pointedly, jabbing at the page with his right middle finger:

"Ephesians 5:22. *Wives, submit yourselves unto your own husbands, as unto the Lord. For the husband is the head of the wife, even as Christ is the head of the church: and he is the savior of the body. Therefore, as the church is subject unto Christ so let the wives be to their own husbands in everything.*"

Mother eyed him warily from across the table, searching for any movement showing a lunge in her direction.

After his diatribe, Daddy lamented, "Now look at this situation . . . arguing in front of the children. Why, my parents always settled things behind closed doors. They never disagreed in front of us."

My eyes widened in shock, but my lips parted only slightly so Daddy wouldn't notice the astonishment on my face and call it disrespectful.

Doesn't he see that he's doing exactly what he's complaining about? I thought.

"Why," he continued, "when my father beat me at sixteen and I started to get up, he said he wasn't finished and beat me some more. And when I went to my room, Mother came and checked on me. She lifted the sheets and saw the bruises on my back and legs, and she said quietly to my father, "Don't you think you were a little hard on him?"

"'Jessie, be quiet,' my father ordered," Daddy said triumphantly. "Now that's how it should be. You have to know who's in charge. There can only be one boss. Why, we always knew who the head of the house was."

I glanced at Mother, but she didn't say a word.

"But now our children don't respect their father. I must bring this out so that our children can see how wicked their mother is so they can see the truth for themselves. And so that you, Gale, can see the error of your ways and stop breaking your marriage vows and prostituting yourself in the name of Christ and five hundred Mennonites. Then you can come back and be a proper wife."

Like Mother, we monitored Daddy intently for the tiny clues that signaled increasing violence. Some days prior, Mother had taken the .22 stored on top of the china hutch for safety and hidden it away. After both Daddy's and Mother's families had seen what he had written to many members of the Church, they felt he should not be allowed to have a gun.

Daddy was incensed by this action. "I could kill my family with my bare hands," he told Mother. "If anyone's afraid, they should cut off my hands." He then demanded his gun be returned. When he eventually found it and put it back on top of the china hutch, Sharon looked up at him with her innocent blue eyes and asked, "Daddy, are you going to shoot Mommy?" He didn't reply, just as he didn't seem to be aware of our existence in the room. Instead, he thumbed to another bookmark.

"1 Corinthians 11:3–16. *But I would have you know that the head of every man is Christ; and the head of the woman is the man; and the head of*

Christ is God. Every man praying or prophesying, having his head covered, dishonoreth his head. But every woman that prayeth or prophesieth with her head uncovered dishonereth her head: for that is even all one as if she were shaven. For if the woman be not covered, let her also be shorn, but if it be a shame for a woman to be shorn or shaven, let her be covered. For a man indeed ought not to cover his head, forasmuch as he is the image and glory of God: but the woman is the glory of man. For the man is not of the woman: but the woman of the man. Neither was the man created for the woman: but the woman for the man. Judge in yourselves: is it comely that a woman pray unto God uncovered? Doth not even nature itself teach you, that if a man have long hair, it is a shame unto him? But if a woman have long hair, it is a glory to her: for her hair is given her for a covering."

Daddy paused in self-satisfaction.

"Why, it's pathetic how you women are so hypnotized by the great and mighty bishop Henry Fisher. He said to me with a knowing smile when he was at our house that I was strong and healthy and would soon be back in the Church. I got the message. They think that a wife is like candy and the men in the Church can control me."

And then he started talking about a wife's conjugal duties and rocky mountain oysters. I didn't know what those things were, but I imagined it was about sex because Mother always said with disgust, "Oh, Robert, don't be so vile."

He thumbed to another bookmark.

"And it says here in 1 Corinthians 7:2-5 . . . *'Let the husband render his conjugal duties to his wife, and in the same way also the wife to her husband. The wife hath not power over her own body, but the husband.'* When are you going to render your conjugal duties?" he demanded. "Any farmer knows he's in for trouble when he teases his cattle as this Church has teased husbands and wives. A farmer knows he will have fences to repair and bulls to separate from cows, and that is a job, if he partitions them off from one another and they are able to 'look but don't touch' the other. Young heifers don't even need to see a bull and they will get out and roam the countryside looking for one. It takes good fences to keep in heifers."

Daddy often talked about women like they were animals. He had even demanded of the ministers that they "give me back my heifer!", which meant

Mother. When he got really agitated, he would describe animal mating practices to make his point and talk about Mother being naked. When he talked like this, I wanted to vomit and disappear.

Daddy always lost control at some point during these lectures. Sometimes it was a short acceleration followed by an explosion, but on that day it appeared it would be a long lecture first.

"It says here in 1 Corinthians 7:34 . . . '*but she that is married careth for the things of the world, how she may please her husband.*'"

He flipped the pages backward. "And Matthew 19:4–6 says, '*Have ye not read, that he which made them at the beginning made them male and female, and said, For this cause shall a man cleave to his wife: and they twain shall be one flesh? Wherefore they are no more twain, but one flesh. What therefore God hath joined together, let not man put asunder.*'"

Daddy lobbed these heavy Bible verses from his scriptural catapult in an attempt to pulverize Mother's walls of resistance until she surrendered her thinking and saw the error of her ways, submitting into unity with him.

But instead, Mother launched a brief defense: "Yes, and it also says, '*husbands love your wives, even as Christ also loved the church, and gave himself for it.*'"

"Why, I *have* loved you," he said indignantly. "I've given you a fine home. A neighbor lady said when we were first married, 'Some farm wives wait an entire lifetime to have a home like that.' Show me where I haven't loved you."

"You're violent," she said.

"I'm not *violent*," he said, dismissing her with contempt. "You were hardly hurt. Why, I barely touched you. If I really wanted to hurt you, you wouldn't be alive. You needle me to violence, Gale. Some women need to be put in their place. They need to know who's the boss."

Daddy *hated* to be called violent or accused of any wrongdoing. When Mother dared cross that line, he would get so wound up that it was hard to tell what he would do. On this day, however, he simply stormed off.

No one knew if Mother would be gifted with such an abrupt exit the next time.

Previous Agitations

Summer settled into an uneasy routine of escalating violence and increasingly open warfare. Daddy would get agitated and then suddenly begin railing, which we finally found out was why he was excommunicated. In the Bible, railing was not permitted.

Not long after The Trouble began, we children learned that Daddy had been excommunicated once before, in 1964, right around the time Uncle George, the brother he was closest to, was killed in a car accident. Then, like now, he had found fault with the ministers. He insisted they were not in unity, and when he would not let go of his accusations, they put him on probation and he finally got kicked out. And Daddy never protested anything only once. He always made his objections a campaign and refused to back down until others would agree with him that they were wrong and he was right.

(When I was maybe five or six, I remember his complaining loudly and contemptuously that a bishop from Canada allowed his daughter to wear her skirt a little too short. He didn't stop pontificating until Mother finally agreed with him.)

What we discovered was that when excommunication occurs, the person is shunned by the remaining members, which typically includes the member's entire family: parents, grandparents, adult children, and extended family. (None of us children were old enough to be members, so the shunning didn't apply to us.) Shunning was a biblical practice meant to bring wayward members back into the fold so they could go to heaven. For a community as enmeshed as our Church, shunning was a serious punishment, yet defined as an act of love.

During a shunning, the congregation was not allowed to have "intercourse" of any kind with the wayward member, which meant doing business, eating at the same table, or offering the kiss of peace greeting. However, because my father sold our crops far and wide, the business part of shunning didn't affect him much.

Daddy was constantly accusing the ministers of being hypocritical and not pure enough in their beliefs. He was scornful of the way the women in the Church listened so raptly to the ministers and gushed over their sermons. Mother claimed he was jealous because Uncle Glenn and others were chosen to become ministers but he was not.

"I never wanted that job," Daddy snorted.

But the linchpin of his current battle with the Church had actually begun the previous fall. He had protested that the ministers had allowed a married couple—whom he thought were in disagreement about something and therefore not in complete unity—to take communion. It was not right, he insisted. The ministers always preached that when you had a problem with someone else, you should "go and tell it between him and thee alone." Daddy, though, had chosen to take his grievance to the ministers. When they didn't agree with his conclusions, he insisted upon a hearing in front of the entire congregation. They offered to have his concerns heard by a dozen bishops, but he refused; he wanted everyone to hear what he had to say. When he wouldn't let it go, they put him under reproof, and once they saw that he had no intention of backing down, they excommunicated him.

When Daddy was excommunicated the first time, Mother was excommunicated too—over her objections. She had protested that she had done nothing wrong, but they kicked her out so it would not cause any problems between husband and wife. This second time, however, Mother protested vehemently, insisting she was blameless and refusing to be excommunicated again for his behavior. Daddy saw this as a betrayal.

"You should take my side and stand behind your husband no matter what," he spat.

When she didn't, thus began a summer of chasing . . . and seasons of running.

Declaring War

Daddy resumed farming after the chaos the excommunication had wrought, but the work of the farm didn't fully occupy his brain. He would ruminate while driving the tractor or plowing, and then he would suddenly stop working and return to the Home Farm in the middle of the day to confront Mother and try to grab her. He even foamed at the mouth as he ranted, whether chasing Mother or standing his certain way while delivering his tirade, with his right foot planted firmly and his left leg out front, making a T shape. He would extend his left hand, palm up, and use his right middle finger to jab his palm as he made a point with his arguments, repeating how his parents worked things out behind closed doors and then presented a united front to the children. That's what he wanted: a united front.

Mother was much more agile than Daddy, but when he did catch her, he would slap, push, and strike her. Each time he insisted she had brought this all on herself. What was most terrifying, though, was something he did in his most frothing moments: aggressively grope Mother's breasts. His hands, hungry to humiliate, would become a whir of pincers and twisters. I knew this machine had again found its target when the scream of pain and humiliation pierced the normal background noise of scuffling and arguing. After several of these instances occurred, Mother discovered a lump and visited a surgeon, thinking it might be breast cancer. *What would become of us children if it was cancer*, I wondered. *Who would take care of us?* When the doctor declared it wasn't, I could breathe again.

Daddy was in a war—one in which Mother was his enemy—and he aimed to win. He wanted total control, total victory. The physical battle with her was not gaining him that victory, though. So he decreed that Mother would no longer have access to the family car or the checkbook until she came to her senses and behaved like a good wife. He snatched the keys and the checkbook during one of their arguments and took them to his trailer— except he forgot one important thing: Mother needed the car to get groceries in town, twenty minutes away. When notified of this wrinkle, he ordered Mother to make a grocery list that he would first have to approve, and then he would make the trip himself. He was foiled in his plan, however, when he discovered he didn't know what some items on the list were, nor where to locate them in the store. He solved this problem by taking us along with him so that we could point out where everything was. Disgruntled as he was by it, he kept it up for a good spell.

And Mother, mildly amused by this "punishment," delighted in the fact that grocery shopping became one less chore on her long to-do list.

Driving the Tractor

Throughout the summer, we children worked on the farm as we always did. Daddy assured us repeatedly that this "trouble" wouldn't last long, that he would get it all straightened out and we would return to being a family again soon. I sure hoped so because I couldn't wait for the day when everything would get back to normal.

This was also the summer I decided I was ready to pursue a particular milestone: learning to drive a tractor like my brothers sometimes did. Though I was only eight, I thought it looked easy as I watched my father sit ramrod straight in the seat and move the steering wheel back and forth.

Aside from the Farmall—one of the smaller tractors we had, which had been around for as long as I could remember—we were John Deere people. The Gutshall dealership, located in Carlisle at the point of a triangle in the road, was a familiar place. Throughout the late 1960s and early '70s, it seemed my father bought a shiny new tractor regularly, each model bigger than the one before. And each time he made a purchase, the man in the dealership handed us children a sturdy metal toy tractor in the distinctive green and yellow paint. We added it to our collection of John Deere Tractors, Tonka dump trucks, Tinker Toys, Lincoln Logs, and Erector Sets that lived in our wooden toy box. From this rich treasure chest, we constructed towns and entire economies in the gravel canvas of our large driveway. Roads appeared with the sweep of a hoe, and we drove our tractors and dump trucks between towns. A rake magically produced a fresh, blank canvas whenever we desired.

Driving a tractor looked like fun to me, *and* it looked a lot easier than most of the other farm jobs. I sincerely wanted that job, and I must have pestered Daddy enough because he finally agreed.

Starting me on the old red Farmall, Daddy sat me on his lap and showed me where the clutch and the pedals were. I turned the wheel this way and that, just as I had seen him do, and we snaked across the road far to the left and then far to the right. Eventually, I learned to make little corrections enough to stay on the right side of the road, but working the clutch and brake was a little trickier. I got them confused one day, and the tractor rolled back into the sprayer, which made Daddy angry. Though it did not do any permanent damage, it left me shaken and sobered at the impact of machinery. Nevertheless, I loved driving the tractor and leaped at every opportunity to practice. My goal was to be able to drive solo on the farm. I knew it would take two to three years before I was allowed to do it by myself, but I was determined to master it and prove to Daddy I wasn't the dummy he thought I was.

Baby Possums

Some days, Daddy seemed like his old self and he'd sing "Happy Days Are Here Again," the phrase President Franklin Delano Roosevelt would say during the Great Depression. At the end of the tune, he'd add another favorite of the president's with a booming laugh: "The only thing we have to fear is fear itself."

One morning, David, Benny, Leah, and I went out with Daddy to hoe around the pumpkins planted in the field directly in front of the house. The sun wasn't high yet, and it was still a pleasant temperature. Daddy was in one of his cheerful moods, whistling a tune that made him sound like a young boy. It was going to be a good day, I thought, just like old times. *Maybe everything really would soon return to normal.* I wanted desperately to believe that. Perhaps he did too.

Surveying the field, I mused that we would have a pretty good crop of pumpkins this year. We always liked carving pumpkins for Halloween, and we could do as many as we wanted because they were free, which made me feel rich. The fields stretched out green and fertile before us, and I remember drinking in the beauty of it. But it was not long before Daddy's whistling changed. The best way I can explain his tone was that it sounded like no one was in his body. David glanced at Benny with a warning look, Benny caught me with his eyes, and I caught Leah's. With a small nod from each us, we silently agreed on a plan.

As if on cue, Daddy turned to leave. "Now you children stay here," he said.

We gave him about twenty paces and then dropped our hoes to follow him. He was always so intently focused on his inner world of grievances that we knew he wouldn't notice us disobeying his orders. Our biggest concern was hoping Mother would see him coming . . . and if not, that we would get there in time.

But neither of those hopes came true.

By the time we got there, he was on her. Mother must have let down her guard, assuming Daddy would be occupied longer than the twenty minutes he'd been gone. If there was a chase this time, it must have been quick because she was already caught in the grasp of his meaty hands, with Susie and Sharon crying and tugging at his pant leg.

"Daddy, get off, get off," they screamed. "Leave her alone!"

The four of us who'd come in on the scene jumped on his back and pulled at his arms. We were like baby possums he could easily slough off, but eventually our weight on his back caused him to stumble. When he reached out to keep from falling, he lost his grip on Mother and she slipped away to safety on the other side of the table.

Summer was a monotonous series of scenes like this.

We didn't realize it then, but soon we children would become the enemy as well.

Grandma's Funeral

Grandma Bear had had a heart attack not long before, and she had been treated at the Hershey Medical Center where they implanted a new device in her called a pacemaker. I marveled at this new invention—a technological wonder that could replace a heart. But in June, she had a stroke and was now in intensive care.

After she finally returned home, she didn't recognize any of us when we visited, not even Daddy. I've wondered since if she just couldn't take any more sorrow. I knew from the stories I'd heard that Grandma had a lot of tragedy in her life, though she never talked about it. In fact, she hardly ever spoke at all. Her love was communicated through her cooking (her large pans of just-made baked beans with thick strips of crispy bacon peeking out from the bubbling brown buttons were a favorite, as was her creamy baked rice dusted with cinnamon), and through those little handkerchiefs she offered us when we visited. Other than that, she was quiet as a church mouse. Maybe it really was all the tragedy she had endured that made her go within.

When she was a young girl, her mother died of leukemia. After her father remarried, her stepmother was killed when her skirt caught fire heating water for laundry in a kettle over an outdoor fire. Later, her grandmother died after being struck by lightning in the attic, and her father lost his life during a cave-in in the sand mines where he worked. As if that was not enough, her self-confessed favorite son died in a car accident, leaving a widow and four young children.

I like to believe that one of her greatest comforts was letting Leah and me braid her hair. We would take out the pins that held her cap, unroll the bun she wore, and then slowly and gently brush her thin, white hair for a long time. She would close her eyes and smile while we did this, and then we would braid her hair into two pigtails. After we were done, we would put her cap back on because a woman's head is supposed to always be covered.

I had no idea that only two months after her stroke, Leah and I would never have the opportunity to spend that special time with Grandma Bear again.

After she died, Daddy drove to Papap and Grandma Bear's home in his potato delivery truck. Normally, we children would sit on the truck's bench seats, feeling important sitting up high and bouncing along over dips in the road. But that day, there wasn't enough room in the cab for all of us children, so Leah and I had to sit in the storage area of the truck. I remember that when we arrived, Daddy turned the truck around in the gravel driveway with the back end pointing toward the house, as if positioning a getaway car.

When Papap came out to greet him, Daddy started in on him right away, jabbing his finger the way he always did and making his points about shunning and the Church. Papap, who had always been so stern and hard that I hid behind my father's pant leg when we visited, started sobbing. Hearing this unfamiliar sound, Leah and I shoved up the rolling door and jumped out.

"She's only been dead for three days," Papap pled through his tears.

We grabbed at Daddy's sleeves, trying to tug him away. "Stop, Daddy," we begged. "Let's go. Please. Please."

Eventually, he finished his tirade, jumped in the truck, and roared away with us kids feeling terrible for Papap. But that wasn't the end of Daddy's harangue. He came back with a vengeance at Grandma's funeral.

Mother was seated beside the six of us in the front row with our cousins, aunts, and uncles when we heard a loud commotion at the back of the funeral home. I turned to see Daddy ranting and jabbing. No member could call the police, though. It was against our beliefs of non-resistance. So, we all just sat there while he poked and shouted. I remembered being embarrassed to my core, thinking, *How could he do this at a funeral? Especially his own mother's?*

Who Do You Love the Most?

As was so often the case in those days when Daddy paid attention to us, he was agitated, unstable, and had an agenda.

One day, he loaded all six of us into the car and didn't tell us where we were going. When we pulled into the driveway at Uncle Glenn's house, I knew it could not be good. He hated my uncle.

"Glenn, open up," he bellowed, pounding on the door until I thought he might break it down.

When Uncle Glenn finally acquiesced, his tall frame blocked most of the doorway, protecting Aunt Mary Ellen standing a safe fifteen feet behind him. But he knew it was futile to refuse my father, so Uncle Glenn invited us all in.

I admired their house as I always did. Decorated in soft greens and blues, and with family heirloom antiques adding an unmistakable sense of quality, the house was always immaculate. Aunt Mary Ellen's meticulous sampler hung on the dining room wall, and they even had a bathroom in the hallway just for guests, with soap that smelled divine.

Because Uncle Glenn was a prominent bishop, his and Aunt Mary Ellen's home was the site of many company meals for visitors. They also ran a successful plant and farm market business just across the road from their house. From their driveway, you could see long greenhouses in rows, and beyond the greenhouses was their retail store, Ashcombe. Below the store, they grew acres of strawberries and blueberries. Their landscaping was a manicured vision of flowers and bushes neatly contained by crisp edging.

Uncle Glenn ushered us into his office. My father remained standing, as he always did, and so did Uncle Glenn. David took a seat next to my father, and the rest of us lined up in chairs in age order from oldest to youngest. Daddy began with his usual list of grievances.

"I can't believe Gale has sided with the Church instead of me. And I can't believe she has prostituted herself to you and five hundred Mennonites," he snapped. "The Church is keeping her, dangling her to get me back in line."

Uncle Glenn tried to reason with him, though he knew it was fruitless. Glancing at the six of us, he seemed to wonder why Daddy brought us with him. I was wondering the same. It didn't take long, though, for us to learn why we were there.

Daddy finished his rant and looked at each of us intensely. "Who do you love the most?" he asked. "I want you to state clearly who you love more, me or Uncle Glenn."

I froze.

Uncle Glenn had a gentle demeanor, and he always remained calm. He never got worked up in church, and he and Aunt Mary Ellen made us feel special. Sometimes they let one of us drive to church with them, and Aunt Mary Ellen always carried candy with her—caramel creams, licorice nips, or peppermints from their store that she would slip us in the car or in church.

I didn't want to hurt Uncle Glenn's *or* Daddy's feelings. The idea of seeing a look of pain in Uncle Glenn's eyes when I said I loved Daddy more, or the bruised, angry look in Daddy's eyes if I said I loved Uncle Glenn more was enough to make me feel sick to my stomach.

Think, think, think, Patty. Hurry. Hurry. There are only two brothers answering before he reaches you. What can you say that won't hurt anyone?

But my mind felt trapped in a room with no door, making me frantic and a bit furious too. I didn't know what the right answer was, and it didn't feel like a fair question to me. No matter which way we answered, we would upset someone. I thought about the story Daddy frequently told that when I was little, I would throw myself into his arms and demand, "Daddy, do you love *me* the best?" I didn't remember doing this, but it sounded like something I would do. The truth was that I never felt loved by my father. At best I felt invisible, and at worst, female.

Daddy called on David first. "Who do you love the most?"

"Uncle Glenn," came the defiant answer.

Both my brothers must have been angry because Benny, without hesitation, answered the same way.

Then it was my turn. I still hadn't figured out how to answer, so I went with a safe "I don't know."

With a look of irritation, Daddy moved on to Leah. "Uncle Glenn," she said, as did Susie.

He looked at two-year-old Sharon, hesitated at her blank stare, then circled back to me.

"Who do you love the most? Answer me," he demanded.

Again, I replied, "I don't know."

"All right," he said with disgust, then turned to my siblings. "Since you love your Uncle Glenn more than me, I'm leaving you here with him." And he did. For almost a week.

Me, he took home with Sharon.

I thought I had negotiated an untenable situation as well as could be expected. But Daddy didn't agree.

The entire forty-minute car ride home he vented his disgust at my indecision.

"What's the matter with you, Patricia? You don't even know your own mind. Why, it's a simple question and you can't even answer it."

I hung my head as he berated me, the miles passing slowly outside the car window. I didn't say a word out loud, but I thought to myself, *I do know my own mind. I just hate your stupid game, and I didn't want to play.*

But Daddy was making it increasingly clear that you were either with him or against him. There would be no middle ground.

Being Bad

In September, I begin third grade with Miss Clevenger, who had been a favorite teacher of my two older brothers and would soon be mine as well.

Miss Clevenger was young and pretty with straight red hair that fell to her waist. She was an engaging teacher, but more than that, she was nice to us. I daresay we all had a crush on her. Her house was alongside the road between the Other Farm and the gas station in Bloserville. When Daddy drove past, we'd toss gifts of gourds and strawberry popcorn on her lawn from the back of the pickup truck. In class when the lights were turned off to watch *The Electric Company*, I slid gifts beneath her desk—small boxes I'd filled with clipped pictures of flowers from seed catalogues my parents got. But although I adored Miss Clevenger as a teacher, I thought pulling a little prank would be funny. So I enlisted her student teacher in helping me carry it out, never thinking it could possibly be detrimental.

Lunch money was collected each morning and placed in a green drawstring bag, which seemed the perfect nesting ground to place a rubber snake with its head just poking out of the drawstrings. The student teacher kept the secret, and when Miss Clevenger went to count the lunch money, she reeled back upon seeing the snake and almost hit her head on the wall. Of course, I had to confess to being the perpetrator. As punishment, I had to spend recess standing with my head against a brick wall rather than playing kickball with my brother and his friends.

"Don't worry," Benny said, comforting me, "it's just for one day."

The truth was, I didn't mind not playing kickball so much. What I hated was getting in trouble for almost hurting someone I truly cared about . . . and who seemed to sincerely care about me.

An Ugly Meeting

Since Daddy was excommunicated, Mother was no longer allowed to eat at the same table with him. But the Church had told her to nonetheless treat him with lovingkindness, so when he would come home, she would set the table for him and for us children and take her plate to another room. But Daddy always indicated he could see through their agenda; no matter how Mother treated him, nothing seemed to satisfy him. Whatever she did, he labeled as "prostitution" meant to get him back into the Church. If she was nice to him, he sneered in suspicion, and if she stood up to his treatment of her, he became agitated and violent. It maddened him not having her complete loyalty. After all, she was *his* heifer, not theirs.

It seemed to me that the ministry hoped he would eventually calm down, take his medicine, learn his lesson, and return to the Church, or at least move past his grievances. Daddy's lips, however, curled into a sneer at their naïve efforts. Daddy was itching to get his day in court. He wanted the entire congregation to listen to everything he was upset about, and he made it clear that Mother had a key role in this strategy. "She'll just need to suffer a little pain for the sake of her children," he said ominously. "That's just the way it is."

He was determined to expose her and to show how sick the Church was.

Toward that end, he enlisted his lawyer friend, Richard Wagner, to set up a summit at the Longeneckers Meetinghouse in Lancaster so that Daddy could argue his case. On the day of the meeting, Mother, Daddy, and all of us children piled in the car for the long drive. At the meetinghouse we found a small crowd: Richard, two bishops who had driven down from Canada for the meeting, plus three Pennsylvania bishops (including Uncle Glenn), and another minister. Adding to the assembly were two of Daddy's brothers—Uncle Francis, who was a member of the Church, and Uncle Lehman, who had never joined—plus their father, Papap Bear. Further, Daddy had asked his aunts and uncles to join the meeting. These people were strangers to us; in fact, we had so little contact with relatives not in our Church that I was under the impression *everyone* joined the Church. Even decades after this meeting, I was surprised to learn that Papap Bear was the only one out of seven children to join.

Richard Wagner led Daddy's aunts and uncles into one of the two anterooms, with the goal of getting Uncle Francis, Papap Bear, and Mother to see things my father's way. Meanwhile, Daddy disappeared into the other anteroom with the bishops and ministers.

Though we children did not sit in on the meetings, the atmosphere felt heavy with drama and dread. Daddy would later record the events of this day, which would paint a picture of the proceedings and shed light on a long-term mystery.

In the meeting with the bishops, Daddy had immediately exploded about his many grievances, including his newest one: being accused of rape.

It seemed Mother had told Uncle Glenn that Daddy had tried to rape her, which led to Uncle Glenn alerting Uncle Francis and Papap Bear and telling them to look after her, tasking them with being responsible for her safety. Daddy was incensed by this charge and would later write dismissively of his associated actions, characterizing them as a little wrestling, nothing more. He said he didn't consider it a sin to get in bed with his wife, that he figured she wanted the affection and he was just trying to do his duty. However, since Mother had privately confided in Uncle Glenn, and Uncle Glenn had told Daddy's brother and father, Daddy said he felt her intent had been to shame him and make him seem like an animal. He therefore declared he was going to hit back hard and catalogue prurient details he claimed showed she was not shunning him but rather teasing and tempting him. It was evidence, he said, that she was not being a good girl and that she was prostituting herself for the Church.

After his testimony, Mother was summoned before the bishops. She would later relate her experience of being called before this long panel of stern men, including her own brother, and grilled about Daddy's explicit sexual charges. She was asked to respond in minute detail to his accusations to ascertain whether she was in fact "shunning" him in the bedroom, as she understood she was expected to. I will always remember her telling us about this scene. Even when we were older, she could hardly choke out the explicit, probing questions she had been asked. This went beyond the pale, she said.

Humiliated beyond comprehension, she blew up at the bishops. "If you're going to keep asking these kinds of questions, I'm done. I'm leaving." Red-faced and furious, she didn't care what consequences might befall her from defying the authorities.

The bishops and ministers backed down, but Daddy never would. His lewdness would continue for decades.

This charge of rape against my father would become an obsession. He made it the centerpiece of his future court battles, as well as a reliable feature in the pamphlets he circulated to individuals and local businesses. For decades none of us children could figure out what had really happened and what was true. The circumstances were so confusing, and my father's outrage so loud and compelling, that for most of my life I assumed nothing had happened at all.

Prior to the 1970s, it was commonly accepted that after marriage, a man had rights, and that the wife had given up her ability to deny consent. Even Mother, who had listened to more sermons than I had on the subject of women's bodies belonging to men, seemed confused about whether she had any rights. Though the laws had slowly begun changing, rape retained stubbornly low reporting, prosecutions, and convictions, and marital rape was exponentially less likely to be prosecuted. I keenly remember this time period and this controversy being discussed and openly ridiculed. The idea that a wife's consent was relevant was summarily dismissed as ludicrous, as new changes often are.

It was only recently in reading my father's account of these events that I began to wonder anew about this issue that would fuel his campaigns for decades. As near as I can tell from his writings, he took my mother's seeking help for sexual violence in our home as an outrageous invasion of his privacy and therefore retaliated.

What's particularly disconcerting about my father's actions is that strong family pride would have likely guaranteed that his father and brother would never have repeated the charges to anyone; Mother herself told no one else except her brother. Yet Daddy promoted the awareness of these charges to a larger church audience, then migrated the charge out beyond the insular church community to the public, where he amplified it to a national audience. In essence, my father consistently howled with outrage about this rape charge to a wide group of people—a group who otherwise would have never gotten wind of it.

The question was, *why?*

Sleeping in the Car

We never knew when Daddy would move out of the trailer and back into the house, but he usually made an announcement when he decided enough was enough. When this happened, he would assert he was coming back to be the head of the house again—which always signaled trouble.

One fall day, after insisting that Mother was getting too headstrong, he said he was moving back home. Bracing for the event, we heard him pull into the driveway. It was a chilly night, and Mother was sitting at the sewing machine in the utility room making a dress. A face suddenly appeared at the door.

"Let me in," Daddy hollered, rattling the knob furiously against the locked door.

"Only if you promise not to be violent, Robert," Mother said.

Mother knew how triggering those words were to Daddy, but she said them anyway, perhaps hoping it would make him think about what he was doing. In response, he thrust his weight against the solid wood door several times, but to no avail. After more yelling and pointing, he disappeared.

Five minutes later, he was back. He had found one of the hefty round logs that was unearthed when my parents remodeled the house to create the third bedroom for us girls. With this as his battering ram, he directed all his fury at the closed door. When Mother realized he was determined to break down the door, she opened it, after which a long night ensued.

Every room was a chasing room—Mother fleeing, Daddy pursuing and ranting, and we children following and sometimes trying to intervene. Daddy's argument about Mother teasing him and tempting him behind the bedroom doors was sickening and embarrassing, but also confusing. He told *everyone* this. The ministers, the neighbors, business owners who bought potatoes, us. I constantly wondered, *Is this true?* Mother was always running away from him and locking the doors. His claims didn't make any sense.

Somewhere around midnight, amongst the chaos, Mother spotted an opening and fled outside into the darkness. We followed quickly behind as she raced to the car in the driveway. Doors slammed shut, locks were hurriedly pushed down. Daddy fumed at the sight of his family securing themselves against his assault. *Would he break into the car too?* I wondered.

But despite the anger and frustration that Daddy radiated, I noticed something else: he looked confused and hurt. Five-year-old Susie noticed it too and could not bear his anguish. We heard the sound of a lock popping up, unleashing shouts from all of us. But Susie didn't listen. Instead, she got out, walked around the car toward Daddy, and grasped his big paw with her small hand. They quietly walked back into the house together while the remaining six of us spent the night in the car, curled into footwells and sprawled on seats, huddling together against the night's autumn cold.

Escalation

Mother would often quote "October's Bright Blue Weather," a favorite poem of hers, to describe the magic of fall. The vivid colors, the crisp air, the particular blue of October skies, the smell of the leaves, the experience of this harvest time. It was one of those classic October afternoons when we watched Daddy back his big delivery truck up onto the lawn, all the way to the clotheslines.

"What could he be thinking?" Mother fumed. "He'll ruin the lawn."

Every spring, it was the job of one of the three eldest to take the large metal roller, fill it half full with water, and push it over the lawn to smooth the bumps and lumps that arose from winter's and spring's heaving and thawing. But now, the heavy truck wheels sank into the lawn, leaving double tire tracks to the driveway.

From the passenger side emerged Sonny, who had worked for us on the farm for as long as I could remember. Together, he and Daddy approached the utility room, where we all stood in the doorway. Sonny refused to look at any of us as he and Daddy strode past and unplugged the first freezer. When he and Sonny started carrying it out, their mission became horrifyingly clear: Daddy was taking our food. Two chest freezers full of soups, vegetables, and meats that had been frozen for the wintertime were disappearing out the door. He had already taken away the family car, cut off the money, and now he was taking the last of our food?

But he wasn't done yet.

Before he left, he shut down the electricity, the furnace, and the phone too.

Thankfully, Benny figured out how to get the electricity back on, so we were able to salvage the few items in the refrigerator and small freezer above. And we still had canned peaches, pears, red beets, and jam in the basement. But everything else was in those two freezers. We lived on what remained in the cupboards and the small freezer for a few days, and then we children got to thinking, *Where would Daddy take the freezers?* He wasn't the most complicated or clever person. Most likely he put them somewhere obvious, we figured. The insulated area in the barn up at the Other Farm seemed the most likely hiding place. It had a large sliding door where the freezers could easily be concealed inside. It wasn't long before our plan was hatched.

After school David, Benny, and I borrowed Sharon's red wagon with the slatted sides. We waited until dusk and then pulled it down across the bridge, over the millrace and up the meadow, to the spot where the canoe was anchored to a giant sycamore beside the creek. After loading the wagon into the canoe, we paddled upstream to a landing spot on the other side of the creek, where a large patch of stinging nettle we always called itch weed greeted us. We pulled the wagon up the dirt road that wound past Daddy's trailer, all the way up to the potato storage barn. It was fully dark by the time we reached the trailer, and we could see Daddy's lights on inside. We crept silently past, breathing a sigh of relief at not being discovered as his lights disappeared behind us on the dark road.

Arriving at the barn, Daddy's ferocious German shepherd on a chain barked loudly. Even with us, he was always menacing. Benny talked to him in a low voice, and we were able to sneak by him. Ever so carefully, we pushed open the big barn door and made our way to the insulated storage room. Sure enough, both freezers were there, just as we thought. We piled quarts of frozen vegetable soup, along with some meat and vegetables, into the wagon, then inched past Daddy's trailer to begin the long journey home. We made this trek several times a week through the late fall and into the winter, pulling the sustenance-filled wagon through the isolated darkness and increasing cold. The blue-black of the night sky was so vacant and bleak, and I felt so small and unimportant underneath it, that it seemed Daddy wasn't the only one who cast a cold eye on us. As we trudged along the fields, the stars seemed to look down on us with a chilly indifference too.

The Black Tornado

Daddy had begun telling everyone—the neighbors, the hired help, the businesses he sold to, anyone who would listen—that the Church had destroyed his family. He wrote long letters he got a neighbor lady to type up, and he found a printer who would make copies. These he sent to members of our Church locally as well as to the congregations in Illinois, Ohio, Michigan, and Canada. But perhaps most bizarre was that he often sobbed when he talked about how his family had been taken away from him.

We had never seen him cry about anything, and we couldn't help but wonder if his tears were real or if they were fake to incite sympathy. What we *did* know, however, was that he increasingly said things we *knew* were not true.

For one, he told people that his wife and children shunned him, which was impossible because we children were not officially members of the Church yet, hence we were not required to shun him. We knew this. He knew this. Yet he still told everyone we were shunning him too. The more he said these things, the more he seemed to believe them. Mother, however, responded to his assertions by contending he was lying. Of course, this incensed Daddy because he was always declaring how honest he was. In fact, he would often assert that he was the only honest person and that everyone else was lying.

"There must be something wrong with your head, Robert," Mother told him. "These things simply are not true. Surely you know that."

You can imagine how the idea that he might be mentally ill sent my father over the edge.

"There is nothing wrong with my mind," he roared.

In the beginning, it was Mother who had divided her loyalty between the Church and him. But now, my siblings' and my loyalties were increasingly being challenged. Since we had not condemned our mother, we were guilty too.

Gathered in an attentive semi-circle around my father, my siblings and I shivered on the lawn etched with frost as Daddy thundered.

"A house divided against itself CANNOT stand. We must be united as a family. We all must be on the same side."

Just before the usual numbness accompanying his monologues set in, I had an epiphany. *Daddy needs someone to be on his side! That's it!*

Suddenly, everything was obvious to me. If Daddy didn't feel so alone, if he had someone on his side, everything would be all right again.

Like a student eager to shout out the right answer when everyone else is stumped, I knew what I would say as soon as I had the chance: "Daddy, Daddy, *I'll* be on your side." Even though I didn't agree with a lot of what he said, I wholeheartedly believed my strategy would work.

Now that I knew there was a way out, that we could be a family again, I was excited. I waited for him to take a breath so I could jump in and tell him the good news. He didn't like to be disrespected, so I dared not interrupt him. But just as I anticipated him taking a breath and gathered myself to rush in, I noticed something curious on Daddy's shirt. Superimposed over his chest and throat was an image of a dark, swirling tornado. I stared at it, wondering for a moment if it was real, logically knowing it couldn't be. Tornadoes didn't land on people's shirts. Instead, instantaneously and intuitively, I understood this wordless symbolic message as if I was fluent in another kind of language: my father was lost in a dark vortex, and if I joined him, we would both be lost. The message was unequivocal, the warning from the Divine realm crystal clear. I closed my mouth and stepped back.

I wasn't sad in that moment, it simply was what it was: we would not, I knew for certain, ever be a family again.

The Cost of Trying to Keep Warm

Late that fall, peace settled on our house for a time, as Daddy decided it was time to hit the road and take his argument to individual members in other states. The letters he had written and sent out earlier set the stage. Daddy had always wanted a hearing in front of the whole congregation, and he was on a mission to achieve that.

He took one of the men who had worked for him for many years as a travel companion. Surprisingly enough, he seemed sympathetic to Daddy's cause—despite the fact that the letters Daddy wrote were erratic. They started out mostly normal, outlining his issues in a structured way, but soon became a jumble of sentences that began in one place and ended up somewhere entirely different. Varying text size was interspersed with bold type, emphasizing what he might have expressed in person with a forceful jab to his palm.

Winding his way through Ohio, Michigan, and Illinois, he ambushed members with surprise visits at their homes, confronting them like a lawyer cross-examining a hostile witness. He even brought a tape recorder he named "Honest John" so he could record these confrontations.

While we relaxed a bit knowing he was far away, at least for a while, he had left without restoring the heat or the phone, and he refused to provide money to support us. Mother had to face a harsh reality: she needed to find a job, but how with a two- and five-year-old at home? Grandma Gross offered Mother part-time work in her small business, but she would need a car to drive the forty minutes there. She appealed to Papap Bear for a loan to buy a car, but he flatly refused.

"I didn't help my sons," he said, "so why would I help you?"

Desperate to keep the family warm, Mother had taken to using the oven to heat the kitchen, where we could gather without freezing. One day, noticing the door between the kitchen and dining room was open, she exploded in frustration. "I'm trying to keep the heat in," she said, slamming it shut. Suddenly, screams erupted. Unknown to her, Susie had been on the other side of the door, prying a kernel of corn out of the hinges. When the door slammed, the tip of Susie's amputated finger landed by Mother's feet. We all stared at it, not quite comprehending the screaming or what had just happened. Susie rushed to the small kitchen sink. "Don't call the ambulance, don't call the ambulance," she begged as blood splashed into the bowl.

"We're not going in an ambulance," Mother said witheringly.

How, then? I wondered? *We have no car.*

In a remarkably calm manner, Mother wrapped Susie's hand in clean rags and placed her amputated finger in a plastic bag. She and Susie then set out across the frozen fields to find a neighbor who could take them to the emergency room. The rest of us waited at home for hours, wondering if Susie would lose her finger permanently.

When they finally returned that evening, the finger was successfully reattached, but the danger was not over. If it didn't heal properly, she might still lose it; she would need to soak it each day in Epsom salts for the best results. (Fortunately, it did heal, although she'd always have a crooked finger.)

Sometime after that, Grandma Gross loaned Mother the money to buy a used station wagon. She didn't want her daughter to be in such a bleak predicament ever again . . . or at the mercy of Daddy's imposed deprivation any longer.

She Remembered!

It's my ninth birthday, and I can see the shape beneath the wrapping paper. Before I even open it, I know that she remembered. I tear open the paper, and there it is: a real Bible. It's not quite as big as the one my father carries, but it is still an adult version. On the pebbled black cover are the solemn words "Holy Bible Concordance." The edges of the crêpe-like pages are dusted in gold, and as I flip through them, I see that the words are mostly black except for some sections that have a lot of red words. There are pictures too—not children's pictures, but photographs of the places where Jesus walked: Jerusalem from the Mount of Olives; the Desert of Sinai; the Plain of Esdraelon, a Dead Sea Scrolls cave site; Nazareth, the serene water where Jesus was baptized; the Garden of Gethsemane. And color maps of Palestine, of Jerusalem, of the Exodus, of the journeys of St. Paul and the tribes, and of the kingdoms. I thrust my face into the pages to inhale the delicious scent of ancient and new. It's the most beautiful thing I have ever seen or smelled.

"Look in the front," Mother nudges.

Amidst elaborate blue and tan, green and cranberry scrollwork is Mother's beautiful cursive handwriting: To Patricia Elaine Bear, with my birthdate. I always wished I could have such pretty handwriting, but mine never looks like this no matter how hard I try. Then she motions for me to look in the middle. Placed squarely between the Old and New Testaments is a grouping of documents encased in scrollwork matching the front. One is for Holy Matrimony, and one is for births. I put Jesus's birth right at the top, and then Mother's and my siblings'. The last page in this section lists deaths, so I put Grandma Bear and Uncle George on that page.

Opening to a book of the New Testament, I ask Mother, "Why are some words red?"

"Those are the words Jesus spoke," she says.

Right away, I take my Bible and curl up in a corner to read those red-letter words of Jesus. I love his stories, and his words make me feel good inside because he was so good. Once I read most of the red-letter words, I set about to read the rest.

All that fall and winter, by the warmth of the fireplace, I read and read. It wasn't long, though, before I grew alarmed—and then so hurt and angry that I didn't know what to do.

I had heard the ministers often say that Eve tempted Adam, and that she was responsible for all the sin in the world. I had also heard them say that childbirth was our punishment for tempting Adam. I listened to them end-lessly quote scriptures where women were the property of men, and I had heard my father say over and over that my mother tempted him with her body and that women controlled men with their bodies. Wives were sup-posed to submit to their husbands; the man was supposed to rule over women. Women weren't supposed to preach like men but were commanded to be silent. I knew none of the bishops, ministers, or deacons would ever be a woman, and I also knew that nobody listened to what women thought be-cause they were second-class citizens made from the rib of Adam.

I'd heard all these things in sermons a thousand times, but they hadn't seemed real until I saw them there on the page.

Could this really *be true?* I wondered.

Was having children a curse?

Were we inferior to men and therefore stuck forever being ruled by them?

I particularly hated the Apostle Paul. I thought he was the worst toward women.

One by one, I began examining the men and women I knew and con-cluded that the men did not seem any smarter to me. They certainly were not any wiser, braver, or kinder. I couldn't see *any* way they were superior except for muscles. Plus, women could produce a miracle through birth, just like Mary.

Overall, I couldn't see any real-life evidence that we were inferior to men. But just in case, I decided I would reread the red sections to see what Jesus had to say about it. I couldn't find anything bad about women in his words, so I made up my mind that I would only read the red-letter parts from now on and ignore all the other nonsense.

In the upheaval of our lives during that time, Mother never did get around to asking Uncle Glenn if I could be a convert.

And after my discovery, I didn't remind her.

CHAPTER THREE

1973

Silence encourages the tormentor, never the tormented.
—ELIE WIESEL

BEFORE WE GO ANY FURTHER IN THE STORY, I BELIEVE IT'S NECESSARY TO share the circumstances under which my parents met and decided to marry, and the opposing perspectives they held about their union throughout their years together, to give a fuller understanding of what led to the explosion of their marriage.

My father grew up in the Church and became an official member at twenty-three, but it wasn't until he was on the cusp of twenty-nine that he decided to take a wife. His two older brothers, as well as his younger brother and sister, had been married for several years, but my father would not be pushed into marriage through either family or religious pressure. He knew well the longstanding rule that one must only marry another member of the Church (a "fellow sister in the faith," as they were called), and he chafed at what he deemed his limited choices.

In our community, there was no dating in the traditional sense; rather, there was a courting ritual, if it could be called that, that went like this. A member (either male or female) stated to a minister their desire to marry another member. The minister then contacted the person of interest to query if they were also interested in marriage. If the party agreed, the two people corresponded in writing or visited in person, usually during Sunday gatherings for several months, after which they would set a marriage date.

My father, in the book he would publish sixteen years after his wedding day, wrote about the years he spent as a bachelor and his search for a wife.

One time I was pressing a 'sister' to make up her mind about marriage one way or the other and, of course, a family member felt the need to censor our conversation. This time it happened to be her father, and he said he would take me to their bishop. I said it would suit me alright to go to the bishop, so the father, mother, daughter and I went to talk to him. When we got to the bishop's home I was in for it, for before us all he said I had offended him but he wasn't free to talk with me at the time. When I said I never heard of such a thing, he said he would tell me privately, so we went upstairs to a little room. He then told me I was guilty of being interested in marrying and making overtures to two Reformed Mennonite 'sisters' at the same time and he didn't see how I could be a brother in faith and carry on like that. Someone had told on me and I needed to face the Canadian music. I was never accused of being 'too familiar' with any sister. It was just a matter of procedure, but before it was all over most of the church's bishops were involved for I had offended the honor of the Canadian branch.

After the bishops took the liberty to read some of my letters to a minister's daughter and questioned me as to the exact date, with proof that I suspended acquaintance with one and renewed acquaintance with the other, I was able to convince them it may have been very close but I didn't have two girlfriends at one time. I needed to travel alone to Canada and before four bishops answer for what I'd done. I wasn't the most popular in the bishops' eyes but did squeak through, and to top it off, lost both 'sisters'. I must confess I didn't shed many tears, for the overly sheltered daughters of Reformed Mennonites made me weary and the lording of bishops made me even more tired.

Our father owned four farms but he absolutely would not sell any of us a farm unless we were married. All things considered I thought I would try to get acquainted with a prospective wife. Since

I wasn't too excited about the idea, I chose one who lived in Lancaster at the time rather than bother to go all the way to Canada. I followed Daniel Musser's instructions and informed a bishop and he in turn talked to the 'sister' who agreed to a meeting at his home. I went to Lancaster at the agreed time and the bishop said he and his wife were going out for lunch, that we should just talk as long as we cared to and then lock the door when we left. I tried to follow Musser's instructions. We didn't visit much more than an hour and then we both left. Soon the 'sister' sent me a letter stating she did not care to marry me. About a year later she changed her mind and wondered via the same bishop if I was interested. My father encouraged me to be interested, telling me that I needed a wife and would learn to love her. I was loading irrigation pipe the next morning, and I thought what it would be like to be married, and I just decided right there I was not going through with it.

I then talked to the minister who had taken me to Canada concerning a Canadian 'sister'. He insisted he would write proposing marriage, and I said I only wanted to get acquainted. He insisted that to propose marriage was the only proper way to do it. He believed since all were 'in the Lord' any female Reformed Mennonite was well suited to marry any male Reformed Mennonite. He wouldn't have it any other way so I agreed.

But this marriage was not to be either.
He continues:

It seemed I was always impatient and 'sisters' always wanted to wait a long time. My thought was we don't get to know each other very well anyway and waiting was a waste of time. Then that summer she and her family visited our home, all very secretly, and she still couldn't make up her mind but expected to know in a week or so after they visited Lancaster. I made up my mind I didn't want to marry her and told our bishop. He gave his approval. When she came from Lancaster, she had her heart set on marrying! I told her I didn't want to get married . . .

Again my father and I were having differences, and I told him I was thinking of buying a farm. Then after dinner one day when I was resting for a few minutes I overheard my father tell Mother, I said I was thinking of buying a farm, but my father reassured her by telling her I was "afraid" to buy a farm. When I finished resting, I told my father I accidentally heard him say I was afraid to buy a farm. He said, "and you are afraid". I told him he was mistaken, that I would finish out the year but in the meantime, I would buy a farm. After this he tried to change my mind until he saw there was no use; then he helped me find a farm with good land but poor buildings.

I wouldn't have left my father, but he knew the prospect that I would maybe never be married loomed before me yet he pressed me hard at home and, to add the final straw, said I was "afraid". Before I decided to leave home, he said he knew me better than I knew my-self. After I left home, he never said this for he realized he had made a mistake and pushed me too far. I would have rather died than work for him after he said I was afraid.

My father did buy this farm—one hundred acres with a ramshackle house we would later call the Home Farm.

Around town I was known as Bobby sometimes and the man who sold me the home farm said "Bobby, you have good land but all I can say for the house is it won't fall down." Those first five years were dreary and lonely. The house had no heat except for a cookstove in the kitchen. I stored potatoes in the house during the winter, filling the living room with potatoes to the ceiling, and the dining room was filled with potatoes in bags with just enough room to open the stair door and go upstairs to bed. Once, my uncle came into the kitchen and saw a groundhog run across the kitchen floor. And there were rats. Lots of them. One neighbor said, do you think he can make a go of it? Another said, "well if anyone can, Robert can." I had a good first year and after that I never had to worry about money again. Minister Willis Weaver came to visit and saw how I lived. He said I'd need to change a lot when I got a wife.

The ministers told my father that he was known as a heartbreaker and that he was too picky. He was always looking for perfection, and they warned he wouldn't find a wife if he was too particular. But he wasn't getting any younger, and the years on his farm were lonely. He thought about breaking ranks and leaving the Church while he was young, but he decided to stick it out. Seeing the local girls when he took crops to market, he figured he could easily have found a suitable wife if that was allowed—and he was probably right. The local women who came to the Carlisle Farmers Market were overheard describing him as "that hunky Mennonite." However, being a member, that avenue was now closed to him.

The book goes on to say:

> Into this dark situation a glimmer of hope came during a visit to the Gross' home in nearby Camp Hill. In our conversation their eighteen-year-old daughter was interested enough to stay and take part in our general discussion. She was attractive. She was interesting and planned to go to college. I had seen lots of girls and didn't think much about it until she wrote telling me how much the family enjoyed my visit and I should come again. Though not a Church member Gale was a Reformed Mennonite daughter and knew the steel door of religious beliefs separated us from anything more than simple friendship unless she would become a Reformed Mennonite. After a few more visits and some interesting discussions about different ideas, not much religious discussion, she wrote to tell me she was thinking of becoming religious and wondered whether I would care to explain how I believed. It was a situation where even the stiff and strait-laced Canadian bishops couldn't find fault, for how could I help it if she didn't ask a minister or bishop to talk to her about religion but asked me instead? Gale was a cheerleader in high school, and so to change from 'worldly' dress to the cap and bonnet and 'plain' dress standard uniform of Reformed Mennonite women, she chose a trip to Canada for her debut.
>
> Gale was now a 'convert' and she could expect to be a convert for about a year before being baptized and becoming a member. Before she was a member, she was ineligible to be married or even

acquainted, through the help and approval of the ministry, with a prospective husband. I went to see our head bishop and told him Gale was my kind of girl and asked him if it would be alright to go see the family sometimes, to which he gave his unofficial approval. Sometime after I had been making my visits, Bishop Henry Fisher said he thought I shouldn't visit the family of a young convert too often. I asked him if he thought I had been going too often. He said I hadn't, but he just wanted to 'caution' me.

Mother has her side, too, of her path to this marriage.

In the 1950s, it was commonly assumed that girls only went to college to get their "MRS" degree, as it was then called. College was not where girls prepared for a future that eagerly awaited their talents, intelligence, and experience; it was where they paid for the privilege of mingling with the most eligible young men. But Mother didn't want to go to college to meet a man. She wanted to become an archaeologist. The lure of traveling to locations around the world and exploring ancient civilizations inspired her. Unfortunately there was not enough money for her to attend college. The money that was available had been allotted to her eldest brother, who wanted to study horticulture so that he could make a living and support a family.

The humiliation of my grandfather's near bankruptcy and the financial instability it visited upon his household left deep scars around financial insecurity for Grandma and both her daughters. None of the three women wanted to live through those kind of money troubles again. And since financial independence was not only discouraged but actively barred for women in our culture, finding a capable provider for her daughters was highly important to Grandma—and top of mind for her daughters too.

But because of the unique circumstance of the collapse of her husband's business, Grandma was given leeway to earn money through a market stand at the Lemoyne Farmers Market. Her creativity, resourcefulness, and astute business sense made her successful, which she likely inherited from her father, who had done well enough to give Grandma a house as a wedding present. Grandma was a formidable force too. Had her culture and the times been different, she would have been the one asked to take over her father's business rather than her husband—who, in a surprising moment of self-awareness, declined the offer. Instead, it was Grandma's lot in life to throttle back her considerable talent so as not to commit the unforgivable sin of noticeably outpacing, overshadowing, or outshining her husband. But despite her efforts to confine herself to the women's corral, her very presence gave the lie to what my father viewed as the "natural order of male superiority and domination." His outrage at her obvious and easily won competence rankled him for years—an outrage that frequently peppered his rants. And yet Grandma recognized in my father the same entrepreneurial acumen she possessed and urged her eldest daughter to see that my father would be an excellent provider. She would have a different kind of life, Grandma expected, one that was financially secure and serene. And though Mother had vowed never to marry a farmer, she found Robert Bear handsome and was confident he would make a stable provider.

My parents married on December 14, 1958, just after Mother turned twenty. The marriage ceremony was the usual no-frills church service, with the exception that the sermon and songs were focused on marriage and the service slightly modified for the exchange of vows. The bride did not wear a white wedding dress, nor did she have any attendants, flower-bedecked pews, or a petal-strewn carpet to the altar. Instead, she wore a deep navy dress—the same women's uniform worn every other day—but in a more refined fabric.

Of his satisfaction at the culmination of his long journey of searching for a mate, my father wrote in his book:

> For the first time I could go to town and see lively, enthusiastic girls
> and know Gale wasn't a 'make do' and I was very thankful.

I got the sense from listening to my father that he believed he had married up, that he was proud he had bested the average Mennonite man. And yet the very concept of marrying up also made him feel small and inadequate. He frequently told us that Richard Wagner, his staunchest supporter, said we children got our intelligence from our mother's side of the family. I thought it was an oddly mean thing for one friend to tell another—and odder still that my father repeated it so often. It made me notice something I otherwise would not have.

My father was smart. He was good in business and had good common sense. But despite his insistence that we think for ourselves, nobody would have confused him with an adventurous or independent thinker. Instead, he stuck to familiar ground, speaking with the confidence of those well versed in rigid certainties.

It was Mother who encouraged learning and reading and adventure. She had been raised in town and was more comfortable in the larger world than my father who, as long as I could remember, carried an ill-concealed complex about being a country boy. However, he was as ambitious in love as he was in business. He wanted the best, and he faced the choice that all those who are ambitious face: either raise your game or level your partner so that you never feel insecure. In my father's case, he had won his prize. His work was done.

In the decades to follow, Daddy would never tire of repeating that Mother said their life together was idyllic right up until the last excommunication happened. Then, he said, everything changed. He insisted the change occurred because she was more loyal to the Church than to him. Other times he would unknowingly contradict himself by describing the marriage as stormy, relating indignantly how Uncle Glenn had warned Mother before her marriage that Daddy would probably leave the Church one day.

For her part, Mother often described the Home Farm as idyllic, but never, ever her marriage. When we were older, she confided that my father's admiration of her had not even lasted one week after the wedding. She quickly realized, too, that he carried an emptiness that made him incapable of intimacy. Within the space of six months, Mother had made two irrevocable, lifelong commitments: joining the Church, and marriage. Leaving the Church was unthinkable and divorce was forbidden, hence Mother would feel trapped in a life where she had to learn to "make do." No one was probably better equipped for this life, though, for Mother had the heart of a survivor.

It seemed that my father's working concept of marriage was this: the woman's role was to give, and the man's role was to take. What's more, it was the woman's job to make her husband happy. In response to Mother's angry protests at my father's callous and entitled treatment toward her, he'd often say, "The worse I behave, it means the more love I need." His bad behavior was never an opportunity for *his* self-reflection, of course, only hers.

The truth is, Mother had begun having doubts before they were married. But as the wedding date approached, it had seemed too late to change her mind. In the week after they wed, her father-in-law's oft-quoted maxim rang through her head: "Marry in haste, repent at leisure."

She described that first year of marriage as the grimmest of her life. She would coach herself through it, saying, "You've made your bed, now you'll have to lie in it." She admitted she had never felt so alone in her life, and that she would not begin to feel less alone until we children arrived.

In the aftermath of the madness that erupted in 1972, Grandma apologized to her daughter profusely and often for the advice she offered about marriage. Though our people are culturally more practical than loving in their manner, in ways large and small, Grandma tried to repair the damage she felt she had done with this advice. She knew, though, that it was too late.

I did not realize until years later how much I ingested from watching the relationships I was submersed in as a child, and how they appeared to be a one-way street. There was always a giver and a taker, and those roles rarely switched. The powerful person was almost always the taker, and the least powerful person was usually the giver. The unfortunate thing about it was that this was my role-modeling of what was called "love." Eventually, though, I got wise and called this kind of love what it was: an imposter.

You're on Your Own

In January of 1973, Daddy returned from his cross-country travels and decided he was going to move back home. He sounded optimistic about reconciling with Mother, resuming farming in the spring, and returning to normal as a family.

But his behavior during the previous year had raised suspicions around another kind of normality.

Years before, as a bachelor farmer, my father had been involved in a farm accident. A piece of machinery had swung around and hit him on the head, knocking him unconscious for three days. There had been some question about whether he would live or not. As each violent scene unfolded at home and my father's behavior became more unpredictable and radical, the

Church and Mother began searching for an explanation that might make sense of his behavior. They had begun to wonder aloud if something was indeed wrong with his head—if the head injury had caused a mental illness that was now emerging.

Of course, my father deeply resented this implication and refused to consider the possibility. However, in the spirit of resolving the differences between him and Mother and of clearing himself of the suspicion of mental illness, my father finally agreed to visit a psychiatrist.

"But only if you go along to be evaluated too," he insisted to Mother.

After the appointment, I saw their car crest the hill of the lane, but Daddy was alone. It wasn't until a bit later that Mother stomped up the lane.

"See, there is nothing wrong with my head," he crowed to all of us.

Mother's explanation of her absence in the car was that the psychiatrist blamed everything on her. In his exultation, Daddy was simultaneously echoing the psychiatrist's lecture on her culpability and grabbing at her when she couldn't take it anymore and leaped out of the car.

After this vindication, my father eagerly sought out other psychiatrists who would concur that he was of sound mind.

"If this shunning continues, though," he was told, "it will most surely result in long-term mental issues for your children and might cause you to become psychotic."

Not surprisingly, Mother would refuse to ever meet with a psychiatrist again.

In the face of this lunacy, the financial losses were mounting, so Mother proposed to Daddy that they find a way to live together and run the farm as normally as possible under the circumstances. Like many farmers, they would take out loans each spring to plant and tend the crops, which were then repaid after the harvest in the fall.

"We should put everything in my name," he declared to Mother. "And you should cosign the spring loans like always."

But with all that had transpired, Mother was not convinced that was the best plan. She was still contemplating the arrangement when a letter arrived in our mailbox.

January 29, 1973

Dear Mr. Bear,

This is to confirm, as your public relations counsel, recommendations made orally to you during our recent conversations in this office.

The story of your excommunication by the Reformed Mennonite Church and its effects on your family life is extremely interesting. Most Americans would be fascinated, and many would be shocked to learn of the arbitrary powers exercised over its membership by the leaders of this church in 1973. Because of this, in our judgment, it would not be difficult to bring this to national attention through the press and I believe it might also be feasible to try to interest one of the national television networks in doing a feature on it.

Further to this point, it seems likely that if the matter were brought to the notice of the American Civil Liberties Union on the ground that your civil rights have been interfered with, that body would probably add to the publicity and might even undertake legal action which you cannot do because of your principles.

Therefore, in our judgment it is entirely feasible to undertake a publicity campaign designed to bring public opinion to bear on the matter.

Our understanding of your situation is as follows:

1. You are resolved that you will never return to this church, no matter what happens, because you believe your conscience cannot be at peace under a discipline which can arbitrarily divide families and undermine respect of children for their parents.

2. You are determined not to submit yourself or your children to much further endurance of a home condition which you believe to be degrading and you have therefore resolved that you will plant no more crops on your present farm until your family can join lovingly together in the work as you formerly did.

3. Research by Mr. Richard Wagner into the writings of Menno Simons and other church leaders, as well as a letter from one of the bishops of the

Reformed Mennonite Church, has convinced you that
your wife is not required by church doctrine to
shun you but may, if she chooses, return in good
conscience to you in complete love and loyalty
according to the marriage promises while you
remain under excommunication.

4. You are convinced that your wife would return to
    you as a wife and restore unity to your family if
    the church authorities would counsel her that she
    may do so with a clear conscience, which they have
    obdurately refused to do.

5. You have no wish for revenge against the church
    for what you believe to be its arbitrary and
    despotic use of an excessively cruel psychological
    weapon against you and wish only to be left in
    peace united with your family. If they remain
    obdurate, however, you are determined to try every
    open and honest means of depriving them of this
    power of causing a person to be shunned by his
    immediate family.

As I told you, Mr. Bear, we believe it is feasible to
arouse public opinion against this practice of the
Reformed Mennonite Church because of the many aspects of
the story which would make it interesting to the mass
media. Current national concern about civil rights would
find a new and perhaps startling aspect of the problem in
considering the exercise of repressive authority by a
church. Because of the somewhat exotic nature of the
Reformed Mennonite Church to the average urban American
the story would take on an especially colorful aspect.

We would be willing to give you professional assistance
in this if need be.

However, we must point out to you that such a publicity
campaign might have some affects you would not intend:

1. It would tend to arouse public indignation and
    perhaps derision against the church and its
    leaders in a manner somewhat similar to the
    shunning practice you deplore. It would possibly
    cause discord in the church, especially among
    younger members.

2. It might be a cause of lifelong embarrassment to
    your wife and could be destructive of the normal
    relationship between her and your children if, in

later years, they take the view that she deprived
them of their father.

3. Although, as you believe, your wife now shuns you
   only because of misguided love, the public might
   not be so understanding and would perhaps think
   this not loving behavior. Therefore, a publicity
   campaign might create pressures on her which could
   change this love to hatred and permanently destroy
   the chance that you could be peacefully reunited
   as you wish.

I know you feel that conditions cannot be worse for you
than they are now and are ready for desperate measures.
However our counsel to you is to without action at least
until time to put the potato planting in the ground in
hope that the bishops of the church will see fit to ease
her mind by counseling her that she can, in good
conscience, give up shunning of you and restore your
family to its former peaceful unity.

Failing that, we will be willing to begin preparations
promptly to bring this whole matter before the public. We
further recommend that fairness requires that copies of
this letter be sent to Mrs. Bear and to the authorities
of the Reformed Mennonite Church so they might not be
mistaken about your intentions. In the meantime, it will
be helpful if you will compile a list of the names and
addresses of those who have personal knowledge of the
cases you mentioned where suicide followed
excommunication and shunning by the Reformed Mennonite
Church.

Sincerely yours,
(s) Clarence C. Smith
Clarence C. Smith, PRSA Accredited
Executive Vice President

As the public relations counsel had indicated, they copied this letter
and sent it to Mother and all the bishops. Its arrival suddenly painted a far
different picture of the anticipated use of the loan money than my father
had indicated.

Mother, who had been cosigning loans for the business for years, began
to suspect that the money would not be used for farm income; rather, it
would fund a significant escalation in my father's campaign against the

Church. Knowing this, she refused to cosign any loan. In retaliation, my father charged that Mother refused to cooperate in the running of the business and therefore prevented him from financially supporting his family.

In early spring, he declared that he couldn't take it anymore and announced he was leaving. This time he would head to Delaware, where he was going to live and work for a friend of his near Dover, providing advice on that man's potato crop.

The scene of his leaving and his words as he left would forever be burned in my memory.

Standing in the driveway by the garage, just before he opened the door of the Galaxie 500, he turned to all of us and pronounced, "You're on your own."

His words were so simple, so stark, and so final that I was stunned. Right away, I contemplated with curiosity the surprise that he was going to work for someone else when he had always disdained being an employee. My curiosity provided a temporary buffer for the out-of-body panic that arose next.

Mother now had a part-time job one or two days a week, which Daddy disapproved of although he refused to support us. When he decided to live at home, she got up before he arose, crept toward the second-floor porch, and together with Susie and Sharon slid down the porch posts to the lawn. She would push the station wagon silently out of the driveway and toward the lane. When she was far enough away not to rouse my father, she would start the ignition and drive to work at Grandma's house in Camp Hill. Uncle Glenn had rented some space in the greenhouse behind our home to provide a little additional income for us, but Daddy had exploded when he found out.

"How dare Glenn use *my* greenhouse?' he bellowed.

Unfortunately, none of Mother's efforts amounted to much money.

How, I silently panicked, *could we possibly survive on our own?*

Homecoming

While in Delaware, strategizing the next steps of his campaign, Daddy hired the publicist he had contacted and began plotting ways to attract publicity for his story. He had made it a habit of announcing his homecomings, but this time, he didn't inform us of the exact date. So when he returned in the late spring, it was in dramatic fashion, crashing Sunday meeting (as was his habit) to make his points before a captive audience of the assembled congregation.

My father's public tirades were both predictable and alarming in their menacing—and increasingly vulgar—accusations. He would yell at the ministers, quote scriptures at length, and vent his disdain at the congregation for being accomplices to breaking up a marriage and family. While his private whirlwinds often lasted for hours, his public ones were blessedly shorter, rarely lasting longer than the service normally would, which was plenty.

After Daddy's twenty-minute diatribe and subsequent departure, I heard sobbing from the men's side of the church. I turned and looked behind me across the aisle to discover it was Benny, sitting beside Uncle Francis, with his chest heaving and his head bobbing so low it nearly touched his belly. When Daddy had announced he was returning, though the date was unclear, I knew Benny had been quietly looking forward to seeing him again. But Daddy had come to church, said his piece, and never once looked at Benny—or any of us children for that matter. When he abruptly pivoted and left, the toxic mix of anticipation and disappointment bubbled over.

Benny's sobbing caught me by surprise—not because he was crying but because it startled me into noticing how empty I felt. I realized in that moment that I didn't miss Daddy. I wanted our family to be whole again, but Daddy was so unstable and disruptive and frightening that I enjoyed the peace when he was gone. Plus, he was so obsessed with his campaign that even when he was around, nobody else mattered.

Is there something wrong with me? I wondered. *Why don't I feel anything like Benny does? Why do I feel nothing at all?*

Publicity Storm Brewing

At least since 1964, Daddy had been raising arcane issues with the Church that he said indicated their hypocrisy and lack of purity. And for years he had felt frustrated at being unheard and not taken seriously. Even after the latest excommunication, he had gotten little traction when telling outsiders about the Church's impurities. And yet, as the excommunication began to seem increasingly likely, he told Mother triumphantly that he thought he had finally found a way to take down the Church.

Daddy's brilliant plan was to focus on the issue of shunning and breaking up marriages. I mentioned before that he told neighbors, relatives, business customers, anyone who would listen that his wife and his family were shunning him, that the Church was taking away his family to punish him. But now, with the dramatic increase in public interest he had garnered, his claims further captured the public's attention and outrage.

Though Mother had only suspected that his interest lay in his campaign rather than farming, it would turn out that Daddy had for some time been approaching newspapers. Many had declined to cover his story, but he had noticed that a nearby town newspaper, Chambersburg's *Public Opinion*, often got their stories picked up by the larger newspapers. So, he focused his efforts on getting published in this outlet—the first to deem him newsworthy. This turning point signaled what was to become a media avalanche headed our way.

In late spring, my father's first front-page headline arrived.

PUBLIC OPINION, MAY 5, 1973

Chambersburg, PA

Far-reaching Effects of Church Doctrine
Church 'Shun' Disrupts Ref. Mennonite Family

The religious 'shun' or ban, which most people think exists only in folklore, has sent an area man into self-imposed exile, left a 400-acre farm uncultivated for a time, threatened the man's family relationship, and may lead to a legal suit against the church. . . . Bear was excommunicated by the church a year ago in a dispute over doctrinal procedure. The 'crime' for which he was excommunicated is 'raillery'. He criticized church doctrine and accused the church authorities of unjust behavior in a situation not involving his family.

The article goes on to describe that my father is all right with the loss of buyers for his farm products and of a long-time employee, who is a Church member. But the major problem, it explains, is the relationship between Bear and his wife.

Mrs. Bear, allegedly following the precepts of the church as she understands them, has continued to care for the home and family, cook for her husband, but has refused to eat with him or have conjugal relations with him.

The article further describes the purpose of shunning as a form of love, the aim being to bring the excommunicated person back into the fold in repentance and therefore ensure the salvation of his soul. It also paints my father's aim to break the "shun" and for Church leaders to persuade Mother that her reaction is not required by Church doctrine. Toward this goal, the article reported that my father hired a lawyer and a public relations firm, and that he approached several newspapers.

The public relations firm is planning a publicity campaign which may involve radio and television exposure, a possible book, and even a suit through the American Civil Liberties Union.

The Church would be on record as insisting that each member was simply following their own convictions, rather than being coerced to take any particular action.

Yet, when asked if Mrs. Bear would face any penalties or repercussion from the church should she decide to resume marital relations with her husband, the bishop said, "I do not answer hypothetical questions," adding that he preferred to deal with matters after they happen.

This article would soon be followed by other front-page stories in the towns and cities surrounding our home: *The Evening News* in Harrisburg, *The Intelligencer Journal* and *New Era* in Lancaster, and the *Baltimore Evening Sun* in nearby Maryland.

On May 13, 1973, the story would reach the front page of the *Philadelphia Inquirer*—alongside a headline of Soviet leader Brezhnev coming to visit the US for the Summit on Arms Control.

Daddy's publicity goals had officially reached the pinnacle he craved.

A Major League Story

By July, the story of this little-known religion, its strange practices, and the tale of the persecuted man at the center of it all, exploded onto the national stage with another front-page article, wherein my father was introduced to the American public as "the model of raw-boned American Gothic."

THE NEW YORK TIMES, JULY 23, 1973

Mennonite Dissident Shunned by Church and Wife

By WAYNE KING

CARLISLE, Pa., July 22—At 44 years of age, a prosperous, soft-spoken Mennonite farmer and father of six, Robert L. Bear seemed oddly cast as a heretic, excommunicated from his church and angrily challenging the faith of his fathers.

. . .

Most painful, however, is that his 35-year-old wife, Gale, who continues in the faith and daily wears the traditional plain, long blue gown and cap of the sect, will share neither his table nor his bed, and by Mr. Bear's account, will hardly speak to him.

His six children no longer have faith and trust in him. He has moved from his farmhouse to a sparse bachelor's trailer. Most of the church, including his father and a younger brother, think he is unstable at best. Some think he is flirting with Satan at worst. And much of his farm lies idle because he has been unable to plant the bumper crop of potatoes he has brought forth every year for the last 20 years, earning up to $40,000 annually.

"They're doing this in the name of Christianity," said Mr. Bear, "but I will not knuckle under."

"The bishops and I are like two stags on a mountain. My wife is the doe standing at the top. A fight is inevitable."

. . .

"They think I'm insane, possessed of Satan," said Mr. Bear.

Contrary to church doctrine he has engaged an attorney to counsel him on legal means to stop the shunning. On the attorney's advice, Mr. Bear has visited three psychiatrists as well as a medical doctor to assess his mental state. All considered him normal.

Again, the Church will be quoted for their official position:

Bishop Gross contended that Mrs. Bear's own interpretation of the Scriptures, not fear of the church, had caused her to shun her husband. On the other hand, he said: "We are not to love anything more than Christ (although) it may cause a hardship. If she, or anyone, would not observe the ban, they would violate the Scriptures."

Would Mrs. Bear, who was allowed back in the church after the 1964 incident, then be excommunicated again?

"Well, not immediately, he said. "But if she lost the teaching of Christ, she would be excommunicated."

My father described shunning as "a living hell of torture," and in his determination to fight back, he said, "We must lift the skirts of these plain clothes and give the world a peek underneath. Those plain garments had pride in the corruption of power."

The bishops, he insisted, must be discredited and proven wrong.

The *New York Times* story represented a tipping point, as the story was carried on the AP wire to newspapers throughout every state in the nation. Small-town as well as big-city newspaper headlines shouted such statements as: "Farmer Loses Wife for Criticizing Church." "Outcast fights back." "Wife Shuns Farmer Who Defies His Church." The accumulation of publicity led to television interviews for Daddy on Pittsburgh and Hershey stations. He even did an interview with the Canadian Broadcasting Co., which received such an extensive response they considered a follow-up interview. By late July, the story would be carried in Canadian newspapers as far away as Saskatchewan.

Daddy was elated by this explosion of publicity and the support he received. Sympathetic letters poured in from all over the country and overseas. A soldier based in Germany read the story in the military's *Stars and Stripes* magazine and wrote to Daddy vowing support and solidarity. People called long distance to offer their compassion and encouragement. A Jewish man traveled from New York in his camper and offered to work on the farm. Not accustomed to farm work, however, he ended up assisting Daddy by talking to a bishop, our neighbors, and other supporters of my father. When he left, he promised to stay in touch with Daddy and return later if he could be of help.

The Pennsylvania chapter of the ACLU also agreed to review his case at their next meeting and consider taking it on. In June, they determined in an 18-1 vote that none of his constitutional rights had been violated. Undaunted by this vote and buoyed more by the enormous outpouring of publicity and the support he had received, Daddy became even bolder in his belief in the rightness of his actions.

On Aug 11, 1973, the *Public Opinion* again reported on his case.

> Somewhat overwhelmed by all the publicity, Bear still feels that no effort is too great to restore the unity of his own family and possibly avert the practice of the "shun" on another "erring" member in the future.

The publicity seemed to invigorate him far more than farming, and it reinforced his justifications for his violence at home. It also cemented his status as the injured party and his family as tormentors.

Meanwhile, reporters repeatedly called our home and showed up without warning in the driveway with cameras and recorders, demanding a comment from Mother. Again and again she refused to say anything. Distraught by the narrative my father was presenting to the public, I pleaded with Mother to tell them what was *really* going on.

"Jesus commands us to turn the other cheek" was her reply.

We were supposed to be passive, to be conscientious objectors who never fought in war nor offered any resistance. But I did not like the idea of always turning the other cheek. It didn't seem right.

We should fight back, I thought, *and at least tell them the things Daddy is doing . . . how he's* really *behaving beyond the picture he's painting of himself as the victim. Someone needs to set the record straight.*

I just wasn't sure who that someone would be.

Home Alone

Between our precarious economic situation, the unpredictable violence from my father, and the searing publicity, Mother reached the limits of her ability to cope. Though I was normally finely attuned to her needs, I was unaware of just how close to breaking she was until one day in late summer.

I was concentrating on the chores of wash day, moving the clothespins from the pockets of my apron to mouth to clothesline with conveyor belt–like efficiency. The plastic-lined bushel basket sat by my side with its soggy weight of laundry making an indentation in the soft grass. Rows of shirts, pants, and underwear in parallel lines waved behind me in the breeze. As one row dried, I would replace it with a wet row. Before the day was over, all four lines would be pinned more than once, with the dry clothes taken in, folded, and put away. An ironing pile and a sewing repair pile would be set aside for later. As you might imagine, with a seven-person family, wash day was an all-day affair, but I didn't mind it so much. I enjoyed the sun on my upturned face and the caress of the breeze. Plus, I could think while I pinned. On that day, however, I wasn't thinking about much of anything when Mother suddenly appeared from behind a bedsheet I'd just hung.

"Here," she said, thrusting a sheet of lined notebook paper at me, her neat handwriting filling the entire page with columns of lists.

She did this so casually that I didn't register her meaning at first.

Then she said, "I need a break. I just can't take this anymore. I'm taking Sharon because she's too young to leave here and I'm going to Aunt Linda's."

At that, a jolt ran through my body. Aunt Linda lived six hundred miles away in Illinois, a twelve-hour drive or more.

"I'm taking a bus and will be back in a week," she said.

A whole week? my mind screamed. *Who will take care of us? And what if Daddy comes around when you're gone? What will we do then? Even though Daddy's living at the trailer right now, who knows what he might decide to do.*

But before I could verbalize any of my concerns, she said briskly, "I'm putting you in charge while I'm gone. When I get back, I want everything on this list to be done. Do you understand?"

I stared at the list. None of the chores were for children.

Pick beans and freeze them.

Bake bread.

Clean the whole house.

Mow the lawn.

Weed the gardens.

Do the laundry.

And *I* was in charge? Granted, I knew she chose me because she was certain everything would get done. But it violated the order—as the eldest, David was supposed to be in charge, then Benny, *then* me. I knew immediately that my brothers were *not* going to like it and that I was going to pay the price for it.

Exactly one week later, Mother called to say she was coming home. We all climbed onto the potato storage roof to get the first glimpse of her driving down the road and turning into our lane. As I stood there, only two things occupied my mind: 1) that everything on the list got done, thanks to me badgering and driving my siblings until every last chore was completed; and 2) that my brothers and sisters hated me for it.

It's All Mine

Though Daddy sobbed when he told reporters that the Church took his family away from him, at home I often wondered if Daddy *wanted* us to leave.

Who could blame me? It seemed he cut us off from supplies and made life difficult so that we would *decide* to leave, that it would look like *our* choice. He sermonized often how he was here first, that he spent five years alone here before *she* moved in. *He* bought this farm. *He* built the business.

The farm was *his*. The business was *his*. The money was *his*. She (Mother) didn't do anything, so *she* should pack up and leave with nothing. Never mind that there were six children to consider.

My father moved in and out of the house so many times, it was difficult to keep up with his decisions, or to understand any pattern to them. But in September, he made a big announcement in his usual dramatic manner: we *all* had to leave the farm. Not *him*. Mother and all us kids. He didn't specify just where we were supposed to go, so with only a small bag of clothes, we fled to Papap Bear's. For three weeks, he drove us to our elementary school each day in his car that looked like a big black antique with its winged back end, until finally Daddy cooled down enough for us to return home.

Daddy's actions had incited talk amongst the proud extended Bear clan, who did not receive well the news that Daddy wasn't providing for his own children. It wasn't until the excommunication that we began visiting Daddy's eldest brother, Uncle Lehman, who was the only sibling of Daddy's who had not joined the Church. We kids would sit in the living room and watch *Hee Haw* and *The Lawrence Welk Show*, with the band members in their blue leisure suits, while Uncle Lehman and Daddy talked. (Even though these were old people's programs, we didn't mind because at least we got to watch TV.) Uncle Lehman was kind and sympathetic to Daddy as he listened to his troubles, but he was also firm about his responsibilities. He said repeatedly that Daddy needed to provide support for the children he brought into the world, that what he was doing wasn't right. But Daddy seemed unmoved. He had his reasons and that was good enough for him.

That December, Papap Bear died from cancer. Predictably, Daddy pitched a fit at his funeral, just like he did at his mother's the year before. And Papap, who wanted to be fair to Daddy but had likely recognized he would spend his inheritance on his campaign rather than to support his children, had reworked his will: half of Daddy's share of his inheritance went directly to Mother. This money went toward paying Grandma back the money she'd loaned us for the car, and it also kept us, at least for a time, from having to scrape to buy gas and food. Though Daddy no doubt resented us getting *his* money, Papap Bear's monetary gift was ours, and there was nothing Daddy could do about it.

The Clarinet

The start of fourth grade in the fall of 1973 marked a move to the wing housing the two upper-grade classrooms—which not only brought a feeling of growing up but also a new and unexpected opportunity: every student was invited to join the band and learn to play an instrument.

I wanted so badly to play the flute, which looked elegant and refined, with its notes so sweet, graceful, soft, and gentle. I begged Mother to let me play it, but she said we didn't have the money for an instrument.

"But," she offered, "Grandma might still have a clarinet somewhere in storage."

Sure enough, Mother found the long, brown case that opened to reveal a nickel clarinet resting in a cushion of red velvet.

"But all the new clarinets are black," I protested. "I'll stand out like a sore thumb with this instrument. It will be embarrassing."

"Take it or leave it," she said.

I took it.

Mastering the reed so that it blew into the instrument rather than creating an awful screech that hurt all my siblings' ears was an enormous challenge. They were not at all thrilled about my practicing, even with the door closed. But it was difficult to figure out which keys to press at the same time I was trying to avoid the squeal. I was just barely getting the hang of it when it was announced that we were having our first school concert.

Mother sewed me a brand-new plaid jumper for the big night. She didn't come to the concert, though, because she wasn't allowed to. There was always an invocation at school events, and members of our Church are forbidden from being present when any other minister is preaching. Just by being present gives the impression that the Church member agrees with and is in unity with those other ministers. And since our members cannot be in unity with anyone except for our own Church—and doing otherwise could get you excommunicated—Mother merely dropped me off for the big performance.

The cafeteria, which doubled as an auditorium, boasted a raised stage set up with rows of chairs for the orchestra. Taking my seat, I felt proud and important being up there, and I felt stylish in my brand-new outfit. As the lights dimmed on the audience of parents and teachers, the illumination became focused on us. I was excited but also fervently hoped I wouldn't squeal my clarinet in front of all the parents.

As we began playing, an awful screeching sound escaped, the kind that makes a person instinctively clap their hands over their ears. It was loud, grating, and unmistakable whose instrument it came from. The nickel clarinet stood out in a sea of black clarinets, and my red face, I was certain, stood out too. Contemplating the risk of any more humiliating notes bursting from my instrument, I quickly decided I couldn't bear it happening again. So, for the rest of the concert, I merely pretended to play.

As far as everyone in the audience knew, after that initial squeal, I gathered my formidable skills and played with perfect elegance. I was the only one the wiser that I kept the concert from being ruined—though I think my teacher may have had an inkling.

No Field Trip

Mother's back had been getting progressively worse, with her spasms so severe that sometimes even slight movements would trigger intense pain and render her incapacitated. At first, she tried to feel better by taking a large piece of plywood and putting it under the mattress in the double bed in the girls' room, where she took to sleeping with us because it felt safer than my parents' room. But even with the modified mattress, the spasms were so bad that she sometimes could not get out of bed.

The stress of our family situation was clearly taking a toll on her health, and Daddy crowed that her pain was a sign. He was sorry for her failing health, he claimed, but that was just the way it had to be. What's more, it represented one more indication that he was right, and she was wrong.

"I intended to break the back of the Church," he said pointedly to Mother, "but it seems to mostly be affecting *your* back."

One day, as she lay in bed unable to move, I asked her to sign my permission slip for our class field trip to Indian Echo Caverns. Like most kids, I loved the adventure of visiting new places and seeing the unusual, and I especially looked forward to the chance to buy a trinket in the gift shops with money from my piggy bank. But when I handed her the paper to sign, she snapped at me.

"Of course you can't go. Can't you see I need help? Plus, I need you to stay home and change my bedpan."

I could see that she couldn't get out of bed, and that she frequently winced in excruciating pain. But missing an awaited field trip crushed me. I knew, though, that my staying home was not just about changing Mother's bedpan. She was terrified that Daddy would come to the house while we were at school and find her helpless, paralyzed, and alone. He would most certainly attack her. She couldn't run. She couldn't defend herself. She couldn't even reach a phone.

I knew Mother's decision was final, and I understood that in her broken state, she needed protection from Daddy.

I had already been to Indian Echo Caverns once, I reasoned, so it wouldn't be a big deal to not see it again.

Suing the Church

On November 13, 1973, Daddy filed suit against the Church and two bishops for depriving him of his wife and family. He asked the court for an injunction to prohibit the Church from its current shunning and from all future exercise of this practice. He also declared he was suing for damages resulting from loss of income from farming. He claimed in his suit, as well as in interviews, that his children didn't respect him anymore because of what the Church did to him and because Mother had poisoned us against him.

Daddy had been receiving pro bono consulting from attorney Richard Wagner, a distant relative of his, but now he officially hired an attorney, Mrs. Del Duca, to represent him in the suit. When I heard this news, I was shocked by two things. For one, we were not allowed to sue in a court of law. I had been taught that this was wrong, that it was against the Bible. *How could he change his beliefs so quickly?* I wondered. And two, he hired a woman attorney. I didn't even know there was such a thing! Plus, I found it odd given Daddy's opinion of females.

Benny called her Mrs. Del *Puka* because we didn't like the people who helped my father spread his lies.

"Don't talk about your father or his attorney like that," Mother said sternly. "He's still your father. You must speak respectfully about him."

But she wasn't fooling anyone. Respect for our father had, as he had claimed—and as he himself had systematically caused—gradually faded for all of us kids, even if we were terrified to admit it.

CHAPTER FOUR

1974

You're gonna be happy, said life, but first I'll make you strong.
—ANONYMOUS

THE MONTH OF APRIL CARRIED FRESH HEADLINES ABOUT THE OUTCOME of my father's suit against the Church begun the previous autumn.

INTELLIGENCER JOURNAL, EDITORIALS, APRIL 6, 1974

Lancaster, Pennsylvania

Robert Bear's Dilemma as an Excommunicant

The Cumberland County Court has said "no" to Robert Bear in a great many words that leave a number of nagging questions.

. . .

We believe Judge Weidner, as did Pontius Pilate, washed his hands of the Bear case by taking a stance behind the First Amendment.

It is impossible with the amendment so clear on the issue, to quarrel with a church's right to excommunicate a member or members of its congregation. It may indeed. But how much freedom of religion does the amendment provide?

Can excommunication be carried outside the precincts of the church? Can it be permitted to destroy a man's relationship with his family or his livelihood?

. . .

The church could well have been destroyed by an attack on its doctrine in the courts culminating in an adverse ruling.

On the other hand, there is Robert Bear, his wife, four bright-eyed children and his conscience. Must they be sacrificed to the unbending rule of the church, a rule that has been described as barbarous and archaic in a 20th century setting?

Robert Bear might overcome his conscience and petition to be taken back into the church. The church may forgive his straying, lift the order of excommunication, and Bear might resume a normal life.

That is impossible. Bear is a man of deep and abiding conviction. His conscience and his principles deserve the protection of the courts as much as does the doctrine of the Reformed Mennonite Church.

Judge Weidner's ruling, in the case of Robert Bear, appears to give the church not only the freedom from interference guaranteed by the Constitution, but permits it also to wield influence in areas outside that guarantee.

The ruling is simply too fuzzy, too imprecise and Robert Bear, as he should, is expected to appeal.

THE EVENING SUN, APRIL 8, 1974

Baltimore, Maryland

'Shunned' Mennonite Loses Court Battle

Robert L. Bear, of Carlisle, Pa., will continue to live as an outcast in his own home.

A county judge has ruled that the law cannot stop the Reformed Mennonite Church—and Bear's wife and family—from "shunning" the farmer.

Bear had complained to the court in January that the

"shunning"—an old church practice of avoiding an excommunicated member—was ruining his marriage and business, and he asked the court to order an end to it.

But Judge Clinton Weidner ruled that it was "both idle and vain" to suggest that the court could "coerce" improvement in Bear's marital or business relationships.

...

Richard Wagner, a semi-retired lawyer and Bear's friend, said the judge had ruled that as long as the teachings of the church were "merely persuasive" and did not involve the use of force, there was nothing the state could do.

. . .

Meanwhile, he will go on living in the spacious farmhouse on his 400-acre, $200,000 farm north of Carlisle with a wife "who's friendlier to strangers at the door than to me."

INTELLIGENCER JOURNAL, APRIL 11, 1974

Lancaster, Pennsylvania

Gentle People?

To the Editor:

For the benefit of the reading public and also for all the free world to read, do not the events of the Robert Bear story and those of Russia and Alexander Solzhenitsyn's exit appear similar?

Can this happen in our country?

I greatly admire Solzhenitsyn's wife and family who chose to exit with him, even as "outcasts." Nuff said.

I await F-L-A-C-K.

Are the gentle people as they are called, really gentle?

Maybe we should boycott their wares as they have Robert Bear's?

—Just Wondering

After the inferno of publicity in the summer of '73, the story had died down a bit. There was not much to fuel the public's continuing interest beyond the outlines of the original exotic nature of an obscure religious sect and its unusual practice of shunning. But the suit and its dismissal generated new headlines and put my father and his case back in the spotlight. Renewed interest in "the injustice being done to this poor man" surged and generated more outrage, deepened sympathy for him, and grew a wider group of admirers and supporters.

Increasingly, the newspapers also reported that we children were members of the church and, as Daddy had erroneously claimed, shunning him too. He rarely bothered to correct this misunderstanding of our status as noncombatants. Instead, he fanned the flames, shaking his head mournfully as he told reporters that because of the Church, we had lost respect for him and spoke disrespectfully to him. Sometimes he poured it on thick with the reporters, saying, "I just can't take it anymore," as the tears coursed down his cheeks.

With the renewed media coverage, my father's supporters were even more agitated by the unfair treatment of him by the Church and his family. He received further letters of support and visits from strangers at his trailer; more people stopped him in the street, invited him to meals, and wrote letters to the editor. Daddy frequently told us children about these supporters and how many people were on *his* side. When we went to town with Mother, we would encounter these crusaders of Daddy's, some of whom would see Mother's plain clothes and recognize her face, then throw us looks of contempt. Others would pointedly ask, "Are you any relation to Robert Bear?" Still others would send letters to our mailbox telling us what terrible people we all were and that we should be ashamed of ourselves.

It seemed so unfair. I could not understand what any of us had done to deserve this level of public scorn, particularly us children.

Undaunted and Determined

Though the judge dismissed his suit, Daddy, as the newspaper correctly predicted, decided to appeal his case. Not only would he not stop in the courts, but he told us he was writing a book about his trials and tribulations so that more people could understand what had been done to him. He crowed that he transcribed all the confrontations from his "honest John" tape recordings of Church members from his months on the road in the fall and winter of

1972, plus he recorded confrontations where he had ambushed Uncle Glenn and other bishops. Not only was his book going to be filled with these documentations, he said, but also stories from his childhood we had heard about a thousand times, not to mention his usual array of cringe-inducing intimate bedroom tales featuring our mother.

"I have to expose her," he said. "I'm sorry, but that's the way it is. I must expose the naked truth of her and this Church."

The book, we were told, would be titled *Delivered Unto Satan* because the Church "damned him to hell." He planned to self-publish and distribute it to local bookstores, sell it from his truck, and give away copies to supporters—anything to get the word out about the injustice that had befallen him.

We took in this announcement with dread and despair. This book would mean more publicity. More humiliation. The whole world would, no doubt, place even more belief in him. And worse, nobody but us would have a clue about his true actions toward his family.

Kidnapped

I always liked walking down our long lane to pick up the mail. Somehow it felt like traveling somewhere exciting even though it always ended in the same place: the mailbox that kept company with the plastic newspaper holder, sitting beside the main road (which wasn't very "main" at all, since hardly anyone ever drove by except the school bus, the mailman, or a neighbor or two). Nevertheless, I liked venturing out beyond our borders and observing what was happening in the millrace community adjacent to the lane. The long walk also built the anticipation of seeing what letters might arrive in the mail.

One day back in February, the mailbox had no exciting letters or even seed catalogues for me to peruse; instead, the newspaper delivered shocking news: Patty Hearst, the newspaper heiress, was violently abducted at gunpoint by a terrorist group who was now demanding a ransom. That someone so wealthy and prominent could be kidnapped from her home was astonishing to me. Maybe I took notice because our names were the same, but regardless of that, I was alarmed and frightened for her.

As the days marched on, I kept checking the newspaper, hoping it would report that she had been rescued. But weeks and months had now gone by and still she hadn't been found. I didn't know her, and I wasn't sure why her story struck me so hard and made me so sad for her, but it did.

Candles and Sandals

Daddy no longer planted nearly as many crops as he used to, favoring mostly corn, pumpkins, and cabbages rather than potatoes, probably because those crops didn't require as much intensive care as potatoes, and also because he was always so preoccupied by his campaign against the Church that "plant them and forget them" crops suited him better. It had become clear that his prior dedication to and love of farming had been replaced with relishing his campaign. It seemed to be all he ever talked about, and his excitement over this "great cause" was non-ending. It is no understatement that he ruthlessly and ceaselessly beat the subject into the ground.

Like a man who had broken his fast with a gorge, my father continued spending long hours writing his pamphlets and offering money to people to type them and print them for distribution. Judge Weidner's name and his sin in ruling against Daddy and being complicit with the Church were inexhaustibly inked into scathing diatribes, which landed on the doorsteps of Church members, as well as local area businesses and homes. Whereas Daddy used to devote considerable time to delivering potatoes, he now mostly delivered pamphlets, gave interviews, and engaged in long, devilish strategy sessions with his attorney.

One result of Daddy's shift in focus from farming to sought-after media personality affected the shed in front of our house. In the past it had been used to maintain farm machinery and was once constantly bustling with repair work. Welding, greasing, and fixing the tools and machinery necessary to keep the farm running had always made this shed unsafe and mostly off limits for us children. But now, as it became increasingly clear that the shed would see no more repair activity, we kids had slowly been transforming it into our own kind of workshop.

Pooling our money, my siblings and I bought cake pan–sized slabs of wax, along with bayberry scent, and began making candles. We arranged a two-burner stove on a workbench, and cleared another bench to assemble candle molds. In the beginning we mostly made tapers in the antique candle mold someone gave David. But after we became more adept, we collected milk cartons from school. These we filled with ice, attached a wick, and poured colored wax over top to create a unique candle filled with nooks and crannies that formed as the ice melted. In an effort to help us earn more money, Uncle Glenn allowed us to sell them at his store. Once we sold the initial lot, we took our profits and bought more wax and molds.

As winter was nearing, we started with Christmas-themed molds of Santas and Christmas trees. For the trees we dyed the wax green and filled the molds. When the candle cooled, we took plain white wax and dripped it over the branches to look like snow. Eventually, we acquired more than twenty molds that covered all the different holidays, as well as various animal figures and other objects.

The shed also served to inspire a fashion project I conceived, and that Benny helped to bring to fruition.

I thought it would be nice if we girls could wear sandals, but I knew Mother wouldn't buy them even if I begged. They would probably be considered frivolous and unnecessary, not to mention a drain on the little money we had. So, building on our resourcefulness, each of us girls traced the outline of our foot on a piece of wood. Then, Benny cut out the shape with a jigsaw. I rummaged around until I found the wide green-and-white-striped plastic strips that Mother used to repair the lawn chairs. In a spark of creativity, I had Benny use some leftover upholstery nails to secure the plastic to the wooden outlines, and in no time we had sandals.

Daddy may have been preoccupied with walking his path to vindication, but we had carved a path too: one on which we were discovering new talents, and where I imagined we looked quite fashionable as we clop-clopped on the macadam, a sound that carried a certain delightful feeling of independence.

Equal Pay

Stuffed into the front cab of the pickup truck, some of us uncomfortably sitting on our sibling's laps (I was perched on David's), Daddy drove us home for supper after working at the Other Farm. We pulled abeam the little copse in the woods where a Civil War cemetery sat, with little American flags sticking up through the dense brush; alongside the cemetery, buried in the woods, we always turned right at this T in the road. But just before we did, one of David's curious wonderings erupted from behind my back.

"Daddy, why do you pay us boys a dollar an hour and only pay the girls a dollar a day when we all do the same work?"

The question briefly suspended time as I digested his words.

I didn't know we didn't make the same amount of money! Is that true? Are they getting paid more?

He was right about the work. The four eldest children worked in teams of two, side by side: Benny and David, Leah and me. We did the same tasks at the same time, and they weren't easy. Among other things, we hoisted thirty-foot long irrigation pipes up over our heads and pushed them perpendicularly through the towering corn stalks, each of us holding one end. Holding the pipe high made it easier to push through the corn, which was less dense at the top, but it also left our underarms exposed to the brutal edges of the leaves and the irritatingly sticky, sandy film of pollen that fell from the plant.

As you may recall, Mother and Daddy argued once about how the boys shouldn't have to do "women's work," but Daddy had never restricted the girls from "men's work" on the farm. We cut cabbage with our brothers. We filled fifty-pound bags of potatoes and hefted them up onto the conveyor belt that took them into the delivery truck. We threw cantaloupes, watermelons, and pumpkins from the field up to Daddy, who stood on the wagon and caught them. David, Benny, and I drove the tractors sometimes. We did all the dirtiest, grittiest work our brothers did, only we girls also helped Mother at home, cleaned Daddy's trailer regularly, and cooked for him sometimes too. Daddy never had any problem if we girls worked in the house *and* the fields. No work was off limits to women. *So why didn't we get paid the same?*

I was intrigued by this question, but I didn't have to wait long for Daddy's response. His answer came as a hand flying off the steering wheel toward me, but was aimed for his real target behind me: David's mouth.

"You shouldn't be disrespectful of your father," Daddy fumed.

David dodged out of reach as the truck swerved.

Nothing more was said, so I remained puzzled by this question.

But not long after, we girls started getting paid by the hour too.

Resignation

In early August 1974, we children were working alongside Daddy at the Other farm around midday, but none of us, including Daddy, were getting much work accomplished that day. We were all glued to the news emanating from the radio perched on the near-empty wagon meant for corn (it was supposed to be filled with ears stacked in crates several feet high, but that's how little work we had gotten done).

Like everyone else in the country, we had been following the saga of the Watergate scandal for some time—the drip, drip, drip of information that ignited the questions: Would Nixon survive? Was he telling the truth? We wanted to believe the President hadn't done anything wrong and was being truthful about saying so, but secret tapes had been found that revealed beyond a shadow of a doubt that he had been lying, that when he had confidently denied all involvement with a straight face, he had been deceiving the entire American public.

President Nixon, it was announced, was going to resign tomorrow.

Even though my parents didn't vote, it was still a momentous and sobering announcement for all of us.

"The president will give a speech this evening," the radio announcer added.

It was then that Daddy said we would go to town and watch Nixon's speech on TV.

That night, we found our familiar spot in the line of televisions at Montgomery Ward. The clerks didn't shoo us away; even they were huddled around watching. While Daddy stood transfixed, we all sat cross legged on the floor, witnessing the historic moment and feeling the heaviness of the grave time it was for the country.

What I remember most, though, is the sense that Nixon didn't appear very sorry for what he had done, only sorry that he got caught. I felt the worst for his wife and daughters having to bear the public shame of his misdeeds. Somehow, it was a familiar feeling.

A Badge of Authority

Jim had been a school rival for several years, and we had gone head to head in various academic contests. In third grade, Miss Clevenger held a contest to see who could write the most Roman numerals, and I knew he was my only real competition. We both filled several pads of lined yellow paper, but in the end, he edged me out. My competitive spirit always liked to take the lead in something, though, and this year, I finally got the chance.

The principal, Mr. A.B. McCarter, had asked at the beginning of the school year which fifth graders would like to volunteer to be school bus crossing guards. Even though our Church forbad women members from assuming any position of authority, I knew immediately that I wanted to be a guard and hoped I would be chosen. Shortly afterward, Mr. McCarter handed me an orange belt, badge, and identification certificate with his signature. Words could not express how thrilled I was.

That next day, as we neared my old Roman numeral rival's stop, which was several stops after my pickup, I arose from my new front-seat assignment and stepped off the bus. My bright orange plastic belt lay diagonal across my chest and fastened around my waist with a metal clasp, and my prominent silver badge that looked like a police officer's gleamed in the sunlight. With all the authority and pride I felt, I raised my hand in the universal halt sign toward the approaching car, allowing my classmate to walk safely across the road and climb into the bus.

I don't recall the expression on Jim's face, but I do remember the distinct feeling that things were beginning to turn around for me. I also felt like I was somebody important—and as a girl with few opportunities to feel that way, I quite liked it.

Singing Naked

Rounding the corner from the utility room, where we four oldest kids normally took off our dirty work clothes, we had a long, straight view into the kitchen. On this particular day, we were met with a shocking sight at the end of the corridor: two little shivering figures standing so close they looked like one puddle.

"What happened?" we all blurted out as we rushed toward them.

Susie and Sharon remained huddled with their shoulders touching and heads lowered. Sharon clutched her blankie, and they both looked as if they would fall without the other's body for support.

"What happened?" we asked again quieter, yet more urgently.

"She just started singing a hymn," Susie whispered. "Naked. Right there in the bathroom."

Despite asking for more details, we could not get any more out of them.

"She was singing naked," they kept repeating in horror.

Singing didn't sound so bad to me. *What was the big deal?*

And then, haltingly, fragments of the story emerged.

Susie and Sharon were in the bathroom to keep Mother company.

Mother was taking a bath.

Daddy broke through the bathroom door.

Mother was caught naked.

Daddy was looming over her, screaming vulgarities.

Eventually, we got the remaining horrifying details.

Mother had been so frightened that she climbed onto the bathroom counter and curled into the fetal position, her hands trying to protect her private parts. As Daddy became increasingly agitated, Mother began to sing a hymn in a high-pitched voice as if she had gone far, far away. The girls had stared at her in horror, and then just as suddenly as Mother had leaped to the counter, she swooped like a wraith beneath our father's arms and seemed to fly out the door.

Susie whispered that Mother had lost her mind.

Later, Mother confessed that she knew then if she continued to stay, she would go insane.

She had been pleading with the ministers and bishops prior to this for permission to leave, but they'd suggested that she try a little harder to work things out in her marriage.

As we older children talked among ourselves and pieced together the events of the day, it quickly became clear that we had fallen for one of Daddy's subterfuges. He would sometimes put us all to work on the other side of the creek and then slip away to the Home Farm to chase after Mother, assured that we were too far away to offer resistance or to arrive quickly enough to protect her, if we could even hear her cries for help. And then he had the nerve to publicly state that while his wife shunned him, she simultaneously teased him sexually. He even went so far as to tell reporters that "she lets me see her naked in the bath" and "it's like living in a girlie show."

How Mother endured this blatant and relentless gaslighting without losing her mind, I'll never know.

All the Way to the Pennsylvania Supreme Court

Daddy was once again in the headlines and editorials as word of his appeal, set to be heard by the Pennsylvania Supreme Court, found its way to small-town and big-city news markets.

THE LOS ANGELES TIMES, DECEMBER 3, 1974

Los Angeles, California

Un-Bearable He Says of Church Ouster

Mennonite farmer Robert L. Bear claims two bishops of his church, Glenn M. Gross and J. Henry Fisher, "willfully and intentionally urged" that he be shunned and boycotted by other church members. So, he is suing.

THE PHILADELPHIA INQUIRER, NOVEMBER 14, 1974

Philadelphia, Pennsylvania

State High Court Gets Case of Shunned Mennonite

A Mennonite farmer from Carlisle, Pa., shunned by his wife and his church, since he was excommunicated by his church more than two years ago will get his day before the Pennsylvania Supreme Court later this month.

The case of Robert J. Bear vs. the Reformed Mennonite Church is on the court's list for the November session.

Lawyers for both sides see it as a classic church-state question that could end in the U.S. Supreme Court.

LANCASTER INTELLIGENCER JOURNAL, DECEMBER 3, 1974

Lancaster, PA

Court Hears Case of Shunned Man

The Pennsylvania Supreme Court heard arguments yesterday in the case of Robert L. Bear, Carlisle R4 farmer, who has been expelled by the Reformed Mennonite Church.

...

Attorneys for both said the Supreme Court's decision is not the end of the matter. It will go back to the Cumberland County Court and from there they say, to the Supreme Court of the United States.

...

Bear claims his freedom of religion and right to marital privacy have been denied unconstitutionally and in violation of the Civil Rights Act by the shunning order of the church and its two bishops.

The State Supreme Court took the case under advisement. It did not indicate when it would hand down an opinion.

Leaving

Daddy tended to build steam from ruminating until it reached an intense pressure, and then blew shrapnel everywhere. Afterward, he would often retreat to the cave of his trailer until the next time he emerged hungry—and seething—from his hibernation. Sometimes that hibernation lasted only days, other times weeks. At this point, he had been hiding out in his trailer since September. Whether he was buoyed by his case being heard before the State Supreme Court, or it was simply part of his natural cycles of behavior, the bear was about to emerge again.

I'm forced to rely on court records, newspaper clippings, and my siblings to understand what happened the morning of December 5, 1974. Logically, I know that I was in the kitchen packing my lunch box alongside my siblings when Daddy walked in. I also know that we children must have chattered fearfully about Daddy's impending violence as we walked down the lane to the school bus. But I have no actual memories of that morning.

The newspapers and court records would later report that Mother left early that morning as she did every Thursday for her part-time job preparing food for Grandma's market stand. She took four-year-old Sharon with her, and Daddy would say that he came down from the trailer to find the other five children home alone packing their lunches and getting ready for school. He would claim that he had been upset about us being left alone before school like this for two years and was determined to stop it, announcing right then that he was moving back home, this time for good. We could stay if we liked, he said, but Mother couldn't come home again, so now was our time to leave if we wanted to.

"If she did come back," David asked, "will you promise not to be violent."

No, he said, he wouldn't promise that. In fact, he claimed he had sent a telegram to a bishop in Lancaster to alert him that he was bringing Mother's clothes to his home. After this announcement, Daddy headed out the door for Lancaster where he followed through on his promise and dumped Mother's clothes on the bishop's lawn.

As soon as his car disappeared down the lane, David and Benny put in an urgent call to Mother, apprising her of the danger should she come home again. He was serious, they told her.

Later, Daddy's lawyer friend Richard Wagner testified that he called me at my elementary school and David at his middle school to ask if we really felt we were in danger. According to him, we told him no. Though he must have called, I have no memory of it.

What I do remember clearly was being summoned out of class to the principal's office around midday and walking down the hall in an agitated haze. I'd been in minor trouble with teachers before, but I'd never been called to the principal's office. Now, heading down the hallway, I searched my mind frantically for what I might have done wrong so I could be prepared. Upon reaching the lobby, the principal was standing outside his office surrounded by Mother and my sisters.

The green station wagon was parked beneath the school's carport and I noted several bulging black trash bags in the rear. Before I could comprehend what was happening, Mother said, "Let's go, we've got to hurry. We have to pick up the boys too." With a nod toward the back of the car, she told us that when she got the phone call from the boys, she dropped work and rushed home to grab some clothing for all of us before Daddy came back from Lancaster. Then she announced that we were going to live with Grandma and Papap in Camp Hill and that this time, we were leaving for good. I didn't know what to say or even think.

That past summer, Mother had gathered us kids around the kitchen table for a family meeting. She told us we needed to be prepared for the possibility that we might lose the farm. I didn't believe her, not even a little. What she was saying was impossible, unthinkable. *This is our home*, I thought, *the place we love more than anywhere.* We had continued ducking Daddy, surviving, and going to school. We had fled home briefly on several occasions and twice gone to either live with Papap Bear, or to hide somewhere else when things got too dangerous, but we had always come back home when the coast seemed clear.

As the months passed, that summer warning faded and I forgot about it. When we got on the bus that morning, we expected to ride it home. But that wasn't what transpired.

By midday, we would leave everything behind, never to return. Yes, we would go back to this property again, but it would never be ours. It would never again be home sweet home.

A new routine began for all of us as we settled into Grandma's house. At night I would lie awake in the bedroom that I shared with Leah and watch the shadows of the headlights from the nearby four-lane highway circle the ceiling of the room like train tracks. Sometimes the wail of a passing ambulance would startle me, but the gentle, predictable shadows making their way across the ceiling would usually lull me to sleep.

I missed our farm terribly. But I was also experiencing something that had eluded me longer than I realized. Nestled in that bed, despite the foreign sounds and missing my old bedroom, I was beginning to feel safe for the first time in a long time.

Punching a Time Clock

Even though our father had not been consistently supporting us financially for a while, earning money became more urgent than ever—and all of us who were capable of holding down a job found ourselves working at Uncle Glenn's store. Every day, after school and on Saturdays, Papap Gross or Mother would drive us the twenty minutes out to Ashcombe.

We were used to working, but punching a time clock was new. Somehow, the timecards made the hours seem interminable, but we needed the money, so we did our best not to complain and to do a good job in our assigned tasks.

Leah and I worked together as a team, and Benny and David worked in different areas on their own—always behind the scenes so that Daddy wouldn't spot us when he came to confront Uncle Glenn and Aunt Mary Ellen, as he often did. Most after-school nights, Leah's and my job was to wash the plastic flats that held potted plants. We donned yellow rain pants and raincoats and used a garden hose to systematically wash old soil from the bottoms of the flats. I hated that job. The dingy darkness was only lit by a few overhead light bulbs, and it was wet, dirty, cold, and monotonous—so much so that our other main job, the back-breaking work of bending over to label rows upon rows of trays of potted plants, felt like a welcome reprieve.

My sister and I labeled every different kind of plant among half a dozen different greenhouses. Some of the flowers I could already name from my mother's garden, but I also came to learn the common and Latin names of indoor and exotic plants that were not native to the area.

And I learned something else too. I learned to numb out. To suck it up without protest. To put one foot in front of the other and trudge along, neither sad about the past nor thinking about anything but surviving another day. Without ever intending to, I shut off my feelings, and after a while, I become so good at it that I was not aware of having any. "I don't know" became a safe place to live, and over time, I discovered that numbing out was quite an easy state to enter, and even one I had a talent for. Much later in life, I would understand it within a new context, as something I learned from ice skating on frozen ponds and warming frozen feet: being frozen is uncomfortable, but it is nothing compared to the burning agony of thawing.

Losing a Job

On the last day before Christmas vacation, it was the school tradition for all the students to gather in the lobby before the buses arrived to sing Christmas carols from paper copies printed by WGAL TV 8 in Lancaster. I could not sing on tune at all, but I was an enthusiastic caroler. In fact, I treasured this tradition so much that every year Leah and I wrote to the station and requested additional copies for singing at home too.

After the caroling, the principal would hand out enormous dimpled navel oranges that smelled like the sun smiling. Although we take for granted having oranges year-round today, a Christmas orange was quite a treasure in 1974. So, too, was the fresh Hershey's chocolate bar he handed out with the oranges.

Each morning since December 5th, Mother had driven us girls to Plainfield Elementary and the boys to their school so we could finish out the year there before the Christmas break. On the last day, however, she arrived before classes ended, fearing that Daddy might steal us from school and return us to the farm.

When I spotted her, all I could think was that we would not get to sing, and that we would not receive our oranges and chocolate either. But Mr. McCarter didn't forget about us. As we walked toward Mother, he handed each of us our Christmas treasures.

But our exchange wasn't only sweet, it was bittersweet as well.

Because we were going to have to change to a school near Grandma's in Camp Hill and therefore wouldn't be coming back for the second half of the school year, and because I would no longer be riding the school bus, Mr. McCarter also held out his hand for my crossing guard uniform.

"You can keep the badge," he said, "but I do need you to turn in your crossing guard belt."

Reluctantly, I handed the shiny orange belt to him—and with it, the symbol of a job that had made me feel significant, like I really did matter. I loved the feeling that when I put up my hand, all the cars stopped. It was a thrill I never tired of, and it had lasted such a short time.

Seemingly, in a flash, I was back to being nobody.

Papa Bear's Revolt

During the last week of December 1974, various headlines, all essentially lionizing the heroic nature of Daddy's quest, blanketed the nation's towns and cities. Bringing this tumultuous year to a close, the writers could not help professing their profound sympathy with the loss of this man's "rights" and his courage in fighting to reclaim them.

Tom Tiede's column appeared under numerous banners throughout every state in the nation. This is merely a small sampling:

Court Test May Alter 'True Church' Power
The Pittsburgh Press

One Man vs. His Church
Hanover, Pennsylvania; Lafayette, Louisiana; and
Blytheville, Arkansas

Church Anger Is Powerful
Marshfield, Wisconsin

Shunned Mennonite Battles His Church
Hilo, Hawaii

Church Tramples Man's Rights
Cedar Rapids Iowa

Man Exercising His Guarantees
Napa, California

The article began with a recitation of the story of my father's ordeal and the resulting expense of battling it in the courts, as well as how he had been denied the strength and companionship of his family all this time.

He closed the article on this note, beginning with a quote from Daddy:

> "I have to prove I have rights as a man. I have to prove to my children I'm right. I have to prove only God can put my marriage asunder."
>
> Yet even if he wins in court Bear may lose, in fact. Obeying church orders, the farmer's wife has read nothing of his heroic struggle, nor of the larger community's support for it; thus any decision against the church will likely be conveyed to her by the church as further evidence of Bear's unworthiness.
>
> If she believes that, and so far she has believed everything of the church, Bob Bear's mistreated family may never get back together.

Under the charming headline "Papa Bear's Revolt," another columnist, George G. Connelly, writing for the Berkshire Eagle in Pittsfield Massachusetts, added his own take on our situation, lamenting the plight of "farmer Bear, alone in his trailer in the Joyous Season."

He also reminded his readers of the stakes involved:

> In his complaint he alleges that when the little Bears visit him they are "disrespectful" and that Mama Bear not only denies him connubial rights, but calls him "repulsive." He will not seek a divorce as he opposes it on religious grounds."

Adding the flourish of a literary reference, he remarked:

> Hemingway used to write indignant complaints to Cardinal Spellman and instead of addressing him as "Your Eminence" he began "Your Arrogance."

He concluded the article with:

> The world needs more Papa Hemingways and Papa Bears.

And all my family could think was, *If only these reporters knew the truth.*

CHAPTER FIVE

1975

Sometimes when you are in a dark place, you think you have been buried,
but actually you have been planted.
—CHRISTINE CAINE

Pilgrims' Progress

Mother, my sisters, and I ascended the wide steps leading to our new, brick-encased school. With its elegant white architectural details, it reminded me of Williamsburg—pretty, solid, refined. I liked it immediately and allowed myself to imagine that this school might offer us invisibility, a clean slate. The chance to be normal. But my hope was quickly dashed.

"Look, there's a pilgrim," shouted an astonished third grader.

The four of us girls tried to shrink out of sight behind Mother's long skirt. We hadn't even made it into the principal's office to enroll before I felt the familiar red tide engulf my face and the despair of sticking out once again.

Schaeffer Elementary was where I would complete the last half of my fifth-grade year. Susie and Leah would finish second and third grade there, while the boys would attend middle school at another location. Sharon had just turned five and was the only one not yet in school.

Schaeffer was subtly different from Plainfield Elementary, which was populated with mostly rural kids like us. Although we stood out because of my mother's clothes, and we girls always wore dresses, we did not look significantly different from the other children. Here, though, there was a noticeable contrast. For example, one girl, whose clothes were pretty and obviously new, got dropped off at school in a black limousine. Few children were chauffeured to school, but many wore clothes like hers.

It didn't take long before I felt naked and exposed. Could everyone see what I saw? That I was a country bumpkin?

But despite that, a boy who was nice, good looking, popular, and a star on the soccer team chose me to be his girlfriend. Except for nice, I possessed none of his qualities, so I was proud that out of the whole school, he picked me. Since he also lived near my grandparents' house, he often walked me home from school.

I was happy about this new relationship, but I was conflicted at the same time. I found myself obsessively anxious as my brain got tangled trying to make sense of feeling simultaneously terrified and utterly mystified as to why this popular boy liked me. I felt certain he would wake up one day, notice my plainness, and realize he had made a terrible mistake.

In an effort to delay this inevitable fate, I made a stop at the grocery store each day on my way to school and bought a large bag of candy for him with the money I earned from working at Ashcombe. I figured if I kept him happy enough, he wouldn't wake up, at least for a little while. Eventually, I saved up enough money to take him, along with my siblings, for a whole meal at Gino's hamburger restaurant on the way home from school. It took a lot of my earnings to treat everyone, but it felt good having money to spend. I liked the ability to feel like I could influence my own life.

Having a popular boyfriend helped me fit in at my new school, and so did playing the clarinet (which I no longer screeched when I played). Not far into the school year, the band director approached me.

"I don't have any students to play the alto clarinet," he said. "Would you be willing to play it if the school lent it to you for free?"

I leapt at the chance with an eager "Yes!"

I loved being a special member of the band. I also loved that things seemed to be changing. Life was good. Well, mostly.

One day after school, I was in the front hallway hanging up my coat when Benny quietly opened the front door. I looked up to say hello and noticed his head was down. He seemed to be trying to conceal bruises on his face.

"What happened to you?" I asked, rushing up to him.

Benny's school was a little farther away from Grandma's than mine, but we used the same two general routes. The front route crossed the highway at an intersection with a crosswalk; the back route required us to dodge cars to cut across the highway in front of the house, then cut through a neighborhood by a park behind the library. This neighborhood was generally a safe area, but that day when Benny walked by the park on his way home, three boys he had never seen before jumped him and beat him up.

"Did you tell Mother what happened?" I asked.

"No." He shrugged. "It's no use. It won't matter anyway."

I stared at his face. The bruises, the shame, the sad, almost brokenness. I couldn't bear to see him like this. *How could someone do this to him after everything we've had to endure?* My heart broke for him.

I was thinking about how I thought it would be safe here when I started to feel overwhelmingly helpless.

And then, I got mad.

I suddenly wanted to go find these boys and beat them up. I fantasized what I would do to them. I'd get them on the ground and pound them until they wished they'd never picked on my brother. Then I ruminated that maybe if I had been walking with him, I could have prevented the attack by jumping on them and scaring them off. Rationally, I knew this was futile, silly even. Benny was bigger than me. He was strong and athletic. If he couldn't fight off three boys, I surely wouldn't be able to. Nonetheless, from then on, I kept a lookout for three boys in the park, though I hadn't the faintest idea what they looked like. *They better hope I don't find them*, I thought.

The helpless feeling was the worst. So, in the weeks that followed, I continued to imagine pummeling them. And each time I envisioned the scene, those boys were beaten and fled for their lives.

A New Normal

After many years of bedlam, life begins to have a have a rhythm again. Though we are not playing in the woods and streams of our beloved Home Farm, there are several good things about living at Grandma's.

One is that the Dunkin' Donuts is just down the back alley, well within walking distance. Another is that when it snows, we children walk all over town knocking on doors and offering to shovel driveways and sidewalks for a fee. Mother says we have to shovel Grandma and Papap's property first, but after that we are free to expand our business as much as we want. By the time it gets dark, our pockets are full of money and we are starving. So we head straight for the warm Dunkin' Donuts shop, where neither of our parents can remind us to eat healthy, or limit how many donuts we can eat, and we blow all our money. We sit on the pink stools and enjoy hot cocoa as we inhale one donut after another before trudging home.

Another good thing about living at Grandma's is that the library is just on the other side of the highway on the route to and from school. We can go anytime we want, and even though it's close, I always check out the maximum number of books allowed at one time.

One day, I eye the shelves in the children's section and realize with a deep sadness, and with a faint panic rising, that I've read every single book in the Childhood of Famous Americans series. These heroes, adventurers, inventors, artists, healers, and explorers have been my dear companions. These pillars of character and courage have inspired me and electrified me. Across the mists of time, their life stories have guided me.

I am bereft and lonely without my beloved and colorful companions. *What will I do now?* I wonder. *What will I read?*

Daddy's Book

In March, big-city and small-town newspapers, such as the *Hawaii Tribune Herald*, *The Boston Globe*, and *Arizona Republic*, once again report on Daddy's cause.

The Atlanta Journal and Constitution, March 9, 1975

Shunned by Church, He Sues for Relief
By JULIE DUNLAP (AP)

"We hope to grow vegetables this year."
Robert Bear, 45-year-old Mennonite farmer in Cumber-

land County, Pa, shyly apologizes for using "we" instead of "I."

"I lived alone for five years until I married, and "we" isn't nearly as lonely as "I," he explains.

. . .

But Bear, in his enforced solitude, is fighting back. This spring's potato planting may be delayed because he is busy with a suit filed against the church in the State Supreme Court, and with a book he has written about his "gruesome punishment."

. . .

Bear has hired lawyers and a Harrisburg public relations firm to publicize his case. His book, "Delivered Unto Satan," came out in January. Bear published it himself.

He said that if the State Supreme Court decides in his favor, the church will "take a martyr stance," claiming interference with freedom of religion.

[Bishop Glenn] Gross says he is worried neither about the book nor the coming court decision.

"When the whole truth is exposed or revealed, people will see it isn't entirely as it has been publicized. The scriptures teach us to believe in God. We want to believe in the powers that be, but if our beliefs are judged unconstitutional, we would have to follow Christ," he said.

Both men deny there was any personal animosity between them before the religious difficulties arose, although Gross hints that the matter "is not all a church dispute."

Bear says:

"A year or so ago I said I would move away if I lost the court case, but the situation has changed. Since my wife and children went away it's been such a relief not to have that burden of the closest people to you thinking so evil of you."

Shortly after the articles are released, David comes home from the library waving a book. "Guess what I found?" he announces. "Daddy's book!"

Crowding around him to see what up until now we have only heard about from Daddy, the cover features the title in a stark, uncompromising font, boldly proclaiming *Delivered Unto Satan*. Accompanying it is an artist's rendering of a black hat like our people wear hanging on a wooden meetinghouse peg rack. Beside this hat, a thick noose hangs from another peg over the reflection of a meetinghouse window. Congregating along the bottom of the cover, Daddy's artist has drawn a row of Mennonites in their hats and bonnets. In front of them stand six children, my siblings and I easily recognizable. I shiver at the ominous cover as David opens the book to reveal the interior. Glancing through, I see nothing new. The writing is an echo of every confrontation we have heard about and every diatribe we have witnessed. Still, seeing his disordered thoughts in print somehow feels much more sinister.

David is undaunted by this grim discovery. Instead, he is unable to contain his glee. "Guess where I found his book?"

Before we can answer, he chortles, "It was filed in the fiction section!"

It seems a small triumph amidst a deluge of Daddy's propaganda—not to mention a gullible public.

Nobody Will Notice

Mother has a surprise for us.

"We are moving in a few days," she announces, "as soon as school is out for the summer." Six months with a half-dozen rambunctious children running through their halls and bounding up the stairs two at a time has been hard on Grandma and Papap's nerves.

"But we're not going back to the farm," Mother informs us. "We're moving into a house of our own."

She adds that because we won't be living in this school district in the fall, we will be attending new schools.

I deliberate about mentioning our move to my boyfriend so he knows we will be leaving. On the one hand, I feel silly at the thought of bringing it up. *Why would my leaving matter to anyone?* I think. On the other hand, it does seem rude not to inform him.

On the last day of school, I'm still debating what to do when the bell rings. The doors sweep open, and everyone streams toward home. I spot him talking with his best friend and contemplate joining them. *But I'd be interrupting their conversation.* In a flash, my decision is made. I slip away, taking the back route to Grandma's house. I reason he won't notice I'm gone and that he will probably be happier without me anyway.

I never do see him again.

Assuming I don't matter, and either not showing up or silently disappearing, becomes a bad habit I will never entirely conquer.

The Vow

A small road off busy Route 74 that runs between Dillsburg and Carlisle leads to a T junction where Mother turns left. We drive along a ribbon of blacktop that winds through trees along the small hills that form the base of the south mountain. Beside the road, homes that look like summer cabins on the Appalachian Trail with their dark brown logs and white chinked mortar dot the landscape. These dwellings give way to a neighborhood tucked amongst dense trees and comprised of split-level and old ranch-style homes with nondescript yards. The car slows near where the neighborhood dead ends in a forest.

Down a short, steep driveway lies a ranch house painted an uninspiring shade of deep brown with white trim, and some shabby outbuildings off to the right in a matching color scheme. There are no colorful flower gardens, or gardens of any sort for that matter. Only a few scraggly bushes and a steep, but large serviceable lawn with occasional bare patches reside behind the house. Below the lawn, a row of pine trees guards the lower edge of the property, concealing the house from view of anyone driving along Route 74 below.

Before we enter the house to inspect the inside, Mother tells us the reason for choosing this one: it has a multitude of doors to escape from.

Inside, the house is as dispiriting as its outside. Dark, knotty pine paneling appears to cover every surface. Staleness battles the pervasive smell of mothballs, which seem to have been placed in every closet and on every shelf. The only real positive feature in our minds is a dishwasher, a convenience we've never had before. But Mother quickly shoots this down.

"I have six dishwashers," she says. "There will be no need to use this and waste electricity."

In every way, this house is a far cry from our beloved farm with its magical meadows, creeks, and acres of land fueling our imagination. Still, there is one thing that gives me hope. Where the yard bends into the woods lies a clearing with a handsome outdoor fireplace made of stone. I imagine that perhaps we could re-create the open-fire cookouts we children used to have in the meadow and roast marshmallows here.

To prevent Daddy from having any claim to the house, since my parents are still officially married, Grandma purchased the house in her name and provided a mortgage for Mother, who used the $10,000 she had inherited from Papap Bear and the $2,000 the church loaned her as a down payment. But still we had no furniture. Everything was left behind when we fled, and Daddy refused to allow us to safely retrieve anything. Relatives and members donated used furniture, so we moved into a sparsely furnished house with only a few places to sit, a table, and some beds.

Since we have our own home now, but very little money to live on, Mother confiscates Benny's and David's savings accounts, as they are the only ones with any money to speak of. I am astonished to learn that they each have $5,000 in their bank accounts, an astronomical sum to me. Despite being forced to save almost all our earnings, I don't have even a fraction of that. Against my brothers' indignant protests, Mother is adamant, saying there is no choice and that we need their money to survive.

"And you boys will have to help support the family, too," she adds. Then she softens a bit. "I promise to repay you with interest sometime in the future as soon as I'm able."

Mother institutes other decrees as well.

We cannot afford to eat meat more than twice a week, so the dark-blue-and-orange metal tins of Spam become a staple—we slice and broil it until it resembles bacon. I've been a reluctant meat eater ever since I saw the bloody steer carcass hanging on a hook in our neighbor's barn, so this doesn't trouble me much. The milk restrictions are a different story, though.

To save money, Mother insists we make powdered milk and dilute it equally with real milk. Besides the strange taste, the lumps of powdered milk remain suspended in the regular milk unless you take a whisk and beat it furiously. Even then you almost always miss some. A long, cold drink of milk on a hot summer day is invariably interrupted by an unexpected ball of powder that evaded the whisk and gags your throat.

To earn money to support us, Mother has been working for both Grandma's market business and in the greenhouse at Ashcombe for Uncle Glenn. To supplement the new expenses of a home, she bakes small cakes, as well as batches of banana nut and pumpkin bread to sell at market. I help to wrap them in plastic and label them for sale. When they're all assembled and ready to go on the transport tray, I note that Grandma charges $1.30 for each loaf, and from that, Mother must pay for the supplies to make them as well as the labor and electricity. I know that Grandma also has to make a profit on them to cover her market stand rental. As I do the math in my head, I can feel the anxiety rising just looking at these pint-sized breads. They look so inadequate to feed us and pay the mortgage. But the sight of them, along with my panic, furthers a fierce resolve in me: I will never, *ever*, marry a man for money. Finding a good provider was a strategy that did not work out so well for my mother, and it strikes me as ironic that Daddy is the exact opposite of my mother's father. Daddy is a capable provider; he simply refuses to be one without an oath of blind loyalty from his minions.

For the first time, I wonder what other strategy might work. I am certain I'll do *something* different, though I have no idea what or how. All I know is, I will never be left with six kids and no means of support.

Suddenly, the rows of little loaves are cast in a new light. It occurs to me that Grandma and Mother were *forced* to make their own money. But me, I will *choose* to do so. In that moment, I intend with every fiber of my being to become financially independent.

Yes, I decide, *I will depend on no one but myself.*

Making It Ours

Ever since we moved in, none of us kids have been remotely impressed by this dingy, dated, stagnant-smelling house that is our new home.

"You're all ungrateful," Mother says.

As I survey our surroundings, I know she's probably right. But I'm too cranky to feel bad about being ungrateful. Right now, all I want to do is brighten up this dowdy house and put our stamp on it.

Since we don't have the resources to do much inside the house, my siblings and I create a space for ourselves. We commandeer one of the tiny sheds as a playhouse, clean it out, and give it cheer with a base of pale green paint, accented by brushstrokes of bright yellow and pink flowers. I sew curtains for the miniature windows, and my sisters and I decorate the walls with pictures from calendars.

In one of the other small sheds on the property, we find a chunky, wooden telephone cable spool that can easily double as a table. As we're rolling it out onto the lawn to clean it up, the lady from next door wanders over to introduce herself. She asks lots of questions about who we are, where we come from, and why we moved, all of which we parry with narrowed eyes and vague misdirecting answers. Plus, Mother always reminds us not to air our dirty laundry in public, not that we would ever want to.

Besides, Daddy is doing enough of that without our help.

A New Routine

With school out for the summer, now that we have our playhouse looking spiffy, we focus on improving and brightening up the house where we can. We also work six days a week. Ashcombe is only three miles away from us now, and a train track below our house leads most of the way there. Sometimes Mother drives us, but just as often we walk along the railroad tracks to and from work. We always keep an ear out for oncoming trains and jump out of the way when the lookout yells "train coming!" We also keep an eye out for glass marbles that are sometimes tucked between the rocks and timbers so we can add these curiosities to our growing collection.

One of the nice things about working at Ashcombe is that along with the indoor plants and other things Uncle Glenn sells, he grows lots of fruits and vegetables. His market doesn't compare with our beloved farm, but it's nice being around gardens since we no longer have any of our own.

In late May, strawberries stretch in long, straight, mounded rows, and bits of red begin peeping from the lush, dark-green leaves. Just as prominent are the rows of yellow straw between the strawberries to keep the weeds down. Together, this contrast of colors creates a patchwork of strawberry fields that can be seen from the road. Beyond these lie more fields, filled with mature blueberry bushes, their bases covered in plump sawdust mounds and protected from marauding birds by strategically placed cannons whose loud boom scares them away.

The boys mostly do general farm work, while we girls pick strawberries and blueberries with a large crew of teenagers recruited from the local neighborhoods. Strawberry season arrives first, then a short raspberry season, followed by blueberries. We fill our flats as fast as we can, competing with other kids to see who can pick the most. The competition makes the time go faster, and we earn more money that way. These kids who race with us become our closest friends.

As we resign ourselves to our new home, we find things to appreciate about it. Swimming in the creek has always been one of our favorite pastimes, and just beyond the railroad tracks below our house lies a creek called the Yellow Breeches. Out on the farm we had two swimming holes: one in the creek by the meadow where Mother would often come read a book while we swam to make sure nobody drowned; and another above the dam with a rope for swinging out over the water and dropping in. In no time at all, we spot the telltale signs of a local swimming hole: the large bare mud patch beside an enormous tree, with a hanging rope knotted at the end. Sometimes in the evenings, Mother takes us down there to do Tarzan leaps into the water just like we used to back home. We also find a swimming hole below the fields at Ashcombe, and our new friends swim there with us in the afternoons after we finish our berry picking.

Though we adjusted to our new surroundings, years later in the family photo album, I will come across the picture of us children posed in the living room next to the hand-me-down chair. All of our faces are homogeneously blank, unsmiling with our eyes emitting a haunting, deeply bruised quality. Each of us looks deflated, yet stiff. Even our skin has a pale gray deadness, as if it has been drained of vitality. Perhaps most disturbing, though, is what I can only describe as a reflection of humiliation and despair so normalized, it has seeped into our very character.

As I stare at the photo, something about these children's misery feels dangerous, like I might get dragged back into that picture after all these years if I gaze at it too long. Shivering, I turn the page quickly, ashamed by my cowardice, and yet afraid those children's desolation might be contagious.

Live to Fight Another Day

Newspaper articles flood the United States and Canada—*The Miami News, Fort-Worth Star Telegram, The Sacramento Bee, The Baltimore Sun, The Charlotte News, The Vancouver Sun, Calgary Herald, Edmonton Journal,* and many others—reporting on the ruling of Daddy's case before the Pennsylvania Supreme Court. These articles are accompanied by a photo of him deep in thought, surrounded by books and writing materials, pensively staring out the window of our house on the Home Farm.

Here is an excerpt that encapsulates what all of them publicized.

THE PHILADELPHIA INQUIRER, JULY 8, 1975

By AARON EPSTEIN
Inquirer Staff Writer

Robert L. Bear, a husky Mennonite farmer from Carlisle, Pa, has won the right to a trial on his petition for a court order to stop his church from "shunning" him.

. . .

But when he asked the Cumberland County Common Pleas Court to order the "shunning" halted, his case was thrown out on the ground that a court cannot interfere with the free exercise of religious beliefs.

Yesterday, however, the State Supreme Court, in a 5-1 ruling, reinstated Bear's case which could become a classic clash of Church and state.

Religious freedom is not an absolute, the court majority said, and the government can regulate a religious practice that poses a substantial threat to public safety, peace, or order.

Although the Reformed Mennonite Church and its bishops still may prove that they had acted within their constitutional protection, the court declared that Bear had cast sufficient "doubt" on that defense to entitle him to a trial.

. . .

Bear, 45, described himself as a lonely man whose church-going family is gone, whose neighbors have nothing to do with him and whose profitable farm work is being neglected because of his "ordeal."

He wants an injunction and damages for alienation of affection, invasion of privacy and interference in his business and marital relations.

Custody Hearing

We have been in our new home barely a month when Mother is served with papers: Daddy is suing for custody of us children.

He has consistently asserted in court and in the newspapers that his wife has poisoned his children against him and now he demands full guardianship.

I'm not sure who is more frightened: Mother, or us.

The public sympathy and support for him has been overwhelming, and now a judge will decide our fate.

Will he believe Daddy too?

* * *

In late July, we put on our Sunday clothes and Mother drives us to the courthouse. We are told that the judge will hear testimony from Mother and Daddy and their lawyers: Mrs. Del Duca and Mr. Ball. Afterward, he will call each of us children into his chambers.

I share the transcript that follows of our day in court to illustrate just how skewed the questioning was at times. (Note that I have omitted and condensed some sections for brevity where it contained mundane questions of fact, such as addresses, ages, occupation, repetitions, or tangential details. Omissions and condensations are indicated by ellipses [. . .])

Daddy is questioned first by his attorney.

MRS. DEL DUCA:

. . .

Q: And, what occurred on December 5th, 1974?

A. I lived in a trailer about two miles away . . . I started before daylight and . . . reached our home where we originally all lived, just at daylight, and the five children that went to school were there alone getting their breakfast and getting their lunches packed for school.

Q. Did this upset you?

A. Yes. I had been concerned about that for just about two years until December the 5th.

Q. To your knowledge, where was their mother?

A. I believe she was helping her mother at Camp Hill.

. . .

Q. Had you asked your wife not to leave the children alone in the early morning before they went to school?

A. Yes. Repeatedly.

Q. To your knowledge, how many mornings would the children be alone in a weekly period?

A. It was variable, but I understood always on Thursday, Gale would leave, winter and summer, and as near as I could tell, it may have been as much as sometimes three and four days a week that she had been away. It would seem that it was very variable.

Q. Now, what did you do on December 5th as a result of this?

A. I first called her brother, the Bishop. I had talked to him before about this situation and finally he said, "Let's talk things over." I said, "I'm tired of talking. This has gone on long enough." So, then I wrote a telegram and sent it to the Bishop's house, the minister and deacons of the church, and told them I was taking Gale's clothes down to the head Bishop in Lancaster and I was throwing her clothes out. I wasn't throwing Gale out. She was welcome to come home, although I stipulated in the telegram that we would have some neighbors and relatives present to try to get this matter straightened out.

Q. Did your children return home after school that day?

A. No.

Q. Have you seen your children since December 5th, 1974?

A. Yes. The third Sunday in December 1974, I saw the children, and I saw Benjamin and David last Friday.

Q. Do you know where they are presently living?

A. . . . I'm not certain. From the information I've gotten, they may not be always living at 130 N. 32nd Street in Camp Hill. I do know that I asked Gale's mother where they were and she said, "That's for me to know and you to find out."

Q. Did you, in fact, visit your mother-in-law's home in Camp Hill in an attempt to see the children?

A. Yes

. . .

Q. Did your older children assist you in the farm work?

A. Yes.

THE COURT:

What do you mean by the older ones? Could you be more specific?

MRS. DEL DUCA:

Q. What kind of farm chores, say, did your older children, David and Benjamin, perform on the farm?

A. They would help to gather our crops, drive the tractor, and they were just getting where they could lay an irrigation line, start up the pump, and take care of all it.

. . .

Q. What kind of farm chores did your two daughters Patricia and Leah, perform on the farm?

A. When we grew potatoes, they helped to pick potatoes and helped to harvest potatoes.

Q. I assume your other children, Susan and Sharon, were too young to take on farm chores?

A. Pretty much, yes.

Q. You stated that you had been living in a trailer on your farm for a period of time. Is that correct?

A. Yes.

Q. Did the children help with house cleaning in that trailer? Did they help you in any way?

A. Yes. Quite a bit.

Q. The children would take care of household chores?

A. Patricia, Leah, and Susan, yes.

Q. What kind of work would they do?

A. They always washed my dishes, and they used the vacuum cleaner and scrubbed for me, washed the floors.

Q. Are you presently living in the house which was the family residence?

A. Yes.

Q. Do you do your own household chores?

A. Yes, except now I have a 14-year-old boy that is very capable and helps me.

. . .

Q. Have you had a good relationship with your children?

A. I would have thought so.

. . .

Q. Did you ever use excessive correction methods?

MR. BALL:

Objection, Your Honor. That's a leading question, I believe.

THE COURT:

Well, I think you've covered it. He said he had a good relationship with them and he corrected them when necessary. I think that covers it.

. . .

Q. Are you requesting the court to have permanent custody of these children?

A. Yes.

Q. How do you propose to look after them?

A. My sister-in-law said that she would help to look after them, and one of our very near neighbors, Mrs. Ronald Carper, said that she'll help to look after them in her home when I'm not present.

Q. Are you also able to look after them yourself?

A. Yes. I did quite a bit of cooking when I was at home for our children and for my mother, and our girls are very capable, too.

Q. Is your home located on the farm?

A. Yes.

Q. Is your schedule flexible?

A. Yes. And, especially if I would have custody of the children, I would certainly try to set our crops that would grow. The children would be the first concern.

Q. Would they be attending the schools they've always attended?

A. Yes.

Q. You mentioned your sister-in-law. Is this your brother's wife?

A. Yes.

Q. And, how far away does she live?

A. About six miles.

. . .

Q. Do you love your children?

A. Yes.

Q. Do you love your wife?

A. Yes.

Q. Is she welcome to return home at any time?

A. Yes, I think I've always made that plain that she was.

CROSS EXAMINATION BY MR. BALL:

Q. Mr. Bear, do you now send support for your six children?

A. No.

Q. For how long have you failed to send them support?

A. I'm not quite sure.

THE COURT:

Q. Well, have you sent any since they left?

A. No.

. . .

MR. BALL:

Q. Have you at any time previously, Mr. Bear, failed to send them support?

A. They weren't away before, oh, except for one week the church took them away.

Q. During the period from October 1972 to January 1973, did you send them support?

A. They were at home.

Q. Mr. Bear, how much of a financial saving do you feel that could make by having your children on the farm performing work for you?

MRS. DEL DUCA:

I object to the question, Your Honor.

THE COURT:

Overrule the objection. I think it's relevant.

MR. BALL:

Q. Can you give us an estimate of what you would save if these children, these two children, were with you? If you can't, say so.

A. I don't like to look at children as an item like that.

Q. Well, can you answer the question? Can you tell us, whether you think of it or not? Can you give us an answer to the question? If you can't, say so.

A. Their support and their pay would probably cost more than to hire someone else.

Q. That wasn't my question, Mr. Bear. You don't think you can answer the question. Is that right?

A. . . . Not without figuring it out, no.

Q. Yes. Mr. Bear, did you ever order your wife to leave the home?

A. Yes. I think I did on a number of occasions.

Q. You've mentioned trouble with the church. Was this on account of your own religious views with respect to the views of the church?

A. That I ordered my wife . . .

Q. Yes . . .

A. Only because I believed that she felt the need to show that I was a sinner.

. . .

Q. Mr. Bear, what was your income in 1973?

A. I had a net loss.

Q. How about 1974?

A. A greater net loss.

Q. Did you retain Edward C. Minchner Public Relations Firm in respect to your campaign . . .

MRS. DEL DUCA:

Object, Your Honor.

THE COURT:

What's the relevancy?

MR. BALL:

I would like to ask the witness whether he expended funds in retaining him because it relates to his capability to serve the family, and one of our points is that the campaign against the church is costing money and it helps to diminish resources for a man who reports a net loss for the support of his family, especially in view of the fact that he is not supporting his children at present.

MRS. DEL DUCA:

Your Honor, this is not a support proceeding. Mr. Bear has admitted he has not supported the children since they were taken away by the mother.

MR. BALL:

Q. Mr. Bear, you were speaking of your work schedule and its flexibility. How many days a week do you work in operating your farm?

In a series of replies, he will submit that he works from 6 a.m. to 9 p.m. and that his evenings are free after 9 p.m.

Q. Mr. Bear, last year, you authored a book of 331 printed pages . . .

MRS. DEL DUCA:

Your Honor, I object to the question.

MR. BALL:

. . . May I explain why I brought this matter up? Mr. Bear has stated he's going to produce a second book and . . .

THE COURT:

I don't care if he writes a million books, if he's fit to have these children and father these children, he's going to have his rights. I did say you could ask him questions as to his ability to support them, feed them, and clothe them.

MR. BALL:

May I say that depends upon his time? If he's devoting his life in large part to a campaign against the church and managing a farm and playing mother and father to these children, how is he going to do the last-mentioned item? These things take time.

THE COURT:

I know, but I must assume that being the father of these children, that will come first and, if necessary, he won't write any more books. And if they don't come first, his rights will be terminated.

. . .

THE COURT:

Q. You testified when you're not present, there would be others to look after the children. Do you mean you're absent from the residence any extended periods of time?

A. Yes.

Q. For how long? Weeks at a time, that you're away from the residence?

A. Oh, no. It's just that I'm on another part of the farm.

. . .

Q. You testified you have published things and discussed things with other people derogatory to your wife. Have you ever published or discussed anything derogatory to your children, anything that would show you didn't have natural love and affection for them?

A. No, Your Honor.

MR. BALL:

Q. In reference to Judge Weidner's last question of publishing things derogatory to your children and on this matter of publications, Mr. Bear, these things . . . do you think likely that these publications concerning your family would have come to the attention of your children, especially your older children?

A. I would think in time, as a man said, he hopes they will be able to read the book when they get older. I would hope that it would.

Q. Do you think that if the kind of publications you have made concerning your wife came to the attention of your children through other people, this would embarrass them?

A. I would think there's that danger.

. . .

Richard Wagner, Daddy's attorney friend and supporter of his cause, testifies on his behalf:

MRS. DEL DUCA:

. . .

Q. So, you have observed Robert with his children?

A. Yes. Quite frequently.

Q. What was the relationship of Robert with his children?

A. Well, it was a perfectly normal and seemingly happy father and child relationship, from everything I've observed.

Q. On December 5th, 1974, when the children left the home with the mother, did you have occasion to talk to one of the children that day?

A. Yes. I called the school at Plainfield to talk to the children. I talked with Patricia that day. I may have talked to another, but I remember distinctly talking with Patricia, and later I called the school at Big Spring and talked with David.

Q. And, what was the nature of your conversations with the children?

A. I told them I had received a call from their mother and learned that that their father had come to the house that morning and said that he was planning to come back and stay there, and I asked them if they were afraid, because I got the impression from the call I received from Mrs. Bear that there was concern and fear of what might happen because of possible arguments or disturbances. So, I asked them whether they were afraid.

Q. And what did they say?

A. No. They said not.

MR. BALL:

Q. Mr. Wagner, have you been aware of any incidents of violent behavior by Mr. Bear toward Mrs. Bear?

A. I've been told that on some occasions, Mr. Bear pushed or slapped Mrs. Bear.

Q. Did you believe these stories?

A. Yes, I did. Mr. Bear himself told me that this was true.

Our neighbor from the farm, Mrs. Carper, who has four children of her own and whose son was in my class at Plainfield, testifies that she is willing to assist Daddy in caring for us. She also testifies that she is willing to take care of us, even if it is for the entire day.

Next, Daddy's friend for the past year, Mr. Beachey, testifies that he has seen us when Daddy has brought us with him. During the time we were at the Beachey's house, he and my father talked all afternoon while we watched TV in another room. Nevertheless, Mr. Beachey testifies that our relationship with our father is very "natural and normal." He further says, "I sensed in the children a respect for him as well as for other adults, and I didn't sense any strain or any difficulty between him and his children."

Next, Mother is called by her attorney to testify.

MR. BALL:

. . .

Q. Would you please now give us the exact details and circumstances under which your departure took place?

A. On the morning of December 5th . . . the children called me while I was working to support them at a part-time job at my mother's. They called me and were very agitated, saying that their father had come in saying he was moving back in the home and that I was to leave and that I was not welcome to return. And, the children asked him, "If she does try to return, will you promise not to be violent?" And, according to the children, he said, "No, I won't promise that."

Q. Now, have you ever been previously asked by Mr. Bear to leave the home?

A. Yes. In 1971, before he was out of the church, on Thanksgiving Day in November, he had the whole family leave the home.

Q. This is 1971?

A. 1971. He insisted that we all leave, which we did. He insisted numerous times in subsequent years that I leave and at times he insisted that . . . at times, he included the children, that they should leave too. We were forced to leave again in September 1973 for a period and I can't . . .

Q. All right, Mrs. Bear. After December 5th, 1974 . . . where did you and the children go?

A. We went to my parents' home where we had been told to go numerous times.

. . .

Q. Do you live at your mother's home now?

A. No.

. . .

Q. Did you apprise Mr. Bear of your location?

A. No, I have not . . . I did not do so for the peace and tranquility and safety of our family. But, we can be reached through my family, which he has on occasion done, in Camp Hill.

Q. Have you ever denied Mr. Bear the right to visit his children?

A. No, I have not.

Q. After your removal in December 1974 from the home, did you get any word to him concerning how he might see the children?

A. Yes, I did.

. . .

Q. Now have you offered any other arrangements to your husband with respect to settling all family affairs?

A. Yes, we have. We have offered a settlement, which you worked out in 1974, I believe it was . . . But, it was an offer of a complete settlement whereby he could have unrestricted opportunity to run his business, to maintain his family and occupation.

. . .

Q. Now, I want to ask you some questions, Mrs. Bear, concerning your fitness in terms of support of the children and also relating to the petitioner's claim for support of the children. Did Mr. Bear at any time in the past fail to send support to which he has testified?

A. Yes, he has . . . In October 1972, he took away our food supply, both of our freezers. He took away the family car. We had no means of transportation. He turned off the electricity. We had no heat at that time of the year, it was the end of October. He left the premises . . . not the property, he left the home without leaving any financial support whatever for our maintenance . . . There are more but if you feel that's sufficient I'll stop.

Q. Mrs. Bear, since leaving the home on December 5th, how have the children been maintained?

A. Well, we've been residing in the home of my parents and . . . I've been working as I had before and they're maintained by my earnings, by theirs, by the older boys and, of course, the facilities which my parents offered.

. . .

Q. Did you receive financial support from any other source?

A. Not in the form of support payments, no.

Q. Yes. Now, Mr. Bear has testified with respect to your spending three or four days a week, which he states was variable, but he seemed to average it out at three or four days a week, when you would be working and leaving the children alone. Is that a correct statement?

A. No . . . I had one regular working day a week that I worked for my mother, and the children, the school-aged children, were left alone. The younger children remained with me. They were only left alone for two or three hours at the most. The rest of the way I earned money was through baking at home. The work was done in the home with the children. There was a period, I think, of two months when Robert first left the home in October 1972 when there were two days that I left in the morning.

Q. What does it cost you to maintain the family now per month?

. . .

A. Well, the best I could average out would be between $0 and $600 a month.

. . .

Q. I would like you now to speak to the question of your husband's relationship to the family in terms of his being home. He testified that he was pretty constantly available, and has this been the pattern of his conduct in the past?

. . .

A. Oh, I see. You weren't just talking about visiting away. Yes. He left the family five times. He was in and out of the home, in two years, moving in and out of the home and none of those times did he ask our interest or consent, whether we wished him to go or not. He left in October 1972 for a period of some months, returning in January, leaving again that spring to go to Delaware, and when he left he said, "You're on your own," and left. He returned again, I believe, in May. He left again that late summer or fall. He returned again the following spring. He left again the following summer.

Q. Mrs. Bear, have you been able to observe the effect of these departures and returns and so on, on the children?

A. I think . . . It has not been a good effect for a parent to move in and out of the house. It creates, I think, a feeling of insecurity, instability.

Q. They've said these things to you?

A. Yes, they have. And, you can tell it in their expressions. It's uneasy for me to go through.

Q. Now, Mrs. Bear, I want to ask you, has Robert behaved peaceably toward you in this period of time from 1971 forward?

. . .

A. There have been incidents of violence to the point where it was necessary to visit the surgeon at one time as a result of an injury, to call in the help of family and friends and talk to lawyers.

Q. Do you think, Mrs. Bear, it's possible for you and your husband to have a home?

A. I really don't feel [we can] under the present circumstances. When you have your most intimate family relationships and affairs taken and hung before the public as ours have been . . . and to live in fear of your personal safety and to the point where you, especially with the children, where the privacy of your person is not respected in front of the children, I feel it would be impossible to live in the same home with him.

At this point our physical health is questioned and our report cards examined. Then, Mrs. Del Duca cross-examines and asks about whether

Mother has refused sexual relations with her husband and whether she has refused to cooperate in the running of the farm.

Mr. Ball objects that "We are, indeed, here to determine the fitness of the parents to have custody of these children and we are here to determine the welfare of these children."

THE COURT:

Q. You stated that the two older boys were working for their uncles?

A. That's correct.

Q. How many hours a day do they work?

A. Oh, they would average about eight or less hours a day.

Q. And that is six days a week?

A. It is not more than I would say roughly forty hours a week. There's variation in farming.

. . .

Q. And what are they being paid?

A. They're being paid according to the minimal rate . . . I believe that's $1.80 or $2.00 an hour.

. . .

MRS. DEL DUCA:

Q. You stated that you were receiving money for the earnings of the children. Who else is giving you money? . . . What are you living on?

A. We are living on my earnings and the children's.

Another line of questioning about Mother's work hours and whether they are in or out of the home ensues—as well as if we children get to work on foot, by bike, or are driven there.

Then, Julia Fantino (who has worked for Grandma Gross as a cook in her business for many years) is called as a character witness to testify on behalf of Mother's fitness as a parent. She's asked her religion (Roman

Catholic) to verify she is not a Reformed Mennonite and testifies that she has known Mother for 25 years.

Q. Do you know the plaintiff, Robert Bear?

A. Yes, sir . . . since they're married.

Q. To your knowledge, has there been any violence by Robert toward his wife?

A. I've never seen it, but I have seen her with a black eye and a black jaw.

Q. Do you know who created those? . . . Do you have a belief that this was by Mr. Bear?

A. I would presume so, that's all.

Q. What circumstances would lead you to presume that?

A. Because we looked at her and she just hung her head.

The court recesses for lunch. We exit a side door of the courthouse to avoid encountering any reporters and walk up the street to George's pizza shop. After lunch, the judge has some questions of his own.

THE COURT TO GALE BEAR:

Q. What is your approximate income, from your work?

A. Last year it was about, I think, $5,000, and the year before, maybe $3,000.

TO ROBERT BEAR:

Q. Mr. Bear, you haven't paid any support to these children since December 1974. Is that correct?

A. Yes.

Q. What are your plans for the future?

A. . . . Certainly, I would be glad to support them.

Q. How much? I want to make it clear, this is not going to affect your rights if you don't support them. This is for my information and also to determine your credibility. What are you willing to do?

A. At the time, we offered, I said I think it should be skimpy. I thought $100 a week.

Q. Is there any reason you haven't done that? Is your reason that you haven't seen them?

A. No. The reason is just one thing. I asked of Gale that she would be with the children before school and when they came home from school. I stipulated one condition and I would be glad to.

Q. You mean where they're living now?

A. No. Where they had been living.

Q. Well, but do you feel if you weren't supporting her, and she has to work, that you can dictate the hours of her work?

. . .

A. I was mainly concerned that the children wouldn't be left alone . . .

THE COURT:

Q. No. The question was were you providing adequate food and support for them in the home at the time she took this job, or was this at the time you shut off the electricity and took the freezers and so on that she started to work? Was this at a time that . . . did she start this one day a week work at the time when their provisions were taken from them?

A. I think it was before that, if I remember. It was a cross situation. Gale also refused to . . . we owned everything in joint ownership and Gale would hold that up before me, "You aren't willing to provide for the children," and she would refuse to cooperate in business. And, also she would tell people that she wouldn't believe anything that I would say to some of our customers even, and it was a most futile situation.

THE COURT:

All right. You may step down. Now, we'll talk with the children in chambers. I wish the oldest to be brought and then in order of their age back to chambers individually. After I've talked with them, I'll call counsel in and talk with them again and you can ask questions. What exhibits do you have?

. . .

MR. BALL:

We have three letters here, which Mrs. Del Duca has seen, and these are letters dated March 6, 1974. [We also have] a printed letter from Mr. Bear, which is one of three communications of this kind which show a constant effort to propagandize matters of marital privacy, and we believe there is a likelihood that rumors and talk coming out of these things have come to their ears and caused them embarrassment. The language is extremely violent and corresponds to the kind of thing that someone this morning testified to they would be ashamed to have made public.

The court asks if Mrs. Del Duca objects:

Yes, indeed, I do, Your Honor. I object to the use of the word violent because I think it has nothing to do with the fitness of either one of them to be a proper parent.

As we are getting ready to speak to the judge alone in his chambers, Mother reminds us to mind our manners and of the stakes. She says to make sure we state clearly who we want to live with. And then she adds, "He doesn't really want you children anyway, he's just trying to make trouble." Her statement hits my body like a sledgehammer. I'm instantly alarmed. I look around quickly to see if anybody might have overheard her. If someone did hear, she would get in severe trouble and she might lose custody. Daddy calls her names and accuses her of awful things all the time to us and in public. But if she's critical of his behavior or points out a lie, he makes a huge deal out of it and says she's turning his children against him. Because the courts and the newspapers zoom in on his charges, I know she needs to be more careful. And besides, I already know this. Daddy just wants to win. He can't be bothered to feed us. He's not interested in us. He never talks about anything but himself and his campaign against the Church. Plus, he wouldn't have the faintest idea how to take care of us if he did get us. We'd have to cook and clean for him, make sure HE was happy. We'd end up taking care of him, like we always do.

Still, it's shocking to hear the truth out loud. To have to face it.

We've been nervously anticipating this court date for weeks. Mother has been desperately trying to get David and Susie to stop biting their fingernails, using various methods and imploring them to stop just for a short while. She doesn't want the judge to think they aren't getting enough to eat and find her an unfit mother. Benny and David, however, have already decided they are simply going to run away if Daddy gets custody. Benny declares he will run away as many times as it takes. This makes me feel better. At least we have some options.

David enters Judge Weidner's chambers.

THE COURT:

Q. Do you know these people? This is Mrs. Del Duca and Mr. Ball.

A. Yes.

Q. Well, David, are you happy where you are?

A. Uh huh.

Q. You would be happy to visit the farm?

A. I would visit, yes, but I don't want to go back.

Q. To stay?

A. Right.

Q. What's the reason?

A. Because life is too unstable back there, and this gave us a chance to leave with our mother and if we would go back, we wouldn't be able to go back with her. Anyway, and I would rather stay with her than him.

Q. You said he gave you a chance to leave?

A. In December when we left, he gave us our chance to leave, and he said we could go with Mother, but if we came back, he threatened violence. So, we went with her.

Q. Did you hear that?

A. Yes. He told every one of us. She wasn't there, but we were. He threatened to hurt her.

Q. You don't think he would hurt her, do you?

A. Yes. I think he probably would.

Q. He wouldn't hurt any of you children?

A. No, he probably wouldn't.

MRS. DEL DUCA:

Q. How would you feel about working for your father during the summer?

A. I think if he's not supporting us that we would rather work where we are working.

Q. Suppose he was supporting you, how would you feel about working and living with your father during the summer until school starts?

A. No. I wouldn't like to.

Q. How about five days a week?

A. I wouldn't like that.

Q. Three days a week?

A. I would rather go out and visit like one or two days a week. How many days?

THE COURT:

Q. You asked how many days. What do you mean?

A. Well, how many days we would have to go out there . . . I would rather not go out there all the time because we don't get the same care there. It would be kind of the same as living out there all the time if we went out a whole lot, and we have to keep our jobs.

MRS. DEL DUCA:

Q. What do you mean you have to keep your jobs?

A. We have a job here and we have plenty of work, and there's no use going out there, really.

Q. Suppose your father paid you what you're earning now for the same amount of work?

A. I still would rather stay here.

THE COURT:

Q. Where are you living in relation to the farm, from Ashcombe, the store?

A. I'm not exactly sure I could tell you how far away it is.

Q. Do you live toward Williams Grove or toward Mechanicsburg? Dillsburg?

A. It's over past Williams Grove.

I recognize here my brother's vagueness, his wary and wily answer to avoid revealing where we lived to Daddy's lawyer so that he couldn't find us at our new house. And from my father's previous cagey testimony about where we now lived, I suspect the detective he hired had already found us.

Q. Do you walk to work?

A. I have a bike, I usually ride that, or she takes us to work, and she packs us a lunch and then we come home and get supper.

Next, Benny enters the judge's chambers.

THE COURT:

Q. How old are you, Benjamin?

A. 12, going on 13.

Q. Where do you go to school?

A. We probably will be going to Cumberland Valley.

Q. Are you looking forward to that?

A. Yes.

Q. Are you ready to go tomorrow?

A. I don't know.

Q. Or would you rather have a vacation first?

A. Vacation first.

. . .

Q. You like where you're living?

A. Yes.

Q. Did you like to live up at the farm?

A. It was okay.

Q. Would you like to move back there?

A. No.

Q. Would you like to visit up there?

A. Maybe about a day a week or something.

Q. How about overnight?

A. I wouldn't mind that either.

Mrs. Del Duca:

Q. Would you like to go up and work with your father a few days a week during the summer?

A. A week? No, not really.

Q. How many hours a week are you working now?

A. Anywhere from 32 to 40.

Q. What time do you start in the morning?

A. 7:00.

Q. What time do you stop?

A. 4:00. In the winter, it's from 8:00 to 5:00 like Christmastime and stuff.

THE COURT:

Q. And Saturdays?

A. Yes. We have a day off.

Q. What day is that?

A. Saturday.

Q. Do you work every Saturday?

A. No, I don't, unless I don't have my 40 hours in or if it's pressing.

MRS. DEL DUCA:

Q. Why wouldn't you want to work for the summer for your father?

A. Because, well, my mother needs providing for and we have better work down there.

Q. What do you mean by better work?

A. We do more stuff I like to do. We drive the tractor and stuff and that got boring, where down here, we do a variety of jobs.

Q. Do you love your father?

A. Yeh.

And then I am called into chambers.

THE COURT:

Q. How old are you, Patricia?

A. 11. I'll be 12 in three months.

Q. Where do you go to school?

A. Cumberland Valley.

Q. Have you been there or are you just starting there?

A. We're going to be starting there.

Q. You went to Camp Hill before?

A. Yes.

Q. How did you like Camp Hill?

A. It was okay.

Q. You like it down where you're living now?

A. Yes.

Q. Very happy?

A. Sure.

Q. Do you like the farm also?

A. Yes.

Q. You love both your parents, don't you?

A. Well, I guess you could say.

Q. Well, you love them both?

A. Well, I like my mother better.

Q. But, you love your father, also, don't you?

A. He's okay.

Q. What are you doing this summer?

A. I play sometimes with my friends and sometimes go out to my uncle's.

Q. And work in the garden?

A. Uh, huh. We have a garden out there.

Q. Do you bake pies?

A. Not me.

Q. You didn't learn yet?

A. I know how to do stuff, but I don't like to bake.

Q. You would rather be outside?

A. Yes.

MRS. DEL DUCA:

Q. Would you like to spend the summer with your father on the farm?

A. No.

Q. Would you like to go out for visits?

A. It's okay with me.

The judge sits in a big chair in his office while I sit in a chair facing his desk, feeling younger than I am. I know we need to be polite and well behaved and to say all the right things, but what I really wanted to tell the judge was that I wanted nothing to do with my father. I didn't miss him, ever. I had no desire to see him. I never looked forward to spending time with him, and I couldn't really say that I loved him. I just wanted to be as far away from him as possible and to be relieved of his unrelenting chaos and violence. Still, the judge and Daddy's lawyer seemed to think it important that I say I love him. And they seemed to assume that only the boys have jobs, that I'm mostly playing in the yard instead of punching a time clock. I guess that's the answer they want, so I don't clear up their misunderstandings. Nor do I tell them that I have been making dinner for twelve when we have company for a couple of years. I just don't happen to enjoy baking.

The judge then calls my three younger sisters in and speaks to them briefly about school, and then we wait to learn the outcome.

THE COURT:

I'm going to make a temporary order today . . . This will be a temporary order and we'll have to look it over again before school starts. I'm doing that also because he hasn't been with these children for months and what I'm going to do is start weekends, allow him to have them Saturday afternoon until Sunday evening until he gets acquainted with them, and if anything changes, we can modify the order.

MRS. DEL DUCA:

For the record, I want to raise the question of the Tender Years Doctrine, in view of the Equal Rights Amendment, that a father and mother have equal rights to custody of young children.

THE COURT:

Okay, You've raised it.

. . .

MR. BALL:

I have this problem of support.

THE COURT:

I have no authority to make an order of support, but we have on the record that he'll voluntarily contribute $100 a week for these children. I, of course, couldn't turn him down on visitation for not paying, but if I find he hasn't been paying, it will indicate to me that he wasn't sincere in what he said in court.

MR. BALL:

He has no indication as to when he is to start to pay.

THE COURT:

He promised it today.

MR. BALL:

But, to start when?

THE COURT:

That'll tell me how truthful and honest he is and what he thinks of his children. If he doesn't start paying within a week, I'll assume he would say anything in court. There's another factor here on his part, that's another reason I would hesitate to take these two older boys away from her, is that she certainly needs their income to support themselves in her home. Her income isn't adequate to support six children.

Almost forty-five years later, I read the court transcripts and recognize how close we came to the unthinkable. Worse even than Daddy gaining full custody would have been for us children to get split up. To have lost the boys and for them to have lost us would have been devastating. We had always thought of ourselves as "the six of us against the world"—a tiny community navigating a shared nightmare nobody else understood.

Getting Our Things Back

As part of the custody agreement, the judge orders Daddy to allow us to go pick up our things from the Home Farm and for him not to be present when we do so. Mother rents a truck, and when we pull into the driveway for the first time in over six months, the flower gardens are overgrown with weeds, the shrubs need to be trimmed, and the house looks like it has not received a regular cleaning in a long time.

Duke, our faithful German shepherd jumps and barks excitedly as we tumble out of the car and hurry into the house. We move quickly through the rooms, assessing what to take, unsure when Daddy might return. Stung by Daddy's accusations that she only wants to take his money, Mother leaves behind much of the furniture, including a lovely walnut spool cabinet that held the white linens used for Sunday dinners. Though she always admired that cabinet, and though Daddy cares not a whit about antiques, she says it came from his side of the family and she doesn't want to be accused of pilfering his things. Instead, she takes only a few pieces of furniture they received as wedding presents: one of the two matching Pennsylvania House cherry beds, the dining room table and hutch with matching chairs, and the piano we've been taking lessons on. The kitchen table, chairs and couches, our beds, and the washer and dryer must be left behind.

Making haste, we gather the clothes from our closets and a few personal items. I retrieve my treasure box with the field day ribbons and the handkerchiefs from Grandma Bear. David grabs his tomahawk, his antique taper mold, and a few of our newer candle molds. Someone packs our antique train set and an old ship model that was Grandma's. Before we load our bikes and Duke into the truck, we take a last look around. My eyes fall on the mantle, where our piggy banks are lined up in age order from oldest to youngest. David's big brown fuzzy bear bank has always been the largest, then Benny's, followed by my little Snow White wishing well I'd been so thrilled to receive for my birthday one year. On the roof of the well it reads, "Wishing and Saving will make it so." It felt like magic each time I dropped a coin into the slot in the top. It was here that I'd saved enough money to buy my beloved Schwinn bike.

"Come on, kids," Mother calls urgently.

As much as I want to scoop up our piggy banks and take them with us, I realize in that moment that we've outgrown them. They've been replaced with jobs and bank accounts, along with all the mundane concerns of surviving.

I take one last sweeping glance, savoring the memory of the enchantment that winged its way throughout this home, danced down the meadows, lolled in the creeks, and cavorted across the land like dragonflies entertaining a fairy audience sitting on the millrace bank.

Now, my eyes meet only a dull reflection of reality. Somewhere in time, while our attention was transfixed by endless, inescapable dramas, the sparkle of this property had quietly slipped out the back door unnoticed.

Postcards from Hell

I've always loved the ritual of retrieving the mail, but shortly after the custody hearing, Daddy's campaign letters begin showing up in our mailbox. As we suspected all along, Daddy's complaints that he can't afford to support us have no merit. He can apparently afford a private detective to find out where we live, not to mention the scores of typists, printers, artists, and stamps that fuel his mailings.

On this day, I arrive at the mailbox to discover a postcard-sized mailing that sucks the air out of my chest. It boasts a black-and-white drawing on the front, featuring a starkly violent drawing by an artist Daddy hired. Harsh strokes create an exceptionally stern, stone-faced woman wearing a black bonnet, with long horns protruding out both sides. On each side are three children—the six of us kids, clearly recognizable as individuals, dripping blood from being gored by Mother's horns. Turning the horrifying image over, I find that every inch of the back of the postcard is covered with a closely spaced, incoherent diatribe filled with my father's usual vile sexual accusations.

A few weeks later, a similar postcard with this artist's trademark dark creativity arrives. It shows Daddy kneeling with his hands tied behind him, his head lying upon a tree stump, exactly like the scene when we butchered chickens. Mother is depicted holding a hatchet over his head with Uncle Glenn urging her on, while a group of Mennonites and we children solemnly watch.

Daddy proclaims he sent these postcards because everyone has refused to read his letters.

Though Mother has forbid us from opening or reading any more of Daddy's mail, the walk to the mailbox becomes a dreaded one. I can't help wonder what drawing might greet me, or what action might follow.

We obey Mother's order for a few weeks, but Daddy's letters often give clues to what he will do next. So, despite the feelings of wariness and assault we feel each time we receive something from him, we know we can't afford to ignore reading them forever.

Onion Rings and Movies

In mid-summer, an unexpected invitation arrives. Our Great Aunt Helen (Grandma Gross's sister), who is not in the Church, invited Leah and me to spend a week at her and Uncle Ralph's home in Lancaster. (Uncle Ralph is retired from the newspaper business, but his son runs one of the Lancaster newspapers that publishes articles sympathetic to Daddy, despite Mother's personal protest to her cousin.) We have never been to their house before, so we anticipate it being a treat.

Upon arrival, I can't make up my mind if I like their split-level, rather contemporary home, which is a style I've never seen before. I'm also not sure what to make of my shocking discovery in their recreation room—a beer tap! Aside from the wine at communion, our people don't drink alcohol, and I've never seen anybody who does. It seems so worldly and sinful, but Aunt

Helen isn't self-conscious about it at all, so I set aside my fears about her going to hell and almost immediately fall in love with her.

To begin with, she lets us watch television all day if we want to—and we do!—without any lectures. She only interrupts the TV shows for mealtimes, to point out something interesting in the yard, or to drive us to the nearby town. On Wednesday, she takes us to see *Benji*—our first-ever movie at a real theater. And on Thursday, she drops us off to see a second movie, *The Three Musketeers*. On Friday, she and Uncle Ralph include us in their weekly ritual, dinner at a real sit-down restaurant. As I'm perusing the menu for something familiar, I stop at a strange item.

"What are onion rings?" I wonder out loud.

"Go ahead, order them," Aunt Helen says. "See if you like them."

I do. And they are divine.

Aunt Helen is not only jolly and interesting, she's also impertinent, which is a welcome reprieve from the harsh and stodgy solemnness we are accustomed to from elders and the general heaviness at home. The irreverence must run in the family, at least a little, because Grandma Gross once said "shit" in front of my sisters when she was upset. They were so surprised that they told the rest of us siblings about it. When they asked her about saying such a bad word, Grandma said unapologetically, "Well, sometimes that's the only word for it."

Aunt Helen is earthy like Grandma, but she is more outspoken. On our last day before we have to return home, she opens a hall closet filled with bright cocktail dresses in shades of pink, electric blue, red, orange, and teal. It looks like a closet belonging to a princess. She lets Leah and me try the dresses on and parade around like Cinderella at the ball.

"I don't wear them anymore," she says casually, "so you're welcome to take them home if you want to for playing dress-up."

We both look at her wide-eyed.

"Really," she says, as if it's no big deal to give away beautiful dresses, the likes of which we've never seen. "Take as many as you like."

And then suddenly, her lightheartedness shifts to seriousness. With a fierceness I will never forget, she says, "Whatever you do, don't ever join that damn Church."

Getting an Upgrade

In September, I enter sixth grade at Cumberland Valley Middle School, which is located in a large complex with the ninth-grade building and the high school. The Cumberland Valley school district is commonly called Cow Valley because it was formed only about twenty years earlier from the consolidation of dozens of small, rural country schools, many of them one-room public schools. But Cow Valley is hardly an appropriate name for it. It doesn't seem provincial to me, and it is a long way from Plainfield Elementary, or even Schaeffer Elementary in Camp Hill. The high school boasts a big, modern building with a domed gymnasium and is sometimes called a "Taj Mahal" school. The suburban growth in the area has increased the enrollment so fast that it is greater than the surrounding schools, with more than 600 students in the graduating classes. Such large enrollment has given the district superiority over the surrounding districts in academics and athletics, but it doesn't stop our rivals from referring to us as Cow Valley.

Unfortunately, there are other aspects of the size and scope of the district that are beyond belief. For example, several girls in the middle school, including one in my sixth-grade class, are pregnant. I cannot wrap my brain around the thought of how a sixth grader could have a baby. Other students are regularly busted for illegal drugs. Teenage conflicts—by both boys and girls—are often settled with fists at the end of the school day, at the flagpole near the buses. (Eventually, I was challenged by a girl to meet at the flagpole, but I just shrugged in reply to her taunt. There was no way I was going to become involved in a ridiculous, undignified spectacle like that.)

Another reason Cow Valley is a silly name for our district is that my classmates don't look at all like they live on a farm. The administration pulls students in from all over the county, which includes several wealthy neighborhoods. Perhaps as a result of this, and my time in the Camp Hill district, I am becoming even more aware of style. I don't want to look like a poor country mouse anymore, and I chafe at Mother's narrow choice of wholesome styles and colors—navy blue, Kelly green, and brown—that haven't changed since first grade. In any case, it's clear to me that it's time for an upgrade.

"I am thoroughly sick of Goodwill clothes," I passionately announce to Mother.

She doesn't skip a beat. "If you don't like them, then buy your own clothes."

So that's exactly what I do.

From this point forward, save for rent and the food we eat at home, I become self-supporting and relish the freedom. It gives me the opportunity to experiment with items Mother never indulged before, but has apparently grown weary of policing now. With my newfound independence, I buy heels with braided leather uppers from Super Shoes; pretty dresses from discount stores in various colors; and pantyhose (which, to my great embarrassment, I can never seem to keep from getting long, ugly runs in). I buy Gee Your Hair Smells Terrific shampoo that all the popular kids are using and revel in its worldly smell. Exploring fashion more boldly with sewing projects, I spend hours perusing the latest styles in the fabric-store catalogues of Mc-Call's, Butterick, Simplicity, and Vogue. The money I earn indulges a thirst for creativity and endless clothes-making projects. I even purchase a simulated pearl necklace. I know wearing jewelry means I will surely go to hell, but it is so pretty that I think it worth the risk. (Plus, I reason, if I don't wear it all the time, perhaps it's not so damning.)

Cumberland Valley opens our social world, too. After years of religious isolation when it came to having friends, we now meet kids in our neighborhood and on the school bus. On our first day, I am captivated by a set of fraternal twins, both strikingly beautiful, one with long blonde hair and the other with long brown hair accented by natural golden highlights. The latter is named Sandy, and she not only has a wide smile but is friendly and warm. I like her immediately and come to think of her as my friend, even though she is a grade ahead of me.

We are also greeted by neighbors, or we receive friendly waves from their windows, as we walk to the school bus. Most of the adult neighbors are nice except for one or two. One house we pass belongs to a mean old man who is quite religious. This must be the reason he doesn't approve of us; he believes our mother is divorced. I resent even the suggestion of this, because my parents are not actually divorced, they're only separated. Nevertheless, he sometimes yells at us when we walk by.

One day, David gives the old man the middle finger, and the man wastes no time in complaining to Mother, who then yells at David for being disrespectful.

Considering the way the man shouts at us when we walk by, I don't think David was being all that disrespectful. But we don't want to catch any more wrath from Mother, so we resort to just giving him dirty looks.

The Trailer

Now that we are no longer living at the farm, Daddy moves freely between our old house and his trailer—and during our first weekend with him after the judge granted visitation rights, we are staying at the trailer.

My father, by his own admission, has never been much of a housekeeper. Surveying the trailer in horror, we look at each other in silent agreement and know what must be done: if we hope to have a decent place to stay, we will have to get busy cleaning.

All four of us girls attack the job of the kitchen, which is particularly appalling, while the boys straighten up the two bedrooms. We scrub everything top to bottom, inside and out, including the pots and pans, which are littered with stray mouse dirt. We yank out the burner covers and scrub them with a steel sponge, then do the same to the caked-on grease and food on the edges of the stove. We meticulously dismantle and clean the oven, sink, and microwave, then pull all the dishes out of the cupboards and wash them too. We finish the kitchen with a good scrub of the floor, leaving a pail full of water that looks like brown creek muck after a flood.

After tidying the bedrooms, the boys tackle the bathroom, which is even worse than the kitchen. It looks like it has never been cleaned since we left the farm—and it probably hasn't. Daddy mentions offhandedly that a rat crawled up through a hole in the floor of the shower and ate part of his soap. (After hearing this, I decide I don't need to take a shower all weekend. I sleep in my clothes and try not to go to the bathroom very much if I can help it.)

Once we vacuum the living room rug, the trailer becomes marginally fit for us to stay there. We're all starving by now, but there's not much in the refrigerator. We have plenty of potatoes, though, which I don't mind in the least.

"You can cook them faster in the microwave," Daddy tells us. "That's how I do it."

So we try it. He's right that they cook faster; the problem is, the food doesn't taste the same. The potatoes have a funny flavor, and the skins don't get crispy. So we try making grilled cheese sandwiches in the microwave, but they turn out limp and just lie damp and greasy on the plate.

I survey the mediocre food with a sigh. Even though I know I shouldn't indulge in self-pity, I allow myself to feel sorry for us. After all, we have to clean the whole trailer for our visit *and* make our own meals. And the microwave is not a sign of progress to me; it's merely another symbol of how far our family has fallen. My pity party ends, however, with a hopeful thought: Now that we've cleaned up the entire trailer and eaten lunch, perhaps Daddy will want to know how we're doing in school and how each of us has been getting along since we left home. *Because that's what fathers are supposed to do*, I imagine.

But Daddy has other plans.

"You children, come, sit down," he orders, as if he has an important announcement to make.

We gingerly take our seats on the couch and chairs that used to be in our real home, looking at their dingy condition with suspicion. *What might be on our seats, or in them?*

Straightaway, it's clear that Daddy has no interest in asking about us, our school, or our new lives. Instead, he starts in with "*your* mother this, and *your* mother that." This leads to a slippery slope of all the usual offshoots and accusations that arise from these headwaters: *our* Uncle Glenn, hypocrisy, the Church, etc. As usual, he goes on a rant where he gets really worked up, and the place he started tends to have nothing discernible to do with where he ends up.

Today, his family grievances morph into stories of war with gruesome, gory details. The Germans. The Russians. Battles. Wars. The Civil War. I try to follow the thread and the meaning he wants to convey, but I have no idea where it's leading. I know that any sign of inattention or disputing his version of events will be taken as a sign of disrespect, warranting a smack on the face or across the mouth. David, however, still ventures an occasional thought and gets cracked, and Benny makes faces when Daddy isn't looking.

By the hour-and-a-half mark of his monologue, I am glassy-eyed from trying to maintain the required eye contact. I envy Benny and Susie, who have excused themselves to the bathroom. I think it's a smart way to take a break from Daddy's relentless verbal battering, but I am paralyzed. Suddenly, I imagine myself witnessing this scene from the trailer's ceiling, seeing myself pinned down like one of the struggling bugs we capture and pierce for our insect collections for school projects.

I'm contemplating my life as a skewered bug when Daddy unexpectedly veers away from the subject of war injuries to WWII and Hitler, saying something about being from the superior Aryan race. This catches my attention and wakes me up. *Aryan?* I'd never heard him use that word before. Daddy does believe that his family is superior, but Aryan? It is a horrifying thought that he could be an admirer of Hitler. He has often said that the ordinary German people were nothing like the Hitler youth—he always emphasized that with the young ones, it was "absolute loyalty" and "blind obedience," that you couldn't convince them of anything different. You had to kill them, he always declared resolutely.

Eventually, his tirade predictably ends with a lecture about how weak we children are, just like our mother, and how we should know the difference between right and wrong. He is right, he insists, and everyone else is wrong.

"Why, you can't even think for yourselves," he sneers with a curled lip. "You're all dependent on believing the Church and your mother."

Perhaps to his fevered mind, we are just like the Hitler youth.

Who Will Marry Us?

On Sunday afternoon, Daddy loads us all into the car to take us back to our grandparents' house in Camp Hill. Even though we don't live there anymore, and even though his detective has found us, Mother insists upon this spot as the exchange point so that Daddy won't feel emboldened to personally terrorize us at our new home.

As we set out on the forty-minute drive from the trailer to Grandma's house, my father treats us to one last lecture. When we reach the bridge beneath the turnpike—having endured the usual laundry list of crimes our mother and uncle have committed—he suddenly veers off with some life wisdom for us.

"Never marry anyone from a broken home," he advises thunderously.

As he expounds on his theme, I wonder, *What on earth is he talking about? Who does he know from a broken home?* His parents stayed married until they died. Mother's parents are still married. Everyone we know has been married forever. *Who is he referring to?*

And then, as if with the whoosh of a locomotive sweeping past, I understand.

We are from a broken home.

Although we're not supposed to interrupt while he is talking, an anguished wail erupts from my mouth before I can stifle it.

"But, Daddy, who will marry *us* then?"

He doesn't reply, but I know the answer.

We are damaged goods. Nobody with any sense will want us now.

Daddy's Date with History

After two long years, Daddy's day in court has come.

His suit, first filed in the fall of 1973, then dismissed in the spring of 1974 without being heard, was appealed to the Pennsylvania State Supreme Court in the fall of 1974. A ruling issued in July of 1975 found that shunning may, in fact, be an excessive use of Church authority. Having overturned the lower court's dismissal of the suit, the State Supreme Court ruling that the suit can go forward is finally bearing fruit.

Because of the unusual nature of the combatants, and the possible constitutional implications of a church-and-state dispute, as well as the possibility this case could eventually reach the US Supreme Court, Daddy once again has a national audience for his grievances.

Reporters from the biggest-name newspapers in the country arrive at the courthouse to document the proceedings. For three consecutive days, *The Boston Globe* covers the case, the first two articles landing on its front page. Both days feature a picture of Mother in her black bonnet entering the courthouse, surrounded by Aunt Mary Ellen and a Canadian bishop's wife.

On the third day, the story is run on an inside page—with a picture of my father in a suit with an open-collar shirt, looking straight into the camera and bearing a striking resemblance to movie star Paul Newman. Below his photo is one of Mother captured as she came through reporters to enter the courthouse, again in her bonnet, with head bent low and the caption: "I wish him peace."

The excerpts that follow highlight the increasingly wider disparity between my father's words and his actions, and between his public assertions and our private reality. They also show the role of publicity in fueling his behavior. Each time he twisted the truth a little further and received validation and sympathy for it, he seemed to become more genuinely convinced that what he said was "the truth." And the more confident he became in his so-called truths, the more charismatic and convincing he became to the public. The elevated public support seemed to encourage his belief that any means were justified to reach his ends. And, rendered more and more invisible in the argument between a man and his church was the personal perception of the woman at the center of this maelstrom.

THE BOSTON GLOBE, NOVEMBER 25, 1975

Outcast Mennonite Goes to Court

By ROBERT SCHWABACK
Knight News Service

CARLISLE, Pa. The Reformed Mennonite Church went on trial in the Court of Common Pleas here yesterday—accused of collectively and individually destroying the business and family of one of its former members.

In a courtroom overflowing with members of the church, friends, enemies, and the curious, Robert L. Bear, a potato farmer from Cumberland County, took the stand for most of the day.

. . .

"I'm sorry it had to come to this," Bear told his wife at one point in yesterday's proceedings. His wife Gayle, dressed in a severe long gray gown and a white starched cap, did not answer.

. . .

Bear often lapsed into lengthy discussions of faith, love, and eternal damnation. It was when he spoke of love of his wife that she made her only sign of emotion during the day, moving her hand quickly to her eyes and hiding it there for some moments.

But Bear said he found that his wife Gale's love for the church was stronger than her love for him. She tried to force him to repent through denial of sexual and social contact and turned their children against him, Bear said.

He testified that she also punished him by refusing to cosign loans needed to run their 400-acre farm, causing their gross income to fall from about $100,000 in 1972 to about $20,000 a year later.

"I didn't think the practice would be so bizarre. I was well prepared for her not to unite with me as a wife, but I was not prepared for her not to unite with me in business so I could provide for my children," he said, choking back a sob.

. . .

He later testified: "How can my brother Glenn who has no children, sit there without a sign of emotion and destroy the lives of my children?"

The Boston Globe, November 27, 1975

Outcast Mennonite Testifies Even His Wife Shunned Him

Gale, 38, a slight woman dressed in a plain blue dress and starched white bonnet, testified in Cumberland County Court for nearly an hour against her husband, Robert, 48. She was the leadoff defense witness for the Reformed Mennonite Church which is opposing a suit filed by Bear.

"Do you love your husband?" asked church attorney William Ball.

"I do certainly love his soul and I wish him peace, but the building stones of marriage—confidence, trust, love, and respect—have been deeply damaged," Gale replied.

Why did you shun him? Ball asked.

"For his spiritual welfare . . . and so that he might see himself and correct his errors."

Bear has said his wife and six children were forced to shun him by Gale's brother, Bishop Glenn Gross.

. . .

But Gale said she felt required by God, not the church elders, to shun her husband.

"Of all the counsel I received from the ministry in this regard, the most important thing was that I treat him kindly and that I walk in love to him," she said.

Their years together were sometimes unhappy because of his fights with the church and because he occasionally "treated me with violence." "It was pretty difficult at times primarily because of my husband's deep dissatisfaction with me and sometimes because of his problems with the church," she said. "But if Robert would have been satisfied, I would have been satisfied."

The *New York Times* even weighed in on the case for the second time since it came to public attention. Note the additional emotional details highlighting my mother's testimony, in contrast to the article above. Note, also, the discrepancy in reporting my father's age, which along with misspelling of names, happened frequently in the press.

THE NEW YORK TIMES, NOVEMBER 27, 1975

Mennonite Wife Says First Loyalty Is to God

In cold, dispassionate tones, the estranged wife of a farmer excommunicated by their church told a court here today that her first loyalty was to God, not to their marriage.

Do you still love him? She was asked, and for a rare moment in her testimony, she hesitated, drawing a deep, audible breath. Finally, she answered, her voice cracking as she did.

"I do certainly love his soul," she said, "and I do wish him peace; but . . . those building stones of a marriage . . . have been damaged."

Mr. Bear, 43, a tall, ruddy man, sat impassively in front of her at his lawyer's table and heard her tell the judge that their marriage had not been healthy for several months before he was excommunicated because of his constant dissatisfaction with the church.

The church ruling against him came after he questioned

the authority and infallibility of the church's five bishops, including his brother-in-law, and Mrs. Bear's "shunning" began immediately, she testified.

PHILADELPHIA INQUIRER, NOVEMBER 25, 1975

Church Is on Trial In 'Shunning' Case

. . .

[Bear] claims that because the 400-acre farm is owned jointly with his wife, the church prohibition against his wife having any dealings with him has prevented him from obtaining the necessary bank loans to carry on his business.

During a court recess, however, he said, "To tell you the truth, I don't really care about the money at all. What I want is for them to admit they have not acted as Christians."

CHAMBERSBURG PUBLIC OPINION, NOVEMBER 24, 1975

"They are the chosen few, I am damned"

Robert Bear approached his wife, Gale, outside the courtroom in Cumberland County Courthouse. "I did everything I could to keep it from coming to this," Bear said to her.

Gale, 36, dressed in a plain coat and gray bonnet covering a white prayer cap, stared at the floor.

Bear, 46, extended his hand to the ministers of the Reformed Mennonite Church as they passed in the hallway. The ministers wore black suits, black bow ties on white collars and were carrying black hats as they walked past Bear.

"No hard feelings," Bear said to Earl Basinger, a senior bishop in the church. Basinger avoided him and would not shake his hand.

None of the Reformed Mennonites acknowledged Bear's presence. Bear was visibly shaken by the experience but kept smiling.

"They are the chosen few and I am the damned," Bear said looking hurt.

Since the "shun" was imposed, Bear's wife of 15 years has refused to sleep or eat with him. His six children have been told that their father is a non-person and that he is damned to hell.

MORGANTOWN DOMINION, NOVEMBER 25, 1975

Man Battles Mennonite Church "Shunning"

During four hours of testimony Monday, Bear emerged as a man who may be a victim of his own complex and sometimes violent emotions—a man torn between love for his family and the desire to destroy the Reformed Mennonite Church.

During his testimony Bear was both defiant and compassionate, angry and on the verge of tears.

. . .

When William Musser, an attorney for the church, asked Bear why he didn't love his enemies (the church) as the Bible commands, Bear shot back, "I love my wife and she's my enemy."

But he admitted that Gale took the children and deserted him in December 1974, because he acted in angry frustration and cut off their support.

He also admitted writing a fiery letter in which he compared Gale to a French prostitute because she attempted to use sex to bring him back into the church.

Bear said that after Gale began shunning him, he slapped her once or twice, shook her violently and pushed her out a door.

He later said the violence was caused by uncontrollable frustration brought on by Gale's refusal to compromise her religious morals and be a total wife.

And he acknowledged spending $3,600 for a public relations firm, $750 for a private detective and $17,000 for the publication of a book designed to publicize his cause and show the church and its elders are morally corrupt.

THE BILLINGS GAZETTE, NOVEMBER 20, 1975

Mennonite Shunned by Family Takes Church to Court

Bear says the problem is that you have to marry in the church.

My father wanted me to marry another woman when I was younger and said that I would learn to love her.

"But I have seen how some of the church's "make do" marriages work out and I wanted to marry for love. And when we married, Gale and I were both very much in love.

Bear says that his life with Gale was idyllic from their wedding in 1958 until June 1964 when he wrote a paper challenging church doctrine and both he and Gale were excommunicated for a year.

"That broke her spirit," he said. "She was a diehard Reformed Mennonite, and she thought I had led her wrong. Our marriage was never the same after that. The church set her against me."

Bear said while his marriage was strained, it was still peaceful until 1972, when he was again excommunicated. This time he refused to repent.

Bear said he decided to leave in the spring of 1973 when his wife refused to co-sign a loan he needed to continue farming that year.

"When I went down to the house to say goodbye, little Sharon who was three at the time, threw her arms around me and begged the other children to stop me from going," he said.

"But two years later, she said to me, 'I wish you weren't my daddy. I wish I had another daddy.'"

Then his wife moved out, taking the children to her mother's. He had to sue to get visitation rights.

Bear then decided to fight back. He hired a public relations firm, published a book at his own cost, and filed a suit against shunning in Cumberland County Court.

THE DAILY NEWS, NOVEMBER 26, 1975

Lebanon, PA

Mrs. Bear to Relate Her Story

For three years, Gale Bear suffered in silence while her husband publicly accused her of ruining their marriage and alienating their six children.

But she plans to give her side of the story today as

Robert Bear, her husband, resumes a legal struggle he hopes will "break the back" of the Reformed Mennonite Church and win back his wife and family.

Bear has asked Cumberland County Judge Clinton Weidner to ban "shunning"—the 400-year-old practice of ostracism the church uses to punish excommunicated members.

But William Ball, one of the attorneys representing the church, said, "The picture will change dramatically once the full story is out."

Ball has indicated through his cross examination of Bear that the defense will contend that Bear forced Gale and the children to leave and that she shunned him for more than just religious reasons.

THE DAILY NEWS, NOVEMBER 27, 1975

Lebanon, PA

Mrs. Bear's brother, bishop Glenn Gross, testified he did not order her to shun her husband and never tried to interfere with her marriage.

Both he and Mrs. Bear said that if she had not shunned Robert, she would have violated God's word and she herself could have been excommunicated.

Judge Patty's Ruling

Judge Weidner, who presided over this case, would not hand down his decision until the following year. Though I had been hearing this litany of arguments for years, the only missing piece I had awaited was what the Church had to say under oath about the voluntary or involuntary nature of shunning.

Mother had told us about her testimony in court (as we were not present), how the Church testified that she was led by the spirit to shun her husband, and that she did it out of her own free will and was not coerced.

When I heard this, my judgment was immediate.

What a crock.

From everything I'd overheard, I didn't think Uncle Glenn cared so much about the Marital Avoidance doctrine. The letter of the law would have been satisfied for him by the Bible's explicit injunction not to eat together, but there had been hardline bishops in Canada and Lancaster who were not satisfied with this. Nevertheless, the idea that shunning was voluntary was ludicrous.

Even at the age of twelve, I knew members were not permitted to have a mind of their own, if those thoughts in any way deviated from the infallible word of the ministers and bishops. Everyone was required to be "in unity," or else. Mother would say that she never thought the ministry should be allowed to invade the bedroom and tell her what to do. And yet, she could be at times unquestioning of authority and a bit of a true believer. Still, she was not "led by the spirit." That was silly. She knew exactly what would eventually happen if she didn't do what she was supposed to do. She would be excommunicated and shunned too.

For me to know this as a child, I could hardly bring myself to believe the Church would deliberately mislead like this under oath. It would be years before I heard the term "quibbling," meaning that the deliberate omissions and misdirection to create a false impression was every bit a lie as an outright untruth. But despite not knowing the term at the time, this was a textbook case of quibbling—if not outright lying—and I was astounded.

And for my father's part, he would insist that he loved his wife and children, that he was doing this all for us. He would continually assert that the *only* reason his wife didn't come back—either out of stunning ignorance or deliberate misleading, which one I was never quite sure—was because she didn't have the Church's permission to return.

This was also a complete and utter crock.

After what I'd witnessed in our home, I couldn't imagine any wife who'd want to live with a man who behaved like he did. I knew *I* never would. Frankly, I could never figure out how she put up with it for so long. I was eternally grateful that we finally left.

In fact, watching my father had brought me to make my second internal vow: no husband or boyfriend would hit me *even once* and get away with it. One or both of us might die in the process, but I would never allow it to go unchallenged and unpunished. I'd sooner be dead than tolerate that.

Behind all the drama of the byzantine religious themes swirling about, I realized with complete disgust that the Church and my father were, in fact, engaged in nothing more esoteric than a basic property dispute. Both were arguing over who the wife and children belonged to: Daddy with his "two stags on a mountain fighting over a doe" machismo, and the Church with its slippery denials of iron-fisted control. Sometimes they acknowledged the practice of shunning, but they always took cover behind my mother's skirts to evade any culpability for the effects of it. As for my father, it was pathetic how he publicly howled about being stripped of his entitlements as a man while privately abandoning all responsibilities as a father. Both he and the Church were so intent on asserting their rights that it never occurred to either one of them that we did not belong to them.

They didn't own Mother, my siblings, or me.

We belonged only to ourselves.

CHAPTER SIX

1976

You have to grow from the inside out. None can teach you, none can make you spiritual. There is no other teacher but your own soul.

—SWAMI VIVEKANANDA

Pairs Ice Skating

Visiting Daddy one weekend at the Home Farm, he announces we are going ice skating on the pond up at the Other Farm, which is a couple of miles from the house.

"We're going to walk," he says.

The six of us eye each other in shared surprise. Why he has decided to cross the creek rather than take the truck up to the pond, I'm not sure. Perhaps he thinks the walking is good exercise, or being out in the cold air is good for us. In any case, he warns us that while the pond is frozen, the fast-moving creek will not be solid yet.

We've grown up knowing how to look at the color of ice to gauge how thick it will be, and we know how to test the solidity of the ice by throwing rocks in incremental distances to see if the middle holds before venturing out on our skates. We have also acquired a finely tuned ear for the subtle variations of the sounds of ice cracking. So, when we see the leaves floating just beneath the thin ice on the creek, we are instantly wary.

"It'll be fine," Daddy says, noticing our hesitance. "Just follow me and do what I do."

So we get down on our bellies like he does and shimmy single file (to reduce weight on the ice) slowly and carefully behind him across the frozen creek. Every bit of expertise we have gathered over the years tells us this is a reckless thing to do, but probably less dangerous than defying my father's orders.

Face to face with the ice, the leaves floating below look even closer, and ahead of us, we can see the ice bending beneath Daddy's body. This is near our swimming hole, so I know the water is deep. If we fall in, we could drift under the ice toward the dam below, and in a worst-case scenario, get trapped between the ice and the dam. As Daddy inches slowly forward, I hold my breath each time the ice bends and our little procession comes to a halt, waiting to see if the ice holds.

Eventually, we reach the other side safely. With huge sighs of relief, we pull ourselves up the bank and start on the dirt road—the one we have hauled the little red wagon along so many times, filled with rescued food—toward Daddy's trailer. This time, we make a right and head to the pond.

It is a frigid day, but Daddy peels off his shirt. "It's nothing," he insists with a booming laugh. "We Bears come from hardy stock."

I stare at him. *Hardy stock?* I am always cold. I can't imagine taking off my coat, let alone my shirt, on a day like today. But for him, the colder it was, the more exhilarating he found it. He even likes to sleep with the windows wide open when it snows. He says he sleeps best that way.

Today, Daddy is in a jolly mood, the kind where he whistles a happy tune. After we build a fire so that we can periodically warm our hands and feet (which means we can skate on the pond as long as we want), Daddy says, "Why, here, I'll show you how to skate with a partner."

Putting his arm around my back, he tells me to grasp his left hand with mine, then he takes my right arm. We push off in tandem to the left, and then to the right. Pretty soon we are expertly gliding in unison.

As we skate around the pond with the sun on our shoulders, the crisp air adding to the exhilaration, and the feeling of competence at skating so seamlessly together, I imagine we look like a couple from the era of Louisa May Alcott's *Little Women*—something straight out of an old-fashioned drawing.

After a while, I wander off to explore the smaller frozen tributaries leading in and out of the pond as Daddy sets about teaching my sisters how to pairs skate too. Weaving between the low-hanging branches, I follow the narrow passageways wherever they lead through the woods, thinking about what a wonderful day it is. Daddy's ability to skate in pairs surprised me because he didn't seem like the type to partner well, but I don't think about that too deeply. I am just grateful for the day, one of the unusual days we spend with Daddy when I allow myself to hope that he might care about us after all.

Back in Hiding

What fresh act of violence or mailed threat precipitated our move into Uncle Glenn and Aunt Mary Ellen's basement, I no longer remember. All I knew was, it was clear that it was not just for a weekend, or even for a week, because our schools were notified that this was to be our new bus stop.

Aside from failing Daddy's loyalty test in Uncle Glenn's office and being left here for nearly a week back in 1972, we have taken refuge in Uncle Glenn and Aunt Mary Ellen's unused upstairs before. Those stays had their upsides. For one, they had Alpha Bits and other kids' cereals we were not normally allowed to eat because they had too much sugar. Plus, the breakfast table perched by a sunny window made me feel rich just looking out at the manicured front lawn and gardens. Even in the wintertime it looks elegant. And no matter the time of year, their house always feels peaceful and smells of the fragrant lemon soap Uncle Glenn uses.

But this time, we are not staying upstairs in the sunny areas. The basement has been freshly remodeled to become living quarters (due to our situation or not is unclear to me), and Mother says we are not to mess it up. Aunt Mary Ellen's grimace emphasizes this directive as she eyes our motley clan's arrival. I can't really blame her. We can be kind of wild, and as Mother frequently says, "I can't keep *anything* nice with you kids around." We tend to be hard on our surroundings, to ding walls when we fight and spill on carpets, but we vow to behave in this brand-new space.

Except for the lack of windows and light, the basement is ideal for our situation. Its entrance door is hidden below a steep hill from the main driveway that abuts Williams Grove Road, and Mother can even park her car out of sight. Nobody would know we are here unless they pulled into the driveway. This is good because Daddy cruises this road quite often, since Ashcombe and Uncle Glenn are two of his favorite targets, besides Mother. (She's in charge of the fern greenhouse at Ashcombe's, and though Daddy often hunts for her there, she has the advantage; if she receives warning, she can usually escape to another greenhouse or hide between two, out of sight.)

Another positive of living here is that we children work right across the road, so all we have to do is walk a hundred yards to the warm greenhouse after school. Plus, because Uncle Glenn is health conscious and takes an evening run inside during the winter, he runs laps after closing hours through the wide store aisles and concrete walkways that zigzag the retail greenhouses, allowing all of us, including Mother, to join him. I like zipping around the dark corners and through the open doors where customers normally walk, seeing how many laps I can run and who can run the most. (When it gets warm outside, Uncle Glenn lets me run beside him on the busy road by his house if I get up early enough. We run a mile or two, then circle back, sometimes chatting a bit, though I can never run and talk very well.)

But one day, it seems that Daddy has gotten a little too close for comfort to our hiding place.

When the bus reaches our stop, we are alarmed to discover that none of our cousins are on board. Mother's other brother, Bob, lives with his wife and three children next door to Uncle Glenn, so our cousins get on the bus right before us. But not today.

For a long time, Daddy has mailed and handed out long letters detailing his grievances, but when his targets have refused to take them or read them, he has resorted to a new tactical maneuver. Armed with heavy-duty wood glue and his pamphlets, he plasters the garages or front doors of his enemies. The wood glue makes it impossible to remove the flyers without damaging the surface, and the large lettering that screams out from the flyers is visible from the road, serving the purpose of publicly humiliating whomever receives this treatment.

Uncle Glenn's garage had received "the treatment" many times, as had our garage. But today, it was apparently Uncle Bob's turn. Daddy plastered their trailer with his flyers from top to bottom, and the school bus driver, knowing nothing of this, arrived at our cousins' house, peered at the spectacle, then assumed they had been quarantined by the health department and refused to stop.

We may bear the brunt of Daddy's aberrant behavior, but it's almost more humiliating to witness how it affects the people around us who are nothing more than innocent bystanders.

A Haunting Vision

One day in late spring during a weekend visitation at the Home Farm, I wander up the hill beside the potato storage barn to a spot I've always treasured. It is here that my sisters and I gathered in a circle on the ground and patted mud into pies, sipped imaginary cups of tea, and echoed the conversations we'd overheard from women members. "Pray for me," one of us would intone solemnly. "And pray for me too," the rest of us would reply gaily as we elevated a pinky finger and reached for a dirt delicacy.

It is on this hilltop, barely within the embrace of our home yet just on the perimeter of the fields, that I stand looking across the rolling hills of this land that once was our home. In one direction, beyond the rolling farmland and hills, is the north mountain and endless blue skies. In the opposite direction, also across fields, lies the other perimeter of the Home Farm property marked by a black raspberry patch confined behind a wire fence and backstopped with a forest of assorted trees.

I have an uncharacteristically empty mind as I drink in the panorama of fields, farm, and distant hills, registering the empty fields and what used to be. A slight breeze is blowing when an image of a large black bonnet suddenly appears in front of my face, so close that I pull my chin into my neck. Stepping back a bit, I focus until I can see the entire image. Beneath the bonnet is a grotesque sight: a female skull with hollow eyes staring directly and unsmilingly at me. This vision carries a discernible message that I comprehend instantly—when women get married and have children, they die. I know, of course, that women do not literally die, but I understand symbolically that when they get married, they cease to exist as individuals. It is *as if* they are dead. I receive the message as another clear warning and further guidance on my path.

I know that we have to get married; that is just the way of things. But it makes me profoundly sad when I consider how young that is to die. So, I determine on that very spot that I will wait as long as I possibly can. I make a promise to myself that I won't get married until I'm twenty-eight, because that age seems to be the precise edge of spinsterhood—the last minute a woman can wait before she has to choose between life and death.

Will Daddy Kill Us?

Some memories are the freeze-frame type, where time is frozen like a video, and I will always remember exactly where I was when that event took place as if I were still there in that moment in time. One video memory took place on a day we were driving along Route 641 on the way up to the farm for weekend visitation.

As Daddy was issuing one of his standard monologues about the Church, *your* mother, and Uncle Glenn, I was listlessly staring at the houses passing by outside, nose pressed against the backseat window. Since Daddy couldn't very well drive and police our attention, I tuned him out and took note of a nondescript one-story red-brick house; it seemed it must be exactly opposite the little Bear cemetery I knew lay on the other side of the turn-pike, just behind this house. The tiny cemetery was filled with small, white tablets enclosed in a low, stone-stacked wall. Sometimes the cemetery got mowed and sometimes not. I wondered if the grass was overgrown or if somebody might have mowed it.

Right in the middle of Daddy's monologue, he switched gears, pulling me away from thoughts of my departed ancestors.

"You know, my friend says he doesn't know how I stand it. 'I'd shoot that brother-in-law of yours,'" he said.

Daddy added a special emphasis on the word "shoot," then continued just as casually with the remainder of his friend's advice. "If it were me, I'd take a gun and shoot the wife and the whole family."

I jerked my eyes toward Daddy, wondering about his choice of friends. *Who in their right mind would say something like that?* I stared at the side of his face trying to discern what *he* thought about his supporter's remarks, but his face was smooth and bland, giving away nothing. The questions in my mind jostled roughly against each other.

Will he shoot Mother?

Is he going to shoot us children?

Is Daddy gonna kill us all?

Susie said that when she first saw the hanging rope on the cover of Daddy's book, she was sure he was going to kill us.

But would he really do that? Would he follow his supporter's encouragement? However, instead of providing further explanation, he simply moved on to his next topic.

It was a story, though, he would repeat often.

I always allowed for the possibility that Daddy was so unstable, he was not entirely in possession of his mind. I figured he probably didn't account for the extent of the consequences of his behavior, but his supporters and co-conspirators amplified his worst inclinations. These people included champions of his cause who suggested violence to a dangerous man; printers who helped him publish his vilest accusations; artists who lent their skills to create his gory, terrifying images; and the detective who helped him find the family who was hiding from him. For them, I could find no excuse.

But if I owned hell, I thought, *there would be a special place for the people who suggested he shoot his own family.*

No More Visits

After Easter Sunday, 1976, Daddy told Mother she didn't need to bring us for visitation anymore. He didn't care to see us.

But for the May 2, 1976, issue of the *Philadelphia Inquirer*, he told a reporter something entirely different.

> "Easter Sunday I had the children here, but they have no respect for me. When they come here, I think they come for whatever money they can get." Bear's voice broke. "I just can't take it."

When I read this, I was shocked.

What on earth was he talking about? We came for the money?

Except for Sharon, who was six years old, we all had jobs. We had been working after school, on the weekends, and during the summers for years. Even for him, this was a low accusation.

My father had never given us an allowance. In fact, he had never given us money except as pay for work we did, and even then he was perpetually tight-fisted.

The truth was that we came for visitation three weekends a month because the judge ordered us to. At least that's my truth. Perhaps my other siblings wanted to go, but I only went because we had to. In the car ride to his trailer for the weekend, there was a crossroads just outside Carlisle. Every time we passed that point, it felt like a demarcation of an alternate reality we weren't entirely sure we would return from. A fugue seemed to settle over the car at the boundary line, and the fingers of a fog-like gloom invaded our mood.

Puzzling over Daddy's statement in the newspaper, the only thing I could think of was the $100 a week in child support he had told the judge he would pay. *Could he really be that deceptive?* His record of erratic and extremely reluctant support, and his knowledge that Mother would not go to court to enforce child support, meant that he paid one $400 check right after the custody hearing to look good for the judge, then sporadically after that, eventually quitting altogether. Plus, we knew being openly disrespectful to my father meant certain and overwhelming punishment. We were not generally that dumb. He simply confused respect with blind, unquestioning loyalty. Maybe he didn't feel he was getting what he had hoped for or, perhaps in his mind, what he had *paid* for. In any case, after this declaration, he would never pay another dime of child support.

No doubt, six children three weekends a month was a tedious imposition on his freedom. Nevertheless, though he declined the regular court-ordered visits, he would call from time to time and insist upon the right to see us. Whether he sincerely wanted to see us, or merely hoped to get Mother on the phone to engage her in an argument, only he could answer.

Looking back, I realize something pivotal. My father's excommunication happened squarely in the mid-life crisis years: the early forties. Sometimes in this precarious stage, people abruptly shed long-time responsibilities in a passionate bid for liberation, and the life that was is burned to the ground. After a period of chaos, many people build new lives on the charred ground and assume new responsibilities. But for my father, after his explosive bid for freedom, he seemed ever after to be allergic to responsibility. I've often wondered if his lost childhood years, when he was forced to work so hard, contributed to a reversal in adulthood. He seemed to assume a child-like longing to come and go as he pleased, to do what he wanted, when he wanted—without consequences—and to have no responsibilities to others weighing on his young shoulders. I suspect he longed for a more carefree life, but my father, who despised cowardice, never admitted this, or any motivation other than the need to be vindicated as right.

Lost Case

Eight members of the press, including a reporter from *Time* magazine, attended the session on April 26th where final arguments were made by both attorneys in the lawsuit that had begun in the fall of 1973, and the eventual trial in November of 1975. Now, closing arguments would be made before the judge's final decision was rendered.

Daddy's attorney argued that everything was harmonious in our home until the excommunication, and how "now his wife and six children put him in a lower position at the home." She also claimed that Daddy had not been aware of the implications of excommunication in our religion until they happened to him.

Judge Weidner interrupted Mrs. Del Duca at this point. "By his own testimony, Bear testified he was aware since age 22 of the doctrine of avoidance."

The Church's attorney, Mr. Ball, argued that ruling in Daddy's favor would open the floodgates so that "anyone in dispute with his church could come into court and seek an injunction, like a Catholic who didn't like his bishop." He pointed out that "Bear was raised in a Reformed Mennonite household, and when he chose to enter the Reformed Mennonite Church at the age of 22, he knew its laws. It's almost impossible to believe he never heard of the doctrine of avoidance." He further noted: "The children do not avoid the plaintiff. They are not members of the church."

In June, 1976, Judge Weidner issued his ruling on Daddy's case, dismissing the suit while noting: "The church's case is even stronger now. My God, he brought this all on himself." Judge Weidner's unflinching rebuke would earn him a permanent vitriolic mention in my father's printed screeds, along with a spot on his voluminous distribution list and a public questioning of his manhood.

PUBLIC OPINION, JUNE 25, 1976

Chambersburg, PA

"The judge came down pretty hard on me, didn't he?" Bear asked yesterday.

"You'd think he was a man that has never been a man. You would think he would have an idea what it is to live with a woman like that," Bear said of the judge.

Bear appeared particularly disturbed by a quote in a newspaper story, taken from the judge's opinion. Referring to Bear's children, the judge said they have been "silent observers of this most unfortunate controversy except where the plaintiff (Bear) could use them in his plans to destroy the church."

"Look at that, will you," he said to a visitor who was selling him farm supplies.

Before the visitor arrived, Bear had gone off to another room to take a nap.

Trying to doze off, the events of the day noticeably appeared to be swirling through his head. He talked of an appeal.

"Do you think it will do any good?" he asked.

"The judge seemed to think I was out to destroy the church," he said.

"Are you?" this reporter queried.

He was slow with an answer but admitted "yes," it is part of his aim.

He added, "Since you can't seem to reason with them any other way."

He also told a reporter from the *Philadelphia Inquirer*:

"I believe this is the first time in the history of Pennsylvania that the state has sheltered a form of prostitution . . . They (the bishops) said the stated plain price (to get my wife back) is to return to the church. 'If you repent, Gail would be duty bound to sleep with you then.'"

As I researched this case almost 45 years later, I came across one tiny, precious quote buried in a newspaper article and was surprised to find myself overcome with emotion. Everywhere we children went, we encountered the curiosity of others: teachers, classmates, neighbors, coworkers, strangers. Our mother's distinctive uniform and our much-publicized last name meant that we were constantly recognized, but never for anything good. The Bear name was a sure response for a suspicious squint and the inevitable question: "Are you any relation to . . ." Even before the end of the question escaped our inquisitor's mouth, we always knew what was coming next. My father told a compelling story of persecution, and we were not sympathetic figures in his tale. I dreaded the red tide that crept up my chest, tinged my throat, and blanketed my face like a rash I could never control in the wake of those questions.

But most frustrating of all was that hardly anybody seemed able to discern the truth. Even within our church, there seemed to be a whisper campaign of blame. My sisters overheard one female church member exclaim in exasperation, "If she would have just been more submissive, none of this would have happened." At the time, I suspected she was not the only member who shared this opinion, blaming Mother for my father's aggressive behavior. I resented that member for her ignorance and betrayal for years.

How could anyone possibly *not* know about the violence in our home? My father regularly disrupted church services. He physically attacked members and choked his youngest brother in a pew in front of the entire congregation. He had physically attacked and choked our aunt at Ashcombe amidst a busy shopping day right in front of customers. Surely what was happening in our home could not be a secret. If anybody should be able to see the truth, it would be the Church members, I reasoned.

And, most painful of all, Uncle Francis and his family now kept their distance. We had grown up with his children; many Sundays were spent playing with our cousins, ice skating on their farm's pond, and even gleefully escaping a charging bull as we tumbled over the fence. We played in their barn and spent entire days reveling in our lively cousins' inventiveness in constructing go-carts. They raced them on the dirt lane and let us drive them too. Now we were no longer invited to their home, as if we had a highly contagious disease. Mother said Uncle Francis probably hoped that if he kept his distance from us, Daddy would leave him alone. We couldn't blame him. Who could bear a delusional relative showing up at his farm and choking him? Yet I suspected there was more to his coldness.

The extended Bear clan was a proud one. They didn't like that Daddy refused to provide for his own children. It was a stain on the family honor. They were angry, too, about the publicity and my father ruining the family name. But we heard that Uncle Francis would tell people it wasn't the Church, nor my father, that was the cause; rather, the fault lay with the marriage. To me, this was code for *her* fault. After all, men weren't responsible for relationships. That was women's work.

Everything felt upside down. Even the people we should have been able to rely on could not be trusted. My father had twisted the truth so effectively, with such confidence and utter certainty, that others appeared to quietly blame us for the situation. Like innocent suspects who are interrogated for hours on end and come to question their culpability, *I* even frequently wrestled with the invitation to accept blame, thinking maybe we *had* done something wrong. If everyone else seemed to think we were to blame, perhaps it was true.

The worst part was that nobody seemed to possess the ability to pierce the illusion, least of all those charged with the duty to report truth to the public. My memories of the county courthouse are of circuitous routings and being ushered out back doors, trying to evade the crowd of jackals that clamored for comments from us to populate their newspaper stories—stories that never approached our reality, stories (it seemed to us at the time) written by people either too dumb to apprehend the truth or, more likely, who cared more about printing a juicy story.

And so, staring at a relic from 1976, a tiny jewel of sanity buried in a small-town newspaper article made me catch my breath.

> During the trial a reporter from a major wire service casually referred to Bear as a "media manipulator." (*Chambersburg Public Opinion*, June 25, 1976)

A veritable wave of relief washed over me. Someone *had* seen through the chimera, even then. There was a witness.

It shouldn't matter so much after all these years, I think. Yet it does. Remembering all the years of feeling crazy, there is no way to measure the gratefulness I feel for that singular voice.

A Turning Point

The lost court case has gone as high as it can go in the system except for the US Supreme Court, for which Daddy says he does not have enough money to pursue an appeal. Undaunted, however, he insists he will not stop waging his crusade. And since he must replace the level of publicity that has accompanied these cases, he vows to take his campaign to the court of public opinion.

His first homegrown publicity effort involved wrapping his large potato delivery truck entirely in sheets of black mulching plastic, used to grow cantaloupes on our farm. This neutral background formed a canvas to scrawl imposing hand-painted words in white that wrapped around the truck, shouting a litany of reasons for why he would not repent and go back to the Church. He drove the truck to the Ashcombe parking lot where he parked his tour de force and held court for an entire day while customers entered and exited the business.

His aim was to embarrass Uncle Glenn—whom he continued to hold responsible for his court costs—at his place of business, proclaiming he now owed Daddy (including interest) $700. A picture of Daddy standing proudly beside his billboard truck ran in our local paper.

THE SENTINEL, MAY 4, 1976

Carlisle, PA

Piled on the ground behind the truck, in neat stacks, were copies of Bear's book "Delivered Unto Satan" available to interested store customers strolling through the parking lot.

Bear hadn't sold many by late afternoon (he had been there since morning) but selling was not his primary reason for being there, he said.

"I think the reason this (shunning) has gone on for 400 years is because husbands haven't stood up against it," he said. "Now with the ease of communication today, it seems an ideal time to bring this forth."

"I see law, like beauty, is in the eyes of the beholder," he said. "I saw how futile the trial was."

The steely gray-haired ruddy-faced Bear was glad to speak about what he calls "the living hell" of separation from his wife and family.

"I have visitation rights with my children," he said. "But my wife is so pro-church I can't be a father to them. Of course, anytime I'd got back to the church, my wife would go to bed with me. It's that mechanical."

And Bear now feels his only recourse is "the court of public opinion" out in the windy parking lot of Ashcombe's.

A woman on her way out from the store stopped and asked the price of a book. Bear calculated price plus sales tax and told her. Sold.

"One other thing," she added. "Could you sign it for me?" Bear happily obliged.

Though we may have hoped reaching the end of the legal process signaled the end of the road for Daddy's quixotic quest—and that he could then move on with his life and us with ours—we would come to learn that it merely signaled a dangerous shift in tactics. Abandoning his stated goal of getting the courts to ban shunning and order his wife and children back home, he turned to various forms of guerrilla warfare in his determination to be declared "right." By the end of the year, he would turn to criminal behavior, seeking to get arrested to win more public sympathy. This in turn would further evolve to a long-term strategy of committing crimes designed to provoke jury trials and the publicity exposure that came with them. It was a strategy he would cling to into his nineties, while steadfastly insisting that his sole aim remained to restore his family to him.

Bicentennial Wagon Train

Like scouts running ahead of an expedition party, the exciting news of the approaching Bicentennial Wagon Train reaches us before the procession does in late June. For the past year, it has moved eastward from Washington state across the plains and midwest and into Pennsylvania, as the entire country charted its progress. Retracing routes that early pioneers followed as they moved westward, the wagon train plodded toward its eventual destination and mission—to mark the 200-year anniversary of our country at Valley Forge on July 4, 1976.

Like so many other Americans, we are enchanted by newspaper pictures of these Conestoga wagon replicas on their journey. It is as if the entire country is having a colorful, jubilant, old-fashioned sidewalk party. Imagine our delight when we discover that this procession will pass right below our house on Route 74. Our good fortune to have front-row seats to this moving monument to history is inconceivable to us.

Sandy, one of the twins I befriended at school, lives even closer to the main road than we do. After talking her into a summer job picking strawberries and blueberries with us at Ashcombe, she often bikes or walks to work with us, and we all go to the swimming hole below the blueberry patch after work. Sometimes she even comes to our house to play, and on days we don't go to the swimming hole, we frequently all bike together to the Boiling Springs pool after work, or watch movies at the theater where her mom works in Camp Hill.

This particular summer, as the wagon train approaches, Sandy and I set up a lemonade and candy stand on the porch within her compact, white-picket-fenced front yard. We've purchased candy in bulk that we plan on reselling at a profit to make money, and we pour Kool-Aid and our home-made minted lemonade into pitchers of ice. While we wait for customers to arrive, Sandy brings out her Barbie Dolls, which she shares with me. We never really had dolls on the farm, except for a treasured Raggedy Ann I got when I was three. Our toys were mostly shared Tonka trucks, Erector Sets, and Lincoln Logs—all of which I loved—but I also wished we had dolls. Sandy and I have a ball dressing the dolls in various outfits and having imaginary conversations through them. I enjoy playing with the Barbies so much that I buy patterns at the store to make a stylish wardrobe for Sandy's Barbies.

With front-row seats to history, Barbie adventures, movie theater trips, and a tiny business with a worldly friend, without my noticing, I have begun a westward expansion of my own.

A Dirty Old Shoe

One Sunday in early November, after a family dinner at Grandma and Papap's house, everyone moves to the living room to visit. When we are all seated, Uncle Glenn and Aunt Mary Ellen announce they have a surprise for us, after which they disappear, then return carrying a clodhopper that they present to Mother and us children. The dirty, old leather shoe they present has been so well worn that it has holes in it.

All I can think is, *What is this ugly thing and why are they presenting it to us?* But Uncle Glenn and Aunt Mary Ellen are smiling. "Look closer," they encourage.

Digging past the tongue of the shoe, Mother wrestles out an envelope. We all watch as Mother opens it.

"Airplane tickets!" she announces, both surprised and stunned.

I can't believe Uncle Glenn and Aunt Mary Ellen have given us a luxurious gift like this. The tickets are to Illinois, so far away that it seems like a different world, one that is untouchable and safe and elegant. None of us children have ever been on an airplane, and it feels surreal that we'll be flying *all the way* to Illinois to visit Aunt Linda and Uncle Howard. We will spend Thanksgiving at their beautiful house, eat Aunt Linda's delicious food, and get to play with our cousins.

Plus, we will be far, far away from here.

Daddy has been heavy on the warpath since September, when he tried unsuccessfully to kidnap Mother from Grandma's house. He has also been coming more often to church on Sunday to rant and rave. Some new attempt is brewing, and we can all feel it. So the invitation to go on this new adventure and to spend Thanksgiving somewhere else is a remarkable gift.

On the morning of our departure, we dress in our Sunday clothes and walk across the tarmac at the Harrisburg International Airport toward our plane. Up the metal stairs and through the open door, we pass into a different world. Right at the boundary between inside and outside, the air changes. I instantly love the smell of this new world, both artificial and exotic. The stewardess (that's what they were called back then), looking sophisticated in her crisp, stylish uniform, greets us with a smile, as the scent of coffee brewing engulfs us. Once seated, I discover we get served meals on trays—in the air! I love everything about this adventure: the smells, the taste of the food, and the choreographed movements of the airplane from tarmac to takeoff and back again. Plus, it feels fancy. There is simply no other word for it.

Those airplane tickets were not only a ticket out of hell—at least briefly—but my introduction to the luxurious world in the clouds was love at first sight.

Christmas at the Nursing Home

The Thanksgiving vacation in Illinois was lovely. We rolled huge snowballs into forts and sledded and ate until we couldn't close the buttons on our pants. Christmas, however, was a different story.

Daddy's emotional cycle matured into the action phase once again, so we spent the holiday break from school in the vast, dark-brick nursing home in Lancaster endowed by Milton Hershey. I have no independent memory of how or why we ended up here, perhaps because I was in and out of consciousness with scarlet fever. The constant march of colds, sore throats, allergies, anemia, and other illnesses had not abated over the years. It seemed I still got everything that came down the pike, and this time it was so severe that I fainted from weakness. (When I came to, my eyes met the underside of the toilet bowl, with no idea how I had gotten there.) But, just as likely, I have no memory because fleeing was so commonplace in our lives that I didn't register it as unique until it became clear we would be spending the holiday break here, sleeping in the clean but spartan rooms and taking our meals with the elderly residents in the main dining area.

In any case, I shall have to rely on the newspapers to tell this story.

The headlines almost always telegraphed unmistakably where the sympathies of reporters lay, and it was not with us. Furthermore, the large newspapers seemed to only pay attention when misfortune befell what, apparently, both they and my father considered to be the real victim: him. As a result, the big-name newspapers did not report on the following violent episode until a year after it occurred, in conjunction with a development where he was once again a sympathetic figure.

THE WASHINGTON POST, DECEMBER 15, 1977

Victim of Shunning

In addition to the suit, Bear launched a massive publicity campaign, hired a private detective to snoop on church elders and last year broke into his wife's house in Brandsville with a sledgehammer. On that occasion, Bear loaded the children's clothing into a truck and took it to his farmhouse, expecting the children to come home.

The *Philadelphia Inquirer* would later report on the incident that caused us to flee, under the headline "A Man Strong Enough to Lose Everything" (November 14, 1977).

But even after abandoning his legal challenge of shunning, Bear did not give up getting his wife back. In December, he said, he notified her that he was going to try some forceful persuasion to reunite his family. "I told her I would knock on the door and if she didn't open it, I would knock it in."

When he arrived at the house, she and the children ran away, he said. "I brought their things home. My oldest son called the State police. My wife took me to court and the judge threatened to put me in jail."

Mother would testify that after seeing Daddy arrive early that morning in the driveway and putting up a large sign: "I got the children dressed, and we fled. All but one." She said one son was on crutches and remained hiding in the house until he got word to them that Bear had left. (Source: untitled newspaper clipping from Mennonite archives.)

Our local newspaper, however, reported on its front page the details of this break-in in late December when it reached the courts, resulting in Daddy losing his rights.

THE CARLISLE SENTINEL, DECEMBER 31, 1976

Bear 'sorry' for actions, says he'll move from area

While still standing firm against the practice of shunning, Robert Bear expressed regret for harassing his wife and said he'll move from the area. This came after a custody hearing in Cumberland County court yesterday where Bear repeatedly avoided Judge Shughart's questions as to whether he would continue his conduct.

Gale Bear, Robert's wife, testified at the hearing that Bear, since July, 1975, has engaged in such "conduct detrimental to the best interest and welfare of the children" as mailing hate mail to her, breaking visitation agreements, and on one occasion trying to carry her from her parents' house.

Shughart ordered Bear's visitation rights withheld from him and the district attorney's office later in the day said state police were investigating the possibility of criminal charges against him.

Acting as his own attorney, Bear's testimony consisted largely of criticism of the court for upholding the church shunning practice. "Our children will grow up (believing) that a wife teasing with her naked body is "love and concern," he said, quoting now retired Judge Clinton Weidner's opinion [on] June 23, dismissing Bear's suit.

This morning, in a telephone call to The Sentinel, Bear was more repentant.

"I'm sorry I've caused so much trouble and I think I should recognize how weak I am," he said. "I can't properly cope being so close to my wife and my family . . ."

"Yes, I haven't borne this very well," he added. "But the Reformed Mennonite Church doesn't know what they do to others when they ask of others what they themselves haven't proven they can do."

When asked where he plans to move, Bear said, "It's a

big world." He said he doesn't know when he will move or whether or not he'll continue his appeal filed in Commonwealth Court.

"I will pay whatever debt to society I have to," he said in reference to the criminal investigation against him. "I won't hurt anyone in prison . . ."

Mrs. Bear said Bear told her last Easter he didn't want to see the children but then began appearing at her parents' home, where she was staying with the children, demanding to see them at times other than agreed upon through the July 1975 custody order.

In Nov 1975 she said Bear disrupted church services she was attending with the six children, "saying embarrassing things about me and the children causing us to leave."

In September this year, Mrs. Bear testified her husband came "unawares into my parents' home and tried to carry me off." He had also mailed literature to her, with such titles as "Young, Beautiful, and Diseased." "In essence it compared our religious belief to a venereal disease," she said. She said the children saw this and other such documents.

On Dec 20th, she said Bear confiscated produce in the market stall she keeps at Ashcombe's Vegetable Farm. That same day she and the children had to flee the house when Bear drove up, apparently to make good on his previously mailed promise to "come for you and the children before Christmas."

One child on crutches had to hide in the house until Bear finished erecting a large sign on the lawn and left the property, she testified.

Although now staying with various friends and relatives, Mrs. Bear said the family has returned several times to the house to find a door splintered open, bureau drawers, clothes, sheets, towels, mattresses, "and I think the springs gone."

She said the children have been unable to attend their schools, Cumberland Valley Middle School and Monroe Elementary, and face possible illegal absence. She said her belief in non-resistance has precluded her from calling the police even though she fears for her children's and her own safety.

NEWSPAPER CLIPPING FROM MENNONITE ARCHIVES WITH
NO IDENTIFYING INFORMATION

Court cancels Bear's right to visit children

'shunned' farmer's wife describes break-in

Describes Judge Dale Shughart canceling earlier visitation
rights awarded because he had

- Tried forcefully to carry her away from her parent's
  home.

- Distributed pamphlets describing her in a "disrespectful, distasteful way."

- Broken into her home near Brandtsville early the
  morning of Dec. 20, taken all the mattresses in the
  house, [and] carted away the children's clothing and
  most of the drawers in the house.

- Later that day removed food items from her delicatessen stand at Ashcombe's Vegetable Market,
  Williams Grove.

- Caused her and the children to fear for their safety,
  so that the children are now scattered among relatives and friends.

- Disrupted a church service in November 1975 saying
  "disrespectful things" about her.

"I direct you to cease the kind of conduct that has been
described by your wife. When you indicate to me that you
are going to treat visitation as it ought to be treated, we will
consider visitation," the judge said.

Bear, who claimed he had used up his money in the
former case and was acting as his own attorney, refused to
question his wife after her testimony. "I feel it's a hopeless
situation," he said.

Shughart warned Bear he might face criminal charges
and advised him to get a lawyer, court appointed if necessary.

. . .

Shughart refused a request from Gale Bear's lawyer,

William Ball, that his order include protection of the family,
who Ball said have begun to fear for their safety.

Despite Daddy having declined to see us for weekend visits earlier in the
year, I am immensely relieved when the judge formally terminated his visitation rights. We are officially no longer required to go to the farm and stay
with the man who has gone from being our father to being our tormentor.

CHAPTER SEVEN

1977

Transformation isn't sweet and bright. It's dark and murky, painful pushing.
An unraveling of the truths you've carried in your body. A practice in facing
your own demons. A complete uprooting before becoming.
—VICTORIA ERICKSON

Aftermath of an Ambush

The new year began with a flurry of newspaper articles continuing the coverage that arose out of Daddy's Christmas ambush, offering new details on his experience and shifting motivations. It also gave a window into his future plans.

Though one of the central grievances of my father's campaign revolved around the issue of hypocrisy, reporters never seemed to notice the fluctuating nature of the stories he proffered, nor how those stories sometimes diverged substantially from what other news outlets quoted him regarding the exact same event. For example, in December Daddy told reporters the break-in was to bring his family home. But six months later, he claimed to another reporter that he merely came "to retrieve bedding and other community property his wife had taken with her when she left." It always amazed me that no one seemed to witness these disparities he so brazenly displayed.

Most astonishing perhaps was that no journalist remarked on the absurdity of a man who had smashed in the door of his family's home and hauled away all their possessions (including clothing and textbooks that prevented his children from attending school), yet claimed to be the real victim.

The Los Angeles Times, January 31, 1977

Disowned by Wife, 6 Children

Shunned Mennonite Gives up Fight Against Church

He [Daddy] said he bought the three younger girls wrist-watches for Christmas and the three older children an electric typewriter. He said he didn't receive any presents, or even cards from them.

"That's part of the punishment," he said. "And it hurts because I still love them."

These first-of-the-year articles also introduced a new controversy that would lay down a marker for events that would impact us all in the months and years to come.

Referencing the "most recent episode" of breaking and entering, another newspaper described a doctrinal controversy ignited within the Church because of the legal proceedings that arose out of the Christmas events. As you will remember from the robbery incident on the Home Farm, church doctrine forbids members from "going to the law" for any reason, including suing to redress grievances, seeking protection, or pressing charges. Mother, at her wits' end after the violent home invasion, employed some legal gymnastics in the hopes of safeguarding our home in the future while still obeying Church law. When her lawyer had the custody case reopened to bring attention to the violence and to seek an order of protection from Daddy, he was of course quick to label this hypocrisy. Daddy immediately confronted the Church about where it stood on this issue and questioned them loudly on why they did not punish Mother.

Intelligencer Journal, February 2, 1977

Lancaster, Pennsylvania

. . .

Mrs. Bear took him [Daddy] to court and Bear was stripped of his visitation rights, but the court did not press charges of breaking and entering.

He said Tuesday, "There are only two judges in the country (Judge Dale Shugart and former Judge Clinton R. Weidner, both of the Cumberland court) who have gone so far in blessing a thing like this.

"So, I do not want to live in Cumberland County anymore."

Bear said there is deep concern in the church over his wife "taking him to law." Reformed Mennonites are forbidden by edict to institute court action, he said.

Bear said the Lancaster congregation has been told his wife did not "go to law" and there is considerable debate on the question. She could be excommunicated for instituting the suit to end Bear's visitation under a strict interpretation of church law, Bear claims.

Mostly, though, the story of the break-in is eclipsed by the larger story of Daddy's concerns and, once more, his decision to quit his crusade. He tells reporters in January that he is giving up the fight for good and that he is moving elsewhere because his children don't respect him and question whether he is mentally sick. He says he will go to Florida and work his way north with the potato crop, buying and selling potatoes in each successive state.

In March, I opened the mailbox to find a postcard with a peaceful picture of the singing tower in Florida. On the back, it read:

Dear Patricia,

Hope you are all well. I could easily live here in Florida. My friend refuses to allow me to pay for my motel or our fine meals. I must visit another friend for a day and then I expect to leave Florida. Be sure your father loves you and thinks often of his Patricia.

Your father

I held the postcard in my hand and turned it over slowly, feeling both relieved and sad. I was glad he was out of the immediate area and that we could let down our guard, but at the same time, he suddenly seemed so far away, and his decision so definitive, that it felt as if he had died.

My Highest Ambition

Though I am only in seventh grade, by now I know the work of the home as well as any woman. Nobody must tell me what to do or when to do it. I hang the endless loads of laundry on the clothesline. I clean the house and organize cupboards. I make bread and homemade jam, sticky buns, and desserts. I create menus and grocery lists, sew my own clothing, and even make curtains for the house.

By eight years old, I had been helping to make everything in the kitchen. By eleven I could, just barely, manage the orchestration of the timing of a large meal. Once, when we still lived on the farm, Mother allowed me to stay home by myself from church to make the entire dinner for company. By the time everyone arrived, I was frazzled but I'd cooked an enormous spread of food that covered the entire table: mashed potatoes, creamed corn, creamed onion casserole, fresh green beans, carrots in a glazed butter and ginger sauce, homemade rolls and jam, plus dessert.

Mother took one look at the table and asked, "Where's the meat?"

I thought serving all vegetables meant that I was making a healthier meal. Her comment, however, made me realize I'd made a similar mistake before, though it took me a moment to connect the dots.

One time, when I was around nine, I'd wanted to surprise Mother by making a cake for her birthday. Since we were always supposed to eat healthy, I made the chocolate cake with half whole wheat and half white flour, just like we did with the bread. It tasted rather rough, and I learned my lesson about cakes!

But now at age thirteen, my cooking skills have graduated to a higher level. I enjoy making elaborate menus and I always include meat. I also think having company is a perfect time to experiment, though Mother told me it was best to test it out first. My theory is that guests are more likely to be appreciative of my attempts than my brothers and sisters, not to mention a lot less vocal if the experiment flops. Most of the time it works out, but it drives my siblings crazy that I use every dish, pot, and pan in the kitchen for my culinary efforts. The rule in our house is that whoever cooks, the other children have to do the dishes. When I am done with a company meal, I'm exhausted and the kitchen looks like a hurricane has swept through. It would take me years to learn the art of making an "Aunt Mary Ellen meal"—that's what my mother admiringly calls it, anyway. Aunt Mary Ellen served a perfectly cooked meal, and she did her dishes as she was cooking so that when dinner was served, the kitchen was calm and the only washing needed was for the plates afterward.

Despite the whirlwind I leave behind, my love of menu creation and willingness to cook means that making meals for company increasingly falls to me (which is actually fine by me, since I don't have to clean up the mess afterward).

One Sunday, Uncle Howard, Aunt Linda, and my cousins are visiting from Illinois. The table is set for thirteen, and as I bring platters and bowls of food to the table (and a basket of rolls, which I take great pride in making from scratch and not taking the easy way out with those inferior store-bought rolls), Uncle Howard looks up with a wide, approving smile and pronounces, "You'll make someone a good wife someday."

Immediately, I bristle inside. I know he means it as a high compliment, but the patronizing suggestion that this is the pinnacle of ambition for a girl evokes murderous irritation in me. Before I can stop, I say, "Oh yeah, that *is* my *highest* ambition in life." I string out the words slowly and deliberately, smothering them in a sarcastic gravy so there is no mistaking how I feel about being issued this preassigned life goal.

Mother, who has also been carrying bowls to the table, is standing beside me. I'm sure she'll be angry at me for talking to my uncle disrespectfully. But as I await her reprimand, I'm met with silence, as if she didn't even hear it. In fact, no one at the table makes a single remark, and Mother doesn't lecture me later, which shocks me even more.

I might as well have said nothing at all.

Growing Ever Weary

After being called out of math class, I make my way down the long hallway that connects the middle school to the ninth-grade building, wondering why I've been summoned to the principal's office. Once I arrive, there is Daddy.

He has tired of both Florida and his campaign retirement pledge and has returned to resume his previous activities. In short order, that has included marching into the middle school and high school, demanding to see his four older children.

But his first stop was Susie and Sharon's elementary school—not for a parent-teacher conference or to see how they were doing in school, but to occupy the principal with a recitation of the rights he had been denied as a husband and father. After his rant, he barged past him in search of the girls. Our schools were not locked down, so he made his way to the crowded cafeteria and presented his case to the fledgling court of public opinion, much to my two youngest sisters' horror and humiliation. Apparently, he reasoned, elementary school children needed to know "the truth" too.

Fortunately for the rest of us, our schools are too large and sprawling a campus to track us down, so he demands the principal call each of us in. We have a brief, disconnected encounter, and then I make the trek back down the hallway to resume math class, where I slump in my seat.

All I can think is, *Can't we ever get away from this man? Can't we ever have any peace?*

I am so weary of this endless saga, a few uncharacteristic tears escape down my cheek. I hope the teacher doesn't notice me crying; that would be humiliating. But more than that, I hope she doesn't call on me because I haven't heard a thing she has been saying since I returned.

"*Patty*," she says sternly.

I look up at her blankly, not having heard her question.

Irritated, she repeats the question more forcefully. I imagine she can see my uncomprehending look, which is why she called on me. She's one of those teachers who seem to get pleasure out of making students feel dumb, which to be fair, is not a difficult task with me.

Still, I wonder about teachers.

Everybody seems to know our business, so why can't the teachers see what is going on? How come nobody seems to care about how this is affecting us?

In Disguise

In the summer of 1977, Mother temporarily traded in her Plain dress and black bonnet for sweat suits, sunglasses, and a wig, over which she wore a white bandanna secured with Velcro, serving as the mandatory cap all women had to wear. She took a long-term reservation at the Range Inn Motel in Dillsburg for the summer, and to top it all off, she rented a red car.

What precipitated this drastic solution was a recent visit Daddy made to Grandma's house. While I wasn't there when he dropped by, because of the consequences for all of us (and doubly so for Sharon), the story became somewhat legendary.

Mother had brought seven-year-old Sharon to work with her one late spring day. But it was such a beautiful morning that they decided to kill two birds with one stone: they'd drop off business papers at Mother's accountant's office several blocks away while taking a reprieve from the dark and dreary basement where all the market food was made. They set out on foot down the alley that ran behind Grandma's house, admiring the flowers bursting with color in the neighbors' gardens, breathing in the fragrances and enjoying the soft caress of the breeze. They passed by the Dunkin' Donuts and dodged the cars on busy Market street, completed their errand, and started back to work at a leisurely pace.

Their carefree mood, however, came to an abrupt halt when after retracing their steps up the alley where it branched off into Grandma and Papap's driveway, Mother, always alert to danger, sensed something amiss. There in the glass-enclosed back porch, like a lion waiting to pounce, sat Daddy. Because he had parked his car several streets away, snuck up silently, and opened the door without a peep, even Grandma and Papap did not realize his presence. Mother tensed and began weighing her options for escape. Sharon froze.

Daddy, who had noticed the station wagon in the driveway and waited patiently as he stalked his prey, spotted them almost immediately and leaped up to give chase. Grandma's garden had enough winding paths that Mother knew she could evade him for a brief time, but not forever. When she spotted a straight shot to the door he had just left, she made a beeline for it, intending to reach safety and lock it behind her. Sharon, who had not known what to do, ran toward Mother, who made it to the door with Daddy breathing hard right behind her. She would have been able to get in and lock the door if she had been alone, but she held the door open for Sharon, who could not run as fast. The extra few seconds were just enough time for Daddy to thrust his arm in the door and wedge it open. Immediately, he pounced on Mother. Her body half inside, half outside the door, he forced her to the ground and straddled her while foaming vulgarities as he mauled her breasts, squeezing and pinching as she screamed.

Sharon could do nothing but stare in disbelief and terror. After several seconds, she ran as fast as her little legs could carry her, dashing past Grandma and Papap, who had heard the commotion and rushed out. Sharon scrambled up the stairs and dove for cover beneath our grandparents' king-size bed, where she waited, trembling, feeling guilty and wondering if Mother would be killed. She knew that none of this would have happened if she had just run a little faster. Terrified that Daddy might come for her too, she lay there until she heard Grandma's shaky voice below in the kitchen.

"Please come quick!" she pled.

Grandma, unable to stand the sight of her daughter pinned to the floor being assaulted, had broken the rules and called the police.

After what seemed like forever to her, Sharon heard a mix of voices at the bottom of the stairs: the policeman's calm questioning; Daddy's defensiveness; and Mother's disoriented, dazed, and traumatized voice as she struggled to tell the police what had happened. Finally, Daddy's agitated ranting faded into silence. *Was he gone?* Sharon wondered. Still not sure it was safe to come out of hiding, Sharon continued to wait, but then she realized that in the mayhem, everyone had possibly forgotten about her, inciting a different kind of panic.

Worried she had been abandoned, she cautiously crept back down the stairs to find our shaken mother and grandparents. She was relieved, but she would never forget the fear of being forgotten.

Although she had never called the police, Mother had called Crises Intervention over the years, even when we lived on the farm. She had complained bitterly that our farm neighbors' response to the violence had often been a philosophical shrug of "Well, a man's home is his castle." Few people seemed to take Daddy's terrorizing us seriously enough to stop it—not the police, not the neighbors, not society. Nobody would do much about this man who stalked us everywhere we went and broke into homes at will. And that included Mother.

When my brothers called the police, she would not press charges because of the Church's doctrine about turning the other cheek. Further, the newspapers would report that the ministry forced Grandma to stand up in church and apologize to the ministers and congregation for calling the police that day.

And so, with no protection, hiding behind a disguise and in a motel seemed the only viable solution for my beleaguered mother.

Summer Plans

For years we had been hiding in various ways. For example, when we stopped for lunch at the McDonald's in Carlisle after attending Middlesex meeting, we never ate inside the restaurant or even in the parking lot in case Daddy might drive past and spot us. We always drove across the street to a large wooded cemetery, past all the headstones to where the road dead-ended before we stopped to eat our meal, assured of our invisibility beneath the gloomy shade. When we drove on any road, we always kept a lookout for Daddy's truck. When he was sighted, the scout's urgent yell echoed through the car. "Duck, duck, it's Daddy, it's Daddy!" Sometimes we'd peek above the rim to see if he recognized our car. But he was almost always oblivious, lost in thought, on his way to his hunting grounds.

This summer, however, was another level of hiding, and it was clear it was going to last much longer.

Mother could take no chances after the assault inside Grandma's house. The red car would grant her the element of surprise and anonymity when she went to work, simply because Daddy would never imagine that a Mennonite would drive a red car. He also would not recognize the unfamiliar car sitting in Grandma's driveway and, not seeing our station wagon, he might think Mother was not there and just leave. At least, that is what she hoped.

The Range Inn was an ideal place to hide. Facing the road, it looked like a regular one-story motel. But if you drove around to the back, there was a lower level with rooms looking out over dappled woods. A cheerful little stream ran through the park-like setting and seemed to skip as it went on its way. Here, it was quiet and peaceful, a respite from the relentless terrorism. Another perk was that she could park a car there without being spotted from the main road, which was vital. Plus, it was only three miles away from where we lived, which meant that David, Benny, Leah, and I, who would live at home alone for the summer, could walk or bike to the motel to visit—or David, who had just gotten his license, could drive us there.

A couple times a week we would go to visit Mother, Susie, and Sharon (who also lived there) at the motel. It smelled funny and was kind of dingy and dark, and the room itself did not have much going for it except a television. We usually tried to visit on the evenings when our favorite shows were on. That summer we watched *Happy Days*, laughed at *Three's Company*, marveled at *The Incredible Hulk* and *Charlie's Angels*, and treasured *Little House on the Prairie*.

To Mother's credit, she tried to make things as normal as possible. The room had a small refrigerator and a hotplate that she used to cook meals. Even with these rudimentary tools, she often made delicious home-cooked meals. We ate as a family at the picnic table by the stream, or if it was raining, on folding chairs in the narrow, covered walkway between rooms.

In June, amidst the disguises and hotel hideout we were executing, a frequent sympathizer and chronicler of Daddy's heroic cause ran an article about *his* summer plans.

INTELLIGENCER JOURNAL, JUNE 13, 1977

Lancaster, Pennsylvania

Robert Bear Stays Optimistic

On Friday in a telephone interview Bear feels the family will get back together.

. . .

Bear has promised to take his family on a month's vacation if they can be reconciled.

. . .

The report was the most optimistic that has come from Bear in years. He said he is an eternal optimist. Pessimists are beaten before the race begins.

The older children run away at his approach, and he said, until Thursday he had not seen any of them for six months. He has seen and talked with Susan and Sharon, however.

. . . He said he is spending the summer trying to understand what has happened to him and his family.

Part of the optimism he feels is based on a letter sent to a banker indicating she [Mother] is willing to sell the farm. She sent a copy of the letter to Bear. He feels she has softened toward him a little.

The next chapter in the tortured lives of Robert and Gail Bear and their children is still being written. Bear hopes it will be about the happy ending he has yearned for five long years.

Home Alone 2

Each day that summer, David, Benny, Leah, and I set our alarms in the evening, rose early and made breakfast, then walked the railroad tracks or rode our bikes to begin work at 7 a.m. at Ashcombe. After work, we let ourselves into the empty house, and if we weren't going to the motel that night, we made dinner, cleaned the house or mowed the lawn, and got ready for the next day.

For Leah and me, it was the third summer of picking blueberries and strawberries, and the number of pickers had grown to between fifty and seventy teenagers. Besides the small group of pickers who returned every year, there was a fresh crop of teens hired each season because the work was hot, tiring, and—unless you picked fast—didn't pay well. Down on our hands and knees, crawling on the bed of straw between the rows, we would push the flats filled with quart containers ahead of us as we reached beneath the dark green canopies to retrieve the red treasures beneath. There were the same four or five of us who had competed in years past to see who could pick the most: my sister and me, our friend Joanne, plus two boys, one of whom would sing Frank Sinatra's "I Did It My Way" with a great flourish. He had a nice voice, and it always made me laugh when he'd mimic the moves of the singers he featured.

Each day the five of us vied for the lead. Scrambling along the row we'd fill our flats, heaping the quarts high enough for them to count, but not so high that they would be better counted amongst the next flat. We also had to ensure we left no berries behind. Mr. Smith, who supervised the farm crew, was a stickler for picking the row clean and would often make us revisit a section we had missed, which slowed us down considerably. Occasionally, we'd glance up from our picking to check on our competition. We would watch as a rival ran holding his or her full flat over the mounded rows toward the truck, trying not to spill berries, and compare our progress. The runner always made sure they got their quarts recorded correctly under their name before running back to the race still underway in the fields.

Mr. Smith called out the legally mandated break times, and we would try to finish the last quarts before rushing out of the field and up to the retail store, where I usually gobbled down four candy bars and a soda. At lunch we made our way back up to the delicatessen and ice cream shop, which Mother had opened inside Uncle Glenn's business and where we worked when we weren't in the fields. There we could get a barbecue sandwich or sub and maybe some coleslaw or tapioca pudding. (We were only allowed ice cream once a week because Mother said we'd eat all her profits otherwise.) After lunch we'd go back to the fields to work for another couple of hours.

Strawberry season ended with the beginning of blueberry season, where we again raced against each other. Only now, we wore buckets on strings around our necks and used both hands to thumb the blueberries into our containers. Rushing through the rows of berries, holding on to the full buckets so they didn't spill before we could empty them into the flats, we would mark the number of quarts and then race back to our row to fill the bucket again. At the end of the day, whoever had the most quarts of berries won bragging rights, and we started all over again the next day. The competition made the hours go by quicker—and it had the added advantage of making our pay envelopes fatter too. At the end of the week, Mr. Smith called us each by name and handed us tiny, narrow manila envelopes containing cash. You could see who the best pickers were by how much their envelope bulged.

The blueberry fields were much farther away from the retail store, so we usually took our breaks in the fields and chatted amongst ourselves. One day a girl I knew from school casually asked what my father did for a living. She wasn't being mean, only curious, but I didn't know what to say. My father was in the newspapers so often that everyone—teachers, classmates, neighbors, strangers we ran into in town—seemed to know who we were, even if we didn't know them. What was I going to tell her? That he didn't do anything anymore except fight the Church? Or that he's a farmer like he used to be? And then, the answer came to me with a delight I didn't bother to conceal.

"He's an author," I announced triumphantly.

Though I didn't think he made any income from his book, it was the truest thing I could say. Besides, it sounded not only respectable, but rather important as well. I was kind of proud of my quick thinking. It beat getting red in the face and stammering.

After work, we sometimes jumped in the creek by the blueberry bushes or rode our bikes home, grabbed our swimsuits, and pedaled four and a half miles to the Boiling Springs pool. The pool was often quite chilly, so we alternately swam and lay on the hot concrete like lizards to warm our shivering bodies. We bought candy, ice cream, and squares of pizza at the snack bar, and we listened to the jukebox pump out "Cat Scratch Fever" over and over. Sometimes I got up enough nerve to put quarters in the jukebox myself when nobody else was around.

I often observed the characters in this colorful, bustling community and was inspired by them. I watched the high school boys and girls on the diving board, sometimes performing swan dives with their arms outstretched like huge birds before gracefully surrendering to the water. Other times they jumped three or four times, flying higher each time before tucking into a tight ball and spinning until they opened out and entered the water so cleanly you could barely see a ripple. Still others, they took one quick, hard jump and jackknifed into a dive.

I wanted to dive elegantly and expertly like this, but I was too self-conscious and scared to do more than push off the board a bit, trying to dive without my legs collapsing over my head. The tall diving board seemed so high off the water—and everybody watched whenever someone climbed up to it. I didn't want to try anything where the whole pool society would see me flop. Nevertheless, I was determined to learn how to do what they did.

So, I set my sights on the small springboard on the other side of the pool. Though it had a much tighter spring so I couldn't get nearly as high a bounce, it was much closer to the water and commanded no one's attention. Plus, I didn't have as far to fall. I'd been teaching myself gymnastics using the side of the hill at home to make up the difference between my range of motion and the requirements of a new move. I wanted to do backflips like I'd seen a girl at school do, but I wasn't quite there yet. I figured with a little help from the springboard, I might be able to do some flips in the air. Eventually, if I worked at it long enough, I hoped I could look as graceful and masterful as the older boys and girls on the diving board.

After dogged practice on the springboard, I'd nearly accomplished enough rotation to complete a somersault dive and I was ecstatic. I just needed a little more revolution to get a clean entry. To do that, I'd need to coax some more spring out of this board, I felt sure. So, I decided to jump as hard as I could to buy enough airtime to complete my midair roll. This was going to be my moment of triumph, I thought, as I walked confidently onto the springboard.

I took a couple of preliminary jumps like I'd seen the older divers do, then I drove my legs into the springboard with all my might, pulled my knees up quickly, and prepared to roll. The next thing I knew, I was in the water wondering where I was. As I looked around to get my bearings, I saw blood and cartilage spreading out around my head and began to understand what had happened. I'd drawn my knees up so fast and hard that I drove them into my nose.

Humiliated, I looked in the lifeguard's direction, desperately hoping he had not seen the wreckage below his chair. He had. Silently, I pleaded with him. *Please, please don't jump in and rescue me.* Thankfully, he merely looked down and casually asked, "Are you okay?"

After that, I stuck to basic diving.

But despite my humiliating stint at the pool, living at home with only my three siblings *did* have its advantages: it stimulated me to try new things, learn on my own, and savor a sense of independence.

The Ways of the World

On those days spent at the pool, I found myself staring at the popular girls with envy, but mostly with longing. Besides looking sophisticated and confident, something else was different about them, something I couldn't quite place. *It's their legs*, I think. But what *exactly* was different? Their legs were so pretty: tan, smooth, and shiny. I wanted legs like that, but mine were always pale, partly because I wore jeans to work, and partly because my skin was so light that it never tanned, only burned.

No, it wasn't only the tan that set us apart. Looking down at my shins and knees, I noted how they were covered in bruises from the rocks we frequently encountered beneath the straw-carpeted space between the strawberry rows. But it wasn't just that the other girls didn't have bruises. There was something else they didn't have either: hair. *How was that possible?* I wondered. *How did a person get smooth, shiny legs?*

I puzzled over this mystery for weeks before finally concluding that scissors must be the only way. It would be a daunting and time-consuming task to cut each hair on both legs, but I was determined to have legs like the girls at the pool, so I reckoned I'd better get started. Since it wasn't only laborious but boring too, I figured it could be done while watching TV at the motel.

After I pulled out my scissors and began, Mother stared at my efforts dumbfounded.

"What on earth are you doing?" she asked.

It seemed perfectly obvious to me. "Trying to cut the hair off my legs."

Mother tried not to show her amusement. "Well, you use a razor for that."

"Like Daddy did for his whiskers?" I asked.

"Yes, you shave it off."

Now *I* was dumbfounded. It never occurred to me that she would know what to do. She didn't have shaved legs. That would have been considered vanity.

After that, I bought myself a razor, and soon I had legs as smooth as any other girl at the pool.

A Little More Polish

September ushered in eighth grade, and I was feeling somewhat more confident about fitting in with my more polished peers—or, more accurately, not sticking out quite as much. I no longer got long, ugly runs in my nylons. My shoes didn't get *quite* as scuffed, and the straps of the heels didn't break nearly as often. Overall, I was learning to moderate my "just fell off the turnip truck" tendencies. And though I still could not control the humiliating blush that came with embarrassment, I felt like I might be making progress on eliminating a few of the embarrassments themselves.

In sixth grade I had proudly made, in both pink and baby blue, the same outfit: wide pants with a long tunic-like top in a tiny flower print, secured by a matching belt. I'd learned to do smocking on the sewing machine and was quite proud of this intricate detail on my clothing, not to mention the accomplishment of the complicated collar.

One day, however, Benny caught up with me on the way home from school and asked if he could tell me something. When I agreed, he shyly and hesitantly said, "Those two outfits *kind* of look like pajamas." I was deflated and disheartened but recognized his good intentions. When I got home, I looked in the mirror. He was right, they did look like pajamas. *Why had I never noticed that before?*

After that, I began to sew more stylish, trendsetting outfits with crisper lines, bolder colors, and more elegant materials. And, back-to-school shopping now included a trip to the Reading Outlets for store-bought clothes.

During this particular year, I received even more feedback that helped me grow style-wise.

About halfway to school, the bus picked up Cheryl, a beautiful girl with dark hair who was a grade or two ahead of me and on the pom-pom squad with the other popular girls. She lived on a "gentleman's farm," which is what we called a farm that didn't have tractors parked all over the place, or people working when we passed, and the barn was always in pristine condition.

Prior to this year, I doubted she would have even noticed me, since I didn't run in her circles. However, that summer she was one of the blueberry pickers at Ashcombe, and during a work break in the field she suggested to

several of us girls that we all play a game. Each person would take turns looking at something, or someone, and see if the others could guess what that
person noticed was different between them. She volunteered to go first.
Looking pointedly at my head, then at Sandy H.'s, then at my sister's, then at
Joanne's, and finally at Sandy K.'s, she asked what we thought was different.

"Different colored eyes?" someone guessed.

"No," she said. She narrowed her focus to each girl's forehead.

When her meaning still eluded us, she looked directly at each of our
eyebrows. *Yeah, so?* I thought. Some were slightly different colors, but we all
basically had brown eyebrows. Finally, Sandy H. got it and exclaimed, "Oh,
you mean that we have plucked eyebrows and they don't? (The "they," of
course, referred to my sister and me.)

Triumphantly, Cheryl nodded.

*Plucked eyebrows? What was she talking about? Why would anybody do
that?*

Apparently, everyone but us country bumpkins groomed their eyebrows, and now I worried about this telltale sign being noticed by others too.
So, now that my pantyhose crises had largely become manageable, I decided
to tackle this new embarrassment and raise my standards.

I had no idea how one plucked eyebrows. As I stared at mine in the mirror, I wondered how I could get them into the thin, neat lines that both
Sandys had and not the wide bushy brows that gazed back at me. It was clear
I would have to remove a substantial amount of hair, so since the razor
worked on my legs so well, I figured this must be how the other girls did
their eyebrows too. Again, it never occurred to me to ask my mother, whose
eyebrows looked like mine.

My innocent effort was foiled again. Instead of ending up with pencil-
thin eyebrows, I had *no* eyebrows!

At school, I was repeatedly asked by classmates and teachers, in a tone
that clearly suggested it would be a dumb thing to do, if I shaved my eyebrows.

With as much emphatic dignity as I could summon, I said, "Of course
not," as if it was a ridiculous question.

Inside, however, I was immensely grateful that the week I shaved my
eyebrows was the week we were watching the epic movie *Nicholas and
Alexandra* about the last czar of Russia. At least some of the days were spent

in the dark where nobody could stare in astonishment at the defoliated skin where my eyebrows used to be.

Needless to say, I would never make this grooming mistake again.

Unwelcome News

In mid-November, another flurry of articles hit the newsstands, this time about our beloved farm.

Intelligencer Journal, November 10, 1977

Lancaster, Pennsylvania

Shunned Farmer Told His Land to Be Sold

Robert L. Bear, the "shunned" Cumberland County potato farmer, said he was visited by two deputy sheriffs, Wednesday, who told him his farm would be sold at sheriff's sale on Dec 14th.

Bear said Dec 14 will be the 19th anniversary of his marriage to Gale Gross Bear.

. . .

The visit of the officers of the Cumberland Valley Court was not unexpected, Bear said. He told the bank that financed him in the amount of $35,000 he would make no more payments on the loan after December of last year.

Brushes with Law

Since his excommunication Bear has had several brushes with the law and has sued the church in an attempt to destroy the 400-year-old doctrine of "shunning."

In numerous interviews he has said that the police incidents, the suit, a massive letter-writing campaign and other endeavors were oriented toward bringing his family together once more.

But last year he had just about given up hope. The refusal to pay the bank followed. Although still bitter against the church, Bear said Wednesday his wife is more to be pitied than censured. He has maintained she is a captive of the church—"just like the Moonies." But on Wednesday, he said he "could still forgive her, today."

Earlier, he said his brother-in-law, Glenn Gross, a bishop in the church who was instrumental in his excommunication, had read a statement in the church apologizing for having "gone to law" in the Bear suit.

His mother-in-law, Mrs. Israel Gross, Bear said, has publicly apologized for having called the police to restrain him.

But, the farmer said, it was not a change of heart. Gross, he said, had to apologize or face her own excommunication.

Bear said the confrontation with the deputies was very friendly. He laughed as he said they asked permission to hunt on his farm after they did their duty. Why not? was his reply.

Through her lawyer, Mother had proposed several times over the years that she and my father divide up their joint property: once, in 1974, then again at the custody hearing, and again this summer when she learned of the impending sheriff's sale. She proposed that he take the farm with 300 acres on the other side of the creek where his trailer was, and we would take the 100-acre Home Farm.

Daddy had vetoed each proposal.

PHILADELPHIA INQUIRER, NOVEMBER 14, 1977

. . .

Bear's wife also refused to cosign loans needed to buy seed and machinery for their farm, which they jointly own. And, as a result, the farm became less productive and his gross income fell from $100,000 in 1972 to about $5,000 last year, he said.

"I didn't realize that the avoidance would be that rigorous," he said his voice cracking with emotion. "I was well prepared for her not to unite with me as a wife, but I was not prepared for her not to unite with me in business so that we could provide for our children."

With his once-prosperous potato business failing, Bear said, he asked his estranged wife to sell the farm which he figures is worth $400,000 now. When she refused Bear decided that the only way to get rid of it was at a sheriff's sale.

He stopped paying taxes on the farm a year ago and in March stopped paying interest on the mortgage. In August the Dauphin Deposit Bank and Trust Co. in Carlisle, where he has the mortgage, notified Bear that it was foreclosing on the property and obtained court permission for the sheriff's sale.

"I thought, 'Well, let them foreclose,' said the soft-spoken husky farmer. "It was my only way to get out of this. I'm going to lose a lot of money, but I've lost a lot since this whole thing started. What does money mean if you don't have someone to spend it on?

Kidnapped

Monday, December 5, 1977, was a school day that began with a trace of mist in the air. There was a chance of rain in the forecast, but looking out the window, it didn't feel like it was going to be one of those dreary, late fall rains that casts a wet blanket over the entire day. Instead, it felt like the promise of the rarest type of rain—the kind that envelops bushes and trees in a fine mist, where the entire world glints and sparkles and looks like a magical storybook setting. One that gathers you into a sense of mystery and a deep enchantment with nature.

Normally, I'm running late for the bus. Morning always comes far too soon for my liking, and there are few where I don't groan loudly when the alarm goes off (even though I set the alarm as late as possible to still be able to make the 6:55 bus). Consequently, I'm almost always scooping papers off tables and racing around the house trying to collect books and homework. "Has anyone seen my purse?" is a frequent frantic yell as I rush wild-eyed from room to room. Finding the last elusive item, I fling open the door and rush huffing and puffing the quarter mile to the bus, hoping it doesn't pull away without me (which it has before).

Procrastination is a way of life for me. Numerous papers are written and assignments completed on the forty-five-minute bus ride to school. Sometimes I don't even put the finishing touches on a paper until I'm in homeroom. Worse, I study for planned tests but am somehow never prepared when the teacher announces a pop quiz.

Today, however, I am prepared, which makes it an unusually sedate morning. It's about 6:45 a.m. and my books are already in my arms. I even have my purse. I have plenty of time to stroll to the bus. All of this means that today, Leah, Benny, and I will all walk out of the house at the same time and down to the bus together.

Leah is first to the door. I follow closely with Benny right behind me. As Leah opens the front door, I'm thinking about how nice it feels to not be in a rush or to have to run for the bus when suddenly, a man leaps out from behind a bush and grabs Leah. Benny yanks the back of my shirt, violently dragging me back into the house. He slams the door and locks it.

"It's Daddy," he says urgently.

We didn't know it at the time, but he had parked his car a half mile away on the other side of Route 74 early in the morning, snuck up over the fields, and positioned himself behind a large bush by the front door. We had no inkling and no warning that he was in the vicinity. He must have staked out his position on a prior morning, undetected by us, so that he would know which door we normally exited for the bus stop.

Leah is outside the locked door, trapped in his clutches. When she realizes her own father has ambushed her, she shrieks, "Youuuu baaastard!"

Daddy holds Leah firmly and tells her that if she doesn't yell for help, if she comes along quietly and willingly, he won't tell anyone that she swore at him and called him a bastard.

Knowing his threat is serious that he will publish her word (and believing she had no choice anyway, that he would probably forcibly remove her from the property no matter what), she goes quietly.

That afternoon, the state police return her.

"He led me down through the fields below our house, across the busy road to his hidden truck, then drove me back to his trailer," Leah relates.

Mother promptly chops down the bush Daddy hid behind.

In the days that follow, even though Leah has kept up her end of the no-win bargain, Daddy makes no effort to keep his word to her—quite the opposite, in fact. He broadcasts her startled response in the manifestos he distributes, and will continue to broadcast her words to reporters for decades. *People* magazine will publish an article two years later with this quote from him, "My own son told me I was crazy. My little girl called me a bastard."

In other interviews, he will twist the definition of the event—the kidnapping—that morning.

> Once, he recalls, his 12-year-old daughter, Leah, cursed at him when he showed up for a visit.
>
> "I said, 'Well that's enough' and put her in the car and took her home," he recalled.
>
> Within hours the police arrived and Bear landed in a psychiatric hospital for three days "observation" he said.
> (*Gettysburg Times*, Sept 20, 1978)

(A note here in relation to the date of this article: the newspaper accounts of this "event" did not happen until nearly a year later, and in some cases, many years later. Reporters seemed to take their cues from my father about what was newsworthy, hence this day's events did not make the news until my father raised other issues that affected him.)

Despite the false impression he would actively cultivate for years, the reality was that Daddy was not coming for visitation. He couldn't. Judge Shughart had stripped those rights the prior December when Daddy took a sledgehammer to our door. Plus, visitation had always been at his house, not ours. And visitation at 6:45 a.m. on a school day? Arriving via surprise announcement from a shrub? It was ludicrous to the thinking mind.

These public assertions relied on the confidence, and by now certainty, that nobody would question his story. Not reporters. Certainly not his supporters. Not even us.

In the years to follow, I will often imagine what it must have been like for Leah to be just outside our door, with our having slammed and locked it, leaving her behind, protecting only ourselves.

Psychiatric Evaluation

After the kidnapping, Judge Shughart ordered Daddy to undergo a three-day psychiatric evaluation. Surely this time the psychiatrists would recognize that he was not well, we imagined.

Though Daddy had been ordered to undergo the evaluation, he would claim for decades, with never-diminished outrage, that the judge and state police lied about his actions to get him remanded to the psychiatric ward of the hospital. In contradiction, he also claimed that he had gone voluntarily. But however the public believed he got there, Daddy published his mental health records from this evaluation in the hope it would bolster his case that he had been profoundly mistreated.

The intake form states that:

> "The patient came to Holy Spirit Inpatient Mental Health Unit by way of the police. Reports were that he took her [Leah] off with a loaded gun, but the patient denies this entire story. He states that the police had not grounds to hold him. There had been a peace bond placed upon the patient for him not to visit his family or wife, but he states he informed the police that he would go back to get his wife and family as many times as possible and that they would have to arrest him on each occasion. It was felt then that the best thing to do would be to bring the patient in for psychiatric evaluation."

(Note here that nobody in our family has any clue where the assertion that Leah was taken off the school bus with a loaded gun came from. It did not come from any of us.)

The box is checked beside the verbiage:

> "The patient has acted in such a manner as to evidence that he would be unable, without care, supervision and the continued assistance of others to satisfy his or her need for nourishment, personal or medical care, shelter or self-protection and safety. I believe that there is reasonable probability that death, serious bodily injury or serious physical debilitation would ensue within 30 days unless treatment is afforded."

In the supporting detail requested beneath this section it reads:

"Mr. Bear has made threats of killing his children and/or his own suicide. A noose was noted in his barn. Mr. Bear is very distraught and possesses weapons at home."

The order for the psychiatric evaluation coincided generally with the news of the sheriff's sale of the Home Farm and once again caught the attention of a major newspaper.

THE WASHINGTON POST, DECEMBER 15, 1977

Victim of Shunning

. . . He [Daddy] lost visitation rights with the children after the break-in, but last Monday picked up his 12-year-old daughter and took her home. State police came to get the girl and returned her to her mother.

Bear was then taken to a hospital here, where he was voluntarily examined by psychiatrists. Bear says one of the psychiatrists "examined me for a persecution complex, couldn't find anything, and said I was truly being persecuted."

After this, Daddy will publish excerpts of his psychiatric evaluation results often and gleefully.

"This is a mild man who seems incapable of violent behavior."

"An intellectual profile such as this is counter-indicative of emotional disturbance."

"Mr. Bear is capable of thinking in abstract terms but has enough practical orientation not to lose sight of the concreteness of issues."

"There is no evidence of psychotic process in this man. His thinking is clear and his flow of ideas is quite relevant to the issue."

He will report in his manifestos that his examining psychiatrist believed he was innocent of the charges and told him: "I believe you. The only reason you are here is because Judge Shughart doesn't know what else to do with you." Daddy would also report that this psychiatrist offered to find something a little wrong if it would help, to which he replied, "No sir, I came here sane and the only way you can help me is to make sure I leave here sane."

Our mailbox, and no doubt nearby towns, receive a stream of his letters gloating that he had once again not only been found completely normal by the psychiatric profession, but that they sympathized with him, understood his frustrations, and considered his actions a reasonable response to his situation.

I found the results of his examination astonishing, exasperating, mind boggling, hair pulling, frustrating, and all around crazy-making.

A psychiatrist was supposed to be the referee of the fine line between sanity and insanity, or at least dangerous instability. Yet Daddy always seemed able to show up soft-spoken, reasonable, and sane for the "medical professionals." Although it wasn't a demeanor he was able to sustain for long, or in any circumstances that frustrated him, in their offices he projected an image of personable innocence, perennially wronged and unjustly accused by his wife, his children, the police, and the judges.

By now it was clear to me that my father had fallen under his own spell. The ends always justified his means. He was unfailingly the persecuted one, never the perpetrator. He was forever the victim. And yet the psychiatrists also seemed to consistently fall under that same spell. How could they of all people *not* see that there was something profoundly wrong with this man? They were supposed to be able to see through behavior and stories like this, yet time after time, they sided with Daddy, despite the glaring evidence otherwise.

All they had to do was take one look at the letters he pasted everywhere with their bolded words, irregular fonts, and crude and menacing pictures. A simpleton could have recognized that this was not a well man. Even from a distance the letters looked violent. And had the psychiatrist seen any of the prolific writings that Daddy called "love letters" to his wife? Writings filled with sexual perseveration and perverse, violent physical and sexual imagery? Of rationalizations for violence against a wife who would not be obedient? Rants filled with incoherent references to the Russians and the Germans? Of a female Russian writer who wrote about "the Romance of War" in WWII and the "Unhabitual mode of life, living without women, with that constant longing for a woman that was like an unbearable itch"? How it was like a frigid Russian winter for him, too, how he had an unbearable itch to pull the trigger of his loaded gun. This was intermixed with bizarre quotes about Europeans killing each other because they didn't want to eat their dead, Bible quotes on women and femininity, and metaphors of dogs in heat in reference to women.

Did they not read his letters about loaded guns pushed up against the roof of every Mennonite's mouth and the mouths of the judges who ruled against him? The ones where he veered off about being gang-raped by the Church and then proclaimed:

> "Am I too harsh on you and Mennonites? Then just give this trial run in your mind. Just rise up enough to pull the panties of truth only up over your Court of lies and you know every-one of your Mennonite boyfriends and girlfriends will shun you and loathe you more than had you given everyone an incurable dose of genital herpes!"

And let's not overlook his relentless claim to being honest and in sole possession of the Truth, or how easy it would have been for someone to obtain these letters for a three-day inpatient evaluation. Daddy regularly blanketed the surrounding towns with them like paratroopers on D-day in Normandy. It would not have surprised me if he brought some to his psychiatric evaluation to show the doctors how he was being persecuted.

Nevertheless, the psychiatrists always seemed to easily arrive at the same conclusion: that he was of perfectly sound mind.

One of the psychiatrists who evaluated him this time went even further.

> "The question of paranoia ('Delusions of persecution or grandeur') was raised. Rorschach responses and tat stories yielded no evidence of this disorder beyond a slight tendency to be somewhat suspicious and defensive. This was not seen in clinical proportions and may well be real when one considers the situation in which the man finds himself."

Daddy would take particular satisfaction in the psychiatrist validating his persecution as real.

For the next forty-plus years, he would never miss an opportunity to re-mind us that there was nothing wrong with his head. Every psychiatrist who evaluated him gave him a clean bill of health, he relentlessly reminded us.

And the newspapers . . .

It was as if Daddy wrote the articles himself. Anytime the Leah incident was brought up, they merely echoed his description of the events as a "visit" or "picking her up" and taking her back home to correct her language. They highlighted her startled response without any context, just as Daddy would for the rest of his life.

The pertinent detail about the state police being called elicited no more investigative journalism than the splintered front door had—even when Daddy published his own psychiatric evaluation, which clearly states:

> "There had been a peace bond placed upon the patient for him not to visit his family or wife, but he states he informed the police that he would go back to get his wife and family as many times as possible and that they would have to arrest him on each occasion."

No one—neither psychiatrists nor reporters—seemed to wonder about the veracity of a man's story, or sanity, who divulged that he was coming for visitation on a school day with a protective order in place. Or how unusual it was for a judge to order a three-day psychiatric evaluation. His word was simply taken at face value—the word of a man perpetually and earnestly insistent about his honesty.

My father would harp on the outrage of being accused of holding up a school bus with a loaded gun for decades, effectively obscuring his own ac-tions that day completely. The kidnapping became almost instantaneously invisible, buried beneath his wrath, along with the reporters' and public's outrage about what was done to *him* on December 5, 1977.

No kidnapping charges were filed.

No trial was ever held.

Gone Forever

Within a week of the kidnapping, the newspapers carry headlines like **Farmer Loses Family, Farm After Shunning** (Tampa), and sympathetic articles from around the country begin like this one from the *Arizona Daily Star*.

> First Robert Bear lost his church, then his wife and six children. Now he has lost his home and 100-acre farm he started 23 years ago.

On December 14, 1977, our beloved, magical Home Farm is sold at sheriff's auction for $130,000. After debts and mortgages were satisfied, $90,000 remained to be split between Mother and Daddy. Daddy retreated to the 300-acre Other Farm with his money while Mother's share of the proceeds went to satisfy part of the mortgage on the house we were living in and to pay back Benny and David.

The previous week's events and the sale are covered under the same banner.

The Washington Post, December 15, 1977

A Victim of Shunning

Robert Bear, "shunned" by his wife and six children the past five years under the 400-year-old practice of a fundamentalist religious sect, sat alone in the kitchen of his farmhouse today—his 19th wedding anniversary—just hours after his home and 100 acres around it had been sold at a county sheriff's sale to satisfy debts his outcasting had brought.

"I don't know what it is to have a wife that's mine and doesn't come after the church. I'd like to know what it is to have a wife to call your own," Bear said, his voice cracking.

Recapping the history of the suit against the church that was dismissed because the judge ruled that the court can't interfere with the free exercise of religious belief, the article adds:

"Justice is for those who can afford it," Bear said bitterly. "Those people (church) can outmoney me."

The article also briefly recaps the history of the publicity campaign, hiring of a private detective, the break-in at our home last year, his lost visitation rights, and recent events.

> . . . Claiming that "the only thing that can strike me down now is God," Bear says he wants to take his wife home for "deprogramming."
>
> Bear makes it clear that he wants to be arrested and go to jail. That, he says, would give him the opportunity to expose the "shun" policy. He admitted the break-in of his wife's house had been partly in the hope of being jailed.
>
> "The guy wants to be a martyr," said an assistant district attorney here. "I can't tell you what we're going to do. He wants to get in jail and nobody wants to put him there."

Three days later, the personal cost to Daddy of the sale of the farm is reported.

PHILADELPHIA INQUIRER, DECEMBER 15, 1977

A Time to Sell and a Time to Stay and Fight on

Robert Bear, who only a few weeks ago was considering leaving Cumberland County altogether, said yesterday he had changed his mind and that he would continue to farm 300 acres he owns north of here.

"I don't like to run from life. It's what I think I should do," he said. "I guess $130,000 is the price I paid for the use of a wife for years."

The anguish of separation was evident when Bear, 48, talked about the sale yesterday, which coincidentally was his 19th wedding anniversary.

"Children are your best crop," he said in a voice that quivered. "Without them no crops matter."

Though Daddy had bought the Home Farm as a young man and he, too, must have loved it—and forcing the sheriff to sell the farm certainly appeared like Daddy was cutting off his nose to spite his face—we were not remotely confused about why he had refused all settlement offers, nor why he stopped paying the taxes and mortgage on it.

We all understood exactly why.

Revenge.

Daddy knew how much we loved the Home Farm. Selling it was just one more way of punishing all of us for our failure to offer absolute loyalty and blind obedience to him.

Any hope we'd secretly nurtured that we might someday be able to go home was forever dashed.

CHAPTER EIGHT

1978

My soul is my guide.
—RUMI

The Wish

Before we officially rang in 1978, the question of where we would spend Christmas break of 1977 hung over us like an ominous cloud. Gone were the days of excitement leading up to the holiday; those days had now become about where we could best stay hidden from Daddy.

While we had spent the prior year's break in the church nursing home, we took preemptive measures this most recent Christmas, leaving our home to avoid a repeat of last year's frantic departure. Lucky for us, Grandma's employee, Julia, graciously allowed us to stay in her home while she and her husband went on vacation to Florida.

Even during the break, however, we still had jobs to attend to. Since it was wintertime and there wasn't work outside in the fields, we feared Daddy showing up at Ashcombe even more. Instead of being able to see him coming and have enough time to run, being sequestered inside the store offered too little warning to escape. So, to keep us protected, Uncle Glenn sent the four oldest of us to Perry county, which was thirty minutes away, to work where he owned a couple of greenhouses.

With David at the wheel, we set out on a patchwork of roads across the county until we came to the winding road that led up and over the north mountain. Cresting the top, we entered what felt like another world from a simpler—but not happier—place and time. The remote, tiny town of Shermans Dale was dotted with painfully modest houses, evoking an apathy we shared. The only spark of life seemed to reside in a small convenience store gas station that provided the economy of this hamlet, so although we had all packed lunches, we were happy there was a place we could treat ourselves to hot cocoa and snacks on our work breaks.

The greenhouses Uncle Glenn owned here were where seedlings were grown and the plants eventually sold at Ashcombe. However, in early January, there wasn't a plant or worker in sight. Instead, the plastic had been torn from the metal framework, and the greenhouse looked like a creaky, rusty, metal skeleton. Our job was to climb up the poles and paint the frames of the greenhouses with a silver coating that covered the exposed metal and prevented more rust. Not only was it challenging to straddle the high metal poles, it was bitter cold and windy. Plus, the chill slowed down our movements such that to an observer, we probably appeared lazy even though we were maneuvering our frozen limbs as fast as we could.

As I swiped the paintbrush methodically and mindlessly back and forth, I looked up occasionally to survey the desolate location. It appeared to me like sullen gray skies formed a depressing canopy here *every* day. Hour after hour, I contemplated our situation. I couldn't even muster the energy to be angry anymore. Instead, I was resigned. Our circumstances felt hopeless, as if it would be this way forever and we would never be able to truly get away from Daddy. No matter where we went, he stalked and found us. I had become so weary of running, so tired of all of us having to look over our shoulders all the time, so numb from looking intently at every car that passed by to see if maybe it was him.

Mother always cautioned us not to talk about our situation to others, but occasionally we discussed it amongst ourselves. One time, despite keeping our voices low, Uncle Glenn overheard us.

"Now, you children don't need to feel sorry for yourselves," he said. "There are others who have it much worse."

Up on that pole with my paintbrush, even in the freezing cold, I thought about Uncle Glenn's words and agreed that he was probably right. I knew there had to be others who had it far worse. But still, I was sick of our situation and desperately wished it would end. Leaving the farm didn't end it, and moving to a different house didn't either.

It was then that a terrible thought pushed its way into my mind: *I wish Daddy would just die.*

Though I felt a twinge of guilt, I could not imagine any other way out of our nightmare. I sank into the comfort of this thought and felt my body relax into sweet relief. *That would solve the problem*, I decided. But then I thought, *Maybe God will punish me for this sin.* It *was* an awful thing to wish on somebody. I didn't wish for him to get hurt or to be in pain. *Maybe he could get in a car accident where he would never know what hit him and not feel a thing. Or better yet, he could just die peacefully in his sleep like our great-grandmother did. Please, God. Please*, I begged. *Can't he just die? Can't he just go away?*

Planning for the Future

Although I have already vowed that if we ever do make it out of this nightmare, I am never, ever going to be dependent upon a man who could use money to control me; and although I set my intention a long time ago on making my own money, I decide I need even more insurance for the future: I want to make *good* money so that my financial independence will never be in question.

Even though Daddy has always scoffed at any of us pursuing our education past high school, I figure that to make that kind of money, a person would have to go to college. So, I decide that's what I'm going to set my sights on.

I have no idea how to get into college, or what I will do after graduating, but to combat the helplessness I feel, I begin escaping in my imagination. I start dreaming up elaborate five- and ten-year plans where my life is happy and prosperous and independent. *I'll make enough money to buy back the Home Farm*, I think. *I'll live a life of freedom and safety.*

David was an excellent role model for the ingenuity I sought. He was always finding some new hobby or starting a new business. You may recall that he was the driving force behind the candles we made on the farm and sold to Ashcombe. Then, after we left the farm, he had a business removing wasp and yellow jacket nests from homes and selling the dead insects (at a considerable price) for anti-venom production. He became interested in beekeeping too, and now, at the top of our driveway sit two beehives he tends assiduously. He is so knowledgeable about every new task he takes on that he can easily teach us the intricacies. He shows us siblings the fascinating world of bees and tells us about their unique society, how to spot the queen, and about the role of the worker bees. He demonstrates how to put on the full suit and netted hat so that we won't get stung while inspecting the hive, and he shows us how to use a smoker to sedate the bees when inserting new empty honeycomb racks or retrieving full racks of honey. He's even made honey butter and sold it, along with five-by-five-inch slabs of dripping honeycomb at Ashcombe.

This is precisely why David is the perfect person to talk to about my dreams. He is only three years older than me, but he has a way of explaining things, the way a caring adult would, so that they make sense. He willingly tutors us girls, and we often ask for his help when we get stuck, particularly on math problems, which he's extremely good at. I don't know how he knows so much about the world and the way it works, but I figure it must come from the books he's always reading. I am so grateful for all his help that I volunteer to monogram his name and a beehive logo on his white coverall bee suit with the embroidery function on my sewing machine.

On the day I told David I wanted to go to college, he gave me his usual sage advice, in which he always advocated ambitious goals.

"You can do it, but you need to sign up for four years of math, four years of science, and three years of foreign language in high school. And you need to make sure you take all the prerequisites so you can take physics and calculus by your senior year." Then he added, "Oh, and sign up for the hardest classes available. Take all the honors classes and AP (Advanced Placement) classes you can."

Though I always endeavored to be in the highest level classes, I'd never heard of AP courses, which were only offered in high school. These classes sounded exciting, but I would have never voluntarily signed up for four years of math or science if it wasn't required. Still, I never doubted David knew what he was talking about and was determined to follow his instructions to the letter.

After David helped me lay out this strategy for selecting my high school classes for the next year, my first order of business became clear: I needed to convince my math teacher, in whose class I was no star, to give me a recommendation that allowed me to select the highest level math the following year. While I was never as good at math as my two older brothers, I hated to be in anything but the top class (though thus far I usually had to struggle strenuously to get included on the roster). Now, staring at the dubious face of my teacher, I assured her I would study hard and be able to handle the class. Reluctantly, she wrote me the recommendation.

With that piece of paper in hand, my brother's plan was set in motion.

I was convinced I was already on my way to a better life.

The Thrill of Victory

From the early years on the farm, our sibling Darwinian "branding" ritual was to confer less-than-flattering nicknames on each other. Some of mine were "ugly," "dog," and later, "flat." Each additional nickname added a layer of detail about the person until they became a kind of shorthand description. Generally, as evidenced by mine, our labels had a uniting theme. In my case, they denoted that I was nondescript looking. In other words, plain. In fact, I was plain in every department.

Whereas David (though his nicknames were no more flattering than the ones I'd been given) could have easily been called "Smart"—an adjective everyone knew unequivocally applied to my eldest brother—my school report card sometimes said, "Does not work up to potential." I found this intensely frustrating and confusing. I took school seriously, worked hard to keep up with my classmates, and wanted to do well. Yet, when I would come home openly proud of an A on my report card in a difficult class, Mother didn't attribute it to brains. Instead she noted with a wry chuckle, "Well, you *are* very determined."

Actually, trying hard was the one place I *did* stand out. When I wanted something, I was like a dog with a bone. I simply refused to give up. To be honest, I've always thought this trait was my one true genius. And on eighth grade track and field day, that determination paid off and set me on a whole new trajectory in life.

You already know that I loved winning ribbons and thus entered as many events as possible on track and field days. This year was no different. What *was* different was that a new event was being offered: a cross-country race. So, in addition to the field events and the races that took place on the track, I would enter a race laid out on a grass course. Winding its way around the huge school grounds, it was longer—by far—than any race I'd run before. It was technically a separate event for boys and girls, but we would all run together, competing against only our same gender.

When the day finally arrived and the starting gun was fired, we all bolted off together. The race began at a fast clip as eager runners vied for the lead, jostling each other and jockeying for open room to run freely. It was a scorching day already, which felt much hotter as the course turned up the near vertical hill behind the high school. Once we reached the top, down the hill we thundered only to have to chug back up again. The course looped around the wide field hockey grounds and the baseball field, around academic buildings, across parking lots and back onto the grass before heading back for another punishing encounter with that monster hill.

As I huffed and puffed, I stared at the daunting vertical rise ahead. For the first time in my life, I questioned whether I could finish the race. We had been shown the entire course in the orientation walk prior to starting the race, but now, I couldn't remember where the end was. *I hate this awful event*, I thought. My legs were burning and I was gasping for air, drawing deep labored breaths into my aching lungs. *What was I thinking when I signed up for this?* It was so hot I could barely see through my sweat, but I kept stumbling forward blindly, figuring I would go until I couldn't take another step.

I had started out in the middle of the pack, and now I dimly registered that the space surrounding me had thinned, making it infinitesimally cooler. In fact, I sneaked a peak behind me and discovered that no one was around. *Have I fallen that far behind?* I wondered.

Cresting the hill, I raised my eyes toward the salvation of the finish line in the distance. I saw only a couple of runners ahead of me, neither of whom were girls. I couldn't help but wonder if my competition had already finished. But when I reached the finish line, I was elated to learn I had not only beaten all the girls, but all the boys, except for three. Bent over, panting with my hands on my thighs, I was stunned and feeling on top of the world—until I discovered *how* I'd won: most of the runners had dropped out of the race because the course was so difficult.

I had won the blue ribbon by attrition. But it didn't matter. It was mine.

At the finish line, a group of high school girls I'd never met, outfitted in the red and white uniform of our high school track team, crowded around me with big smiles as I received my award. "You should go out for the cross-country team next year," a few of them said. "We need you."

And so, puffed up by their enthusiastic invitation and the confidence of that blue ribbon, I didn't need a lot of convincing to make that hill a part of my life for the next four years.

The Burglar

After years of having virtually no friends besides my siblings, I am overjoyed to now have a group of friends from the strawberry and blueberry fields. We have remained close since we first started working together, and we take turns hanging out at each other's houses (though some parents don't let their children come to ours because our parents are supposedly divorced, which would be a "bad influence").

Our neighbor Sandy H. is one of our closest friends, and she often comes back to the house with us after picking berries. Sometimes, however, we forget our key and have to sit outside till Mother comes home. After one or two forgotten key episodes, we arrive at a foolproof solution. Beside the window of the room Leah and I share is a chimney, and the sides of it are laddered in bricks where the shape gets smaller, just like miniature stair steps. We discover that if we climb up the chimney "steps" to the window (which we've left open a crack), we can push it up and crawl inside. Squeezing through the window behind us, Sandy laughs as we effectively break in to our own house.

One night, Leah and I are in our bedroom when a face suddenly looms in our window. We are so startled that we run screaming from the room.

"It's Daddy! It's Daddy!"

Benny and David hear us and rush into the living room. They reach the couch about the same time we do, bend down to lift the base, and roughly flip it over to expose four baseball bats pre-positioned for just such an emergency. We each grab a bat, and holding them high we head back toward the bedroom to scout out the situation. But no one is there.

Our patrol slinks cautiously out toward the living room, clearing rooms as we move: the bathroom, Mother's bedroom, Susie and Sharon's room.

We are perplexed. Leah and I both swear we saw a face.

As we creep through the living room to check out the rest of the house, the doorbell rings. When we turn around, Sandy H.'s smiling but confused face greets us through the window.

We quickly tip the couch back into its proper place and slide the bats underneath, hoping she doesn't notice.

When we open the door, she seems to sense the fright ignited in all of us. "I'm sorry . . . I was only trying to prank you."

Not having shared anything about our family saga, Sandy could only be aware of what was going on from the newspapers or her parents, but she was too polite to ask any questions.

"It's okay," I say, trying to laugh it off. "We thought you might be a burglar."

None of us tell her that the burglar we were so afraid of is our own father.

Joining the Team

Figuring I should learn more about running before I begin training for the high school team, I purchase a subscription to *Runners World* and devour every article. In those pages I fall into the elite world of long-distance runners: the legendary Bill Rodgers, who won the New York marathon for the third time; Grete Waitz, who becomes my new hero; Alberto Salazar; and Joan Benoit (later Benoit Samuelson), who will win the Boston marathon the following year.

Between the articles, I discover the variety of running shoes available to me, each with a plethora of advertised features. Despite the cost, I invest in a pair of bright yellow Nike running shoes, with a turquoise swoosh and the new waffle soles. Every free moment I have, I put in the miles to prepare for this upcoming commitment I've made, and for the first time, I experience the runner's high I have been reading about.

Throughout the summer I continue to explore the world of distance running through magazines and the marathoners featured. I am both fascinated by the epic achievement of running 26.2 miles and repulsed by the physical aftereffects. For example, the magazine reported that Bill Rodgers peed black after his record-breaking marathon. *Could I really endure that?* I wondered. Though I'm currently logging miles for the much shorter three-mile race I'll be competing in for the cross-country team, I nevertheless continue studying the training tips for marathons.

When the school year begins, I am officially the first person in my family to be on a school athletic team. Both David and Benny would have enjoyed afterschool activities, I know. Benny, in particular, is naturally athletic and excels at every sport, but despite wanting to play football, he doesn't have that opportunity. Instead, he has to work to help support the family. I feel sad for my brothers and their lost opportunities, but I'm also grateful that I have this chance.

Mr. Harbold, the coach for both the boys' and girls' cross-country team, watches us stretch on the grass while he chews tobacco, periodically turning his head to spit in the opposite direction. He's a tough but fair coach who insists that we train hard. We run endless miles on the country roads near the school while he drives alongside in a small white pickup to time our runs and ensure our safety. And we don't just run country roads; we run hills— lots and lots of hills, including that same awful one from track and field day. In fact, our school's cross-country course is famous for this hill.

"Mastering your own course is paramount if you want to win meets during the season," Mr. Harbold says, touting the purpose of the relentless hill drills that end in heaps of exhausted teenagers.

Besides toughening up our bodies, Mr. Harbold teaches us about something I've never heard of before but find intriguing: the concept of mental toughness. He says we should imagine a short rope around the runner in front of us and never let them get farther away than that, because if we allow them out of our range, we are likely to give up. It doesn't take me long to understand that the mental training is almost as important as the physical.

On the weekends I still have shifts at Ashcombe, but when I'm not working I train hard on the plentiful hills in our neighborhood. I also begin to run increasingly longer distances on the surrounding country roads. It turns out that my fascination with marathons has edged out my fear, and I have decided to enter the Harrisburg marathon in November. I want to be well prepared; plus, the more I run, the more I enjoy it as I achieve the invigorating runner's high.

And it's not just the high I get from working out that fuels my new passion; my teammates are wonderful too. Even though we are all competing against each other for starting positions, they are wonderfully positive and encouraging. I love the way the team captain and top runners cheer me on (though I occasionally make the rookie mistake of starting out too fast and then fade as they pass me); it's like having a group of caring big sisters—and the boys are mostly nice too. Even at meets, the girls' and boys' teams cheer each other on.

In the evenings after practice, I get off the activity bus around 6:30 p.m. and amble up the road toward home. Although it is dark, I am tired and happy. Happy to be part of a team. Happy to finally be moving forward and succeeding, as if an exciting future is unfolding.

Another Abduction

In September, with my move to the ninth-grade building firmly established, an article runs that telegraphs Daddy's intentions, though for us it sounds like the same old news.

THE GETTYSBURG TIMES, SEPTEMBER 20, 1978

Shunned Robert Bear Still Seeking Return of Wife and Children

. . . there will be more attempts at reconciliation, and he'll use force if necessary, said Bear who once sued the church in court for alienation of his wife's affections and lost.

"In fact, I think this weekend, I'll go down and bring that little woman and those children home" he said more than half jokingly, "Or they'll put me in jail."

Not long after the article's release, David goes missing. A whole day passes before we somehow learn that Daddy has taken him. We figure he probably took David to the trailer, but we don't know for sure.

Worried, I anxiously ask Mother, "When is David coming back?"

"I don't know," she replies in her usual stoic manner. "We haven't heard anything."

"What will Daddy do to him?"

"I don't think he'll hurt him."

I'm not so sure of that, I think.

By the second day, I can't stand it any longer.

"Mother, *do* something!" I plead. "Call the police."

But instead of mirroring my concern, she says, "Patty, you know we don't do that. We must turn the other cheek. Besides, I've never thought your father would hurt you children."

But her response doesn't placate me in the least. David has been gone too long without hearing anything. All I can think is, *What could be happening to him?* Beside myself with worry, I decide that enough is enough.

"Mother, I don't *care* about your stupid Church rules. *Do* something," I demand. "Call the police."

But still she refuses.

On the third day, we get a call from David, asking for Benny to come pick him up at a friend's house in a nearby town. We are all so excited to hear from him, and I'm *so* relieved he's coming home safe and sound, that none of us ask him any questions.

When we hear the car pull into the driveway, Mother moves to stand at the open mudroom door, and we children line the sides as if we are awaiting the arrival of a loved one getting off an airplane. My heart is pounding as David opens the outside door and I hear his footsteps. Upon seeing us all waiting to surprise him, however, he stops. I stare at him wordless, frozen.

One effect of Vietnam that lingers into 1978 is that all the boys wear their hair long. No one wears a crew cut or anything remotely similar.

David has always had a wealth of thick brown hair that blankets his head so thoroughly, it sometimes looks like a puffy chocolate helmet. But now, except for a couple of isolated spiky tufts like random outcroppings, his skull is naked. All of us are shocked into speechlessness. My brother's baldness is unfathomable to me.

Before any of us has a chance to move, David breaks the silence. He tells us that Daddy kidnapped him and took him back to his trailer. Then, he led David to the most isolated spot on the farm by a wooded ravine, far from the dirt road where no neighbors could see or hear what Daddy was about to do. There in the woods, he held my brother down while he shaved his head bare. David gave Daddy the best fight he could to get away, which is why a few random tufts were left behind.

For two full days, Daddy lectured and berated David while sporadically hitting him. But at some point, David managed to run away, slipping into the woods behind the farm where he could not be easily seen, then making his way several miles across neighboring fields and farms to the house of a beekeeper friend of his, where he asked to borrow the phone and called home.

David relates all of this quickly with a half smirk, as if he isn't bothered by the event at all. But I notice the pale red flush that has again found a home on his cheeks, the deadness of his skin, the dullness in his eyes. It is the same "afterward" face he always wears.

Across the doorway, I see my own shock and horror reflected in Susie's and Sharon's faces. With their eyes fixed on David's head, they crumple almost in unison to the floor, sobbing.

But I feel a different reaction. It erupts like a force of nature as I absorb the ghost-like appearance of my brother. *This is it. No more.* I turn my body away so that no one can decipher in my eyes the decision I have just made.

I am going to kill Daddy. I am going to end this once and for all.

I will go to jail for life, I know. That is inevitable. But I will make sure no one else can be implicated. No other lives need to be ruined. If nobody else knows what I'm about to do, they cannot be held culpable.

Silently, I begin to plot.

How can I kill him? The .22. We still have it for some reason. Yes, that would work. I know how to shoot it.

But my logical mind butts in with its logic, seemingly trying to talk me out of it.

You're not old enough to drive yet. You don't have a driver's license. And you can't get anyone else to drive you because you cannot involve them.

Fine, I'll *run* out there, I vow undeterred. I've been running long miles for months training for the Harrisburg marathon in November. That would work. I could do it.

Someone will surely see you on the roads carrying a rifle and get suspicious, my logical mind counters again.

Okay. Well then, I'll use a knife. I'll get a big one, but I'll conceal it in my clothing while I run. I remember how I traveled on foot to my friend's house who lived out beyond our Middlesex meeting house. It took me hours, and I was exhausted by the time I reached her house. I realize then that Daddy's trailer might be too much of a challenge to reach on foot. It's a thirty-minute drive by car and probably twice as far as my friend's house.

Plus, he's so much bigger and stronger than you. He would surely overpower you if all you had was a knife.

Frustrated, and feeling defeated and helpless, I retreat to my bedroom. My plan is over before it even begins.

That fall and winter, David wears a wig to school. His classmates mock him, but he pretends not to care. He even wears a knit cap at home until his hair grows out a bit. Perhaps the saddest part is that it is his senior year of high school, and since he won't allow any photos taken of him, he is virtually erased from his yearbook.

Sadder still is that no newspaper article will ever mention what happened to David, not even a hint.

There is, however, a sudden flurry of newspaper articles around the nation and in Canada shortly after David returns home. Daddy makes the same charges year after year, but a startling new one catches my eye in the *Los Angeles Times*, beneath the headline "'Shunned' Man Retains Hope":

> . . . his oldest son, David, 17, in a fit of anger, once tried to run
> him over with a tractor.

Since I know nothing resembling this ever happened when we were living on the farm, and since Daddy never missed an opportunity to detail how he was victimized by his wife and children, I can only conclude that some version of this incident happened while he was holding David hostage over the weekend.

Not surprisingly, in record time after he kidnapped David, Daddy has already twisted and quietly repackaged the incident as an assault on *him*. He has always managed to reverse reality so that his victim is painted as the aggressor, and this article mirrors it, saying that "he [Daddy] will keep trying for reconciliation despite repeated failure." It also quotes him as saying, "I intend to get my wife and children straightened around. That's what keeps me going."

Once again, no kidnapping charges are filed.

And once again, no trial is held.

Trying on Careers

The assault on David only deepens the fierceness of my resolve to never accept the life my Mother's culture has allotted her and her children.

I redouble my efforts, imagining a better future where *I* am the master of my destiny. Dreaming is free. I can create whatever I want and then crumple it up, throw it away, and dream even bigger. Each time, I create an architecture for my dreams with a To-Do list of achievements to build these visions. Experimenting with different goals and their feasibility makes me feel like I am doing something, even if nothing is changing right now.

I begin trying on possible careers like trying on outfits at the store to see how they fit.

A doctor would certainly be a good job, I muse. *They make lots of money.* But then I remember that medical students must dissect cadavers. I am too squeamish for that and dry heave merely at the thought. Since seventh grade, I have been 100 percent successful in volunteering to be the note taker for my dissecting groups without anyone catching on. The other students love dissecting, and I plan to continue facilitating their passion throughout high school while I stealthily avoid it.

After trying on a few more professions that I deem unsuitable for me, I arrive at the idea of being an architect and designing houses, and I enroll in an architecture class as an elective. The most important thing in this class, however, is not imaginative design but having a sharp pencil so that the width of our lines on blueprints is exactly consistent. This level of neatness is demonstrably beyond my abilities. It also escapes my comprehension how this can be such a priority in the creative process of designing a home. I promptly cross architect off the list and go back to the drawing board.

In seventh grade, they gave our class an aptitude test to reveal what we were good at. I scored highest on English and mechanical abilities. Yet up until this year, English classes have been a mind-numbing, tedious exercise in grammar and punctuation, so I find this result quite discouraging. *Perhaps I could be a librarian*, I think. But I immediately see the work as too dry and holding little interest for me. At one time, I thought briefly that I might enjoy being a journalist, but "reporter" is a dirty word in our family. Hence, I would never *dare* to even mention this idea out loud and summarily dismiss it.

So I return to the "mechanical abilities" I'm supposed to be so good at.

Of *this* result I had been furious for days, ranting to whoever would listen. I didn't like cars or machines, and I had no desire to be a mechanic. "I don't want to spend my days greasy and dirty under the hood of a car!" I fumed. (Of course nobody had explained what "mechanical abilities" actually meant. It never occurred to me that there was an alternative explanation, and it would be a decade before I understood on a more complex level that I scored high in this area because I was able to visualize how shapes fit together, how one shape might drive another to produce a force or action, and how gears and levers interacted.)

In the meantime, it did occur to me that the test might reflect the years of sewing I had done. After all, I had repeatedly taken oddly shaped pieces of clothing patterns from Butterick and McCalls—a piece of a bodice, a shoulder, a collar, arms, cuffs—from being a confusing array of amputations to fitting together in one whole. Even with the directions, I still had to reason how things fit together, and I had to learn to stitch seams on the wrong side of the fabric while imagining what the result would be when turned right side out.

But I don't envision myself having a career as a seamstress. So, having eliminated all other career possibilities, I settle on one that I think will suit me quite well. I love flowers! I have swooned over them my entire life, finding them intoxicating, beguiling, and soulful. I've recently planted a tiny garden on a portion of a hillside at the edge of our woods, which I bordered with rocks gathered from the woods, then transplanted divisions of succulents (called "hens and chicks") and anything else Mother could spare from her garden. I reason that because I enjoy gardening, and because, along with farming, it seems to run in our family, I should be successful in this field. Plus, I have years of experience with indoor plants at Ashcombe. From labeling the pots season after season, I know all the common and botanical names of each one.

It's settled. I decide to become a landscape architect and design gardens. Furthermore, I set my sights on getting accepted at the prestigious Longwood Gardens college of horticulture. Having a goal and a more detailed strategy for the future always makes me feel good, and I've met several knowledgeable and creative graduates of Longwood Gardens who've worked at Ashcombe. I know it's difficult to get accepted there, but I also have no doubt that it's possible.

Running Scholarship

Cross country is going far better than I ever expected. My teammates remain supportive of me, and I have risen to number three on the team, which means that I will earn a varsity letter my freshman year.

Now that my world is expanding and my dreams are taking shape, however, I begin to understand the implication of attending college. Specifically, how much it will cost. Some cross-country runners talk about athletic scholarships, and I eagerly attach to this idea because I know I will have to pay for everything myself. I figure Mr. Harbold, though he's not a big talker, could give me advice on what I need to do to get one of these scholarships, so I confidently approach him one day at practice.

"Mr. Harbold, I want to get a full running scholarship to college. What do I have to do to make that happen?"

He looks at me and silently strokes his bearded chin over and over. He says nothing for a long time, and I feel my chest sink and my stomach start to hurt. I stop breathing as I see in his eyes that he doesn't think I'm talented enough.

Finally, he says something about needing to win at the state level. His tone, though not unkind, suggests the vast gulf between that goal and my level of talent.

I walk away dejected, processing my disappointment. But then, I quickly shift back into determination, deciding to ignore his indirect judgment of my abilities. *I don't have any other options*, I think, *so I AM going to get a scholarship. What does he know about me, anyway? It's only my first year. He'll see.*

The end of the cross-country season ends with the county-wide meet. Out of eighty to a hundred runners, I come in 20th. I feel good about being in the top 20 or 25 percent for my first year, but it's not nearly good enough in my book. I want to be right at the top.

Soon after, I receive my first varsity letter at the athletic awards banquet. Mother can't come for the same reason she couldn't come to any of the meets—because they always say a prayer. I understand and I am used to it by now. Plus, whatever disappointment I may feel about Mother not being there is eclipsed by my thrill. *Varsity!* I didn't even know what varsity meant when the school year began. I had never expected to be number three on the team; I just wanted to belong somewhere. Next year, though, I want to be number one. *If I could advance to number three on the team, I can get to number one too.* Right then I decide that whatever I must do to get there, I will.

For now, I celebrate this accomplishment by ordering a letter jacket in the red and white school colors like the football players, field hockey players, and other jocks. *I am now one of them.* My name comes professionally embroidered over the heart, with the varsity letter sewn prominently on the right side and "Cumberland Valley Cross Country" announced in a large semi-circle on the back.

I will wear this coat everywhere. To school. To the mall. Anywhere people will see just how beautifully I belong.

Harrisburg Marathon

Sunday, November 5, is the date of the fifth Harrisburg marathon, and my first. I go up a day before to preview the course, just like we do for cross-country races. Then, on race day, I arrive with plenty of time to find my number, pin it to my shirt, and move with the throng to the starting line, sandwiched toward the back of the pack. My heart is pounding as the gun goes off, but nothing happens for a few minutes until the enormous bank of runners in front of me begins to move and I'm able to surge forward. Large packs of runners surround me as I wind through tree-lined city streets. Bystanders cheer us on and hand us water and Gatorade as we fly by. At some point, the course ventures out beyond the city where there are fewer spectators but still lots of volunteers, who stand at the rest points encouraging us and providing more thirst-quenchers.

For a while, I try to keep a mile pace on my watch. But over time, my highest ambition becomes just finishing the race. In fact, I am no longer running, only jogging, as I place one foot in front of the other, ascending hills that feel like they will never end, then letting the descent propel me a little faster, only to meet yet another rolling hill.

Eventually, we re-enter the city streets, where the runners have thinned out considerably. Some have simply quit, but others are hours ahead of me. By the time I reach the twenty-mile mark of the race, I am running alone— and I'm painfully aware of why they call this point "hitting the wall." I've already been alternating jogging with walking for the last several miles, and still there's another 6.2 miles to go. I'm truthfully not sure I can finish. But then, the knowledge that *everyone* hits the wall fortifies me, and I redouble my determination.

When the finish line finally comes into view, I want to finish strong like we're encouraged to do in cross country, but my stiff legs don't produce anything resembling a sprint. Instead, I stumble across the finish line into the arms of volunteers. They wrap me in what looks like aluminum foil, which feels so good on the chilly day.

Buoyed by the congratulatory hugs I receive, I revel in the fact I did it— all 26.2 miles, in a time of five hours and four minutes.

As I'm feeling relieved just to have finished, I'm astonished to learn that I placed fifth in the 18 and under age group. I'm elated when the race officials present me with a medal affixed to a wooden plaque.

I can barely walk for a week, but it doesn't matter. This race has proved something to me that goes beyond pain or discomfort. It has given me undeniable validation that my future knows no bounds.

CHAPTER NINE

1979

Until the lion learns how to write, every story will glorify the hunter.
—AFRICAN PROVERB

Another Kind of Scare

On Wednesday, March 28, 1979, the Three Mile Island nuclear generating plant caused alarm throughout the nation, but most acutely here in central Pennsylvania. At first it seemed there was a problem but no release of radiation. Two days later it was discovered that a bubble of gas had exploded and had indeed released a small amount of radiation. Some combination of a malfunction and human error had caused an emergency in one of the reactors.

Each successive day revealed a situation more serious than previously known, escalating the sense of danger. Residents were advised to stay indoors. School was closed. By Friday it looked like there might be a larger explosion, which would spread a cloud of radiation across the countryside and perhaps much farther. The governor called for an evacuation of pregnant women and preschoolers within a five-mile radius of the reactor. This caused panic, and thousands began fleeing the area. Though we were thirteen miles away, we too began gathering our clothing and a few essential items while we followed the news reports closely. The question was: Where would we go? And then, how far away was far enough? And how would we fit Duke, our German Shepherd, in a car crowded with seven people and their belongings?

We waffled for days about staying or leaving, until President Jimmy Carter, who had been a nuclear engineer in the Navy, arrived in Harrisburg on Sunday, April 1, to inspect the reactor and to calm a terrified state and frightened nation. That afternoon, the experts declared the danger had passed and that we didn't need to worry about an explosion anymore. The reactor was too badly damaged to ever return to service, but it would no longer pose an existential threat.

The news would report that the reactor had come within less than an hour of a complete meltdown. Though we had stayed put, over 100,000 people had evacuated the area—some for weeks, and a few never returned.

Relieved not to have to be on the run once again, even if it wasn't from Daddy, we all returned to school and life slowly went back to normal. As normal, that is, as life could be given the perennial threat of our father's behavior.

Sunshine Gained, Sunshine Lost

It was Monday, April 9. On the cow path between the high school and the ninth-grade building, I was walking when David approached, running to his next class as if he was being chased.

Flying past me, he breathlessly announced, "Sandy is dead."

I spun around, incredulous.

Continuing to run past me, he added over his shoulder, "She died yesterday in a car accident."

His words hung in the air like a cruel joke.

Which Sandy? I wondered. *Sandy H. or Sandy K.?* But David was gone before I could ask. Either way, my heart was crushed with grief. Both girls were dear friends who had picked berries with us for years. Unable to connect with David during the rest of the school day, I was forced to sit in class all day, where I didn't hear a word the teacher said as I wondered which one of my girlfriends had died.

After school let out, I got the news that the girl in the accident was

Sandy H., our neighbor and very first friend when we moved away from the farm. In fact, she was the first real friend I had *ever* had. I couldn't believe she was gone. And I couldn't understand why a wonderful person like her would be taken from the world so young. Her smile lit up her face. Her eyes sparkled. She was easygoing and fun, not to mention lighthearted, effortlessly pretty, and warm. I had loved the times we walked the railroad tracks together, worked in the fields, swam, played, and goofed off. And she wasn't only a good friend to me but to all my siblings as well. She never judged us, not once; in fact, I don't think it would have occurred to her to do so. Somehow, Sandy didn't care whether we were awkward or popular. She simply liked us, and we liked her.

That same week, a service was held for her. A long line of people waiting to pay their respects snaked around the room of the funeral home. While my siblings and I stood awkwardly waiting, we talked in whispers amongst ourselves. At some point, a nervous laugh broke out from our little group, and I glanced quickly at her parents at the front of the room, hoping they hadn't heard us and if they did, that they didn't see us as disrespectful friends who didn't really care about their daughter. Nothing could have been further from the truth.

In the days and weeks following Sandy's death, I picked up the phone several times, excited to tell her something, only to remember she wasn't there to tell. Even worse, the reality would hit me that she would never pick up the phone again.

I missed Sandy terribly. We saw her mother at the movies from time to time, but I couldn't find any words to speak to that kind of grief, to offer comfort, or to tell her what Sandy meant to all of us, so I said nothing.

Later, when her gravestone was placed, it read "Sunshine" across the top.

Clearly, Sandy had brought as much sunshine to other people's lives as she had to ours.

Permission Slip

I search the house for Mother upon arriving home from school. Finally, I spot her outside with clothespins in her mouth, methodically hanging wet laundry on the lines. She looks up at me with a smile as I call "hello" and meet her at the bottom of the hill, handing her a piece of paper with a pen.

"I want to be on the track team this spring," I tell her. "I need to keep running so I can improve my times and work on getting a scholarship. Can you just sign this paper, please? It's the same as the one you signed for the cross-country team."

I'm hoping to save her the time of rereading the entire document, knowing it will be a quick formality for her to sign it. But despite my tidy explanation, she reads the form over anyway.

"No," she says, pushing the paper toward me. "You can't be on the track team. Cross-country was enough. You need to go to work and save your money."

"But, I *need* to be on the track team," I insist. "I need it to get a scholarship for college."

Matching my forcefulness, she says, "If you want to go to college, you need to have a job and earn money."

What began as a routine ask is suddenly becoming a disaster I didn't see coming. I can feel the panic invading my throat as the world shrinks to only my mother's face and the paper in her hand. I know that once she makes up her mind, she almost certainly won't change it, and I can see from her expression that it may already be too late.

So, I take a different tack that I hope will be more convincing than the first. "I'm going to get a track scholarship to *pay* for college."

But the panic and desperation in my voice only confirms her decision. She scoffs at the idea as unrealistic and repeats, "No, you're going to work."

Mother turns back to her laundry but I don't move. *I can't work. I know this is my only solution. I'll never be able to save up enough money by graduation. She can't ruin my plans over something this basic. I will get a track scholarship. I WILL. I don't care what Mr. Harbold says. I don't care what she says. I don't care what anyone says.*

Mother once said to me, out of the blue, "Sometimes you're just too good for your own good." I never knew why she said it or what she meant by it, but I *have* always tried to be a good girl. I'm the one who chides my siblings for saying "My God" and lectures them primly about taking the Lord's name in vain. I'm the one who follows the rules and makes sure the others do too, which generally elicits rolled eyes and resentment from my siblings. I've always been Mother's little helper, quietly picking up the slack without needing to be told. I bake bread, make curtains, clean the house, and insist the others do too. I look around and see what needs to be done. I lighten her load. Determined to be good, I have lived my entire life as a goody two shoes on steroids.

Suddenly, I'm done being that girl, at least in the moment. "If you don't sign this permission slip," I say emphatically, "I'll run away from home."

My fierce promise stops Mother in her tracks and she looks at me hard, searching for cracks in my resolve. I stare straight back. She knows this isn't like me, and I can see in her eyes that she knows I mean it.

With a sigh, she signs the slip and hands it back, with one caveat. "Well, don't say I didn't warn you."

With the permission slip catastrophe narrowly averted, I can now focus on the events I choose to compete in. Like in the past years of track and field day, I want to enter as many events as I can. I try my hand at shot put and even attempt the hurdles, but I quickly settle on four events that suit me better: the mile run, the two-mile run, the two-mile relay, and the high jump.

With this decision made, I buy a pair of gray cleats for the track season and adjust to the feel of running on cinders and small spikes as well as trying to master the unique strategies for the varying race lengths. For the high jump, I watch the boys and girls do the Fosbury flop technique and study their efforts, striving to decipher the intricacies of this skill before setting out to practice it tirelessly.

Overall, I find that track is an entirely different atmosphere than cross-country. For one thing, there are so many events happening at the same time and so many more athletes that it is like a huge circus. For another thing, it is a much larger pool of athletes, so I am competing against runners I've never seen because they play field hockey during the fall.

Lucky for me, the girls on the track team—like cross-country—are all very encouraging and supportive of me and of our teammates. It's a wonderful feeling to be a part of something big like this. And, to top off my first season, I do well enough to earn not only the respect of my teammates, but another varsity letter for my jacket.

A Lopsided Promotion

Due to the oil crisis of 1979, the summer brings long lines at the gas station as Pennsylvania institutes odd-even-day gas rationing. But other than that inconvenience for my mother and brothers (since they are the only ones who drive), our summer is expected to be much the same as it has been every other year: working outside in the fields.

Every winter, I long to work inside at the cash registers in the warmth, and every summer, I imagine how nice it would be to work in the soothing air-conditioned store like other teenagers do. Plus, I could wear nice clothes rather than mud-streaked jeans and clodhoppers, my legs wouldn't get covered in bruises, and most importantly, I would get paid by the hour rather than by the quart. But that aspiration is quickly eclipsed when a sudden announcement is made: Mr. Smith, who has always supervised the seventy or so berry pickers, is retiring. This means his job is open, which means someone will need to fill this job—and it pays by the hour!

With this being my fourth year picking strawberries and blueberries, I have a lot of experience; plus, I'm one of the fastest pickers in the field. What's more, his job looks super easy. Mr. Smith never did anything but drive the truck to the field and stand there with a clipboard. He recorded how many quarts we picked, determined if they were full enough to count, and fired kids who threw strawberries or who didn't show up for work. Even though I'm not old enough to drive the truck, I know I could do his job. Even better, I wouldn't have to be down on my hands and knees hustling so hard to make money.

Right away, I ask Mother if she'll talk to Uncle Glenn on my behalf.

"If you want the job, ask him yourself," she retorts.

So, I muster my courage and approach his six-foot-plus frame. "Uncle Glenn," I say, looking him as much in the eye as I can from my vantage point, "I've been picking berries for a long time and watching what Mr. Smith does. I think I could do his job. Can I have it?"

He thinks for several moments, then says he'll let me know once he's made up his mind.

When he comes back with his decision, he announces that my sister

Leah and I will be given the position jointly, and that (unlike Mr. Smith) we will still need to pick berries when we aren't supervising. I guess Uncle Glenn figured that to be fair, he had to give the job to both of us. I didn't agree. After all, I was the one who took the risk to ask, so I thought the job should have been mine alone. But I didn't argue with him.

And so began a new chapter for Leah and me as co-bosses of the strawberry and blueberry pickers. We started off okay, with us both deciding jointly to fire a kid for lighting off a firecracker near another boy's ear. But when we were faced with firing our best picker, the decision didn't come so easily. Throwing strawberries at other pickers was a well-advertised fireable offense. But in this case, the conscientious boy in question had thrown the strawberry in response to being called a racial slur. It was our responsibility to make a command decision, but my sister thought one way while I thought another. From then on, the co-leadership experiment limped on with considerable acrimony and never recovered. I appreciated the chance to test my supervisory chops, but in the end, I would have much preferred being a cashier.

The Pledge

My plans for college and beyond were going swimmingly—until our family decided to take a road trip.

It wasn't uncommon for us to travel to Canada, where we sometimes visited members from our Church, along with the other half of our extended family. We always looked forward to seeing our aunts and uncles, but especially our cousins, and a road trip to anywhere was always thrilling. But on this particular drive, David was driving with Mother in the front passenger seat when I noted a wistful sadness in Mother's voice as we discussed our approaching visits.

Believing I knew what was bothering her, I asked, "Are you lonely being in the Church all by yourself?"

As if considering this idea for the first time, she thought for a moment and then said, "I am."

Before I could stop myself, I responded by saying, "Would you like someone to join so that you won't be all alone?"

She didn't miss a beat. "Yes, that would be very nice."

Immediately, I was sorry I had asked the question. In hearing her reply, I felt an old, inexorable pull toward a duty for the care and protection of my mother. Without a single thought about the plans I had been making for my own future, I decided on the spot that I would join the Church so Mother wouldn't be so lonely and sad anymore. I didn't make the commitment out loud, but I did feel the need to do something to assuage the disappointment I felt inside for making such a rash decision.

Nothing has to be done immediately, I reasoned, *so long as she eventually gets some companionship.*

That's when I made up my mind that I would delay acting on this decision and buy myself one more year of freedom. I hated to keep Mother waiting, but I also couldn't ignore what Aunt Helen had said to me four years prior: *Whatever you do, don't join that damn church.*

Abduction Attempt

It was not unusual for Daddy to go to the Lemoyne Farmers Market. It was also not unusual for him to time his arrival during the bustling Friday market hours when he was most likely to find Mother there and ambush her. This venue served a dual purpose: humiliating Mother, and giving him a crowded forum for his grievances against both her and the Church.

For some time, Daddy had been promising in his mailings that he was going to come pick Mother up at market and take her away. Furthermore, he repeatedly declared that when he caught her, he would rape her.

In the many arguments we witnessed on the farm, and in the endless monologues since, rape had been a frequent topic. He would often scoff derisively about it and say, "Why, any dumb female animal knows she must put her tail aside before she can enjoy sexual intercourse." Yet, if he was directly confronted about his views on rape, he would always shake his head mournfully and say, "Oh, it's terrible thing, it's a terrible thing." Mostly, though, I always had the impression he thought rape didn't ever actually happen. He would constantly infer that they wanted it, were pretending otherwise, or were lying. And the real topper he would subtly allude to: "How can you rape your own wife when she belongs to you?"

These rape threats were petrifying to me. It was horrible to think about Mother getting captured and raped—but another even more terrifying thought occurred to me. With Daddy, you were either with him or you were against him. It was a black-and-white choice. Since we hadn't taken his side against Mother, we children were considered the enemy too. If there had been any doubt about that, David's kidnapping and assault had erased any illusions.

One day, after another of Daddy's threats had reached our ears, I fearfully approached Mother.

"Would he rape us girls, too, if he caught us?" I asked her.

"No." she said firmly. "He wouldn't do that."

But I wasn't as confident as she was. I knew you belonged in one camp or the other: supporter or traitor. There was no middle ground.

The fact was, Daddy had tried to carry Mother off many times before, from Grandma's house and from market. I lived in constant fear of him catching her and the terrible fate that awaited.

And then one day, the unthinkable happened.

On August 31, 1979, Mother was outside the farmers market in the early afternoon, loading boxes into her van in the parking lot, when Daddy came up rapidly and silently behind her. Witnesses would testify that he dragged her, then picked her up and carried her the length of the parking lot before forcing her into his pickup truck. She screamed to bystanders for help, one of whom called the police. Fortunately, they happened to be nearby and arrived within minutes before Daddy could secure Mother enough to drive away. Police reports stated that there were two knives within reach (but never used), and that he held her by the chest and across the throat with her head on his leg by the gear shift as she struggled to get away. When the police officers demanded he release her, he said he wouldn't unless they arrested him. They continued to try to reason with him, but it wasn't until forty-five minutes after the ordeal began that he was finally placed under arrest and Mother was released.

The events that day were sobering for all of us. What if the police had not come as quickly as they had—or at all? What if he had taken her to his trailer like he did David? Where would it have ended?

Naturally, my father's arrest produced a wearying number of newspaper articles. The *Philadelphia Inquirer* featured pictures of my father's handsome, chiseled features and a closeup of my mother's face framed by her gray bonnet tied neatly beneath her chin, both above the headline: "'Shunned' Man Held in Abduction Try."

The article described the alleged abduction:

> Bear was charged with unlawful restraint, false imprisonment, simple assault, and disorderly conduct. He remained in jail in lieu of $50,000 bail set by District Justice Joseph Zedlar in Camp Hill.

Again, the same unceasing misinformation would be propagated.

> His wife and six children, like other Mennonites, are forbidden to have any business or social contact with him.

One mind-bending sentence buried innocuously in this article, however, would capture the persistent vertigo our family felt because of the way this saga was continually framed:

> Bear has made several attempts to re-unite his family, including an effort to kidnap one of his daughters in 1977.

Shifting the Spotlight

Besides my work duties, I have spent the past summer diligently preparing for cross-country, and my hard work is paying off. Not only have I moved up to the number-two varsity position on our team, but I am increasingly in the number-one position, as our lead runner suffers from shin splints. On September 5, I set a new course record, and as the fall season unfolds, pictures of the runners on our team make the newspapers.

Occasionally, my name is announced on the school loudspeaker for placing first or second in a meet. It is a new experience to be recognized for standing out in a good way. I am so tired of our family being known for bad things, so weary of the public condemnation. So this experience of making the news for my running accomplishments generates a new vow: If I must be known, it will be for something good.

Yes, I am going to make a positive name for myself.

Despite the number of truly talented runners in our conference, I begin to seriously entertain the idea that Mr. Harbold is wrong about my chances of obtaining a scholarship and set my sights on achieving a status no one will see coming.

Final-Straw Letter

For the past seven years, since this whole ordeal began, my father's constant publicity in newspapers, as well as his radio and television interviews, have been compelling enough that his supporters feel the need to reach out to us in the form of letters mailed to our house. Duty bound to express their outrage at what we are doing to him, these champions of Daddy's let us know that it is not only Mother who is evil, but that we children are quite terrible as well.

How could we shun this poor man?

What is wrong with us?

We should be ashamed of ourselves.

Sometimes I wonder if we will be able to survive the public condemnation, or if we will be crushed into nothingness. Between Daddy's constant propaganda, the media's unreflective projection of the story, and the public's unrelenting sycophantic chorus, it all feels so heavy and oppressive that it's like being buried alive.

Every time we've received one of these letters, I have cycled from feeling despair to steaming at the injustice. Usually, I stomp around and fume at the unfairness while marveling at the depth of Daddy's supporters' ignorance.

This particular fall, one of these letters arrives in our mailbox, written by a lady who expresses her indignation and disapproval as a Christian woman, ending her letter with "I'm praying for you." The tone of her letter clearly conveys the depth of our sinning and her prayer for our dark souls.

I'm praying for you?

That did it for me. We had fielded enough of these letters, and I was done ignoring them.

Before we folded beneath the weight of Daddy's cult's judgment or went crazy ourselves, I decided I was going to speak up. I wanted these people to know we were still alive, that the truth was quite different from the upside-down "truths" they had been told.

So, I sat down to craft a reply to this woman. Despite the rage I felt, I told her politely but clearly about the things Daddy had done. How we had to leave the Home Farm because he was violent, how he refused to provide for his six children, how he took an axe to our door, how we had to spend Christmas at the Church nursing home, how he kidnapped Leah and later David, shaving off all his hair to humiliate him. Most especially, I made it clear that we children were not part of the Church. We didn't shun him; we were *afraid* of him. When I finished, I asked my siblings if I could read it to them to see if they thought it was okay to send. I wanted to make sure it was accurate, that it wasn't rude, and that I left no important points out of the narrative.

They gathered round and I read the letter aloud. As soon as I finished, squeals of delight erupted.

"Yes! Yes! Yes!"

"That's right!"

"Tell her!"

I see in their faces the deep satisfaction I feel that we are finally defending ourselves.

Even Mother gives me an approving nod.

I don't expect to hear back from the woman. Daddy's fans are intensely loyal and generally immune to facts or independent thought. But it is enough just to not be passive anymore.

A New Language

Though I'm following David's advice and taking the math and science classes on the college-prep track I've chosen, I like my humanities courses better. In particular, I'm fascinated by the Soviet Union's politics and culture we were exploring in Social Studies. It's frightening the way you must be careful about what you say so that your neighbor won't inform on you to the authorities. Even worse, family members might turn you in, so you have to be mindful about what you say in your own home. It reminds me a little of the stilted conversations and formulaic letters that the members of our Church write to each other. They, too, are careful never to discuss anything too personal, or to express doubts about doctrine or disagree with Church authorities, lest they be reported and find themselves in trouble.

This happened in our own family when last year, Benny and I gave each other wooden Bjorn Borg tennis racquets for Christmas and practiced hitting a ball back and forth on the road above our house. Eventually, we moved our game to the municipal courts by the elementary school. Mother, who had always been athletic and sometimes played basketball in the driveway with us, became interested in tennis too. Playing in her long dress and black shoes, she warned, "Don't tell Uncle Glenn."

Like the Soviet citizens, we kids needed no reminders of the unspoken rules.

Soviet society seems sinister, cold, gray, dreary. Yet the colorful cultural elements left over from old Russia are fascinating, such as nesting dolls and Russian eggs with intricate designs made with overlays of ink and wax. I find learning about cultures around the world fascinating and long to go on one of the student trips to Russia that our teacher Mrs. Bej leads each year. I am disappointed that the cost is prohibitive, but feel a bit of consolation when the next scheduled trip is canceled due to the boycott of the 1980 summer Olympic games.

I have also fallen in love with English class, where I've been introduced to vibrant concepts I had never considered before. My teacher, Mr. Matthews, is in his thirties and is devoted but tough. He also has a little quirk: he dislikes it when students crowd too near him. I've never known someone who asked others to "back up" out of his imaginary space bubble, but that's what Mr. Matthews does when too many kids swarm him with questions after class.

I will actually take several classes from Mr. Matthews (keeping a respectful distance), but Film I and II will be my favorites. In his class we watch *Cool Hand Luke*, *Psycho*, *Citizen Kane*, and other films, where we learn to analyze the themes and motifs woven through them. Rich, colorful, and mysterious, these new concepts are like being introduced to a fascinating hidden world that exists behind ordinary stories: appearance vs. reality, good vs. evil, red herrings, foreshadowing, symbols, metaphors, comparison and contrast, a character's fatal flaw.

These concepts that represent all that goes unsaid and unseen are so compelling a language to me that it will be years before I can simply watch a movie for entertainment. They become yet another layer to giving voice to the inner world I entertain, as well as my growing interest and understanding of the possibilities that await me once I sprout my independent wings.

A Ludicrous Request

In late October, my father was, at long last, formally arraigned.

Outside the courtroom, two television stations arrived to cover the event. Inside the courtroom, Daddy insisted to Judge Sheely that he did not want or need an attorney because, he claimed, he had been previously manipulated into the mental hospital and did not have much faith in the judicial system. Several people had offered to pay his legal expenses to hire an attorney, yet he would maintain his insistence upon acting as his own, expressly so that *he* would be the one to question the witnesses directly, particularly Mother. To facilitate this, he was appointed an attorney who would advise him in legal terminology and how motions were made in court. The arraignment concluded with Daddy pleading not guilty and a trial date set for Monday, December 3, 1979.

Sometime after Daddy's initial appearance in the courtroom, he wrote an indignant letter to the prosecutor and to Judge Sheely (who would also be presiding over his jury trial). This letter petitioned for an "informal request for pre-trial recovery of my wife and six children" and would be included in court records. Under the pretext of this petition, the letter rambled for eight pages, detailing the torment he suffered at so many hands, including his wife and the justice system. It included the usual romp through eccentric tidbits of European and US history, which were apparently tangentially relevant to his cause; some quoted scriptures; the familiar dog and swine comparisons to females; and other outbursts that had little connection to each other. For added emphasis, much of this written document was populated with under-lined sentences, hence the underlined passages that follow.

Upon being informed that the Commonwealth reserved the right to produce the two knives that were found in his truck at the scene as exhibits, he raged:

> "Most anyone should realize I could kill my wife about as quickly with my two hands as with two knives. Besides, a bloody mess is a messy business. Using my hands would not have been nearly as messy a murder."

Further, he contended that he was ripped off.

> "My bail was set at $50,000 for holding my wife in my arms for forty minutes. A Harrisburg man's bail was set at $500 for the charge of rape and attempted rape. Any businessman knows that if a charge of rape is worth $500 bail, I didn't get my money's worth. I have been cheated out of a lot of crime. To get my money's worth I should have raped a hundred women!"

In this document, he also included a lengthy story about meeting the father of the patrolman who arrested him in the grocery store, who he said strongly implied that his patrolman son, despite having to do his duty, was sympathetic toward Daddy, saying he was "a real gentleman." Daddy might have been happy that the man who arrested him was supportive of him and his cause, but instead he seemed outraged that anyone would dare arrest him, asserting that the patrolman's written statement of charges was "na-palmed and his testimony set on fire."

Echoing so many of my father's other responses to limits imposed on him by the law, he didn't dispute the main charge that he carried his wife off.

Rather, he was incensed by the small details that he insisted the police got wrong in their reports and charged them with lying about the incident. As such, he promised to call both the patrolman and his father to the stand and expose the arresting officer as a liar. Moreover, he said that this lying about the details proved that both the patrolman and Mother were (metaphorically) in the same bed together. The patrolman henceforth joined a long list of people who earned spots of dishonorable mentions in Daddy's future publications.

Buried amongst the diatribes was a proffer of sympathy to the prosecutor for being caught up "in the crossfire of this war caused by my Gale's rebellion." He followed this comment up with an insult for the prosecutor who had dared charge him: "You imagine you have a case, and you do—you are a case."

Oddly enough, Daddy followed the insult with a generous offer to "do a little horse trading, which would be to our mutual advantage." When the prosecutor apparently declined, Daddy underlined for emphasis a veiled threat:

> "Just think how that will look if you are so headstrong
> as to try to peddle your petty lies before a jury to that
> extent, and right before Christmas too."

He further reminded the prosecutor:

> "Already, two heavyweight reporters with a nationwide
> audience tell me they intend to have ringside seats at my
> trial. Just think how this will look preached UPON THE
> HOUSETOPS all over the country."

He also taunted the justice system:

> "How many times have I tried to rescue my wife? Do you
> think I will not try again? Of course, I will! It livens
> my life up a bit. I will even let you know when and where
> I intend to hold my wife in my arms the next time."

Concluding this passionate letter and pre-trial recovery petition, Daddy had the gall to appeal to the judge with a final dollop of lunacy:

"I believe in the end I will have my Gale calmed down and
be holding her in my arms. Before beginning this trial
why don't you prove to millions that you are a wise man
and put Gale in my arms—and wish us a happy honeymoon."

Pushing Through

As we await my father's trial, we are shocked when horrifying news is splashed across every newspaper and televised news hour: the American Embassy in Iran has been stormed, and 52 Americans were taken hostage.

I can't imagine what those poor people are going through. But I'm distracted by my own event. In the past year since my first marathon, I have been voraciously consuming articles in *Runner's World* and honing my training strategy, entering 5k's and 10k's to gain more competition experience, and running increasingly longer distances and several half marathons, hoping to peak on race day—which happens to fall on this day of the embassy attack.

There is a pall over the race, but we have all trained so hard for it that hundreds gather despite the unsettling world event. For me, I think of the mental toughness Coach Harbold has instilled in me, not to mention all we've endured with Daddy's tirades and brutality, being dragged through the media, and being repeatedly humiliated publicly. If those things haven't fortified me for the curve balls and hard knocks of life, I don't know what will.

Though this is still a grueling endeavor, the prospect of running 26 miles does not feel nearly as daunting or intimidating this year. I feel more confident as I run, and by the time I cross the finish line, I have improved my time from last year by more than an hour.

Despite the fact that my new time still only yields the same fifth-place medal as last year, I am ecstatic to realize that I am only twenty-five minutes away from qualifying for the Boston Marathon, which requires a time below three hours and thirty minutes. I calculate that if I keep training and improving at the rate I have thus far, I should have no trouble qualifying next year.

The Abduction Trial

The petition to have the judge order Daddy's family returned to him was unsuccessful, and the trial began on December 3, covered by the most famous newspapers in the nation.

Despite the publicity, we all breathed a sigh of relief. *Finally*, Daddy had been charged for his crimes and his case was going to trial. *Finally*, the violence and terror we had lived with was out in the open, and his actions were officially on trial rather than ours. Even though he had pled not guilty, he had been caught red-handed in the act by the police and there were multiple witnesses, so it was an open-and-shut case.

The thought of our father going to jail for his crimes was sobering—even frightening—but we felt confident that he had finally come to the end of the road with his behavior. We also envisioned an end to our exhausted existence living on the run, eagerly anticipating the relief of the legal system at long last, placing boundaries on Daddy's behavior and providing us with the peace and quiet we yearned for.

But, as you will witness, the trial almost immediately veers in an absurd direction that, unthinkably, sides with a known abuser instead of with those who have been indisputably, repeatedly abused.

The prosecution begins by calling one of the three patrolman who responded to the scene. He is asked to testify to the factual details that Daddy held Mother captive in his truck and in a semi choke-hold across his lap for forty-five minutes while the officers' attempted, "at least ten times" to talk Daddy into releasing her.

The patrolman testifies to the sense of escalating danger and of finally making the decision to arrest this man. He further testifies to Mother's condition afterward:

"The whole ordeal, it appeared as though she was both not only physically but emotionally drained . . . When she first stepped onto the pavement, her knees seemed to buckle. And I thought she was going to go down on the pavement."

Daddy cross-examines this patrolman. He begins by insisting that the three police officers are dishonest because their reports said "he dragged her and carried her" when Daddy said he had only carried her. He is intent on trying to get the patrolman to admit he lied. He further argues that because the police officers tried to reason with him, rather than physically intervene immediately, she must not have been in any actual danger.

The patrolman firmly refutes both points.

Next, the prosecution calls Mother to testify.

She states that she has lived separately from Daddy for the past five years. She also states that on the day he accosted her, she did not want to go with him. The reason she did not initially cry out for help was because she was intensely embarrassed about being carried across the parking lot in front of a large group of customers at her place of business. She thought she might be able to reason with him and convince him to let her go. But when he forced her into the truck and said he would be violent if she didn't do what he wanted, that's when she called out for help. She testified that she was indeed afraid and reiterated that she did *not* want to go with him.

Daddy rises to cross-examine Mother. (This is the moment he has been waiting for and the reason he declined an attorney to represent him.)

"Why are we separated?" he asks.

The prosecutor objects.

Next, he tries to impugn the veracity of her testimony with the same diversionary tactic (focusing on tedious discrepancies to portray the witness as a liar) used against the patrolman, by getting her to admit he was walking rather than running when he came up behind her.

"I won't contend," she replies to this nitpicking. "It seemed as though you were running to me or a very fast walk. It doesn't matter."

His next line of questioning infers that since she asked him to put her down, and that she said she could walk, it meant she wanted to go home with him.

The questioning then abruptly jumps to another topic. Daddy asks the judge to have portions of Mother's diary from 1973 entered into the record, asserting it will show she is only pretending to be so deathly afraid of him and is actually just putting on an act of terror in front of us children.

JUDGE:

"You are offering this to show that on the day when you picked her up that she was [really] not afraid of you?"

DADDY:

"That's right. And it is really a psychosis. It is a retreat from reality. And the worst of it is I haven't seen my little daughter—"

The judge orders a ten-minute recess while all parties meet in his chambers to discuss entering the diary into evidence.

After some discussion, the judge says he won't allow Daddy to question Mother about her diary, but Daddy's advising attorney steps in to clarify one reason Daddy wanted it:

"It is his position that the shunning practices of the Mennonite Church are an evil thing and something that he was attempting to liberate his wife from."

The judge ruled that it had no bearing on the criminal charges resulting from the events of Aug 31.

Daddy resumes his cross-examination in the courtroom, trying to get Mother to admit that she didn't really feel she was in harm's way that day.

MOTHER:

"I feared what you might do to me later."

DADDY:

"What did you fear I might do later?"

MOTHER:

"Would you like me to be specific?"

DADDY:

"Pardon me?"

MOTHER:

"Would you really like me to be specific?"

DADDY:

"Yes, please."

MOTHER:

"There are several things I would have feared: physical harm, beating, sexual assault. I believe you shaved David's hair totally six months past. I also thought of that too, which was minor. And the humiliation that it would be to go through those things."

(Note here that my mother's odd phrasing, I believe, reflects the survival dialect of battered women around the world. Born out of fear, it is shaded with minimization, qualifiers and vagueness, and over-deference to authority, as well as colored by a hyper-vigilant awareness of retaliation for exhibiting assertiveness. The opaqueness of this dialect protects the speaker yet also obscures the detail and true horror of her experiences.)

In response to this statement, Daddy veers off again into his rote recitation about sexual teasing. He then quickly leads the court on a merry chase with his favorite topic: the privately made rape charge from seven years ago. Daddy zeroes in with pointed questions toward Mother designed to humiliate and discredit her, suggesting she allowed sexual relations with him after excommunication.

What follows is a voyeuristic and torturous discussion around consent in marriage—before a twelve-person jury and an all-male cadre of judge, assistant district attorney, Daddy, and his advising attorney, reminiscent of the panel of bishops Mother once also faced.

DADDY:

"Describe the time, the circumstances, and just what the rape entailed. You said you weren't certain of the meaning, the specific meaning of rape, and I would like to remind you that you said—"

The judge tells him he is asking too many questions at one time, then asks his own, furthering the quest around Daddy's favorite topic.

JUDGE:

"Would you explain to us what you meant when you said the word rape?"

MOTHER:

"Perhaps I was inaccurate in my definition. I don't know what would be considered that in a legal sense."

JUDGE:

"You tell us what you thought it meant when you said it, in your mind what it would mean?"

MOTHER:

"In my mind, when two people are married it is a free-will offering. When it is no longer a free-will offering but a forced—I can't think of the rest of how you want to say, but when it is not a free-will offering, it is not as it should be."

My father sees his opening to resume questioning on this salacious topic and and pounces on Mother:

"So then we *did* have sexual intercourse after I was shunned?"

The prosecutor objects but is overruled by the judge.

JUDGE:

"We will permit her to answer the question. The question was, was there sexual intercourse after he was shunned?

MOTHER:

"Could I better phrase that as sexual assault and would that be acceptable to the Court? . . . If that's acceptable, then can we leave it at that?"

Note that amidst this circus, the assault and Mother's humiliating capture in broad daylight in a busy parking lot is rapidly obscured by Daddy's expert hijacking of the trial that was supposed to prosecute his crime.

JUDGE:

"You will have to tell us what you meant by it. When you said you feared what he might do later, and one of the things you said was you feared a sexual assault. And that is what we are trying to figure out, what you meant by that."

MOTHER:

"Well, I believe that I said—I don't know how to be specific about this. It is a little hard for me, Your Honor, to speak about things like this. I don't know how to phrase it and to be legally exact."

What follows is a tedious back and forth between the judge and Mother, wherein the judge seeks concrete details of this long-ago (and private) allegation for which my father was never legally charged and for which he is not on trial for today, while Mother tries to avoid getting dragged into a mortifying exchange where she is asked to speak of details of intimate violence that happened years ago. By now she has become so entangled in the web of her accusers' (both Daddy's *and* the judge's) quest for prurient details that it appears never to have occurred to her that all she needed to do to establish the imminent danger she felt was to simply repeat my father's many stated threats to rape her when he caught her.

JUDGE:

"What did you mean when you used the phrase 'sexual assault'? That is what we are trying to find out."

MOTHER:

"To me it is when your person is violated."

And with that, the judge tells Daddy to go ahead with his questioning, for which Daddy needs no encouragement to resume his favorite grievance.

After more invasive questioning before the jury, the prosecutor objects and it is finally sustained, though no redirect is attempted.

The market manager and another police officer are called to testify to what they witnessed.

Daddy cross-examines both of them, subjecting them to his typical nitpicking and contention about the details they recalled. He does this in an effort to suggest that Mother wasn't truly uncomfortable or in danger, then he refocuses attention once again on his reasons for the abduction and assault.

* * *

The second day of the trial begins with Daddy stating that he intends to testify in his own defense. His advisory attorney asks to make a motion to dismiss the charge of simple assault because:

"[Mrs. Bear] was not in any imminent danger, which the statute requires. Additionally, what she said specifically was that she feared such ridicule as having her head shaved, or sexual assault, or a beating, which does not comprise serious bodily injury as it is defined in the statute. For there to be serious bodily injury, it would have to be an injury that created substantial risk of death or that caused serious permanent disfigurement, or protracted loss, or impairment of any bodily member or organ."

Note here that Daddy's advisory attorney has just summarized and masterfully argued the classic abuser's case (which is always to disparage the horror the victim feels and drastically minimize the impact of the abuser's actions). In fact, the statute itself appears to have been written to provide wide leeway for abusers. Victims, themselves, often become conditioned to adopt the abuser's perspective and learn to minimize their own horror and injuries.

The assistant district attorney prosecuting the case argues that she was "legitimately in fear of serious bodily injury because of the threat, and because of past occasions that she mentioned of serious bodily injury."

Daddy's attorney reiterates that the injury she feared was not serious.

The judge agrees that the legal definition of serious bodily injury is a close question but says he will leave it up to the jury.

The prosecution rests and Daddy prepares to put on his defense case. He wants to call Mother back to the stand. He had also given notice that he intended to call other witnesses: Uncle Glenn and Aunt Mary Ellen; a prominent Lancaster bishop and his wife; and Uncle Francis and his wife and daughter. His intention in doing so was to prove that he was trying to rescue Mother from a cult. The judge ruled it had no bearing on justifying the criminal behavior he was charged with from August.

Daddy nevertheless wrangles a promise from the judge for leeway in presenting his defense, then proceeds to give a colorful forty-minute recitation of how profoundly he has been wronged by the Church, his wife, and his children. He never denies his actions on the day in question. In fact, he tells the jury that he had planned it at least several days before. He also repeats dismissively that she was not really afraid of him.

Daddy closes his argument by insisting that neither he, Mother, nor us children have lived as we should have. He maintains that getting arrested and hauling his wife and the Mennonites into court is the only way he can get a hearing for his grievances, and that he hoped the jury might see that he was trying to right a much greater wrong.

In sum, his defense is that *he* is the real victim, and that the ends justify his means.

The Jury Speaks

Reporters from the biggest newspapers in the country will detail their ringside seats at what appears to be the trial of the decade—the outcome of which falls hard on our family: after less than an hour of deliberation, the jury unanimously declares Daddy not guilty of all charges.

Note how this first article characterizes the public abduction as a romantic gesture gone awry.

People Magazine, December 5, 1979

By GREG WALTER

A Shunned Mennonite's Trials with His Wife and Church Take a Bizarre New Turn

"I said, 'Hello, Gale,' and she just said, 'Robert,' as if she were surprised. I picked her up and carried her to my truck. She said, 'Where are you taking me?' And I said, 'I'm taking you home, where you belong.'"

Under different circumstances, it might have been a moment for wandering toward the sunset in an affectionate fade-out. Instead it was merely the latest episode in the bizarre marital saga of Robert L. Bear, a man shunned by his own family and cast out by his church. His hands tremble and his eyes brim over as Bear recalls how he drove to the Lemoyne, Pa. farmers' market where his wife was working last summer and tried desperately to persuade her to return home with him. For his effort, he now stands accused of assault, disorderly conduct, unlawful restraint and false imprisonment—charges that could bring him 10 years in prison.

The article goes on to describe Daddy's argument with the Church and his wife for its readers and quotes:

> "A Reformed Mennonite woman is on call 24 hours a day to the church," Bear maintains. "The church has firsts on her and her husband has seconds." As part of what Bear calls "the lash of the ban," he says she refused to cook for him or share his bed. "They even teach your children there's something wrong with your mind," he says.

After detailing Daddy's efforts to seek redress in the court system, the article continues:

> Finally, last August, Bear took matters into his own hands, holding his wife in the cab of his truck for 30 minutes before releasing her unharmed. Though offers of help came in from all over the U.S., Bear stubbornly spent 15 days in jail before posting a $50,000 bond.

THE NEW YORK TIMES, DECEMBER 5, 1979

Farmer Shunned by Mennonites Is Acquitted of Wife's Abduction

Mr. Bear acknowledged the incident but said that he had not meant to harm his wife, only to obtain a forum for his grievances against the church. He took the stand for 40 minutes today as his only witness.

"What I tried to remedy was far greater than what I had caused," Mr. Bear told the jury in his closing arguments, tears streaming down his cheeks. "What I tried to do was reunite the family. I thought what I did would be excused for remedying the much more serious evil."

The prosecutor, Michael Eakin, said he sympathized with Mr. Bear, but he told the jury it should be concerned only with whether the cabbage and corn farmer had abducted his wife. Judge Sheely also warned the jury that "we're not here to try the Reformed Mennonite Church."

THE WASHINGTON POST, DECEMBER 5, 1979

'Shunned' Man Acquitted

The day-and-a-half-long trial featured dramatic and often tearful pleas by Bear, who acted as his own attorney, that he had seized his wife for the sole purpose of getting arrested in order to bring his dispute with the 500-member religious sect to public attention.

From the beginning of the most recent trial, Assistant District Attorney J. Michael Eakin, 31, fought a losing battle to keep Bear's dispute with the church out of the case. "Although you may properly have sympathy for Mr. Bear's position," Eakin told the jury, "his church is not on trial here." He then produced witnesses to Bear's seizure of his wife at Lemoyne, PA, farmer's market last Aug. 31.

Bear quoted the written works of Menno Simons, the 16th-century founder of the Mennonite Church, that excommunication "would either break a man or cause him to become as a raving, biting dog, or an unclean swine."

At that point, Bear lost his composure. His soft voice broke, and he wept as he repeatedly apologized for breaking down.

"I can't take it," he said. "Why can't you die, why can't they kill you is what you think when they excommunicate you. You are looking at someone who is condemned to hell. I am the living dead."

. . .

"I did this so that the whole world would know that the Reformed Mennonite Church has terrorized me, has pulverized me with the lash of the ban. But I don't think that will help my poor wife.

Many of those in the courtroom, including a woman juror, began weeping softly, and many sat with heads bowed as Bear tearfully told of his frustrations and seven years of loneliness.

After 40 minutes, prosecutor Eakin objected, and county Judge Harold E. Sheely ordered Bear to stop. "I think we have given you ample opportunity to tell your story," he said.

Under cross-examination by Eakin, Bear admitted that he had planned his wife's abduction "for days."

After the jury had announced its verdict, Sheely noted: "Mr. Bear, I consider you very fortunate. If I had been hearing your case without a jury, I would have found you guilty of false imprisonment."

The verdict is a devastating reminder that the public will believe whatever Daddy says. That he can get away with whatever he wants. That there is no accountability. That he can twist things so that even when he tries to abduct someone, he becomes the real victim. And that even worse, he is believed.

Nobody—not the judge, nor the prosecutor, nor any member of the jury—displays a shred of curiosity about the blip of testimony stating what had happened to David. Likewise, the prosecutor doesn't bring up the ceaseless assaults on us for the last seven years that might have established a pattern of behavior and raised a question in the jury's mind about Daddy's false versions of events. If he had, perhaps one person might have connected the dots and looked deeper at the astonishing manipulation of the truth. Even the experienced judge was distracted into following Daddy down the rabbit hole of his grievances. Mother gave few concrete details that would lay out a picture of Daddy's extensive violence: the kidnappings, the many assaults on her body, the interminable fleeing. It was as if she assumed that his behavior was so pervasive in our lives and had been reported in the newspapers so often that everybody already knew. Or perhaps it was just the hesitant answers of a victim who has taken on the humiliation of having been assaulted, and worse, shouldered the shame that should belong to her attacker. Maybe, too, like all of us, she had been so conditioned to the fatalistic resignation that Daddy always got away with everything that no matter what she said, she understood it wouldn't make much of a difference. We had all been trained to understand that we did not matter. Our experience would remain unacknowledged and overpowered by the twisted, but much more colorful, rendition presented by our attacker. In contrast to his dramatic performance, our injuries and persistent terror were framed just as he intended: imaginary, tiresome, repetitive, and above all else, inconsequential. His legal audience was so carried away by the entertaining act of a bully and his compelling story that they forgot all about their duty to justice.

The only newspaper to mention David at all was *The Washington Post.* He had graduated high school the previous spring, and his hair had grown out to a short cut by the time he accompanied Mother to the trial.

> And, in the hallway outside, barely noticed by dozens of reporters covering the trial, wandered Bear's eldest child, David, 18.
>
> "I'm not shunning my father," the modishly [read: modestly] dressed youngster told a reporter. "I just don't want anything to do with him. I don't hate him and I didn't want to see him go to jail. But I did want someone in authority to tell him that he just can't do this to my mother anymore."

Perhaps the most telling comment of all, however, was what Prosecutor Eakin said at the close of the trial:

> "The thing that worries me is that Mr. Bear will now think he has a license to do what he wants in the future."

And that is exactly what occurred.

With the culmination of this trial and the lack of any semblance of justice, we all finally and fully absorb the impact and reality of my father's words so many years ago, and now echoed by the court: "You're on your own."

CHAPTER TEN

1980

As you walk on the way, the way appears.

—RUMI

BUOYED BY HIS DRAMATICALLY QUICK ACQUITTAL AND THE RENEWED national media attention to his case, Daddy pursued a new outlet, which was reported shortly after the trial.

> "Bear is cooperating, for example, in the writing of a second book, this one by a professional journalist in Philadelphia, and reportedly the first three chapters are being considered seriously by a major New York publishing house. In addition, there are reports that movie and television rights are being discussed with a New York agent and that public television is considering a proposal for a national documentary on Bear's life.
>
> If any of this comes to fruition, according to informed sources close to the Reformed Mennonite Church, the church will retaliate with what one church member called "information not made public before that would bring Bear's credibility into question."
>
> The 'informed source' would not elaborate on the information regarding Bear, but said it dealt with specifics concerning Bear's relationships with others long before his rift with the church.

(In reference to the second paragraph, I was never able to uncover what the Church might have "had" on my father. This kind of public threat was highly unusual for the Reformed Mennonites, and I believe this information was openly revealed only because they clearly felt their image would be severely threatened by movie and television deals. Yet no movie or television deals materialized. As for the second book? It never surfaced. However, I did recall hearing Daddy say what he planned to title it: *Delivered from Satan*.)

A Surprise in the Mail

By January 1980, newspaper articles carry Daddy's predictable New Year's assertion: that he is going to permanently quit his campaign against the Church and his wife. It is predictable because often after a terrorizing act (even though he could reliably rest on the press and the public for sympathy for his behavior), he would retreat for several months. Like the battering husband and father he was, he would frequently say, "I'm sorry but . . . I'm going to stop/change, I'm going to move away," etc. It was as if he knew what he had done was profoundly wrong and he was ashamed—until he wasn't anymore. When the shame had passed, he would resume his familiar tactics. As such, none of us actually believes he'll quit his campaign, so we simply roll our eyes over the announcement.

What *does* surprise me, though, is what arrives in the mailbox in early January: a response from the woman whose letter I replied to in the fall.

Dear Gale,

I planned to send you folks a Christmas card with a note enclosed but ran out of time. Hopefully, this will be a short letter.

I want to thank you and Patty for your reply to my letter. And I wanted to apologize to you for not really considering your feelings in this matter. When you mentioned that this is a painful subject at best, this caused a new dimension in my thinking regarding the situation. I'm sorry to remind you again, but I wanted to tell you that in a way I did have my mind made up when I wrote that letter to you. Even though I explored a number of possibilities, I was pretty sure I knew the situation. Was I wrong! It's funny in a way, or perhaps the word should be ironic, but I thought I was writing to encourage you to "see the error of your ways" and return to your husband. Actually, I was encouraging you to feel better about having left.

My husband and I usually stay up late Saturday nights, and for some reason the Saturday following the receipt of your letter, I did something I rarely do. We do not have television, so at 11:30 PM I turned on the radio, probably to see if I could get a weather forecast. I listen to WDAC (in Lancaster?) a lot, but at noon or for the weather I often turn to WHP AM. The radio was tuned to WHP. Imagine my surprise when a lady's voice stated that she was going to interview Robert Bear. Glenn was in the living room napping. He probably thought the house was on fire when I very excitedly awakened him, but after realizing what I was trying to tell him, he hurried to the kitchen. The reception wasn't perfect, but we could make out most of it. It was then that I really appreciated Patty's letter. Without it, I would have been more firmly convinced of my previous ideas concerning the situation. But knowing what she had written, I was able to tell that what he said was not altogether true, and sometimes not true at all. You probably know what was said, and it would take a long time to write it down, so I won't go into any detail. However, if you don't know and would like to know what I remember, I would be glad to tell you what I could.

Speaking of Patty's letter reminds me of two things I want to mention before I close. I never did find your phone number, but if I do run across it, please be assured I won't give it to anyone. In fact, I plan to destroy it. And secondly, although I read some things in the paper regarding your situation, there could have been much I missed reading. I know I never read anything about your husband shaving your son's head. As I stated previously, I had my own ideas about the matter, but just knowing that would have caused me to wonder about my ideas. I'm sorry I wasn't as open-minded as I sounded. Your letter caused a feeling inside me that didn't belong there to simply melt away, and a new compassion to take its place. I almost wished I hadn't written. I never thought about my letter causing you pain, and I am sorry for that. But on the other hand, I did feel the Lord wanted me to write, so I hope it helps to know at least 2 people know and believe your side of the story, plus possibly any others that we might have occasion to tell. And thank you for helping me.

As I stood over Mother's shoulder while she read this woman's letter, I felt so grateful for the small miracle unfolding with each word. Though the jury had disregarded the facts, and even the judge seemed to have allowed my father to take the legal system for a joyride, it indeed helped to know that somebody recognized the facts, pierced the illusion, and heard our side of things. Even better, she had the humility to admit she had been wrong. I tucked this letter away in my treasure box and kept it as evidence that, if given the facts, open-mindedness did still exist within genuinely good people.

A Vacation

Mother has always made sure we take an annual vacation somewhere, even if it's only for a couple of days—and even when affording it, after Daddy told us we were on our own, was not the easiest feat for her to pull off.

That first year, wanting to cheer us all up, we piled into the station wagon and drove toward the Shenandoah mountains in Virginia. We intended to travel along iconic Skyline Drive and then visit the Luray Caverns on the way home. We made it to Skyline drive and parked just off the road before nightfall. Mother had only thirteen dollars to her name, so the seven of us slept in the station wagon by the side of the road, and we children bought Moon Pies for dinner from the gas station with money from our piggy banks. On the heels of this new sadness, we were six miserable children sleeping like skeins of tangled yarn in that chilly car. We woke up even more miserable, cranky, and quarrelsome. Seeing the trip was no use, Mother decided we should just turn around and drive back home without even stopping at Luray Caverns.

Though that trip had not worked out as she planned, Mother was determined over the ensuing years to be as normal as possible on the budget we had. Always frugal, working two jobs and running her own small business, Mother managed to save a little money each year for her retirement, and for the family to get away. Mostly, we drove somewhere local: the free Smithsonian museums in Washington, DC; the Museum of Natural History where we ogled the famous Hope diamond and bones of enormous dinosaurs; the Air and Space Museum with the Apollo spacecraft on display and airplanes hanging from the ceiling; Gettysburg, with its complex panorama of the ever-shifting battle lines played out in colored lights representing North and South; Valley Forge to explore historical figures; and the Hershey Chocolate factory, where we could take a tour we never tired of to see how chocolate was made from start to finish. Longwood Gardens was also a perennial favorite with its beautiful gardens and Christmas displays—and where I hoped to go to school someday for landscape design. We also drove to Canada to visit relatives and other members, and we once spent a week in the sleepy little beach town of Stone Harbor, where we crammed into cheap hotel rooms and brought a cooler so we didn't have to go to restaurants. And when driving somewhere wasn't feasible, we sometimes packed picnics and hiked the Appalachian Trail behind our house.

But this year was different. This year we were going on a *big* vacation. Mother was taking us all to Florida.

When we found out we would be taking ten days off from school, the maximum you could take and still be excused, we were elated. Mother had traded in her station wagon for a large van that better accommodated us as we grew (and doubled as a supply hauling vehicle for her business), and all of us fit nicely in it, including Grandma and Papap, who accompanied us on the highways toward warmer weather. One of my favorite stops was Charleston, South Carolina, where we explored architecture and ambience very different from what we were accustomed to. We toured an aircraft carrier in Charleston, then we visited the antebellum mansions with their meandering expanses of lawn and long avenues of ancient live oak trees covered in ghostly fingers of moss. These wispy tendrils lent the plantations a graceful air, yet a vaguely mournful one, as if the homes were in the middle of a cemetery.

Once we crossed the Florida state line, we made our way to Orlando, drinking in the vast orange groves that dotted the landscape. After stopping at a factory to see how orange juice is made, Mother continued on to the most magical place on Earth: Disney World. None of us could believe we were there.

"I won't go," Mother said matter-of-factly, "because that would be unseemly for a member, but you kids can go if you want."

To be honest, I wasn't too excited. I don't like roller coasters or crowds, and there were hoards of people there. I actually enjoyed the historic stops much more, though my siblings did have fun at the amusement park.

The next day, we toured a few greenhouses along our route. This was because the Church had unwritten rules about vacation. For reasons I never knew, we weren't allowed to go somewhere solely to have fun. The purpose of a trip had to be to visit other Church members or for business reasons. If you wanted to stop somewhere for fun along the way, that was considered acceptable. I was left to suppose that vacations were considered too frivolous—too worldly. So, like an obedient member, Mother made time for this requirement and took pictures of the horticultural businesses we visited.

After Orlando, we headed toward the coast, which would be our last stop before heading back to the cold Pennsylvania weather. Reaching the beaches was like stumbling into paradise. My siblings and I luxuriated on the pretty sand—but not being used to such direct exposure, I fell asleep and woke up so severely burned that even a thick coat of Noxzema didn't relieve the pain. To the disgust of my siblings, I peeled sheets of skin off my arms and back all the way home.

But despite the less-than-comfortable ending, one thing was indisputable: it was an epic vacation none of us would ever forget.

Do You Believe in Miracles?

Two summers ago, we children pooled our money to buy a record player and a few albums. The first two we purchased were the classical *Blue Danube* (probably suggested by Mother) and our own choice of *John Denver's Greatest Hits*.

We swayed to the elegant classical music, but we all sang along with "Take Me Home, Country Roads," belted out "Thank God I'm a Country Boy," and hummed to "Sunshine on My Shoulders." John Denver's sentimental songs and cheerful voice made me remember the best part of growing up in the country: the innocence of dirt roads; the humble, carefree feeling of boundless joy when the sun smiled on you; and the exuberant appreciation of a stack of pancakes drenched with syrup.

Mother hadn't objected to the record player or the early albums, and by the time the boys graduated to harder-edged music from bands like Black Sabbath and AC/DC, they were pretty much too old to be prevented from their choices. (We girls belted out these songs with equal gusto to John Denver's.) But we couldn't believe it when Mother gave the six of us $200 as a joint present this past Christmas, saying she would not buy us a television, but we could if we wanted to. Well, we wasted no time in purchasing one, and we set it up just in time to watch the 1980 Winter Olympics in Lake Placid, New York.

Having grown up ice skating on the creek and nearby ponds, we frequently played ice hockey, hence all of us being immediately drawn to the gutsy, inexperienced US hockey team. (It also harkened me back to a memory I would never shake. In ninth grade, I'd been playing on a local pond with Benny and a couple of his friends when an older guy we didn't know asked if he could join in. For some unknown reason, he hit a slap shot at short range straight into my face. The puck barely missed my eye but struck the bone just beneath, leaving it black and blue. Eventually it morphed into a gruesome mottled green and yellow, and I refused to look at myself in the mirror until it faded. When a teacher asked me in front of the entire class what had happened to me, he looked rather dubious when I told him, as if he didn't believe girls played ice hockey. I laughed to myself. Nobody acknowledged any of the other violence in our home lives, yet this innocent incident drew attention.)

As the Olympics progressed, like most of America we were enthralled with the improbable wins of the plucky US ice hockey team against the powerhouse teams of the world that were supposed to win. As the American team kept turning in victories, Leah and I got so excited that I suggested we drive up to Lake Placid to watch some games in person. It soon became obvious that this was merely a pipe dream. I'd just turned sixteen and only had a learner's permit and no car. She was younger and not even driving yet. Nor had we considered the cost of gas and lodging, or the minor detail of getting tickets to this highly sought-after event. So, we stayed home and resigned ourselves to watching the games on TV with the rest of the family.

The Soviets (though officially deemed amateurs) were a team of experienced de facto professional players with four consecutive gold medals to their name. They had gone up against our professional hockey teams in the past and routed them. Conventional wisdom said that the young American amateur team composed of college players surely had no chance against this behemoth. In addition, the Soviets had already crushed the US team three days prior to the Olympics in an exhibition game.

Even Mother joined our nerve-ridden arena as we watched the US and the Soviets play. Then, the unthinkable happened: we beat the Soviets! Even though it wasn't the gold medal round, crushing the overwhelming favorites *felt* like winning the gold medal. Our living room erupted into exultant cheers and chants of "USA, USA, USA." As we jumped up and down giddily, the television announcer asked, "Do you believe in miracles?"

We all waited anxiously for the gold medal round that following Sunday. With America in the lead 4–2 after nearly all three periods, we held our breath through the final sixty seconds while the US ran the clock down. As the buzzer sounded, the arena burst into cheers, nearly drowning out the announcer exclaiming, "This impossible dream comes true."

This national triumph ignited within me a tiny flicker of belief in the possibility of miracles.

Learning to Fly

Since graduation, David has continued working at Ashcombe and begun taking classes at the community college. He has also continued running his bee and insect removal business, as well as embarking on a new activity he is very excited about: taking flying lessons. He has always been interested in new and fascinating ventures, and he announces he's going to get his private pilot's license. Always eager to share new endeavors, he usually tries to talk someone into joining him—and this time, it's me.

"Why would *I* want to learn to fly?" I ask. "Besides, I don't have any money."

I have so few funds after paying for running gear, clothing, food, and entertainment that one of my new nicknames has become "flat broke Patty" (which is no surprise because I'm always saying dramatically, "I'm flat broke!"). But David is very convincing. He keeps cajoling and says he'll pay for an introductory ride with his instructor, Dan.

So, I agree to go up one time to try it out.

On the day of the ride, David buys me a small black logbook so I can record the flight hour. The next thing I know, David talks me into taking a few lessons "just to see if I like it."

I don't.

We do stalls; I feel queasy. We practice landings; I worry how close we come to the ground before flaring to land and fear I'll never be able to do it. But I continue going.

I still don't have my driver's license, let alone a car, so sometimes I ride my bike the twenty miles to Capital City airport for lessons. Sometimes David has a lesson too. Then we rumble home together in his 1950s truck that looks like the one on the sitcom *Sanford and Son*.

It takes ten hours flight time to solo, so I decide that since I always like to have a goal, I'll take enough lessons to solo, then switch to doing something more productive with my time and money.

I have no idea how those ten hours are going to influence my life.

The Price of Fitting In

Last season's cross-country season pegged me as an up-and-coming runner of increasing prominence, and I come into the spring track season feeling more confident than I had my first year. I'm also thrilled to find out that the girls track team gets their own coach this year—two in fact, a husband and wife team who were highly ranked runners in college. Their expertise and the possibilities for training and improving fills me with excitement, and I want to be the best I can be for them. Hence, I fit training into every spare moment. Determined to be a dominant runner and break out of the pack, I run and run and run until I log a 5:50 mile, which seeds increasing confidence in my trajectory toward a track scholarship.

Between going to school and working on the weekends, plus track practice every weekday, I am often exhausted by the time I get off the activity bus and walk home in the dark. One night, I fall asleep into a bowl of soup at the dinner table; one morning, I lean against the bathroom wall, hoping to steal a few more minutes of rest while mindlessly brushing my teeth, and wake up to find I've succumbed to the bliss of oblivion and have to run for the bus. To make up for time lost at practice, I crank out homework and write term papers on the forty-five-minute bus ride to school.

Despite my fatigue, I find time for a persistent fantasy that doesn't involve earning a scholarship: that the very handsome school quarterback, who is also on the track team, knows who I am because of my wins. I realize this is a silly fantasy; I truly believe I am ugly (my brother's friends hiss "dog" at me when they pass me in school, and other people's reactions have become my mirror of truth). I've cultivated a habit of walking with my eyes to the carpet, only looking up briefly when I come to an intersecting hallway to see which way to go, because I can't bear to see this truth in other people's eyes when they look at me. One day, though, I don't tilt my head up quickly enough and almost run into someone. Startled, I look up and find myself face to face with our star quarterback. In that moment, I see nothing in his eyes but a safe blankness, and perhaps even a kindness. I'm not quite sure which as I duck away red-faced, but I don't see "ugly" reflecting back at me from his expression. *If I were truly ugly, surely he would know*, I reason. The fact that he doesn't flinch or say something rude is a revelation. I allow his non-response to buoy me slightly—not enough to stop navigating the halls with my eyes downward, but enough to give me a shred of hope nonetheless.

The truth is, I try to look as much like the popular girls as possible. Some of them wear hundred-dollar sweaters (which I cannot fathom, or afford), but I try to mimic their styles on my frugal budget. For example, clogs—particularly those with a two-inch heel—are the trendy item this year, and I find a pair at Super Shoes in my price range and wear them to school every day. I have no idea these beloved shoes that give me a semblance of fitting in will be so dangerous.

One spring morning, after a particularly strenuous track practice the night before, my legs are killing me as I walk down the hill to the school bus. A moment later, my ankle suddenly gives way and my clogged foot turns swiftly sideways, making me stumble. It hurts but I've turned my ankle so many times while ice skating that I'm unconcerned. I know it will likely hurt for a little while and then go away. At school, however, I notice swelling with increasing alarm, which is accompanied by a black-and-blue mark the length of my foot. With a sinking feeling, I remember what Mother says this kind of bruising means in a situation like this, so I limp to the school nurse's office. She takes one look at my foot and promptly calls Mother to come pick me up and take me to the emergency room for x-rays. When the doctor slaps the film onto the lighted screen, it's immediately clear that my foot is broken.

"You'll be in a cast and then wear a boot for at least a month," the doctor says.

Glumly, I call my coach to deliver the news. I was building such positive momentum, and now this frustrating development has left me crushed.

Jordan Almonds

Daddy calls the house, not because he's heard I have broken my foot, but because he does this from time to time to try to get Mother on the phone and engage her in an argument about his grievances. He seems to relish conflict, and she usually hangs up on his tirades. But she's not home when he calls; and since I'm the one who answers, I tell him about my broken foot.

He right away responds in a jolly way. "How about I come over and bring some pills along to make you feel better?"

I know what he means by "pills": Jordan Almonds. Anything can be fixed with candy, and Jordan Almonds look like big, pastel-colored pills. I know it sounds crazy that I would have anything to do with him after all the terrorism, but I know Mother will be working, and saying no to my father is still unthinkable. Plus, he seems to be in such a good mood, and I don't want to hurt his feelings, so I agree he can come over for a short while.

When Daddy arrives, he sits in the living room to visit with a few of us children, doling out Jordan almonds to all of us, not just to me. It is times like this that hope springs eternal, or at least beats reality. When Daddy's not on the warpath, his other self seems far away, and for a moment I can forget his ugly side and entertain the idea that he loves us like a real father would.

As you might expect, Mother is irate when she gets home and finds out Daddy has been in the house. She's understandably worried the visit will only encourage his boldness and that he'll feel he can come in the house anytime he wants. She's right, I know, and promise not to do it again. It's just that when Daddy is nice, even for a brief time, he seems sane and somewhat normal. And I can't help but want to hold on to that notion, even though my rational mind tells me that he's probably incapable of ever being normal again.

Hypocrisy in the Mirror

July brings the following credulous article:

THE PITTSBURGH PRESS, JULY 20, 1980

Shunned Mennonite Sneaks Peek at His Children

On Sundays sometimes the Carlisle farmer slips into a shadowy corner of the courtyard to see his children, who never indicate that they notice him.

"In eight years they haven't spoken to me," he said, standing his ground, waging war against what he calls "the hypocrisy of the church and its members."

Bear, 50, has found a Kansas psychiatrist to help plead his case to the church and to his family. Dr. Harold Voth, who has helped one other excommunicated Mennonite get reconciled with his family, has been writing letters to Mrs. Bear and to Mennonite bishops.

"If they want to boot him out of the church, that's their option," Voth said, "but I personally think it's time that family gets back together."

Voth described the family's shunning as the ultimate cruelty and urged Mrs. Bear to consider the consequences.

"To break up the family makes the children pay the highest price and leaves them open to psychological damage. I feel society should step in and help this man."

...

"There are extraordinary pressures on her that make her avoid me," Bear said. "This has gone on for too long for me to engage in wishful thinking."

Yeah, like maybe the extraordinary pressure of your constant terrorism, I think sarcastically.

His adviser Voth confirms Bear's grim outlook: "I doubt he'll ever get his wife back unless he repents," he said. "These people are very rigid and they have been very misguided."

Bear—farming 300 acres of cabbage, cantaloupe, and pumpkins—maintains he loves his family and doesn't want a divorce.

"I keep hoping they will break away from the church and come home to me," Bear said. "It's not nice to be alone."

Ugh, I think in exasperation. *Are all psychiatrists this blindingly ignorant? This willingness to believe whatever story some man tells them without verification. Do you think maybe constantly fleeing our home because of this man's violence might have some psychological impact on his children?*

Seriously, you can't make this stuff up.

Despite any number of publications with "Inquirer" in their name, I'm astonished how little inquiry takes place. *We haven't talked to him in eight years?* What baloney. (And this from a man who keeps insisting how honest he is, and how *everyone else* is lying. Yet, Daddy's lies litter every article ever written, and the public laps it up like a starving kitten at a bowl of cream.)

Add these erroneous articles to the ignorant do-gooders who think they know what is going on in our family, weighing in with advice on what we should do, and you have the perfect recipe for driving a previously sane family out of their minds.

Freedom Comes in Many Forms

We used to be required to go to church, but now that we're older, it takes a lot more energy to force us. Mostly I go to make Mother happy and so she's not alone, but there is always one minister I hope won't be delivering the sermon. He's not a bad or mean person. He's just desperately boring. And he's not only plodding, circular, uninspired, and unimaginative, he repetitively reinforces the inferiority of and need for women to be submissive.

As I sit in the pew on Sundays, sometimes with one or more of my sisters beside me, this emotional, psychological, and spiritual violence rains down on our heads. Whether I want it to or not, I can feel it seeping into my identity and grooming me to accept without protest second-class status, invisibility, silence, and passivity. Worse, I am to accept this relentless humiliation as ordained by God. Hearing these words is stifling; I can hardly breathe. Desperate to escape, I can only stare at the ceiling lights, where I try to blur the torrent of hateful rhetoric. When that doesn't work, I focus on a spot on the wall, willing myself to be anywhere but here.

Seated there glassy-eyed, as when enduring one of my father's monologues, I recall the time I viewed myself with detachment as a pinned insect. Now, however, my mind becomes fixated on the concept of Chinese water torture as I listen to the drip, drip, drip of the indoctrination of subjugation. The torture is relieved only by a few homicidal fantasies (in one, I interrupt the entire sermon by falling on the floor, banging my heels, and throwing a righteous tantrum) and an intense desire to scream.

Of course, I don't do any of those things, I just silently fume.

*I absolutely **refuse** to worship a God who hates women. I will **not** do it. Why on earth would I? We are humiliated, abused, exploited, silenced, blamed for everything, and treated like second-class citizens, all in the name of God. Why would I worship that?*

As I'm thinking about how I cannot tolerate this repetitive propaganda much longer, not even for Mother, and stay sane, I realize in a sudden illumination that it's not *Adam* who was tricked, it was *Eve*! *She* was the one who was handed a poison apple to eat, and she has been under the influence ever since: swallowing her inferiority, digesting suppression, and plastering on a smile to slave away for tyrants. I recognize in a great burst of liberation that hell isn't lurking around some corner after death. For women it exists right here on earth, so why should I worry about it later?

Freedom, I decide, comes in many forms.

With this epiphany, I instantly shed the fear of hell, never again to be controlled by this tactic of manmade conditioning.

Wake-Up Call

As a career procrastinator in certain areas of my life, I tend to put things off to the last moment and then race to make the deadline. It usually works out, but lately it hasn't been working enough as it pertains to my job at Mother's deli and ice cream stand at Ashcombe.

On several occasions this summer, I've arrived five to ten minutes late for work, and today, I am twenty minutes late. This time, Mother is seriously steamed.

"You're fired," she informs me.

I'm fired? By my own mother? Is that possible?

But I need the money to buy my clothing, running sneakers, and a new pair of racing flats for cross-country this year. I also need it for flying lessons.

"Okay, okay," I tell her, "I'll try to be on time."

But she has had enough. "No, you keep saying that. This is it. You're done."

"Okay, fine," I retort indignantly. "If you fire me, I'll go get a job pumping gas at Shillito's."

Shillito's is the gas station right up the road from our house, about a mile away. We've always ridden our bikes there to get chewing gum and ice cream sandwiches. I figure it would be the perfect job and even closer than Ashcombe. I know she won't be thrilled about this job because she thinks a girl pumping gas is not safe from strange men. But I decide right then and there that it will be all right.

"I'm going to do it," I tell her. "I'll go apply tomorrow."

She can see I'm not bluffing, just like the time I told her I would run away if she didn't sign the permission slip for me to be on the track team. "Okay," she backpedals. "You can have your job back, but DON'T be late again."

I promise her I won't be. And I'm not.

Moving Up

I finish the cross-country season in the number-one varsity position and become the team captain. At the county meet I finish sixth, which I consider a huge improvement over my previous twentieth-place finish.

On this particular Saturday, I must report to work at Mother's deli as soon as the race is over. I'm so excited about this improvement that I burst in and blurt out. "I came in sixth in the county!"

As usual, I'm already extrapolating what this portends for a magnificent future.

With an affectionately dismissive laugh, Mother says, "Oh, my little second-place Patty."

I am instantly stung and outraged. "I'm *not* second place," I assert. "I made a huge improvement, and I'll do even better next year. You'll see."

My determination up to that point had known few bounds, but I was about to step it up to a level that even I didn't see coming.

A New Goal

The summer and fall have been a busy time for me. I've been studying a thick book David recommended to prepare for taking my SATs, and he's been helping me with the math problems when I get stuck.

The pace of flying lessons has picked up recently, too. I took my first flight in May. Then two in June, three in July, one in August as cross-country training got underway, and three more in September. Then, on October 23, 1980, my instructor, Dan (who is also my brother's flight instructor), certified in my logbook "Okay to solo." I was nervous, but I was also terrified, not only to be up in the airplane all alone, but that I would crash. It was too late to back out without looking foolish, though. So I started the engine, taxied out, and took off, completing the touch-and-go landings while Dan observed from the ground. After I safely landed the final time, in the time-honored tradition of aviation, a portion of the back of my t-shirt was cut out, and my name and the date of my solo flight was inscribed in sharpie pen. The fragment now hangs on the wall of the flight school where I rent the airplane.

With my first solo flight accomplished, I decide to continue taking lessons and set a goal to get a private pilot's license like David is working to-ward. (David is also teaching me how to ride his motorcycle and suggested I get my license, which I thought was a splendid idea. Mother put her foot down, though. "Absolutely not," she said. For a reason I never understood, motorcycle riding was out of the question but flying lessons were not.)

I am admittedly mystified by this decision to continue my flying in-struction. I make only enough money to take one or two lessons a month, I often feel airsick, and I'm not particularly enamored of flying. David says I picked it up easily, but I can't tell if that's true because I am always terrified of making a mistake.

Despite my father's insistence that we think for ourselves, asking questions of him—or anyone else—has rarely been welcomed or answered. So, I have developed the habit of querying myself. Sometimes, if I wait long enough, the answers arrive.

Why are you doing this? I ask myself, Why would you spend all your hard-earned money for this when you should be saving it for college?

Only one answer comes to me, and it seems flimsy, even to me. *Flying is unique. A positive kind of being different. Something admirable rather than disreputable.*

But flimsy as it is, I'm still intrigued by it. Plus, I have so little money that saving enough to pay for college seems hopeless.

A Final Marathon

All summer and fall, between flying, working, and training for cross-country, I have also been training to qualify for the Boston marathon at the annual Harrisburg marathon in November. Long runs, short runs, hill work on the steep mountainside behind our house, wind sprints on the flat part of the road. I now know a lot more about training and have a detailed strategy for pacing each mile of the race. Normally, I wear my regular sneakers for the long-distance runs on the road, but I figure I need all the edge I can get to reach my goal, so I switch to wearing the thinner-soled racing flats I wear for cross-country meets on the grass.

On the day of the race, I bring a stopwatch and take careful note of each mile time. For the first eighteen, I'm on pace for the 3:30 qualifying time needed for Boston. I'm well in the lead and feeling confident about winning my age group this year when suddenly, my legs start to get tighter and tighter and I can't keep my strategic pace. Pretty soon, I see my competition passing me. By then, my legs are so locked up I can't run. Actually, I can barely walk. I realize the racing flats that work so well on grass over three miles were probably not a good idea for twenty-six miles of pounding on macadam.

As more girls pass me, I look down to see my fatigued legs dripping with blood from where they've rubbed together. Finally, at the twenty-mile point, I accept the offer of a ride.

I don't qualify for the Boston Marathon.

I don't even finish the race.

When One Door Closes

Fall succumbs to the rainy, drizzly days of mid-November. I turn seventeen but feel much older. Worse, all my hopes and plans are disintegrating. After being unable to finish the last marathon, I can feel everything slipping away like water swirling down the drain.

Though I had a good season in cross-country, I'm beginning to comprehend that I'm not in the same league with the most dominant runners I face from our rival schools. In the big races, I start out strong but then slow down. My coach tells me to lower my chin when I run, but I can't get enough air in my lungs that way. Sometimes it gets so bad, and I wheeze so loudly, that my competitors slow down enough for me to see their horrified looks as they ask me if I'm all right. For the longest time, I figured it was because I wasn't in good enough shape, but no matter how much I run, it still happens. (At the time, I had never heard of "exercise-induced asthma," but that's likely what it was.)

Increasingly, I begin to quietly acknowledge that Mr. Harbold was probably right after all. Mother too. I'm not a good enough runner to get a full scholarship to college. And I probably can't get an academic scholarship either. I'm in the top ten percent of my class, but I'm never going to contend for valedictorian or salutatorian, which is who I assume receives the scholarships. I have no money saved, and what I do have goes to flying lessons. As usual, I am flat broke. Mother did say I should have worked and saved my money for college, and now I think I should have listened to her. I have virtually nothing to show for years of running, or signing up for the hardest classes, or even savings from my employment. Dejectedly I think, *All my efforts have amounted to nothing.*

But I desperately want to escape the infamy and shabby future that lurks behind every corner if I stop striving for better. More than anything, I want respect. I *want* to get into a prestigious college, but I have to face the fact that I simply can't pay for that. The local community college will probably be my only option.

One day, right before Thanksgiving break, I go to my locker in front of the guidance counselor's office to exchange books and materials. I have study hall next period but find myself stymied about what to select from my locker. I have no homework to do and no term papers to write. This is so unusual that I am baffled about what I will do with a free hour. I am contemplating this dilemma when an announcement comes over the loudspeaker.

"A cadet from the United States Air Force Academy will be in the guidance counselor's office at eleven a.m. if anyone would like to attend this presentation."

Air Force Academy? *What is that?* I wonder. "Air Force" sounds like it might have something to do with flying, but because of our pacifist background, I know zilch about the military.

Since I have nothing else to do, and the office is right here, I figure I might as well check it out.

As I pivot away from my locker, something miraculous happens. Though it is elusive, it is as if an angel's robe flutters ever so softly against my cheek. The feeling is so gentle that I wonder if I simply imagined it, but the faintest whisper of intuition registers that something momentous is about to happen.

I look at my watch and see that the presentation begins in three minutes, so I hurry into the room and take my seat.

Though I'm sure the cadet talked for thirty to forty minutes, I remember only three things he said:

The Air Force Academy is difficult to get in to.

It's free.

They pay you $487 per month.

I am flabbergasted by my luck.

It seems I have found the holy grail.

A prestigious school. It's hard to get into. And it's free.

I know immediately, beyond a shadow of a doubt, that this is it, that this is my answer.

The announcement by my locker and the soft flutter near my cheek anchors in both the momentousness of the moment and a lesson I will carry with me throughout life: the miracle that doors can open where before there were only walls—but only if you follow your soul's callings and your guidance. Had I not already been prepared for this opportunity, and further, had I not been standing empty-minded, directly in front of the guidance counselor's office, this announcement would have gone unnoticed.

After the presentation, I go to the room next door where the catalogues for all the colleges are filed and pull out the one for the US Air Force Academy. A picture of the iconic cadet chapel, its spires like fingers reaching in prayerful exultation toward the sky, graces the front cover. Inside are pictures of cadets on glossy pages, skiing in the Rocky Mountains and ice skating on the pond at the Academy's private winter retreat in the mountains. Multiple athletic fields stretch in green splendor to the skirt of the mountains jutting directly behind the campus. Everywhere they talk about a commitment to excellence. One entire brochure is devoted to the theme, showing cadets in uniform marching in front of the chapel with this quote beneath: "Let anyone who quits striving for excellence move over for those who will not."

This is what I want. I am utterly certain.

Perusing the majors the Academy features in the catalogue, I don't see much I recognize, but since I'm already taking flying lessons, I guess I'll choose aeronautical engineering. The brochure says that every cadet who graduates is guaranteed a pilot training slot if they are medically qualified to fly. (I will later learn that for some, this is the only reason they want to go to the Academy.) For me however, it doesn't make much of an impression. Flying as a career is not remotely on my radar. As far as I know, pilots are virtually all men. There's only one woman I've heard of who flies for a living—she's nicknamed Judy Jet, and she's an aviator for a corporation out of the same airfield where I take lessons.

I read the requirements to get in: GPA, class standing, SAT scores, varsity letters, clubs students belong to. They also show the percentage of acceptance and the three major elements the Academy looks for: academics, athletics, and leadership. I study the requirements intently and feel confident that I have the varsity athletic portion well covered. I'll have to take a physical fitness test to get in, plus have a medical evaluation and present proof of 20/20 vision, all of which should be no problem for me. The academics require four years of math and science and a minimum of three years of language. Admissions also looks favorably on AP and honors classes. I realize I have all these requirements met, thanks to my brother who told me which classes to take. I already have the necessary class standing, which I'll need to keep and improve a bit, but I have yet to take the SATs, so I note the average scores for those who get accepted and make achieving those a more targeted focus of my SAT prep. I'm also certain the flying lessons I've already been taking will be a plus.

There is, however, one big hole in my resume. I'm late to the game in the area of leadership and clubs. Reading the list of examples from earlier appointees, my heart sinks when I realize I belong to none of the clubs mentioned, except for the National Honor Society. It never occurred to me to join clubs. They not only took up extra time I didn't have, but joining clubs was something my family simply did not do.

I can put down cross-country team captain for the leadership portion, but I realize I'll have to join some clubs that demonstrate leadership. After researching organizations diligently, I volunteer at the Boys and Girls Club of Harrisburg, sign up for PA Youth in Government and Model UN, join the French club, and seek out any other opportunities that I might be able to put on my application.

With an invigorated focus, I vow to put maximum effort into this new goal. (It will become the subject I talk about so much that my siblings will roll their eyes and groan and become thoroughly sick of hearing about it.) I even disregard with a shrug that the Academy requires one other thing that no other college does: each graduate of the institution will owe the Air Force five years of active duty service in exchange for their free education.

I'm seventeen, I figure. Big deal.

CHAPTER ELEVEN

1981

Luck is what happens when preparation meets opportunity.
—SENECA

Fear of Failure

Fresh off the mind-boggling new opportunity the Air Force Academy cadet introduced to me in the guidance counselor's office, I encounter a new wrinkle several weeks into January: trigonometry is *not* my friend. Nor is the trig teacher. He is another one who looks around the room to spot the student with the deer-in-the-headlights look and calls on that student. Between the stress of being singled out and the confusion I feel about the subject, I wear that blank, uncomprehending look too often. My pop-quiz results add to the stress and growing panic that this class is going to pull down my average enough to endanger my quest to get into the Academy. I am so worried that I decide I need to drop another class to make more time to study trig.

While the core classes continue uninterrupted throughout the year, the new semester brings fresh electives I selected prior to adopting my new goal. And since electives seem like less important classes, I figure dropping one elective should be no problem—particularly an English class on how to write term papers. I've written so many already that I know this class will not be difficult for me, but it will take a lot of my time to do research. I'm actually mystified by why I signed up for this class in the first place.

I march confidently to the teachers' lounge to talk to the head of the

English department (who is apparently the only person who can give me the permission I need to drop this class). I explain my predicament and the stakes involved as she listens carefully.

"Will you fail the term paper class?" she asks.

"Of course not," I tell her, then launch into reexplaining my reasons.

She cuts me off before I get very far. "Well, I can't help you. I can only drop a class for a student if they're going to fail."

"But—"

"It's final," she says. "That's the rule."

I meander out, head down as usual, and try desperately not to cry until I reach the privacy of a bathroom. The track scholarship didn't work out as I had hoped, and now it looks like this dream will be doomed too. I know I cannot take both classes and keep my trig grade up.

Leaving the bathroom, I almost bump into Mr. Matthews, the English teacher I've had for several classes and who is one of my favorites. He is good looking, and I have a secret crush on him, but that's not why he's my favorite teacher. He makes the material interesting, and though he demands the best from his students, he also treats us respectfully. I've written several term papers for his classes and received excellent grades.

"Oh, sorry," I mumble.

His eyes narrow as he takes in my face. "What's wrong?" he asks.

I let out my anguish over trig, my fear of not getting into the Academy, and how I can't drop the term paper class unless I'm going to fail it.

He glances away thoughtfully, then back to me. "What period do you have lunch?"

"Fourth."

"I'll meet you in the cafeteria then."

Unable to believe his generosity, and my good fortune, I practically count the minutes until lunchtime. After getting my food and finding a table, I expectantly wait for him.

Not long after, he strolls in and finds me. "You're out of the class," he casually announces,

My jaw drops. "How'd you do that? The teacher said she wouldn't drop it unless I said I'd fail."

Nonchalantly, he says, "I told her you'd fail."

He knew that wasn't true, and I knew he had too much integrity to lie, but he never did tell me what he actually said.

A few months later, when I asked him to write me one of the three required recommendation letters for the Academy, he handed me a fat sealed envelope. What he wrote in that letter forever remained a secret too.

Colonel Etchberger

Filling out the Academy form to request more information triggered a consultation with Colonel Etchberger, an Academy liaison officer assigned to our area. His job was to advise students on the process of getting into the Academy. He was a gruff but kind man who made it clear that getting in was up to me and my efforts but that he would shepherd me through the process.

Like other elite colleges, the Academy required good grades and rewarded athletics, leadership, and volunteer activities. During our meeting, I told him about my grades, as well as my positions in track and cross-country.

"And what clubs are you in?" he asked.

"Well," I said, "when I saw the Academy brochure in November, I realized I was a little late to the game in this area. But I joined every club I could find and am doing everything I possibly can to make up for lost time."

He nodded. I couldn't tell if he was impressed by that or not, but I hoped so.

I told him about my background growing up on a farm and my current job at Ashcombe.

He almost cracked a smile. "The Academy likes kids from farms because they work hard and never give up."

This made me feel much better about my background.

"And your job supervising berry pickers qualifies as a leadership position," he added.

I was both surprised and thrilled and relieved to hear this. I had figured that without something like class president on my application, I was doomed. But he said no, that my qualifications at this point were good.

"And keep studying hard for those SATs," he advised. "Take them more than once. The Academy will take your best combined scores."

And then he told me that there was one more crucial part of the admissions process, which was completely *unlike* any other college.

"You must receive a nomination from your Congressional Representative or one of your Senators."

My eyes widened.

"They're limited to nominating only ten high school seniors. For those fortunate few who receive a nomination, their names are forwarded to the Academy. Of the ten, only one will be offered an appointment to attend the service academy of their choice."

I wasn't sure how to respond. I had *definitely* not seen this part of the application coming.

Colonel Etchberger explained the nomination process, how it included applying to each office and hopefully being selected for an interview. He handed me a card with his phone number and the important timelines for each part of the process.

I thanked him and told him there was one more thing: though I was taking them sporadically, due to my increasingly full schedule with the added club and volunteer activities, as well as training for track, I was continuing the flying lessons I had begun months prior.

His eyes lit up a bit. "Keep taking those," he said. "And get your private pilot's license. That will look good too."

After he left, I realized I had been exceptionally fortunate to "discover" the Academy just in the nick of time, both to make all the deadlines *and* to cram enough clubs onto my application. It seemed I was on the right track; even my trig grade improved enough that it wasn't going to doom my chances, and I began to feel slightly better about my prospects. Though I knew the competition was stiff, I believed I was at least in the ballpark.

Maybe things are looking up for me after all, I mused.

Homesick

I'd been selected for the Rotary Leader's Conference, which was a three-day overnight event at Dickinson College in Carlisle. I was elated to be chosen, and it was one more gold star to add to my resume, but it coincided with a previously scheduled orthodontic appointment—and one hard limitation for getting accepted to the Academy was that all orthodontic work had to be completed before graduation, and therefore prior to basic training.

Mother had a solution: I would attend the conference, but she would retrieve me for the orthodontist appointment, then return me afterward for the rest of the event.

It turned out that I was grateful for the reprieve. Even though it was only ten miles from home, I'd never been away overnight like this, surrounded by so many people I didn't know. I became terribly homesick but felt rescued when Mother came to pick me up. After the appointment (where my orthodontist, to my relief, hatched an ambitious plan to get my mouth ready by graduation), Mother took me out to Dairy Queen, which did the job of helping me survive the weekend.

At the conference, boys and girls my age attended lectures and engaged in activities to develop leadership. I enjoyed it, but I quickly realized that to survive the Academy, I would have to not only up my leadership game a great deal, but I would also have adjust to being a much greater distance from home—not ten miles away, but ten *states* away.

Deadlines and Decisions

Perhaps she didn't take it very seriously when I announced this opportunity, or perhaps like me when I first learned of it, the reality and requirements did not initially sink in, but the bottom line is: Mother is not thrilled about me going to the Academy.

Now that it is a serious quest, she is beginning to voice her objections, beginning with her concerns about me being a conscientious objector.

"We're to turn the other cheek," she reminds me. "And we are forbidden from going to war."

I know all this, and the idea of it *does* trouble me a bit. *Who wants to fight in a war?* But I know this a great opportunity, so I brush the argument off.

"You'll also owe them five years after graduation," she points out, "and then another two after that, including pilot training." She does a quick calculation. "You'll be twenty-nine when you're done. What about marriage and children?"

This troubles me not at all, and I brush it off easily. Twenty-nine is another lifetime. Mother may disagree, but I believe I'll have plenty of time to get married. First, I need to pay for college. The rest I'll figure out later.

The deadline for applying for nominations and to the Academy itself approaches in early summer. I intend to fill out the applications, but for some reason I keep procrastinating. Though Mother has objected to this military path, my procrastination in the face of something I desperately want exasperates her until one day, she explodes.

"If you want to go to the Academy, you better get those applications filled out RIGHT NOW. The deadline is almost here."

Shocked by the seeming support tucked into her heated statement, I get the applications filled out and mailed. Because the Congressmen and Senators interview for all the service academy nominations at the same time, Col. Etchberger said I should indicate my first choice along with my alternate selections (the Naval Academy, West Point, Coast Guard Academy, and Merchant Marine Academy) in the order I wanted to attend.

"But I don't want to go anywhere *but* the Air Force Academy," I told him emphatically.

I almost saw him crack another smile. "Well, you still need to indicate that you're interested in the others too."

I didn't like the idea of being relegated to another academy, but I obeyed his direction nonetheless.

Being accepted into an academy other than the Air Force wasn't the only thing weighing on me, though.

A year ago, I had made that silent promise in the car on the way to Canada that I would join the Church to keep Mother company. The year of procrastination I'd given myself was up, not to mention that the military and the Church were utterly incompatible. This left me with two starkly looming choices: go forward toward the Academy, or go what seemed to be backward to join my ancestors.

If I joined the Church, I'd have to marry someone in the church, I knew. So, the following Sunday, I look around and consider my choices. The number of eligible men I'm not related to is small, even if I include the ones in

Canada. Furthermore, the only ones with any liveliness I can detect are my cousins, and you can't marry your cousins.

My decision is made.

Mother will have to be on her own.

Changing Momentum

Cross-country season of my senior year begins solidly. I'm still number one on the team and the team captain. But there's another girl on our team who has been gaining ground on me. I recognize in her face the same hunger I once had. We remain neck and neck for a little while, but she gradually acquires momentum that surpasses me and I fall to the number-two position.

As the new goal with the Academy has taken shape, I find that I don't care quite as much about running anymore. The constant competition of meets makes me weary. In fact, if it weren't for the varsity letters I need for the Academy, I'd probably try my hand at tennis, which I have come to love. I don't even sign up for this year's marathon.

I've also been learning ping pong for the last couple of years. Benny, who graduated last June, learned to play between his classes at Votech. He built a ping pong table in the basement and painted lines on it. We played all through winter and spring, and I observed Benny's skills: how he served, how he positioned himself to make the best moves, how he slammed the ball in an overhand swipe for a winning shot. I loved playing and spent months in the basement dancing on the balls of my feet to meet his shots. Finally, I drew even with him and now occasionally win a game.

I am doing better in math too. This year I'm required to take calculus, and I really like it. I actually perk up when the teacher assigns a project that will make up a significant portion of our grade. He gives us a set of ten story problems to solve using calculus and says we can earn extra points if we are creative with the assignment. Looking at the little stories, I believe I see a pattern, and with a little massaging I think I can fit them into a theme of nursery rhymes. This inspires in me enormous energy and resourcefulness.

I gather two pieces of yellow poster board. On the front, I use a stencil to paint in blue, storybook letters, "Calculus Through the Eyes of a Child." I cut long strips of dark blue fabric and sew the edges under with large stitching so it looks like book binding, then I attach it to both the cover and the back so that it presents like a fairy tale book. I fill the book with stories and illustrations that echo the math problems. On one page, three ships moving at different rates of speed becomes a problem facing the butcher, the baker, and the candlestick maker sitting in their boats. I paint these characters on the poster board and write out the solved math problem below them. Another page becomes the old woman in a shoe. For her, I cut out brown velour fabric to resemble a boot and use shoelaces for her children to jump rope. For the graph problem, I worry my theme might have run out of steam, but then realize Humpty Dumpty's brick wall can serve as a graph. The coup de gras is the site of Hansel and Gretel's danger. I bake a flat gingerbread house and decorate it in a colorful variety of candy before carefully affixing it to the poster board.

On the day I turn it in, my teacher is so amazed that he shows it to all the other teachers. I earn a grade of 98 on it, and I am thrilled when he sends a letter home saying I am doing exceptional work.

Nomination Interviews

Over the spring and summer, after achieving good scores the first time out, I heed Col. Etchberger's advice and take the SATs a second and third time. Each time I cram for weeks before the test, and each time I do better, finally achieving an above-average median score for the Academy. Now, it's showtime for the elimination process.

I've sent my letters to the Congresspeople, and now I'm waiting to get called for an interview. If I don't get a nomination, my quest is over. No nomination, no AFA appointment. But I don't have to be concerned for long because I get word from Senator Specter that he's willing to interview me.

When the day arrives, it is cold and David's 1950s truck I'm driving to the interview refuses to start. I turn the key again and again, hoping to hear the engine roar to life, but nothing. Pretty soon, knowing I'll be late and that it won't look good, I call the Senator's office to reschedule. Feeling defeated, I figure this will probably doom my chances.

When the rescheduled appointment day arrives, I dress in my spiffiest outfit, pull my long hair back neatly, and drive my brother's truck (which this time I tested prior to leaving) to Harrisburg. Arriving just in time, after getting flustered trying to park in the city, I am ushered into a conference room with several interviewers seated around a table. I've never been to an interview before, but I expect they might ask me why I want to go to the Academy and why I think I am qualified. To my shock, however, they ask me none of that.

"Who is your favorite president, and why?" one of them asks.

My face grows red and my mind freezes.

Why are they asking me this? I wonder. *What does my favorite president have to do with getting into the Academy?*

So, I say the first president that comes to mind: John F. Kennedy. Then, completely unprepared, I fumble over my reasons for why.

They continue to ask other questions that have nothing to do with the Academy, and I leave the interview feeling like the country bumpkin that I am, driving away in my country bumpkin transportation, wondering why on earth they would ask me something so silly and irrelevant.

Of course, on the way home I remember who my favorite president is: Abraham Lincoln. And I know exactly why. This humble man with his bottomless wisdom and wry sense of humor in the darkest times, along with his unimpeachable integrity, has always inspired me. I learned the Gettysburg Address by heart in elementary school and it still thrills me to remember those famous lines.

I sensed that the people sitting around that table were sophisticated in ways I never would be. And I was left to assume they had recognized what I had—that I didn't belong in their world.

A Smaller Pond

Because I *knew* the interview had been a red-faced flop, I figured I would have to focus on a somewhat smaller pond, competing against other candidates from my district rather than the entire state. I had one last opportunity to gain a nomination: my interview with US Representative Bill Goodling.

Mother had gone to school in Camp Hill, and one of her classmates not only knew him, but said she would put in a good word for me.

"Be nice to his secretary," she advised. "The secretaries see everybody, and their opinion can make or break a candidate."

I was grateful for this advice that felt like it was leveling the playing field a little bit, and I made sure I was very polite to her. The interview seemed to go decently as well.

Around Christmastime, I learned (as I had feared) that I did not get the nomination from Senator Specter. (Decades later, I would burst out laughing, disrupting the dark silence of the theater in the middle of the Oliver Stone movie, *JFK*, where it was apparent that Senator Specter loathed President Kennedy.) Furthermore, I had never considered that Senator Specter was a Republican and JFK a Democrat when I gave my answer. Although I had studied government and civics in school, I had no context for politics in actual practice, since our family and culture did not believe in voting. We were to be "in the world but not of the world," which left me with no perspective on political parties—or that the people who belonged to them felt about their party the way our high school felt intense loyalty to our football team and hatred for our chief rival. Even after two seasons in PA Youth in Government, I had no idea who was a Republican and who was a Democrat. It never occurred to me that it might be relevant.

Each day I go to the mailbox to see if a letter has arrived from Mr. Goodling, but none appear.

Perhaps all this has been a pipe dream, I think. *Nothing but another foolish fantasy of mine.*

Back in the News

After 1979's deluge of national attention, Daddy has been relatively quiet (for him) these last two years. He does pop up in interviews on occasion, and this time it's in an article commemorating the anniversary of his acquittal of assault charges two years ago.

The Scrantonian, December 6, 1981

Another Lonely Holiday for Shunned Mennonite

[The article reports that he stopped to ask two teenagers where he might find his son, whom he knew was working on a nearby farm.]

"I haven't seen some of my children for four years. I went to the Ashcombe Farm and asked two girls if they knew where he worked and suddenly, I realized one of them was my daughter," he said.

...

Accordingly, under Church doctrine, his family was ordered to shun him. To this day they refuse to speak with him or even acknowledge his existence.

...

"Some of them run when they see me. My wife runs away."

Two years ago this week Bear was dramatically acquitted of charges he abducted his wife, Gale, to whom he is legally still married. Bear admitted accosting her at the farmer's market and dragging her to his truck, but he said he merely wanted to save her from the "religious tyranny" of the ultraconservative sect. A Cumberland County jury agreed with him.

Later in the article he offers his reflections on quitting his campaign.

"It was a mistake to say I was going to stop," said Bear, who once used an axe to get through the front door of his family's home. "You don't help yourself or anyone else by waiting. If I'm going to be a devil in their eyes, I might as well be a big devil. I don't know what will happen from here on."

While it's still unnerving to see him in the news, in many ways I am beginning to feel a tiny bit less in Daddy's world, or even *of* his world.

CHAPTER TWELVE

1982

Live life as if everything were rigged in your favor.
—RUMI

The Letter

In early January, a letter finally arrives from Congressman Goodling's office. It begins:

> *As I indicated to those of you who I had a chance to talk with, choosing ten nominees for each of the academies, when we have so many qualified applicants, is a very difficult task.*

My heart sinks. This is the way a person writes to let people know they didn't get a slot.

> *We first of all, look at the recommendations of the academies. If an academy does not recommend an applicant as above-average, qualified, or excellent, it would be false encouragement on our part to nominate them. We do this because in all probability the academy will not accept anyone unless they are listed as above average or excellent.*

Now I'm sure I've hit the end of the road, but I feel compelled to trudge on toward the inevitable verdict. All I can think at this point is, I did everything I could think of and it wasn't enough.

Secondly, we look at the recommendations of the Selection Board which interviewed the applicants. If the Board strongly favors an applicant, we will normally nominate him. Also, if the Board highly recommends an applicant, but we are unable to grant the applicant his or her first choice, we will automatically recommend him to the Academy of his/her second choice or to the Merchant Marine Academy.

Now I think maybe they're going to offer me a second-place choice, even though the only selection I want is the Air Force Academy. I begin to consider that I could learn to live with another choice.

Again, let me repeat, we automatically give every possible consideration to all applicants who are listed by the Academy as above average or excellent. I would also like to repeat what I said during the interviews for the benefit of those who I did not have an opportunity to meet. After we nominate ten people for each vacancy, and in this case that means ten people to each of the four Academies, our responsibility and involvement ceases. The final selection is made strictly by the Academies.

And there at the very bottom of the letter I see the official verdict.

I am very happy to be able to nominate you to the Air Force Academy and wish you well as you compete against applicants from all over the country.

A Calling to Liberation

Though I'm elated over my nomination, and proud of myself for reaching this level of the process, I can't help but doubt that I'll get into the Academy. I've been accepted at other colleges, but I can't really afford to go to them either, so I resign myself to my fate: that after everything I've done to get into college and the Air Force Academy, I'll probably end up attending the local community college.

After track practice one night, the family is milling around in the kitchen after dinner when I walk in the door. I ask the standard question, as always half hopeful and half afraid of the answer. "Did anything come in the mail today?"

My family is used to the intensity of my obsession with the Academy, but still I know they sometimes find it annoying and often tease me.

"No letters arrived," David says. "But don't worry. You can drive with me in my truck to the community college."

I take the bait easily and blow up. "I don't *want* to go there."

I know it sounds like I'm putting down where he is going to school, and it is a fine community college with a great reputation, I know. But I'm frustrated because I've worked so hard in high school and have hoped I could go to a prestigious school. My siblings have heard these statements a thousand times before, and they join in a chorus of teasing me about my future life at community college.

Amidst this noise the phone rings.

"It's for you," Mother says. "It's Col. Etchberger."

My heart sinks. I take the phone, figuring he is calling to let me know the disappointing news. "Hello, Col. Etchberger." My voice is flat but polite.

"Hello, Patty," he says. "I'm calling to tell you . . . that you've been accepted to the Academy."

My heart immediately begins pounding so loud I think my family can hear it.

"I have?" I say, trying not to sound as incredulous as I am.

"Yes, ma'am. I wanted you to know right away."

My whole family is staring at the smile I can't wipe off my face.

"But," he continued, "Representative Goodling wants to personally inform you, so make sure you sound surprised when he calls to make it official."

"I will," I say a little too enthusiastically. "Thank you!"

After we hang up, I shout, "I can't believe it! I got in! I got in!"

But something about the looks on my family's faces tells me they already knew, and the confession comes out.

"Col. Etchberger called earlier and told us the news. He said he'd call back when you got home after track practice."

"You guys knew?" I protest. I'm disappointed that they knew before I did, but I feel even worse about blowing up over going to the community college with my brother. That feeling is eclipsed, though, when the news sinks in again.

I'm going to the United States Air Force Academy.

Later that evening, Representative Goodling calls to deliver the good news all over again and my excitement is so genuine that I have no need to pretend to be surprised. When I hang up with him, I turn to Mother.

"There's just one more person I need to tell. I've gotta call Daddy!"

Mother's smile fades. "I don't think that's such a good idea," she says with a warning face.

"But I'm so happy," I counter. "I *know* it'll be all right and he'll be as thrilled as I am. How could he not be?"

Mother's face continues to caution me as I dial the number.

As soon as he answers, I blurt out, "Daddy, Daddy guess what? I got into the Air Force Academy! Can you believe it?" I don't wait for a reply. "It's a *really* good college. It's hard to get into. I just have to give the Air Force five years active duty after graduation, but it's free! Isn't that great?"

There's a long silence on the other end of the line, and I wonder if he's still there. Didn't he hear what I said? I got into THE UNITED STATES AIR FORCE ACADEMY!

Finally, his voice snakes through the line with a powerful venom. "Why, you've *PROSTITUTED* yourself to the Air Force, Patricia."

I am momentarily stunned. *I've prostituted myself?* As he barrels on, I ignore his rant and think, *Seriously? That's what we're calling this? Prostitution? Who was gonna pay for college? You? The man who avoided providing for his own children all these years?*

His harangue continues for quite some time. As always, I wait until he runs out of material and then get off the phone politely. Normally, I would be angry and deflated by his reaction, but this time, something is different.

He doesn't have the same power over me anymore.

As I'm relishing the sense of freedom I feel knowing that I'll be leaving home soon and spreading my own wings, another kind of liberation blossoms within me, one that awakens a burgeoning realization, as well as a sense of grief: Daddy has been a father in name only. I recognize that he has belittled, undermined, and denigrated me and my abilities and efforts unless those efforts directly nurtured *him*. He has never been a true father, one that encouraged, mentored, validated, guided, and protected me, and I begin to finally understand and accept that he never will be. Loyalty, respect, protection, approval, and kindness were tithings his children were expected to make to him. They did not, however, flow both ways. I had been raised to respect my parents, but now I realized I didn't owe his opinion any allegiance. It becomes clear to me that my father is destitute in ways I will never fully understand, that he was so emotionally impoverished and needed so much from his family, he effectively had almost nothing to offer us. He had little understanding of the true nature of love nor of the exquisite pleasure of loving and supporting others. Though he was exceptionally capable at making money in business, when it came to love, he was as demanding as a street beggar.

In the aftermath of that call, shaking off my denial and acknowledging the grief beneath was one of the most pivotal liberations I have experienced. Though I might never stop wanting a father, I realized I didn't *need* one. In effect, I hadn't had a real father all my life and I had survived—even thrived. In that moment, I relinquished my expectations of him, gave him his freedom from his unwanted role, and took another giant step toward my own sovereignty.

A Question of Merit

Having sloughed off the black cloud of my father's insulting reaction to my news, I am once again giddy with disbelief and elation on the school bus the next morning. I can still hardly believe that the journey is over and that I actually got in. But my euphoria is interrupted as I suddenly remember my good friend Dave who has been on this journey with me. The Air Force Academy is his dream as well. I haven't seen him for a couple weeks because we've both been busy, and I wonder what I should say if I run into him. But the dilemma is taken out of my hands when I unexpectedly encounter him in the hallway.

"Hey," he says. "I heard back. I didn't get accepted. What about you? Have you heard anything yet?"

I hesitate. I don't want him to be hurt. I wish we were both going to the

Academy together, but I'm a lousy liar so I simply say, "I heard last night. I got an appointment."

"Congratulations!" he says warmly and sincerely. And then, just as sincerely, he adds, "It probably helped that you're a girl."

Though he doesn't say it unkindly, he *does* say it matter-of-factly, as if it explained everything. *Of course you'd get in because you're a girl.*

I brood over his comment all day and the days that follow. *Did* I get in because I'm a girl? *Was* it unfair? Although we're both in the top ten percent of our class, his class standing IS slightly better than mine. *Maybe he's right.*

Unable to shake that my gender has something to do with my acceptance, I decide to settle the question by logically running a comparison of our resumes.

I've taken all the hardest classes: physics, calculus, chemistry, honors and AP courses. He's taken these same classes, and he's better at math and science. He hasn't taken as many AP and honors classes as I have, though, and I'm not sure what his SAT scores are, but mine are above average for the Academy. I assume that his are too.

I do have eight varsity letters. I've lettered in two sports every year since I was a freshman. As Dave and I were going through the admissions process together, I'd often wondered whether his lack of varsity letters would hurt him. The Academy had a three-legged stool in their evaluation—it said so right in the catalogue: Academics, Athletics, Leadership. In addition to the varsity letters I'd earned in track and cross-country, I ticked off in my mind the many outside races I'd entered and medaled in, including the two marathons. I then added to my side of the ledger being captain of the track and cross-country teams.

Besides all the resume-filler clubs, like French Club or National Honor Society, I had volunteered in Big Brothers, Big Sisters. I was also in PA Youth in Government and Model UN for two years where we passed mock bills in the state capitol and debated issues of the world.

I had filled every square that the Academy said mattered to them, and a couple that weren't mentioned too. I even noted my leadership of the last several years, which I would have taken for granted had it not been for Colonel Etchberger's insistence that I put my job on the application. (I'd punched a time clock since fifth grade, so this was just a part of daily life for me, but thankfully, he had emphasized its value.) In addition, after two years of spending every dime I earned, I would have my private pilot's license, which he would *not* have.

Looking at it all written out, I concluded that while he had the edge on me with grades, he didn't have flying lessons or varsity letters, and he didn't have the same type of club or leadership experiences I had.

I was disappointed for my friend, and I sincerely hurt for him. I wished he could have gotten an appointment and we could have been classmates at the Academy. But the facts didn't lie: I had done much more to get in than he had.

Little did I know, I would get plenty of practice facing the spurious, virulent, and repeatedly exhausting charge that as a woman, I got slots that men deserved, simply because I was female.

A Different Kind of Cross-Country Course

If I hoped to get my private pilot's license before I headed off to Colorado Springs in June, I knew I would have to drastically increase the pace of lessons and solo flights to complete all the requirements for taking my check ride. Over the last two years, I had methodically logged the hours and various types of flying required to qualify, including mandatory flight maneuvers and the necessary night hours, as well as making short, solo cross-country flights. For these I studied aviation charts that depicted landmarks such as rivers, towns, mountains, and towers that would help me to navigate, in addition to radio navaids.

One major milestone that still remained was a three-legged solo cross-country flight, which had to be a minimum of 150 miles. Because I was a student pilot, it had to be plotted to remain out of the busy airspace surrounding the major airports in our area. So, I decided to fly from my home base of Capitol City airport to Morristown, NJ, just outside of New York City, where I would refuel before heading south to Cape May, NJ. After refueling there, I would take off for the return flight home.

On the day I set out to complete this journey, my instructor tells me that if I get in any trouble, I should tell air traffic control I am a student pilot and they will take care of me.

"That's what I do," he says with a hearty laugh, which makes me laugh too.

After my preflight check, I start up the engine of the Cherokee 140 and take off on the first leg to Morristown airport using VOR (Very High Frequency Omnidirectional Range, which is a type of short-range radio navigation system for aircraft) and visual landmarks to navigate. As I pass Allentown airport, which I've landed at before on an earlier single-leg cross-country flight, I think, *So far so good.*

I'm enjoying the trip over familiar territory until I approach Morristown, where New York city looms behind it. I begin to imagine how awful it would be to get lost and overshoot the airport. *What if I end up right in the middle of New York City in that congested airspace with all those big airliners?* But I don't worry for long. I identify the airport and land safely, breathing a sigh of relief. On the ground, I get my plane refueled. Then I go inside to pay and ask to get my logbook annotated to officially verify the trip.

As I make my way out of the New York area and down through crowded airspace in New Jersey, the leg to Cape May appears equally ripe for disaster. I am so concerned with being on course that I overcorrect as I navigate from radial to radial. My instructor has always said not to chase the needle of the VOR, but like a drunken person riding a bike, my corrections are too extreme and I find myself close to the approach path for McGuire Air Force Base. I know I am off course, but I'm too overloaded to find my position with visual references on the plots I've charted. Panicked that I'll blunder into the path of the huge planes on their approach route, I tell the controllers I'm a student pilot like my instructor said to. They don't seem too concerned, however, and I continue on my way, finally getting back on course and vowing to make little corrections from now on.

I am relieved to see Cape May airport come into view and to know that I only have one more leg to complete. Another safe landing and another official notation are entered into my logbook. I buy a sandwich, pay for the fuel, and preflight my airplane once again, making sure to drain water from the fuel tanks as always.

Though stressed and exhausted and ready for this day to be over, I begin to feel more relaxed. This last leg should be much easier now that I'm heading away from congested airspace and over familiar landmarks.

I crank the engine and lift off smoothly. I'm heading out toward the Delaware bay when I suddenly hear an unfamiliar and alarming sound. The engine is sputtering. I immediately look around to see where I might land if the engine quits. One of the first things my instructor taught me, if I found myself in trouble, was to survey the area and pick a suitable field or space where I could set down if needed. But looking down, I see mostly water. Looking back, I see I'm too far from Cape May to return to the airport if I lose an engine.

Dover airport is just across the bay, I realize. *I could declare an emergency and probably make it to a landing there before the engine quits.* I figure that would be the safe choice, but I only briefly consider this option because the thought of it is simply too embarrassing.

I suddenly wish I knew more about engines, but they've always been a mystery I was not much interested in, so long as they worked. But now I needed a solution, and quickly. *Maybe I can lean out the fuel or switch fuel tanks*, I think. I lean out, but it makes no difference. So I flip the switch to only burn fuel out of the one tank. That seems to help as the engine resumes its normal sounds, and I limp toward home relieved that I don't have to humiliate myself and land short.

I am happy beyond measure when Capital City airport comes into view, but the day is not over yet. There is a cross-wind that makes the landing much more difficult now that my fuel tanks have made me significantly lighter on one side than the other. I am cleared to land, but the approach is so shaky that I know I must go around. Pushing the throttles up, I roar back into the sky. The long, stressful day has worn me down and I'm beginning to panic that I might not be able to get this thing on the ground when the controller calmly asks me if I want the other runway. Why didn't *I* think of that? In my tunnel vision, landing on the intersecting runway, where the winds would be much more favorable for landing, simply hadn't occurred to me.

I want to hug that controller for his suggestion, but instead I reply as confidently as I can muster, "Affirmative."

I've never been so grateful to land.

It's Official

My acceptance has felt unreal, but there is no doubt it is real when a letter arrives on April 29th. It is signed by Major General Kelley, the Superintendent of the Air Force Academy, offering me an appointment. In addition, the letter says he is coming to central Pennsylvania to honor the other appointees from the entire region at a recognition dinner in May, at a hotel in Harrisburg.

Immediately, I realize that the dinner is scheduled for the same night as our high school prom. One of David's friends, a freshman home from West Point, heard of my appointment to a service academy and offered to take me to my prom. But although it was a sweet and generous offer, I decide to go to the recognition dinner, which I consider far more important.

On Saturday, May 22nd, I rush home from my job at Ashcombe to shower, change clothes, and drive to Harrisburg for the dinner. I have just enough time to get dressed and pull my hair back into a ponytail, but it's still a little wet when I arrive. In my rush I hadn't thought much about who else would be there, so I am surprised to remember that the invitation included not only the other appointees (my future classmates) but their parents as well. As usual, I am alone because Mother won't attend an event that will have an invocation.

The dinner is lovely, and meeting the major general is exciting, and a few days afterward I get a note from Col. Etchberger. He wants to arrange for me to see flight simulators, and he says I might get the opportunity to fly in a C-141 or some F-type, which would mean a ride in a fighter aircraft. *How incredibly exciting!*

At the bottom of the note, he signs off by saying, "Now don't get a swelled head, but the Supt. was impressed with you."

Getting Ready for My Next Chapter

To prepare me for the days ahead, Colonel Etchberger takes me to the army base at Ft. Indiantown Gap to get the boots, fatigues, and other uniform items I will need for basic training.

When I return, Mother takes one look at the boots and says, "If you're going to be running in those for training, you'd better break them in or you'll be sorry once you get to the Academy."

I realize she's right. So, always a multi-tasker, I decide to break in my boots while mowing the lawn. And, since I feel I need a tan too, I take to the push mower wearing only a bikini and my combat boots. This odd sight incites a bewildered stare from our next door neighbor.

Since I'm already running for track, I don't need to do anything extra in that department, but I know we will be doing lots of pushups, sit-ups, and pull-ups. In the physical fitness test we had to take to qualify for an appointment, I maxed out everything except for the pull-ups, which were a struggle for me. I was only able to eke out the minimum required. So, I set a goal to practice the exercises every day that we'll be doing in basic training and throughout the next four years. I especially work on my weak area (the pull-ups) and focus on increasing the number of pushups I can do because Col. Etchberger says we will be doing a *lot* of these.

Now that I am accepted into the Academy, I technically could save my money and relax. But I figure I am so close to getting my private pilot's license, and I have come so far, that I really want to finish what I started. Rushing toward the finish line, I make four rides in April, five in May, and twelve in June. The principal even let me skip school and excused my absences so I could complete them.

One day, at the airport where I rent an airplane, I meet a guy from the class ahead of me at the Academy who's taking a few lessons on his three-week summer break at home. He has just finished his doolie year (which is what they call your freshman year), and when I tell him about my appointment, he pulls a little gray book from his back pocket called *Contrails*.

"Every new cadet must always carry this on them during their first year and memorize it," he says.

I have never visited the Air Force Academy because I could not afford to fly out there or pay for a hotel room, so I am eager to see something from this new world I will be entering.

I open the well-worn pocket-sized book and drink in the poem on the first page.

HIGH FLIGHT

by John Gillespie Magee, Jr.

Oh! I have slipped the surly bonds of earth
And danced the skies on laughter – silvered wings
Sunward I've climbed and joined the tumbling mirth
of sun-split clouds – and done a hundred things
you have not dreamed of – wheeled and soared and swung
high in the sunlit silence – hov'ring there
I've chased the shouting wind along and flung
my eager craft through footless halls of air
Up, up the long delirious burning blue
I've topped the windswept heights with easy grace
Where never lark nor even eagle flew
And while with silent lifting mind I've trod
The high untrespassed sanctity of space
Put out my hand and touched the face of God.

After I read the last line, my new friend takes the book back and leafs through the pages, giving me a tour of military history, airplane outlines, and pictures of courageous military heroes.

"You'll be required to memorize quotes by famous military and world leaders, and you'll be quizzed on your ability to identify US aircraft and enemy aircraft on sight," he says. "Plus, you'll have to memorize the menus for each meal of the day *and* the names of upperclassmen. Basically, you have to memorize this entire book."

I look at the dense text and can't imagine having to memorize it *all.*

Surely, he must be exaggerating, I think.

Soon enough, I'll find out that he isn't.

344 | PATTY BEAR

Full Circle

On June 11, 1982, I am finally poised to graduate from high school. At the commencement ceremony, I casually flip through the pamphlet and am reading the names of classmates who have received awards and scholarships when I see my name listed as a scholarship recipient to the US Air Force Academy. *I got a scholarship just as I said I would,* I think with immense satisfaction. Yet it hadn't happened at all in the manner I imagined it would.

Originally, I had set my sights on an academic or athletic scholarship, but those weren't what the Universe had in store for me. Instead, I had followed the call of my wild soul, walking the path that opened before me as I took one step at a time. Yes, some doors had closed, but others had certainly opened. And with naive trust, I had walked through.

Perhaps the ironic topper of my graduation day is that it is *exactly* ten years to the day since my father was excommunicated. It was in 1972 that the life I knew was shattered, that the future laid out so neatly by my ancestors was violently dismantled. And yet, here I stood with an entirely different trajectory than the little girl who watched the destruction wreaked by Hurricane Agnes and her own father. As I had envisioned over and over, I would *not* have a life of economic dependence, making me the prisoner of an unstable, controlling, and tyrannical man. Nor would I be yoked to a man for whom I would continually have to shrink myself so as never to outshine him. I would further not be anchored to a rigid gender role and never permitted to grow. Just as the Voice had predicted from the shadow of the woods, the different life—the bigger life—had been born. I was, on that glorious day, standing on the cusp of freedom.

Two weeks later, on June 25, 1982, I passed my private pilot's check ride. To celebrate, David paid for a ride in a helicopter with the dual qualified pilot we called "Judy Jet." We zoomed low over the Susquehanna River, popped up over the bridges that spanned the wide river, then dipped down for a close-up look at the wooded islands perched in the middle of the flowing waters.

Soon after, it would be my turn to take a passenger, now that I was qualified to do so. I was nervous about it, but I knew I had to do it sometime. So, for my first flight as a private pilot, I invited my mother and she accepted. As we flew down toward Carlisle, I pointed out the sights to orient her in the sky: Ashcombe, Route 74, the little airport in Carlisle. Continuing beyond Carlisle, we both searched for the familiar bends of the Condoguinet Creek and recognized the Home Farm. I made circles in the sky above, lingering over a beloved past. On the return flight, we passed by the base of the mountain where we now lived. It was a bittersweet tour of two very different homes.

In three days, I would board a much bigger airplane headed to Colorado Springs—and a new home 1,600 miles away.

On Angels' Wings

Sometime toward the end of track season, I had become aware of a crushing tiredness. Though fatigue was by now a way of life, this time I noticed it was qualitatively different. I remembered David having mononucleosis in high school, and my symptoms sounded like the ones he had. So, I scheduled a doctor's appointment to get tested.

Whether I got too busy finishing my license and canceled the appointment, or the test results did not come back in time (I don't recall which), I believe my tutelary Guides were looking out for me. Had I been diagnosed with mono, I would have been forbidden to join my class in basic training and the appointment would have been annulled.

But, guarded as always by my Guides, on June 28th, 1982, I entered the USAFA graduating class of 1986. The 1,483 new cadets from all over the country (10 percent of them girls) would begin basic training lasting the summer, and then fall academic classes would immediately commence. In the preparation paperwork the Academy sent before I left, they told us that throughout basic training, we would be allowed only one five-minute phone call home per week. Even after basic training was over, we would rarely be allowed to leave the base or dress in civilian clothes for the next year. Parents Weekend, however, would be a small exception to this insular world. It would take place after the completion of basic training, several weeks into our academic term. Parents would be able to visit and go off base with us, but we would still have to wear our uniform at all times.

After reading about this special weekend, I didn't say a word about it to Mother or my family. I intended to be anonymous in my new life. I would be starting over where nobody would see I have a mother who dresses in Plain clothes, and where nobody would see me as different. After so many years of wishing I could fit in, I would be just like everyone else.

Little did I know how naïve this thinking was.

I had no idea what I was in for: the arduousness of the training, the hostile environment toward women that eerily paralleled what I had experienced in the Church, the persistent challenges on multiple levels that would push me further than I ever expected.

Yet at the time, the naiveté and hope that filled me were blessings. Without them, I might have balked at what lay ahead and remained locked in my perceived limitations, afraid to stretch my wings and fly.

Reflections on the Journey

Truth loves all people, heals all people, and is all people, but Truth makes no compromise with fear nor seeks to hide herself in sweetness but rings out pure and clear and with the strength of clarity.

—SPIRIT

TOWARD THE END OF MY SENIOR YEAR, THE PRINCIPAL HANDED ME A slip of paper with a phone number.

"A reporter called the school and would like you to return his call. He wants to interview you about the Air Force Academy appointment."

I had had my picture and name in the newspaper a few times before for cross-country, but this was the first time the entire article would feature me and this prestigious new direction of my life. *Finally*, I thought with quiet satisfaction, *I am being known for something good, just as I had always vowed to be.* I left the principal's office, skipped down the stairs leading to the pay phone by the gym doors, and dialed the number to conduct my first real interview.

It became clear quite quickly, however, that this reporter had recognized my last name and was not nearly as interested in the AFA appointment as he was in getting me to talk about my parents' situation.

The article ran in several local newspapers under the banner "Miss Bear Named to AF Academy." One column detailed my plan to major in aviation engineering, noted the flying lessons I had been taking, and announced my appointment. The other two columns were about being the daughter of my infamous shunned parent and a recap of Daddy's case. The reporter quoted my polite refusal to comment on the past: "I do not want to jeopardize my mother or my father. Any comments I would make about the problem with my father and mother would only hurt them both."

I did not have a comment for that reporter that could encapsulate what my past held for me, as the budding sense of the strange and paradoxical nature of this journey—both mystical and practical—was a perspective only beginning to form in me.

Now, however, as I wing my way toward another landing in a faraway city, I pinch myself in disbelief at having slipped "the surly bonds" of so much heavy conditioning, and I marvel at the irony that the shattering, disillusioning experiences were the identical ones that provided the rocket fuel of determination to escape the gravity I had been born into. In fact, had my father's behavior not been as utterly beastly and prolonged as it was, I would have still become a Church member—marked by the lies that defined my femaleness as inferior and my body a possession of my husband. My goodgirl nature, which longed to excel in the adult world and put faith in what "they" said, would have joined an interminable gray line of women in bonnets. Even more sobering, I would have been one of those female enforcers who help to police their own kind, normalize subjugation, and anchor these cultures that celebrate rigid ignorance under the guise of benign traditionalism. This is hard to admit, and I'm not proud of it, but having been the one who took on that role with my own siblings, I've always known this about myself.

While severing traditional female roles was the exact opposite thing on my father's mind, his actions were like a tornado that destroyed everything in its path. It left nothing and no one standing untouched. And because of that, new foundations were cast, and new lives rose on the ruins of the old that broke the cycle for me and for my children. And, I was exceptionally fortunate that this shock to the system coincided with new opportunities opening for women. Had I been even ten years older, this path would not have been presented to me. I bow my head in gratitude to my courageous military and aviator sisters who preceded my class and blazed a trail for every woman who followed.

I cannot condone my father's behavior. Nothing justified his violence, abandonment of his responsibilities, or his petty, vengeful actions and twisting of the truth. Yet, neither can I ignore that from the devastation he wrought arose a life with more vitality, color, joy, and freedom for me. In the darkest of times, I had felt the terror of my father's message—"You're on your own"—and registered despair and helplessness as I witnessed his message callously echoed by the public and the courts. Now, however, I glimpsed a greater truth shyly emerging: I had never been on my own. The Divine had been in my corner all along, quietly collaborating with the expansion of my soul to orchestrate a bigger, bolder, more fulfilling life for me to step into.

Even more stirring was the understanding that there had always been a plan—that my father's behavior had, unwittingly on his part, goaded me into leaving a world intent on confining me and defining me as less valuable.

And so, as I "dance the skies on laughter-silvered wings," it is the strangest paradox of all to consider: What would I have become without my father?

After graduating from the Air Force Academy, I became an Air Force pilot and served as an aircraft commander in theater in Operation Desert Storm. I married another Air Force pilot, left active duty, and was hired by a major airline. Twenty-eight years later, I am a 777 captain who flies frequently to Europe and Asia. (By the time this book is published, COVID-19 will have caused me to take an early retirement. Having lived through the devastation 9/11 wrought on my industry—and many other life experiences—I try to anchor myself in the knowledge that this is part of the expansion and contraction of the human and spiritual journey, part of the in-breath and out-breath of life.) I have been blessed with a loving husband and two grown children whose character, independence of thought, creativity, and kindness make me privileged to know them.

As I headed off to the Air Force Academy, my mother became a real estate agent. In maintaining her Mennonite uniform, she made an odd figure within the industry, but her work ethic, love of learning, and desire to meet people made her successful. In 1987 she left the Church, and like all members who dare to leave, she was excommunicated and shunned, though she maintained mostly warm bonds with her family who remained in Church. After thirty years of wearing the uniform, it took two full years for her to make the transition to civilian clothes.

As for my father, he is 91 as of this writing and has spent decades of his life in and out of jail to draw attention to the practice of shunning. He has had contact with most of his children for much of that time, however limited it was sometimes due to his behavior.

Five of my siblings graduated from college with either a bachelor's or associate's degree, and three became entrepreneurs. Five of us married, four have children, and one has a grandchild. Though some of us moved away, we all currently live in or nearby the area we spent our childhood. None of the six children ever joined the Church, though we maintained contact with relatives in the Church to varying degrees.

On the outside, my extended family probably looks like a happy story of resilience and achievement. This is true on one level, but psychologically, this is not the full picture. No long-term experience of abuse and terrorism neglects to leave horrific scars—some on the outside, but many more tucked out of view on the inside. Those formative experiences haunted my brothers, sisters, and me in varying ways, impacting every aspect of our lives, including our relationships with each other and with others. Scars on the outside became deep rifts, decades-long estrangements, financial losses, illnesses, and breakdowns. Those on the inside manifested as recurrent and debilitating depression, anxiety, and despair. Nothing, and no one, escaped the long tail of trauma, including me. The demons released in the maelstrom of those years would need to be confronted and wrestled to the ground. Each one represented a daunting hero's journey that continues today.

Of the siblings I am in relationship with, we lived out the challenge of scars as different as each of us is as individuals, yet we all had one fervent hope: that this book would right the profoundly duplicitous story that was told about us.

Stories are spells. Each story is woven with words by a storyteller adept at either black magic or white magic, designed to take you captive or set you free. The most powerful spells are told by dark storytellers with a masterful command of both words and human nature and an agenda to monopolize power. They seem to instinctually know how to prey on the fears, vulnerabilities, insecurities, and desires of others and to hide their real intentions. On the other hand, some of the darkest human stories invite us into disorienting depths so that we can learn to see in the dark. The night vision we acquire brings discernment. It allows us to recognize the outlines of dark spells and their weavers, and how dark storytellers seek to manipulate. We learn to recognize more quickly the difference between darkness and light, and through *these* stories we become not only wiser but fiercer and more compassionate. I hope to have unveiled that to some degree through the events of this book.

One of the more powerful spells we confront on the spiritual journey is the story that anger is not spiritual. To be spiritual often carries an expectation of being sweet, nice, always positive and forgiving, and "loving"; in fact, "forgive and forget" is an especially strong cultural belief in the Plain culture I come from. Forgiveness, as the "great antidote," is offered to victims of all kinds as the promise of a release from pain and anger; forgetting offers the "promise of freedom" and is considered the right—and only—thing to do, regardless of what has transpired.

For decades I kept silent in the face of my father's narrative (and even regarding the Church's treatment of women), but "forgive and forget" has never sat well with me. I always smell a rat when someone pushes this advice, perhaps because I sense that it bypasses justice that might be restorative for everyone, including the perpetrator. Or perhaps because it patronizes the injured and overtly suggests they should "just get over" what was done to them because it's becoming inconvenient for the rest of us to hear about it. Just as likely, though, is that it disturbs me that this mantra is almost exclusively directed at women and children, used as a mask for the prohibition of anger in victims. It conveys that only the abuser has the right to get angry— and it's not offered so much as wise advice but a subtle command. Be silent, or else. Let it go. Never speak of it again. Like so many stories the abuser promotes, it is self-serving.

The truth is that anger is a catalyst. It is an invitation toward transformation and part of the soul's frontline spiritual immune system. Anger has the power to cut through the abuser's disorienting monologue. It helps us to cultivate discernment. To recognize lies. When we've been systematically deceived, abused, exploited, demeaned, and subjugated, anger is the only reasonable response. It gives us the power to protect ourselves and the courage to protect others. Anger can point us in the direction of truth and toward wholeness.

Someone asked me how had *I* been transformed by writing this book. It was an intriguing question because the process of speaking the truth does indeed change us. I didn't have an immediate answer at the time, but later in the quietness I remembered an incident that was new behavior for me.

I had always been an easy mark for the "forgive and forget, be nice, be sweet" command. In the choice between compassion for others or protecting myself, I'd almost always choose others. Because of that, it took me fifty years to interrupt my father's monologue and talk back.

My father never repented or asked for forgiveness. Instead, he spent fifty years doing just the opposite. He minimized his terrorism against our family, and he ceaselessly strove to humiliate others, to "humble" them so they would acknowledge how wrong they were. He seemed to believe that when this happened, he would finally be free. He endlessly repeated his rationalizations, and I spent decades listening to him, thinking it might be healing for him, rarely refuting his twisted version of events. Why did I do this? Because like many abusers, he had two sides to him.

Publicly, my father was generally well liked. Good-looking and charismatic, he was a friendly neighbor with a broad smile. He was a sociable, attentive, polite, and charming farmer with many adoring acquaintances. A man with a generous spot for the elderly and infirm who often brought a gift of vegetables and the company of his colorful stories and his desire to listen.

Privately, however, my father was most often what I have described in this book. He was what the researcher and psychotherapist Daniel Shaw would call a "traumatizing narcissist," a man for whom every conversation, and every need, revolved around him, or else. Incurious and uninterested in his children's and grandchildren's lives, he monopolized conversations with a mind-numbingly unvarying review of his grievances. More than anything he seemed to genuinely believe it was his right to expect close relationships with the people he had incessantly terrified. I was astonished by his confusion and unquestioning entitlement. But I was fascinated too.

Did he have amnesia about all the things he'd done? He'd often say he had searched his conscience, and if he'd been wrong anywhere, he would be the first to admit it. But he always concluded that he didn't see how he could have done anything different, as if his one decision to leave the church set in motion every single other action he took, none of which was preventable.

Yet there was another private side I occasionally glimpsed beneath the bluster: a lonely, hurt, traumatized, and neglected little boy who just wanted affection. A boy who needed, and deserved, love and understanding, and who could not understand why he was getting the reactions and results he got. Why his wife and children ran away. Why they were angry. Why they wanted nothing to do with him.

I saw this lonely boy and wanted to hug him and protect him from ever being hurt again, even as I sometimes simultaneously wanted to beat the adult bully senseless and make him understand how much destruction he had caused. To force him to finally take responsibility for the things he had done. But it was this little boy I could never get out of my mind.

These two perceptions of my father warred with each other. The avenger argued I was giving the terrorist a pass for far too long. The mother insisted I should pay attention to this little boy who needed so much. Usually, the needs of the little boy won. But one day I realized that the needs of the little boy and my own deserved to coexist.

For years I'd stayed silent in the face of my father's confusion, justifications, and rationalizations. I reasoned that if I had done what he had, I couldn't face myself either. Hence, I decided that the kindest action was to not comment, mostly because I sensed this was a small child living in a man's body—a child who as far as I could discern had experienced little to no affection when he was young. He was, in my concerned estimation, a bewildered, heartbroken, and deeply despairing child who did what frustrated children do: throw tantrums. And because I could see that he needed love, I gave him love and kindness, at least as much as I could spare given our history.

When I was a child, his tale of woe and blame-shifting had been confusing as well as compelling. He sobbed. He was outraged and angry. He spoke with such certainty, and with such a committed and consistent narrative of being the victim, that I frequently wondered if I had been wrong in my understanding of the situation. Had I missed something? Over time, I actually wondered if perhaps he *was* driven to violence by a completely unjust situation.

As an adult researching newspaper articles of our family history, I was confronted with an unexpected and almost unwelcome clarity. I had known there was a gap between my father's public presentation and his private behavior, but I had not been aware of how stark and undeniable it was. In interviews, he would repeatedly tell stories where he was the victim in circumstances that I did not recognize or understand. The things he described sounded awful, but I was startled when I began to recognize that the story details he offered to interviewers in fact belonged to private horrors *he* had visited upon our family. Because these private details had never been publicized, he had been able to twist the public facts into something unrecognizable, even to me. It seems odd and embarrassingly naïve to admit that after all these years I was still stunned by what I read. But my father had always spoken about the importance of honesty, and had evinced such force of expression that his cause was about getting the truth out, that I assumed (though he sometimes deluded himself) he was basically committed to honesty. Not until I read the court cases and pieced together a timeline from the newspapers and my own memory did I realize the extent and intentionality of his lies.

Stumbling upon this evidence of his deliberate betrayal, along with the fresh reminders of his many terror attacks, made me extremely angry. Because of my emotional state, I thought it best not to reach out to him and get together as I usually did. After several months, though, I felt able to compartmentalize the reality of the past from the compassion I felt for him as a person in the present, which at the time was when he was ninety.

We arranged to connect on the phone when I returned from London. The call began with short pleasantries, talking about him and a recent fall that had resulted in a broken bone. When he shifted to "I'm so different...," I knew it signaled our entry into the lengthy monologue phase of these visits. So, I settled in for the familiar stories and grievances whose sentences I could finish after two words. Rather rapidly, he followed up his introductory phrase with the equally familiar, "If I could just *see* where I was wrong, I would admit it publicly. But I just don't see how I could have done any differently."

Now, as I said, over the years I've remained silent when he has stated this. But inwardly this statement sends me through the roof. I always see the scene of David walking through the door after he'd been kidnapped. I remember the dullness in his eyes, the red flush creeping over the deadened mask of his face, the way he tried to shrug off the humiliation that had been heaped on him. I remember how kids in school mocked him for wearing a wig. I remember the horror and the heartbreak on my sisters' faces as they looked at their brother's homecoming. I remember how helpless these kinds of scenes felt.

And so every time he makes this statement, I want to get in his face and scream at him. I want to yell, "Really??? Seriously, Daddy? You couldn't have done ANYTHING different? Maybe not kidnap your son and deliberately humiliate him? Perhaps not sneak up across the field and hide behind a bush to ambush your children on their way to school? Maybe not kidnap your daughter? Maybe not bring your hired man to haul away your children's food before their eyes? Maybe not marshal the public to heap scorn on your own children? Maybe . . ."

I'd remained silent before. But not this time.

This time I was tired from back-to-back trips. I'd had a glass of wine and was feeling relaxed. So, when he said he couldn't see where he'd been wrong or what he could have done differently, I heard myself calmly point out that he had abandoned his children, refused to provide for them, terrorized them, and been violent. As I knew he would, he became instantly angry and defended his actions, saying they were caused by my mother and the Church. Though inwardly I noted to myself it was no justification for the pervasive violence toward his wife either, I calmly told him that had nothing to do with his behavior toward his children, that he and he alone was responsible for his choices and actions.

My "talking back" escalated both his response *and* the "ewww" factor as he launched into what was never far from the surface—and what he'd always considered his winning argument: "You don't know what happened behind closed doors, how she sexually teased me."

I thought, *I know what happened outside those doors. She was always locking the door to keep you out, running away from you, keeping her children close as shields to protect herself from you. I know you broke into the bathroom while she was bathing and then told the newspapers with outrage that "she lets me see her in the bath." And I also know you're a man who at 89 felt profoundly persecuted by young female college students crossing the street, simply because they were dressed a bit scantily. You actually thought they were taunting you with their bodies, when all they were doing was trying to stay cool on a hot summer day.*

But I just kept calmly coming back to his justifications.

"Daddy, no one else is responsible for your choices and your actions but you."

When he realized I would not indulge his rationalizations, he abruptly said, "We should probably end this call."

I shrugged nonchalantly. "Okay."

When he hung up, I realized something in me had shifted.

I didn't feel bad!

Not only that, I knew I would never again tolerate in silence the rationalizations for his violence.

I had found my voice and with it the sweetness of freedom.

I'd always hoped my father would one day acknowledge what he'd done to the children he claimed to love was wrong, even though I also realized he was probably incapable of that. But now I knew. I didn't need him to hear me. I just needed to say it.

When I tell the truth, it is not for the sake of convincing those who do not know it, but for the sake of defending those that do.
—WILLIAM BLAKE

We don't tell our stories so that abusers will listen, or so that they will be remorseful or change. That *can* happen, yes, but the reality is it rarely does.

We tell our stories so *we* know the truth. We tell the truth in solidarity with the still small voice within that yearns to trust its own wisdom. We tell our stories because lies and abuse proliferate in secrecy. We tell the truth to put abusers on notice: *I see you. You may still abuse, but I won't let you get away with it without objection. I won't help you hide your dark secrets.*

We tell the truth so that others may have a contrast by which to recognize lies, particularly the young and the vulnerable. We tell the truth as a compass for those who wish to avoid becoming abusers themselves, whose souls long to cultivate the discernment required to live honorably. We tell the truth as a beacon for those who also wish to break the spell of the lies that bind them.

Words are the ingredients of any spell, yet it is words that can break spells too. Speaking the truth can break the darkest, most powerful spells. It's why dictators in the home and around the world enforce silence so rigorously. The truth, whether facts or an inner knowing, demystify the abuser's carefully constructed lies and drain them of their dark power.

All of our lives are different because someone left, someone pressed charges, someone said "no more," someone marched for the vote, someone was beaten and jailed and still marched on, someone refused to sit in the back of the bus, someone insisted on equal rights, someone was a pioneer in a field not open to women or people of color or the LGBTQ community. Someone stood up to the bullies who hold us all hostage with their shrunken definitions of us.

It is the hero's journey these individuals took that paved the way for me and so many others. Most of them never made the history books. Most probably did not live to see the changes they worked tirelessly for come to fruition. Many were simply changing their own lives for the better. I doubt they thought that their setting of boundaries, or leaving, or getting their own bank account, or going to college would impact anyone else in the world.

But it did. I and others have lived the fruits of their labors. My story and the unique possibilities that opened for me would not have been possible for someone ten years my senior. While I was in elementary school, women were knocking on doors and blazing trails into new and often hostile territories. By the time I arrived at high school graduation, six classes with girls had begun integrating the nation's service academies, and three classes of women officers had graduated. Those six classes cracked open the doors, braved the terrain, and left a footpath for others like me to follow. Without the steps countless anonymous women and men took in the service of freedom, and without the brave pioneering of my academy sisters, I would have a different life. Everybody pours their drop in the well and we all drink from it.

As individuals, and as a collective society, we become who we identify with. That little boy who became my father faced two terrible choices that would kill off his innocence before his childhood was barely begun: identify with the dominator or the victim. Subjugate others or be subjugated. He was already conditioned by his gender which path to take.

As a little girl I took the other path, the one *I* was conditioned to take. I would never have guessed it then, but I was the lucky one. For the path of the subjugated is not blinded by "special" status or its addictive entitlements. Rather, this road leads to a dead end where the lies become visible and undeniable. Where the spell is broken. And there, at the end of the road with little to lose, a third path appears. You begin to think for yourself. To obey an inner voice. To own yourself. And to say as Rumi did, "My soul is my guide."

I found, as many before me have, that the path of the downtrodden, the slave, the victim, the outcast, can paradoxically lead us to liberation. It seems, however, that in order to become liberated, we must first recognize the ways in which we are bound. We must come to recognize the force of gravity of our conditioning and "slip the surly bonds of Earth" before we can fly higher. The call of the wild soul always beckons us on a quest toward our higher self. Though this path often winds into darkness and through confusion, the wild soul never leads us toward domination, but always out of captivity.

The wild soul calls us to grand adventures. It invites us to navigate by curiosity. It does not call to obedience to some monologue but rather invites a dialogue with the Divine. Its metaphysical secrets glitter like jewels hiding in plain sight: "Seek and ye shall find, ask and it shall be answered, knock and the door shall be opened." It encourages us to grow, and to develop courage, stamina, and character. It harkens us toward our destiny, to the expression of our soul in the world. It offers a collaboration with Spirit for the flowering of the Divine seed within each person.

Many times in life, I have traveled with my spirit Guides on these journeys down into the depths. There was no coercion, no attempt to control me. My Guides never demanded anything of me except the pleasure of walking alongside me and co-creating this life together. With spirit and matter blissfully entwined, I discovered what they already knew: that though these paths through darkness each traversed different terrains, they all eventually spiraled upward to where I could once again "dance the skies on laughter-silvered wings."

I hope this book has sparked your trust that we *all* have spirit Guides on our hero's journeys throughout our entire lives. It takes practice and discernment to hear the myriad ways they communicate. It also requires that we take responsibility for the choices we make. Though heeding the call of your wild soul always leads to your soul's deepest desire, it is not always an easy path. Little did I know when I boarded the airplane bound for Colorado Springs that I had jumped out of the frying pan into the fire. Or as my husband says with a twinkle in his eye, "Stay tuned for another episode of Saturday's Child."

Non-judgmental witnessing is an immensely healing gift to the traumatized, and I am deeply grateful to you for accompanying me on this journey.

May you be richly blessed in body and spirit as you walk the pilgrimage of your own journeys through life.

Per Ardua ad Astra

"Through adversity to the stars"

PHOTO GALLERY

Aerial view of the Home Farm

Part of my mother's garden on the Home Farm

Me at age two or three in the living room on the Home Farm

Me, probably in second grade

School picture from 5th or 6th grade

The trip to Illinois in 1976. My first flight in a commercial aircraft.

christmas carols

WGAL TV8

1. O Holy Night Db 4/4

O holy night the stars are brightly shining,
It is the night of the dear Saviour's birth.
Long lay the world in sin and sorrow pining,
Till he appear'd, and the soul felt its worth.
A thrill of hope the weary world rejoices,
For yonder breaks a new and glorious morn.

Led by the light of faith serenely beaming,
With glowing hearts by His cradle we stand.
So led by light of star so sweetly gleaming,
Then came the wise men from th' Orient land.
To see the King who made earth' lowliest
  choices,
Yea, chose His throne a manger all forlorn.

Chorus

Fall on your knees!
O hear the angel voices!
O night divine!
O night when Christ was born
O night divine!
O night O night divine!

2. The First Noel D 3/4

The first Noel the angel did say
Was to certain poor shepherds in fields as
  they lay;
In fields where they lay keeping their sheep,
On a cold winter's night that was so deep.

They looked up and saw a star
Shining in the east, beyond them far;
And to the earth it gave great light,
And so it continued both day and night.

And by the light of that same star,
Three wise men came from country far;
To seek for a king was their intent,

And to follow the star wherever it went.
This star drew nigh to the northwest,
O'er Bethlehem it took its rest,
And there it did both stop and stay,
Right over the place where Jesus lay

Chorus

Noel, Noel, Noel, Noel
Born is the King of Israel.

3. Joy to the World D 2/4

Joy to the world! the Lord is come;
Let earth receive her King;
Let every heart prepare Him room,
And heaven and nature sing,
And heaven and nature sing,
And heaven, and heaven and nature sing.

Joy to the earth! the Saviour reigns;
Let men their songs employ;
While fields and floods, rocks, hills and plains,
Repeat the sounding joy.
Repeat the sounding joy.
Repeat, repeat the sounding joy.

4. Away in the Manger F 3/4

Away in a manger, no crib for a bed,
The little Lord Jesus laid down his sweet head.
The stars in the sky looked down where He lay,
The little Lord Jesus, asleep on the hay.

The cattle are lowing, the Baby awakes,
But little Lord Jesus, no crying He makes.
I love Thee, Lord Jesus, look down from the sky,
And stay by my cradle till morning is nigh.

*The Christmas carols pamphlet we ordered every year and sang
from in school*

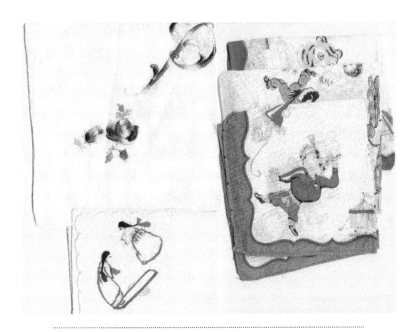

A few of the handkerchiefs Grandma Bear gave me

My badge and patrol certificate. Ha!

Bicentennial wagon train on Route 74 by our house

A typical picture of Lancaster county,
with the horse and buggy hitched up near a store

My mother with
her parents,
Grandma and
Papap Gross

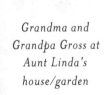

Grandma and
Grandpa Gross at
Aunt Linda's
house/garden

Newspaper photos, probably copied from Mennonite archives

Daddy

Mother is in back, trying to avoid the press

Grandma Bear at her family's stand at Carlisle Farmers Market

The Bear logo printed on the bags of potatoes grown on our farm

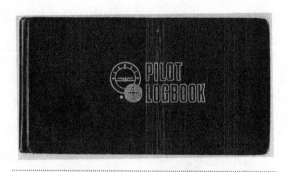

My private pilot's logbook from high school

Air Force Academy pamphlet with Col Etchberger's comments atop

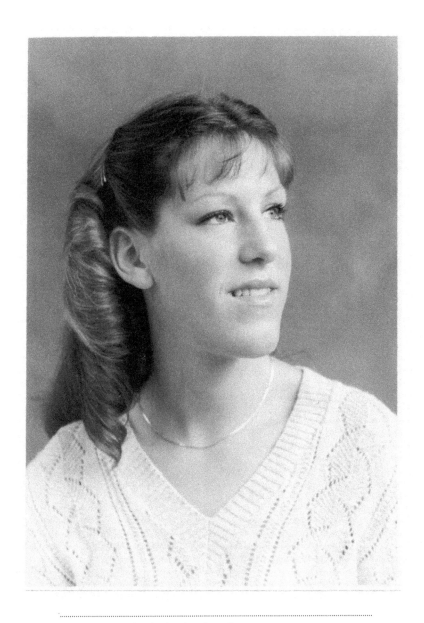

My high school graduation picture

My Air Force Academy graduation photo

My "hero picture" (what these photos were called) from pilot training,
which I went to after graduating from the Academy

*The day I left for the Academy, at the Harrisburg airport
terminal with my mother*

*The day after I got my private pilot's license;
taking my mother up for a ride*

Me in the Harrisburg Marathon

Later in life, the aircraft I flew in the Air Force, a KC–135

ACKNOWLEDGMENTS

To my siblings, Ben, Susie, and Sharon, I am grateful for the willingness to revisit painful memories in the quest for as much independent verification of the accuracy of memories as possible. For providing the crucial details that I did not remember, and for their unfailing integrity in wanting to tell the truth and only the truth about an ugly time. To my sisters, I am grateful for early reads of the manuscript and their validation of this endeavor in speaking a hidden truth, and for encouraging me to include my own feelings in this memoir.

To my mother, for whom this memoir could be nothing but an excruciating reminder of the past (and sometimes still the present), who read the rough draft and gave her imprimatur to "write my story without reservation," and who fact-checked crucial details without malice toward my father and with fairness to the record, often erring on the side of my father.

Several early readers provided valuable feedback that allowed me to make crucial refinements to the finished manuscript:

Kathy Kuser, who remains unconditionally positive and encouraging, while unfailingly presenting nuggets of perspective and insight that enlighten my understanding and offer crucial polish and sparkle to the finished product.

Wayne Shade, who generously spent countless hours poring over the rough draft and offered incisive commentary and suggestions that sharpened key passages and raised questions that were crucial, and who offered rich historical details for me to incorporate.

Stacey Aaronson (www.thebookdoctorisin.com), my editor, cover designer, formatter, and all-around book champion is a person in whose hands you can place your most precious possession (in this case, a life story I've wanted to tell for decades and part of my sacred contract) and trust that it will be handled with exquisite care and deeply appreciated. At the same time, her honesty and professionalism are never in doubt as she delivers needed and sometimes substantial changes with empathy, clarity, and respect. It is a rare combination. I discovered her services years ago in a serendipitous way that had all the hallmarks of another door being quietly opened by my Guides. Today I also count her among my dearest friends.

Sharon Bially (owner of booksavvy.com) and her associate, Lauren Hathaway, are my publicist and official book champions. After the searing publicity my family and I endured as a child, to enter back into this arena was mildly terrifying. But this time I had trusty guides who were not only competent and professional, but joyfully creative as well as warm and kind. They connected me to media opportunities and held my hand as I presented this long-buried story to the public. Plus, it was just fun to collaborate with them.

To my grown children, Morgan and Evan, who patiently provided objective feedback and were simultaneously unfailingly supportive. They are some of my most effective grassroots promoters, advertising the book to friends even before it was fully finished. They read the snippets as I wrote, offered thoughtful suggestions, entertained my countless queries and self-doubts, and were endlessly enthusiastic, supportive, and encouraging of me and this project.

And to my husband, Kevin, my safe-haven and companion in our many adventures. He has always been my most loyal supporter and biggest champion. I credit him with helping me heal so much of this story and its themes through his lighthearted humor, rootedness in kindness and practicality, and his goodness, decency, and equanimity.

MORE WITH PATTY BEAR

INSIGHTS,
INTERVIEWS
&
MORE

DISCUSSION QUESTIONS

1. Which themes in the book spoke to you personally? Why?

2. The book begins with a child's innocent view of her world. Discuss why you think the author provides this stark contrast from later years.

3. Patty heard an unmistakable voice at age seven that told her she would have a bigger life. She also saw a black tornado appear on her father's shirt, witnessed the skull of a Mennonite woman appear before her, and felt the brush of an angel on her cheek, all of which opened a door where there had only been a wall. Have you ever been aware of guidance like this? What methods were used to communicate with you? For instance: a voice, a vision, an inner knowing, intuition, a synchronicity, a strong feeling, a blocked path, a sudden opportunity, someone else's strong advice, etc.

4. Patty grew up in a particular religious environment, yet her coming-of-age experiences weren't so different from "regular" kids. Discuss those you related to.

5. In the book Patty describes wanting to get a running scholarship but ends up instead with an appointment to a service academy. How have the goals you set out to achieve shape-shifted on the way to their final outcome while still retaining the essence of what you want?

6. Did you gain any insight into the mindset of either abusers or victims through reading this story? What were they?

7. What examples of conditioning did you recognize in the book? What conditioning of your own did you become awakened to? How has it affected the trajectory of your life?

8. Why do you think the media, the public, and the jury were so sympathetic to Patty's father?

9. Do you think Patty's soul needed these arduous experiences? And if so, for what possible reasons might her soul have had?

10. In the Preface, Patty briefly mentions the "Acorn Theory" by James Hillman, of which he says that we are all the seed of something. If you had to guess, what are you the seed of? What does your blooming look like? What Gift might you bring to the world?

11. What did you think of the actions of Patty's mother? Did you find yourself frustrated with her or compassionate toward her? Or both? Why?

12. Were you surprised that despite the years of terror, Patty invited her father into the house after she broke her foot, and that she called him when she got an appointment to the AFA? What do you make of this inconsistency?

13. Discuss why you think it took Patty so long to stand up to her father, telling him he was the only one responsible for all his past actions.

14. Patty mentions the comfort she took in knowing that the Voice indicated a plan for her life. Have you felt there was a plan for your life? If so, can you glimpse the outlines and turning points? Has it helped you to be patient with the timing of your life?

PATTY BEAR is an international airline captain, life coach, self-certified master multitasker, garden and interior design whiz, and voracious reader and self-learner.

A pioneer rising out of a childhood in the insular and male-dominated world of the "Plain People," she became one of the early female Air Force pilots during the first decade women graduated from pilot training. She has spent over thirty years dedicated to the study of defying gravity: escaping conditioning, walking the transformational journey, and the practice of following the call of the wild soul. She is a Certified Caroline Myss Sacred Contracts Archetypal Consultant, as well as a Certified Medical Qigong practitioner. In 2016, she coauthored *House of the Sun: A Visionary Guide for Parenting in a Complex World* with Pat Shannon.

Patty lives on the east coast with her family.

www.theflyingclub.com

Patty, this is such a remarkable story of transformation and liberation. Why did you write the book?

One part was as an accountability project. I wanted to expose how abusers operate—their tactics and how easily they fool the public. And I wanted to illustrate the underlying dynamics of the manipulation of public opinion, the court system, and the media.

Equally dear to my heart has been the desire to illustrate the practical mystic's path. To show a real-life example of the magic and practicality of what it looks like to follow the call of your wild soul.

It's almost fifty years after these events began. Why write the book now and not earlier?

The process I experienced as a child taught me that everything has a timing to it, as if there is a choreography happening behind the scenes whose complexity is beyond our comprehension. Part of that timing is a goal known only to our soul, which takes time to unfold and becomes clearer with each step we take. So, part of the answer is that I simply wasn't prompted earlier. However, I will say that once it became clear that this story was definitely on the agenda, I desperately tried to procrastinate. I worried that telling the story truthfully would hurt my father. Part of that resistance was formed by the propagandized belief that abusers instill in their victims: that if you tell what they did, you are betraying *them*.

Another part of the resistance was the deep compassion for my father. I don't know what all happened to him as he was forming, but it has always been clear to me at an intuitive level that he was a profoundly wounded child. While I saw the immense damage he did (and never genuinely repented for), I *always* saw a precious little boy too, one who loved to please, who wore an endearing jaunty smile below sparkling blue eyes, and who carried an enchanting boyish optimism.

As I have come to know the soul as a tough yet compassionate taskmaster leading to a wise and healing destination, I sat down to write the story and trusted that somehow this profound dilemma would be reconciled prior to publication.

And was it reconciled?

For a long time I believed that I had to choose between telling the truth about what happened and compassion for my father. Years ago, I was presented with the phrase: "Truth loves all people, heals all people, and is all people, but Truth makes no compromise with fear nor seeks to hide herself in sweetness, but rings out pure and clear and with the strength of clarity." At the time, I searched for what relevance this had on my present life and could find none. The only thing that was crystal clear was that I was to remember it word for word, so I did. Only later did it become clear to me that it was guidance about how to tell the truth.

The truth is that we don't do abusers any favors by helping them avoid accountability. They accrue the natural karma of their bad actions (as my father did in a lifetime of crippled relationships that were the natural consequences of his behavior) and lack the boundaries and guidance that point toward healing self-correction. I found in writing this that it was possible to simultaneously speak my truth and hold compassion for my father, and that how he framed this was dependent upon *his* consciousness, not mine.

Your frustration with the newspapers and media is evident in the book. Do you think the media coverage of domestic violence is different today, fifty years later?

I think the journalistic profession is a profoundly noble one. In their highest purpose they are a witness to the facts and to the events that shape cultures and the growth of collective consciousness.

I certainly think the *awareness* of domestic violence and sexual violence is greater today, but I don't see a great leap in understanding of the dynamics of domestic violence or sexual assault. Victims are still routinely blamed for inciting the behavior of their perpetrators, and the predictable perpetrator's assertions about the victim lying, projecting motives onto them, and general character assassination is still widely disseminated and treated as an equivalent narrative. Abusers are exceptionally manipulative in shaping public perception, whether that's of the neighbors, the workplace, the courts, or through the media.

I wish journalists would educate themselves on the standard operating procedures of propaganda that abusers routinely use so that they could be more reliable witnesses for the whole truth. In fact, the gaslighting that abusers use to shape perception is such a powerful spell that numerous times while gathering the newspaper articles used in writing this book, I was astonished to find myself falling into sympathy with my father's narrative that *he* was being persecuted, that *he* was the real victim of his wife and children. I literally had to shake this off and focus on the facts of the events described and my own memories of what had actually taken place to dispel this seductive narrative. That is how powerful these manipulative tactics are.

I did, however, find myself with greater empathy for a gullible public. If even *I* could fall under this spell knowing everything, how much more difficult would it have been for the public to recognize?

I believe that a key part of a journalist's sacred contract is to be a credible witness that informs the public in ways that help them to grow in wisdom and understanding so that collectively we become less abusive and grow as souls. A journalist can't do that if their own lack of deeper understanding unwittingly allows perpetrators to hijack the narrative and reshape the story so they become the sympathetic figure we identify with.

You seem to be suggesting that abusers share the same basic techniques?

Yes. Definitely. Those who work with sexual assault survivors and domestic violence offenders identify this standard operating procedure with the acronym **DARVO**.

> **D is for deny, deny, deny.** Deny it ever happened. Deny you did it. Deny it wasn't consensual.
>
> **A is for attack.** Call them a liar. Attack the victim's credibility, smear their reputation, twist their words, claim their REAL

motive is money, attention, fame, or revenge. Carpet bomb the victim until their reputation and credibility is destroyed beyond recognition. Deflect attention from the abuser's behavior and make the court of public opinion about the behavior and motives of the *victim* rather than the perpetrator.

RVO—Reverse Victim and Offender. Having obliterated the victim's credibility, the land is fertile to plant the idea that the abuser has been falsely accused and that this is the REAL crime and he is the REAL victim. This final step is the ultimate revenge on the victim for daring to speak up. It demonstrates to the victim how powerful the perpetrator is and how powerless she is. He can do anything and get away with it. And it's a warning to her and others like her to shut up or else.

Abusers not only share a script for manipulating public perception but they share a script for taking their victims hostage emotionally, and then physically. The investigative reporter Jess Hill talks about this in her book *See What You Made Me Do*—how eerily similar the victims' stories are about their abusers' tactics of "unfathomable cruelty and violence," and what sounds like orchestrated campaigns of control. It is as if the abusers are all reading from the same script and all went to the same school.

If abusers share common behavior, do their victims also share common behavior patterns?

One of the the things I find frustrating—and what I imagine police, the courts, and friends of abused individuals find incomprehensible —is the inconsistent behavior of victims. They will quite often protect, defend, and excuse their abusers. It can be maddening to observers who may conclude that the circumstances of the abused aren't very dire after all. Yet consider this: do terrorists behave in a predictable manner? No. In fact, the uncertain nature of their violence is the key to the terror their victims feel. This not knowing what to expect is the core of terrorism. So, why would victims who must learn to adjust to terror behave in predictable or logical ways? It is antithetical to their survival.

What is the guidance of the Soul around captivity such as this?

The call of the wild soul is always, always leading to liberation and the growth of wisdom. Part of the liberating path is to recognize the heavy conditioning (which is a type of propaganda) one is under because that awareness is a crucial part of the path of one's escape. The heavy conditioning in patriarchal societies, like the one I grew up in, often presents itself as benign and seductively idealistic to those inside and outside the cultures. In reality, it is emotional, psychological, and spiritual abuse to train others to believe in their inferiority and thus to groom them for subjugation.

Rachel Louise Snyder in her book, *No Visible Bruises*, says, "One of the questions that is so difficult to really explain is how abuse slowly erodes a person, how often survivors talk about emotional abuse being so much worse than physical abuse." Would you agree?

In many ways it is worse because it is so insidious that it literally becomes unspeakable. But the soul is a match for this because it has a language that is beyond words. If you remember the vision I was shown about the tornado on my father's chest, or of the Mennonite woman's skull beneath the bonnet, that was the soul raising my awareness. Once enough awareness was raised, I began to make different choices. I no longer lived in fear of hell, which was huge because that could no longer be used to drive my behavior. It simply didn't have any power over me anymore.

How do you feel about the Church of your childhood now?

There's a saying that "hurt people hurt people." Trauma has a profoundly long tail, and its aftereffects can be either internalized as self-harm and self-sabotage or externalized as bullying others. Plus, trauma is not only carried in individual's memories; it is also carried in the consciousness of collectives and passed down through the generations. Of course, that is no excuse for perpetrating abuse on others, but let's remember that this Church's past carries gruesome death-related trauma arising from merely questioning the then status quo's practice of infant baptism. Overall, I do feel that the Church is based on manipulation and subjugation of women, all based in fear.

Your father spent a lifetime protesting the practice of shunning. What is your opinion on this practice?

Like my father who occasionally expressed wanting to do better than his father, I think the Church wanted to do better than its "father" church. They eschewed war and violence, and advocated non-violence even in self-defense. They preached often about being humble and gentle. But they, like my father, succumbed to identifying with the abuser.

I would say that *excommunication,* like divorce, is a healthy boundary to someone who is perpetually disruptive and destructive like my father was. By contrast, the practice of *organized shunning* seems to be more of a tactic of control rather than a protective measure for an organization and its congregation. To me, shunning is spiritual and emotional violence, whose real agenda is revenge and control. Like a vengeful boyfriend who sets out to make a woman pay for leaving and for the audacity of rejecting him, shunning is the Church's revenge on anyone who wants to leave or dares to question the authorities. It is not a loving practice, no matter how many times the Church defines it as such. Calling abuse love is the abuser's standard line.

What is your opinion on the evolution of the court system around domestic violence?

This is a big subject. My mother would say that she is treated differently by law enforcement today than she used to be. I believe some of that is because she became more assertive, and some because law enforcement and the justice system *has* made progress. However, Jess Hill's book that I referenced earlier makes it clear that this progress is merely the tip of the iceberg of what is needed. She describes an encouraging approach adopted by a city in North Carolina fed up with the sickening violence: they adopted a stringent zero-tolerance policy and saw immediate results. I'd like to see much more of what Hill describes in that example. I think there is still far too much excusing this behavior at all levels and far too little understanding of the confusing behavior that arises from people held in violent captivity.

Do you think people play a role in being victimized or not victimized?

That is a wonderful question. First off, the perpetrator is always *entirely* responsible for their abusive behavior. Period. Most of us have been hurt, yet many who have been profoundly traumatized choose not to abuse others because of their experiences. It is a choice to hurt others. Not only that, but perpetrators—if they cannot successfully deny their behavior or lay the blame entirely at their victim's feet—will negotiate with their victim and the public to assign at least equal blame to the victim of their abuse, such as by saying, "I lost my temper, but you provoked me." This desire to equalize responsibility is especially common in cultures where power is not shared equally. For example, in the Church's patriarchal culture, the men held all the power but they projected the responsibility for evil, corruption, failure, and abuse onto women. It was the same with my father, this "gaslighting" technique.

As we shed abusive conditioning, however, we naturally become more powerful because the purpose of conditioning is to strip one individual or group's power so that another can monopolize resources, adopt entitlements, and generally conscript others for profit. But nothing happens in a vacuum. When we reclaim our power, others notice and must give more thought to how they will interact with us, particularly abusers. Gavin DeBecker talks about this dynamic in his book, *The Gift of Fear*. But it's not just abusers who weigh us differently when we grow into who we are, it's also the people who now must make a more conscious choice in siding with the abuser or not. Once we can no longer be taken for granted quite as easily, we become a force to be reckoned with and that changes the balance of power.

It sounds like despite everything, you have a relationship with your father. Have you forgiven him?

For me personally, I don't feel the need to forgive my father. He hasn't asked for it and he doesn't seem to feel he needs it. Allowing myself to be angry is one of the more healing things I have experienced. Too many years of swallowing the rage is not good. That doesn't mean I took it out on him. I didn't. But, as I wrote, I finally told him he alone was responsible for his violence.

All of this is to say that I do not forgive and forget. I don't forgive abusers who don't demonstrate a sincere and longstanding effort to regain the trust they violated or who don't request forgiveness. And I never forget what that person is capable of so that I may be prepared should they revert to their previous behavior. But I will offer them boundaries accompanied by compassion, regardless of their level of remorse.

With regard to the definition of forgiveness as "letting go of the belief that the past could have been any different," I acknowledge and agree that it is healing to oneself energetically to forgive. However, I do feel strongly that the extreme focus on forgiving and forgetting within the Plain community doesn't allow people to break the chains of abuse. Forgiveness may indeed come later to unburden the victim herself, but I believe it is a place a victim must arrive at herself, not be forced by outside influences.

When you decided not to join the Mennonite church, did you feel the presence of Spirit with you? If so, could you cite specific experience where the presence of the Mystical was evident to you and made a difference?

As a child I heard voices occasionally and had visions at critical turning points, but it felt so natural that I didn't even name the experience; I simply took the advice or warnings that were given. It was only when I reached my twenties that I began to recognize this individual guiding presence and learned to tune into my intuition and to collaborate with Spirit deliberately.

You name the behavior toward girls and women by the Church as spiritual violence. How are boys and men adversely affected?

The movement of women reclaiming their Divine rights is a profound chapter in human history. It is opposed, often violently, by traumatizing narcissists and those who identify with their self-centered totalitarian agenda, who see other's freedom as an existential threat to their control, who see equal human rights as a threat to their entitlement culture, and who resist personal responsibility, change, learning, and growth.

Yet, men are as big a beneficiary as women of the movement

toward freedom. They gain freedom from the stultifying roles of masculinity that they, too, have been forced into against their will— that is, being forced to perform the distasteful and corrupt work of controlling other humans. They have, however, been able to share the burden with a partner of the sometimes crushing responsibility of providing financially for those we love, and that has opened a world where the joy of true partnership and companionship that is only found among equals is increasingly enjoyed, and where men can become immersed in joyful participation in their children's lives.

As women reclaim their humanity, it opens a space for men to reclaim their lost humanity as well. Tim Winston, Australian novelist and speaker, talks about how "the unguarded parts of boys are being shamed out of them every day. The dreamy, the vulnerable, creative, sensitive, affectionate, kind, compassionate natures of boys are forced underground." In my experience, the very things that make us unique individuals is what gets oppressed. Both boys and girls are forced to conform to a sick reality. Winston goes on to say, "There's a constant pressure to enlist, to pull on the uniform of misogyny and join the Shithead Army that enforces and polices sexism . . . Boys and men are so routinely expected to betray their better natures, to smother their consciences, to renounce the best of themselves and submit to something low and mean." (Jess Hill, Pg 143.)

You endured years of instability in your home life, public shaming, controversy, psychological abuse, and emotional neglect. Certainly you were impacted by being diminished and unseen as a young child. What would you say were the most important factors that empowered you not only to recover, but to soar?

Well, first I would say that recovering is a life-long process. A fellow pilot once said to me, upon learning a little of my background, "But you're so normal." I told him, "I'm still working on normal." The truth is that I learned how to work on the outside in order to fit in. However, the process of deconditioning—especially when it is this heavy and this targeted at your very being and worth—does not go away overnight or even magically. Healing takes work and often a long time.

The most important factors in the work of deconditioning and healing at some level have been very simple. Here are the three I would put at the top of the list.

1.   Create a nurturing home for your soul to heal and thrive and grow. It must be unique to you. Bring beauty into your environment that resonates with you. For me that was my home and my gardens. I incorporated flowers, colors, organization, functionality, and nature, all of which soothed and delighted my soul. Whatever soothes and delights *your* soul, bring a little more of that into your life. That includes people. Spend less time with the type of people who shame, criticize, and abuse and more with people who accept, share, and encourage.

2.   Question. Question. Question. What is the level of integrity of what you are hearing? Is it true? Is it kind? Is it limiting you or others based on factors of birth? What level of integrity does the speaker possess? And more than anything, question yourself. Self-doubt in a world that reveres confidence is highly underrated, so most of all question yourself. Are your beliefs true? Are your limitations as set in stone as you believe? What else is possible? What else could be true?

3.   Each soul is born into this world bringing Gifts to offer the world. You have something valuable to share. But just like a baby does not come into the world fully realized and must grow and develop skills and practice, so too does your Gift need to be developed. *While* you're apprenticing to your Gift, practice sharing the wealth that lies within you: a talent like singing or organizing, or protecting, or a grace such as kindness, delight, discernment, an encouraging word, compassion, a smile. Your healing is in its advanced stages when you have offered an elixir or Gift to others honed out of your experiences of agony. You will feel this shift.

You talked about the practical mystic's path and the call of the wild soul. Can you define what a practical mystic is? And how do you hear the call of the wild soul?

This is my favorite topic, and I could talk about it all day long! The most elegant answer to this question belongs to the Sufi mystic Rumi who said, "As you start to walk on the way, the way appears." That is the essence of living as a practical mystic. You take steps. You do the work that is before you that appears to be on your path. You look for signs of synchronicity and opportunities, you are open to guidance without straining, and you simply trust that as you walk, the path opens before you. From a lifetime of living like this I can tell you it always does, though sometimes I must say it took far longer than my impatient spirit demanded, and it sometimes matured into radically different results than my naïve original vision had conjured.

How do you hear? In my experience it doesn't take any special practice like meditation or rituals. Instead, it's extraordinarily simple. "Ask and it is answered, seek and ye shall find, ask and it is given unto you" is an enduring metaphysical jewel available to all, but only if you listen. Navigate via curiosity. I just ask the question, then let it go. The answer rarely arrives in the moment I ask, but rather when my mind is not straining or when I've already taken action toward my destination. Don't expect to receive a detailed map of the entire quest, or a guarantee. It rarely works that way. All you need is information around the *next* step on your journey. Use your guidance and know that more will arrive when you reach the point that it is needed. Of course, listening is different from obeying. You are not following a narcissistic guru; you are in partnership with the Divine on a journey to your destiny of which the blooming of your soul is the true aim. So use the logic and common sense you were given, and don't be afraid to question your guidance either.

Will you ever write about *how* to walk this path?

Yes, this is the path of my heart. Ten years ago, I began to try to teach the mindset and skills of the practical mystic's way to three 14-year-olds who formed what I called a flying club. Over the course of a year, my daughter and her two cousins practiced on a year-long goal for each of them that was dear to their heart and felt just barely doable. I created a workbook that looked like an aviation logbook that walked them through developing the practical skills of goal achievement, as well as the skills and mindset of the mystical way.

Next on my path is the book I'm currently writing, *Adventures of the Soul*, as well as redesigning the workbook I developed years ago. I would love to see "flying clubs" of soul friends supporting each other.

How is your quest to change, grow, overcome, and soar relevant to our world today?

I think we are arriving in an era when many of us are less inclined to tolerate a middleman between us and the Divine. We are more ready to entertain direct experience and to walk the practical mystic's path of following our callings and doing the work they require. One of my hopes in writing the book is that it will give a very down-to-earth demonstration that this collaboration between spirit and matter is entirely practical *and* entirely rewarding. It is not magical-thinking hocus pocus; it requires hard work and attention to the signs on the way, as well as patience, for the timing of Spirit is often different than our impatient nature. Additionally, it can be a rather shapeshifting journey. Destinations we arrive at often look different than we had imagined, though they always contain the essence of our desires. Further, I believe we are entering a time period when these skills will increasingly become the norm.

Do you have one message to offer to readers who have endured adversity and desire to overcome, to soar?

Yes. Follow what you love, what lights up your heart. Your unique path *is* the Way. Toward that end, gradually and gently shift your focus from what you don't want and more toward defining what you *do* want.

Those who have endured trauma are habituated to avoiding danger and surviving, which involves a fixation on what you don't want. As a consequence, hypervigilant survival muscles become overdeveloped while the muscles you need for thriving—positive visioning, optimism, and consistent goal-oriented effort—often remain weak. But we all have the capability to develop new habits. Positive habits are a powerful form of wealth that you can steadily accrue and can never be stolen from you.

ADVENTURES OF THE SOUL:
How to Walk the Practical Mystic's Path and
Follow the Call of Your Wild Soul

Follow your bliss and the Universe will open doors
where there were only walls.
—Joseph Campbell

This book is a trail guide for how to follow the call of your wild soul and to manifest your callings. No matter who you are or what you may have already achieved or endured, you probably harbor an unspoken dream or calling that feels impossible, or perhaps utterly impractical—maybe even crazy.

Life often feels like we must choose between settling for security with its banal, stifling practicality or follow what sparks us and surrender our desires for a prosperous life of love, security, or achievement. I believe, however, that our unique callings emanate directly from our own souls. They are an invitation to play the game of life zestfully and earnestly, and to arrive at uncommon triumphs that nurture the spirit and our evolution as a soul. We are continually inspired with quests that invite us on a path to merge spirit and matter—to realize our dreams—and to live a colorful and full life.

In these pages you will find a practical manual for how to marry the mystical and the mundane, and how to cultivate the skills of dialoguing with the Divine: a fertile attitude, hearing your inner voice and the voice of your Spirit Guides who accompany each soul on their adventures, how to read the signs on your trail, accepting the importance of timing and stamina, and recognizing doors that open. You will also learn how to apply the practical aspects of realizing any dream: creating a clear vision, breaking your quest down into step-by-step journeys, taking initiative, understanding the purpose of obstacles and navigating around them, and identifying practical skills you need for any particular quest.

As you practice what you read, you will fall in sync with your soul, allowing you to live a more coordinated, harmonious, and joyful life. As a result, you will naturally find yourself becoming a practical mystic.

Parenting is a calling of the highest order. A humble job, it's also the most honorable and important work in life. Yet you are given so little training to become the kind of parent you long to be. Frazzled by the dizzying changes of today's complex world, bombarded by countless "shoulds," and torn between the experts and your heart's knowing, you watch your best intentions get overrun. What's more, you are expected to simply be a good parent, regardless of the quality of parenting you received.

House of the Sun takes a fresh approach. It suggests that deep within you is a well of natural wisdom that's the key to being a superb parent for your child. Gently, you come to understand why you sometimes parent in ways you wish you didn't—and how to shift, whether your children are four or forty. Guided by a metaphor from Nature, you'll discover the best in you so that you can bring out the best in your child by:

- inviting your natural wisdom to bloom
- building your parenting skills no matter your history
- applying timeless guidance to every age and stage
- calling on a memorable framework even when life is stressful

Whether you long to reverse dysfunctional family patterns or merely refine your current parenting style, *House of the Sun* is a companion and guide to nurturing the well-being of each person in the family, as well as for the development of the "Unique Gift" your child has brought to bless the world.

∽∾

If you would like to connect with other readers of this book
or with Patty, please visit:

www.facebook.com/authorPattyBear

CPSIA information can be obtained
at www.ICGtesting.com
Printed in the USA
LVHW030331150221
679323LV00005B/330